The Kingdom
according to
Luke *and* Acts

The Kingdom

according to
Luke *and* Acts

A Social, Literary, and
Theological Introduction

Karl Allen Kuhn

B
Baker Academic
a division of Baker Publishing Group
Grand Rapids, Michigan

Published by Baker Academic
a division of Baker Publishing Group
P.O. Box 6287, Grand Rapids, MI 49516-6287
www.bakeracademic.com

Printed and bound by CPI Group (UK) Ltd, Croydon, CR0 4YY

Library of Congress Cataloging-in-Publication Data
Kuhn, Karl Allen, 1967-
    The kingdom according to Luke and Acts : a social, literary, and theological introduction / Karl Allen Kuhn.
        pages cm
    Includes bibliographical references and index.
    ISBN 978-0-8010-4887-6 (pbk.)
    1. Bible. Luke—Criticism, interpretation, etc. 2. Bible. Acts—Criticism, interpretation, etc. 3. Kingdom of God—Biblical teaching. I. Title.
    BS2589.K85 2015
    226.4′06—dc23   2014041612

15   16   17   18   19   20   21   7   6   5   4   3   2   1

For Kathryn

Contents

Acknowledgments

W e are blessed to be living in a time and place with such abundant resources—academic, traditional, and communal—for deepening our collective and individual understandings of Scripture. My hope is that the work to follow might contribute something meaningful to the rich dialogue from which it emerges and to which it owes its existence. In particular, I have benefited greatly over the last decade from the insights of colleagues participating in the social-scientific criticism task force of the Catholic Biblical Association. Our study together has enriched my own engagement with Scripture and sowed seeds that germinate in the thoughts offered here. I have also learned much from students participating in my Luke-Acts seminar, especially the spring 2013 cohort, which read and commented on drafts of several chapters. In addition to the assistance provided by these colleagues and students, three individuals served as my readers for earlier versions of the manuscript: Fred Kramer, Kristal Klemme, and Kim Thimmig. To them I owe much appreciation for their generous gift of time, encouragement, careful reading, and insight. Lakeland librarian Joe Pirillo graciously and ably processed numerous interlibrary loan requests, making my research much easier from our setting in rural Wisconsin. I am grateful to Mark Allan Powell for his suggestion to pursue Baker Academic as the publisher and his advocacy on behalf of the project. I also deeply appreciate Baker Academic for their commitment to this study and for their congenial professionalism, especially that of editors James Ernest and Tim West, who ably shepherded the project through the various stages of publication and offered many suggestions that have improved it.

I also give thanks for the many blessings I receive in my ministry of teaching and learning at Lakeland College. As a college of the United Church of Christ with an undergraduate program in religion, Lakeland has granted me many opportunities to shape my understanding of Scripture and faith in conversation with students, colleagues, and members of the wider church community. Finally, I give thanks for my wife, Rev. Kathryn Kuhn, to whom this volume is dedicated in appreciation for her ongoing witness to God's Kingdom as a minister of the church, and for our children, Joshua and Clare, whose support and love in this and many other endeavors are a source of tremendous blessing and joy.

Abbreviations

AB	Anchor Bible
ABD	*Anchor Bible Dictionary*. Edited by D. N. Freedman. 6 vols. New York, 1992
AnBib	Analecta biblica
Ant.	Josephus, *Jewish Antiquities*
ASNU	Acta seminarii neotestamentici upsaliensis
ATANT	Abhandlungen zur Theologie des Alten und Neuen Testaments
BA	*Biblical Archaeologist*
BCE	Before the Common Era
BECNT	Baker Exegetical Commentary on the New Testament
BETL	Bibliotheca ephemeridum theologicarum lovaniensium
Bib	*Biblica*
BibInt	*Biblical Interpretation*
BNTC	Black's New Testament Commentaries
BTNT	Biblical Theology of the New Testament
BU	Biblische Untersuchungen
CBQ	*Catholic Biblical Quarterly*
CD	*Damascus Document*
CE	Common Era
CTR	*Criswell Theological Review*
CurTM	*Currents in Theology and Mission*
DSS	Dead Sea Scrolls
1 En.	*1 Enoch*
EvQ	*Evangelical Quarterly*
GNS	Good News Studies
Greg	*Gregorianum*
HDR	Harvard Dissertations in Religion

HTKNT	Herders theologischer Kommentar zum Neuen Testament
HTR	*Harvard Theological Review*
Int	*Interpretation*
JBL	*Journal of Biblical Literature*
JSHJ	*Journal for the Study of the Historical Jesus*
JSJ	*Journal for the Study of Judaism*
JSNT	*Journal for the Study of the New Testament*
JSNTSup	Journal for the Study of the New Testament: Supplement Series
Jub.	*Jubilees*
LEC	Library of Early Christianity
LNTS	Library of New Testament Studies
LXX	Septuagint
NICNT	New International Commentary on the New Testament
NIGTC	New International Greek Testament Commentary
NovT	*Novum Testamentum*
NovTSup	Supplements to Novum Testamentum
NRSV	New Revised Standard Version
NT	New Testament
NTL	New Testament Library
NTS	*New Testament Studies*
PRSt	*Perspectives in Religious Studies*
Pss. Sol.	*Psalms of Solomon*
RSV	Revised Standard Version
SBLDS	Society of Biblical Literature Dissertation Series
Sir.	Sirach
SJT	*Scottish Journal of Theology*
SNT	Studien zum Neuen Testament
SNTSMS	Society for New Testament Studies Monograph Series
SNTSU	Studien zum Neuen Testament und seiner Umwelt
SNTW	Studies of the New Testament and Its World
StudNeot	Studia neotestamentica
SubBi	Subsidia biblica
SwJT	*Southwestern Journal of Theology*
T. Levi	*Testament of Levi*
T. Sol.	*Testament of Solomon*
VT	*Vetus Testamentum*
War	Josephus, *Jewish War*
WBC	Word Biblical Commentary
WUNT	Wissenschaftliche Untersuchungen zum Neuen Testament

Introduction

The Heart of Luke's Witness to the Kingdom

With a handful of believers clenched in their grasp, the mob screamed, "These men are turning the world upside down!" Paul had been teaching in the synagogue, "explaining and proving that it was necessary for the Messiah to suffer and to rise from the dead, and saying, 'This is the Messiah, Jesus whom I am proclaiming to you'" (Acts 17:3). Some in the synagogue believed. So too did "a great many of the devout Greeks and not a few of the leading women" (v. 4). But others, including a sizable number of Israelites, did not accept this strange, even outlandish, word about a crucified criminal fulfilling sacred oracles of old. In fact, they found Paul's testimony so offensive that they became "impassioned," formed a mob, and set the city in an uproar! Searching for Paul and Silas, they attacked the household of a believer named Jason. Though Paul and Silas were not there, these defenders of Rome grabbed any of Paul's rabble they could find and dragged them before the authorities. They demanded that these outlaws be charged for their outrageous, dangerous, world-overturning claims, insisting, "They are all acting contrary to the decrees of the emperor, saying that there is another king named Jesus" (v. 7). The people and the city authorities were indeed disturbed by what they heard, for few charges could be more serious than this. The authorities released Jason and the other believers, but only after exacting bail. Further consideration was needed. How might they deal with this troubling new movement that threatened to lead many astray?

Three Characteristic Cadences of Luke's Witness to the Kingdom

Even though this story occurs deep into Luke's narrative, it is a fitting one with which to begin. This tale of bold witness, passionate opposition, angry mobs, and disturbed officials represents well the vision of the Kingdom that spans both parts of Luke's two-volume work. It joins with many other episodes composed by the evangelist that make plain at least three prominent features of the "good news" he narrates and proclaims.

First, this account in concert with many others asserts in earnest that the good news of what God accomplishes in Jesus of Nazareth is world-defying news. It shatters established patterns for interpreting reality and ordering society. It is relentless and uncompromising in offering a vision of heaven and earth that turns the tables on what most people in Luke's age profess and live as true. The early disciples—as accused by their detractors in Thessalonica—really were attempting to turn the world upside down.

Second, this account among many others reminds us that our post-Enlightenment tendency to segregate "religion" from "politics" is not an appropriate lens through which to view Luke's world. In his day, life was not compartmentalized into these and other categories of action and thought. In fact, one could justly argue that to merely use the terms "religion" and "politics" with reference to the ancient world is anachronistic. Perhaps the terms should only be employed to say that these domains of ancient life along with others were inextricably intertwined. The reality was that religion and politics did mix in antiquity (and for nearly all of human history), along with economics, social standing, kinship, and most other dimensions of human society. Recall the charges brought against Paul's companions in Thessalonica: "They are all acting contrary to the decrees of the emperor, saying that there is another king named Jesus." To confess Jesus as Lord and Savior had a disturbing corollary. It implied that anyone else who might claim those titles was an impostor before humanity and heaven. Embracing the Kingdom—from Luke's perspective at least—was at once a religious, political, social, and even economic act.

Third, this account among many others also conveys Luke's recognition that the proclamation of the Kingdom elicits highly impassioned reactions. Luke knew well the connection between worldview, storytelling, and emotion. For many in Luke's day, the gospel message was a misguided, even dangerous assault on the way the world is and, frankly, should be. For others, that same word was a heaven-sent, nightmare-ending call to awake to the bounty and blessing of a homeland they had always hoped awaited them despite so many indications to the contrary. Thus, we see some characters in Luke's narrative rant with rage and others erupt in songs of deep joy, some respond with obstinate dismissal and others with awestruck recognition of what it truly means to be blessed. But it is not only the emotions of his characters that concern Luke; he also seeks to elicit an emotional response from his recipients through his own telling of the gospel story. As an extraordinarily gifted writer, Luke uses various literary forms and devices to compel Theophilus and others to experience—intellectually as well as affectively—what is at stake in the allegiances they claim.

Corresponding Cadences of This Guide to Luke's Narrative

This study aims to introduce readers to Luke's two-volume work, focusing on its urgent call for Theophilus and others to embrace Jesus and the Kingdom of God. The three characteristic features I just identified will guide our investigation of the key historical, social, literary, and rhetorical features of Luke-Acts.

Luke's Vision within the First-Century Roman World

The intertwining of numerous social realities in Acts 17 and the rest of Luke's narrative is, as noted above, characteristic of the ancient world. Only somewhat recently have commentators begun to appreciate the various ways in which the testimonies of the biblical authors both reflect and address the social, religious, political, and economic realities of their day. As a result, a growing number of scholars now view knowledge of the biblical writers' social world (including norms, values, characteristic patterns of interaction, resource distribution, social and political structures, religious affiliations, and geography) as vital for understanding how the biblical writings speak to the setting and circumstances of their audiences. Similarly, my discussion of Luke's story of the Kingdom's arrival will be informed by what has come to be called (within the field of biblical studies) social-scientific analysis. Drawing from cross-cultural anthropology, it will use those models and insights that seem particularly relevant for engaging the myriad ways in which the first-century Roman world is reflected in Luke's portrait of the Kingdom.

Part 1 invites readers into Luke's social setting. Chapter 1 reviews the social, economic, and political structures of the Roman world, the role of religion in facilitating those structures, and the character of the Roman Empire as a realm of disparity and want. Chapter 2 investigates the Israelite contexts to the New Testament's (hereafter NT) proclamation of the "Kingdom" or "Reign of God" (ἡ βασιλεία τοῦ θεοῦ).[1] Here I propose that it is best to understand

---

1. I will avoid using "Jew" and "Jewish" to refer to those persons, groups, and beliefs connected to Israelite religious tradition, unless I am citing the perspectives of other scholars or biblical texts that use these terms. Instead, following the lead of John H. Elliott (see "Jesus the

the early Christian usage of this term as signifying not a distinct concept but rich formulations—narrative in shape and function—of the arrival of God's long-awaited reign. The "kingdom stories" proclaimed by Jesus and his early followers were adaptations of those told by Israelites before them. In the centuries leading up to the Common Era (CE), these stories were characterized by both incredible variation and their shared enactment of three fundamental claims: (1) Yahweh is King of Israel and Ruler of the universe; (2) the current order of creation and state of God's people are not in alignment with God's will; and (3) God will act to reorder creation into alignment with God's intentions. Chapter 3 presents my understanding of Luke's social location as a member of the elite (likely the Israelite elite) and the significance of this realization for better appreciating the rhetorical edge of his narrative.

The Artistry and Pathos in Luke's Proclamation

As stated above, Luke knew well the connection between emotion and worldview and the potential to challenge and transform worldviews through the art of impassioned storytelling. I also argued above that Luke was not simply interested in *portraying* emotion as a common reaction to the proclamation of the gospel. Rather, like other writers before him, he frequently *employed* "pathos" (passion) as a rhetorical tool, here to lead Theophilus and the rest of his audience to appreciate what was at stake in their own response to Jesus and the Kingdom of God. Consequently, part 2 will help readers attend to the ways Luke shapes his narrative to engage both the heads and the hearts of his audience. Chapters 4–7 examine Luke's use of a host of literary techniques and conventions, including various generic forms (birth narratives, genealogies, miracle stories, etc.), repetitive patterns and parallelism, the citation of or allusion to Israelite traditions, and character speech (direct and indirect discourse). Thus, part 2 summarizes what many scholars have come to know and appreciate about Luke's narrative artistry.

Chapter 8, however, invites readers into largely uncharted territory. Building on chapters 4–7, this chapter unveils some of the ways in which Luke marshals these and other literary techniques in order to elicit an emotional reaction from his recipients. This is a dimension of Luke's narrative artistry that, in my view, has not been sufficiently explored. As a gifted writer, Luke knew that emotion was an effective, even subversive, means of drawing Theophilus

---

Israelite Was Neither a 'Jew' nor a 'Christian': On Correcting Misleading Nomenclature," *JSHJ* 5 [2007]: 119–54) and others, I will adopt the preferred terminology of Israelites in Luke's day, employing "Israel," "house of Israel," "Israelite(s)," and "children of Israel."

and others into his narrative and compelling them to entertain the vision of the Kingdom it proclaims.

The World-Defying Character of the Kingdom

For a time, it was common for scholars to argue that one of Luke's main objectives in writing his narrative was to demonstrate to Roman leaders that Christianity was politically and socially benign, posing no threat to the current world order, and that it should be regarded as another sect of an accommodating Judaism. As we shall discuss in chapter 10, this view is still held in varying forms by some scholars today. Yet I concur with others who find that Luke intended nothing of the sort. Instead, as indicated regarding Acts 17, the gospel proclaimed by Luke is one that calls upon all humanity to turn their allegiance from Caesar and the kingdom of Rome to another realm and another as Lord. Luke's aim was not accommodation but resistance. He considered the reign of God to be not a benign reality but a deeply subversive and disturbing force that was already undermining the foundations of Rome and all earthly claims to power. Luke was promoting nothing less than an entirely new way of life that offered incredible blessing for both peasant and elite.

Accordingly, after we have unpacked the broad contours of Luke's sociohistorical context and specific tendencies of Luke's narrative artistry, part 3 will review the primary contours of Luke's kingdom story and engage the main rhetorical impulses of his narrative. When the evangelist's narrative rhetoric is encountered against the background of his first-century world and his own social location, these emphases stand out in sharpest relief: (1) the unassailable rule of Yahweh and the advancement of God's Kingdom through Jesus, the divine Son of God and resurrected Lord of all (chap. 9); (2) the manifold ills of this world due to demonic perversion, elite greed and oppression, and the faithlessness of many; and (3) Luke's celebration of God's still-unfolding age, which opens the way for all to turn aside from the darkness plaguing this world and enter into God's realm of blessing (chap. 10).

Author, Sources, Dating, Unity, and Genre

Several other subjects are also important to the study of Luke-Acts, and my judgments on some of these matters shape my analysis in the following pages: authorship, sources, the dating of the work, the relationship between the two "volumes" of Luke's kingdom story, and the Greco-Roman genre to which Luke-Acts most closely corresponds.

Author, Sources, and Dating

Although in chapter 3 I will argue for Luke's social location as a member of the elite, as well as offer some informed speculation that he was Israelite, we are on less certain footing when trying to identify the evangelist more specifically. Several early Christian traditions assign the authorship of the Gospel and Acts to "Luke," likely indicating the companion of Paul identified in several epistles by the same name (Col. 4:14; 2 Tim. 4:11; Philem. 24). Five surviving witnesses dating from the end of the second century into the early third century CE provide this testimony.[2] The title "Gospel according to Luke" is found in the oldest extant (surviving) manuscript of the text P[75], a papyrus codex dating from 175 to 225 CE. The Muratorian Canon, dated by most to 170–90, lists a number of works deemed authoritative by Christians, including most of what later compose the NT; among them is "The third book of the Gospel: According to Luke." The canonical list further states, "This Luke was a physician," presumably alluding to Colossians 4:14. The second-century theologian Irenaeus also names Luke as a companion of Paul and the writer of Luke-Acts, and considers him the same figure identified in Paul's Epistles. In addition, the ancient, extratextual "Prologue to the Gospel," also dating from the end of the second century, attributes the Gospel's authorship (and that of Acts) to Luke and identifies him as "a Syrian of Antioch, by profession a physician, the disciple of the apostles, and later a follower of Paul until his martyrdom."[3] Finally, Tertullian, in his writings opposing Marcion, similarly identifies the writer of the Third Gospel as Luke, a companion of Paul, and describes Luke's Gospel as a digest of Paul's teaching.

Scholars, however, debate the reliability of these traditions because the work itself is anonymous, and the earliest of these traditions date to about one hundred years after Luke-Acts was likely composed. Moreover, some scholars argue that several discrepancies between Acts and Paul's Letters in their respective portraits of Paul and his teaching undermine the claim that the writer of Acts was a companion of Paul. The more salient of these inconsistencies include the following: Paul's Letters do not mention the miracles he performs in Acts; the Letters offer accounts of Paul's movements and experiences that sometimes conflict with or are not corroborated by Acts; Paul's theology as can be discerned from his Letters is in tension with the preaching of Paul as presented in Acts, including subjects such as the use and place of the law, the salvific significance of the resurrection, and the importance of the return of Christ.

2. For the following summary I am indebted to Joseph A. Fitzmyer, *The Gospel according to Luke I–IX*, AB 28 (New York: Doubleday, 1981), 34–41.

3. Cited in ibid., 38.

Despite these discrepancies, the occurrence of the first-person plural ("we") to refer to Paul and his comrades in several places throughout Acts does suggest that the writer of Luke-Acts, whether "Luke the physician" or not, was a sometime companion of Paul and eyewitness to certain events of Paul's ministry. The narrator of Acts includes himself among those called to preach the gospel in Macedonia (Acts 16:10), and then travels with Paul and others from Philippi (20:5–6). From there, "we" journeyed to Assos, Mitylene, Samos, and Miletus (20:13–15), and eventually to Tyre, Ptolemais, and Jerusalem (21:1–17). Later, after Paul's hearings, the writer includes himself in the troop that set sail with Paul (now a prisoner) for Italy (27:1), finally arriving in Rome after a shipwreck at sea and three-month winter layover on the island of Malta (28:11–16). The most commonly held explanation for this grammatical phenomenon is that the writer of Luke-Acts was a companion of Paul and joined Paul on some of his travels. What this potentially tells us about Luke is that he joined the Jesus movement sometime in the mid-50s or earlier and ministered for a time alongside Paul.

In my mind, the discrepancies we find between Acts and Paul's Letters can be explained by Luke's limited companionship with Paul, the amount of time that likely transpired between Paul's ministry and the writing of Luke-Acts (twenty to thirty years), and Luke's desire to cast Paul's character in ways that were consistent with his own perspective.[4] For this reason, I think it best to understand the function of the "we" passages the way they are most naturally regarded by most readers: to indicate that the writer participated in some of the events he describes. For the sake of convenience, and with a slight nod to received tradition that may very well be accurate, I will continue referring to the writer of Luke-Acts as "Luke."

In terms of Luke's sources, I follow the lead of most scholars in adopting the two- (or four-) source hypothesis for explaining the literary relationship between the Synoptics: Luke, like Matthew, used both Mark and another source (commonly designated "Q") when composing his Gospel. Thus, in my discussion to follow, I will sometimes compare traditions in Luke with their earlier counterparts in Mark and, where relevant, their parallels in Matthew in order to illuminate Luke's emphases. Similarly, I will sometimes compare Luke's and Matthew's rendering of traditions they presumably draw from Q. Luke also frequently alludes to or cites Israelite scriptures in both Luke and Acts (see chap. 5) and even occasionally alludes to or cites nonscriptural traditions, including some found among the Dead Sea Scrolls (see chap. 3). In some

---

4. So also ibid., 34–41. For a fuller articulation of this argument, see Karl Allen Kuhn, *Luke: The Elite Evangelist* (Collegeville, MN: Liturgical Press, 2010), 1–9.

of these cases it can also be fruitful to compare the original tradition and its form as reshaped by Luke and integrated into his narrative. Luke obviously used other early Christian traditions (commonly designated "L" material) in his Gospel and Acts. Since we lack a reliable means of determining (or even guessing at) the precise contours of those traditions before Luke used them, I find it best to focus on the form in which they appear in Luke or Acts and not to speculate on how Luke may have redacted them.

With the dating of Luke-Acts, the best that can be offered is a rather broad range.[5] Luke's use of Mark and his apparent awareness of Jerusalem's destruction (see Luke 13:34–35; 19:41–44; 21:20–24) point to a date after 70 CE. Reliable historical markers on the back end include Justin's citation (*Dialogue* 103.8) and Marcion's use of Luke, but these do not necessitate a date earlier than 125. I think that the dating range embraced by the majority of scholars (70–90) is most likely in light of the evidence that Luke was an occasional companion of Paul. The apostle, as most conclude, arrived in Rome between 56 and 61, and this is the last indication from the "we" passages that Luke was with Paul. Even if we presume that Luke was as young as twenty-five during the latter years of Paul's ministry, this puts Luke in his mid-sixties to mid-seventies by the start of the second century. While it is not impossible that Luke could have written Acts at that age, the closer to or further past that date we go, the less likely it seems.

Unity and Genre of Luke-Acts

Several features of Luke and Acts indicate their common authorship.[6] Most apparent, the author addresses a certain "Theophilus" in the prologue to each volume (see Luke 1:1–4 and Acts 1:1–5), and the prologue to Acts characterizes the work to follow as the continuation of the "the first book" (i.e., the Gospel) Luke wrote for Theophilus (Acts 1:1–2). Scholars also note considerable stylistic and linguistic similarities between Luke and Acts. These features, along with the abundant parallelism, thematic development, and shared rhetorical objectives between the two works (as we shall discuss in parts 2 and 3), also convince many that not only are Luke and Acts from the same hand but that

5. For a detailed review of the various arguments concerning the dating range for Luke and Acts, see Craig S. Keener, *Acts: An Exegetical Commentary* (Grand Rapids: Baker Academic, 2012), 1:383–401.

6. Only a few have challenged the common authorship of Luke-Acts; see, for example, A. C. Clark (*The Acts of the Apostles* [Oxford: Clarendon, 1993], 393–408), who argues for separate authors based on what he considers stylistic differences between the two works. See also A. W. Argyle, "The Greek of Luke and Acts," *NTS* 20 (1973–74): 441–45; and J. Wenham, "The Identification of Luke," *EvQ* 63 (1991): 3–44.

Luke's intent was for recipients to interpret both as one and the same story.[7] As my preceding discussion has already implied, I agree with this assessment. For our purposes, the unity of Luke-Acts not only legitimates but also necessitates our attempts to incorporate evidence from both volumes when discerning Luke's objectives. It also directs us to consider that certain aspects of the Kingdom presented in the Gospel may not be fully manifested in the immediate narrative, but anticipate events to come later in Acts (e.g., the mission to the gentiles, first announced by Simeon in Luke 2:25–35, or Jesus' promise of the "power from on high" in Luke 24:49). Conversely, we are also called to recognize that because of Luke's frequent use of parallelism, his characterization of certain characters or developments in the ministry of the believers in Acts needs to be viewed in light of certain characters or events he has portrayed in the Gospel.

The advantage of discerning the genre to which Luke-Acts, as a unified volume, most closely corresponds is that genre provides another indicator helping us to determine the evangelist's purposes for composing the work.[8] The two Greco-Roman genres most commonly proposed are biography and history. Ancient biography testifies to and celebrates the significance of a notable figure.[9] It often casts a subject within a certain historical context, and that person's significance is sometimes set in relation to a particular moment in history. But the chief aim of biographical narrative is *characterization*: portraying the figure in various situations so that his virtues and vices may be illuminated and edify the audience. To be sure, Luke-Acts does in some

7. One of the more detailed arguments for the thematic similarity and unity of the two volumes is Robert C. Tannehill's *The Narrative Unity of Luke-Acts: A Literary Interpretation*, 2 vols. (Minneapolis: Fortress, 1986, 1990). See also Keener, *Acts*, 1:550–81, or the more concise treatment in Joel B. Green, *The Gospel of Luke*, NICNT (Grand Rapids: Eerdmans, 1997), 6–10. Mikeal C. Parsons and Richard I. Pervo (*Rethinking the Unity of Luke and Acts* [Minneapolis: Fortress, 1990]) argue that while Luke and Acts are unified at the *story* level of the narrative, they are not at the *discourse* level; the story content of both volumes is clearly parallel, but the method of telling the story has changed, resulting in a kind of disunity between the two volumes. Hence they refer to Acts as the *sequel* to Luke as a means of signifying the very close connection, yet organic separation, between them. In contrast, many others argue that the separation of the work into two scrolls was simply due to the practical matter of its length; see, e.g., Green, *Gospel of Luke*, 8.

8. For helpful reviews of the debate concerning the genre of Luke-Acts, see David E. Aune, *The New Testament in Its Literary Environment*, LEC (Philadelphia: Westminster, 1987), 17–115; Ben Witherington III, *The Acts of the Apostles: A Socio-Rhetorical Commentary* (Grand Rapids: Eerdmans, 1998), 2–39; or Keener, *Acts*, 1:90–115.

9. Two chief proponents of the view that Luke's Gospel is best categorized as a form of Greco-Roman biography are Charles H. Talbert, *What Is a Gospel? The Genre of the Canonical Gospels* (Philadelphia: Fortress, 1977), and Richard A. Burridge, *What Are the Gospels? A Comparison with Graeco-Roman Biography* (Cambridge: Cambridge University Press, 1995).

measure manifest these biographical tendencies in its portrayal of Jesus, Peter, Paul, and others, whose actions the evangelist likely intends to be instructive for his recipients.

On the other hand, four notable features of Luke-Acts indicate its intent to address broader, historical developments as it announces the arrival of the Kingdom. First, throughout the infancy narrative and the rest of Luke-Acts, events are cast as the advent of God's plan to redeem Israel and humanity; in other words, the focus of Luke's kingdom story is on God's accomplishment of the world's long-awaited salvation, or God's ordering of "salvation history." Second, and related, God is presented as choreographing this fulfillment *through* Jesus; in other words, the focus of the narrative is primarily theocentric and secondarily christocentric. Third, when we transition to Acts, the historical character of the work becomes even more pronounced, as the narrative attends to the development and mission of the early Christian community. Several characters stand at the forefront of Luke's narrative, but none of the ways Luke draws his characters overshadows his overarching concern to show how their faithful actions and perseverance advance the emergence of God's Kingdom. Fourth, in addition to the historical purview and plotting of Luke-Acts, several of the literary techniques and devices Luke employs find closer parallels to the genre of historiography. For instance, Luke uses temporal markers (synchronisms) to date key events (e.g., Luke 1:5; 2:1–2; 3:1–2) and states in his preface that he has investigated sources of information carefully and consulted with eyewitnesses (1:2). Moreover, Luke's frequent allusions to characters and events in Israel's past (see chap. 5), and his widespread use of character speech to testify to the significance of present events within the broad sweep of Israel's history (see chaps. 6–7), show clear resemblances to Israelite historiography.

Ancient biography and historiography were flexible enough to include elements typical of other genres. But the primary factor in determining genre is the overarching purpose of the work as a whole, as evidenced by the contextualization of its constituent elements through repetition, plotting, and thematic development. From the prologue of the Gospel (1:1–4) onward, Luke-Acts tells us a story of "the matters fulfilled among us" (τῶν πεπληροφορημένων ἐν ἡμῖν πραγμάτων). Its chief focus is the inauguration of a new historical era that the faithful are called to embrace and enact with joy, devotion, and sacrifice. To be sure, Jesus' life, death, resurrection, and ongoing ministry are central elements of that story, as are the actions of others. Moreover, Luke's recipients are also called to celebrate and emulate the faithfulness of these characters. Yet the actions of these figures are inextricably connected to and given meaning by the characters' participation in this decisive period of human history. Thus, Luke's kingdom story is best categorized as an instance of Greco-Roman historiography with many formal and thematic similarities to Israelite historiography.[10] For "the identity-shaping, legitimacy-providing concerns that animate reader response to Luke's Gospel and its sequel center on the connection of this history to the history, and particular OT histories, that belong to the Jewish people."[11] In short, Luke's historical narrative is an urgent call for Theophilus and others both to "know the truth concerning the things about which [they] have been instructed" (Luke 1:4)—namely, the advent of God's long-awaited Kingdom in the ministry of Jesus and his followers—and to order their hearts and lives accordingly.

---

10. We will explore a number of these formal similarities to Israelite historiography in chap. 4.
11. John T. Carroll, *Luke: A Commentary*, NTL (Louisville: Westminster John Knox, 2012), 6.

Part 1

Luke and His World

Part 1 invites readers into the political, social, economic, and religious character of the first-century Mediterranean. Chapter 1 sketches distinctive features of the Roman world, including their manifestation in Palestine, drawing from the insights of social-scientific analysis. Chapter 2 then focuses in on Israelite hopes for rescue from the evils of this age and deliverance to God's realm of blessing. Chapter 3 presents my understanding of Luke's social location as a member of the elite and the insight this realization yields for better appreciating the rhetorical edge of Luke's narrative.

1

Imperium Romanum

An Empire of Disparity and Want

As proposed in the introduction, the primary aim of Luke-Acts is to challenge Theophilus and others to abandon their allegiance to the life they know and to some extent still cherish. The world of Luke and his audience was that of the Roman Empire. While cultural patterns and conditions in the vast territory controlled by Rome surely varied from region to region or even from year to year, the survey to follow provides a baseline of what life was generally like for most in the Roman world in the first century of the Common Era. It was a realm characterized by the grossly inequitable distribution of power and resources, leaving the vast majority wanting for life's basic necessities. However, I should also note at the outset that the survey to follow focuses on those dimensions of the Roman hegemony that I believe Luke was most interested in confronting—namely, its distribution of power and resources and the belief system that legitimated those modes of distribution. But, of course, the Roman world—though dependent upon and fueled by this exploitative system—was also more than this. Rome's legacy also includes impressive works of literature, philosophy, politics, art, and architecture that remain influential to the present day. To be fair, we should keep this in mind as we attend to what many would consider the darker sides of Roman rule.

The Rise of the Roman Empire

Power changed hands several times throughout the Mediterranean region in
the centuries leading up to the Common Era. Under Alexander the Great in
the fourth century BCE, the Greeks wrested control of this part of the world
from the Persians, who had themselves overtaken the Babylonians in the sixth
century BCE. After Alexander died in 323 BCE, his vast empire was first divided
between his generals and eventually became three dynastic realms that would
continue for more than another hundred years: the Antiochid in Macedonia;
the Ptolemaic in Egypt; and the Seleucid, from Persia across Syria to Asia.
But in the latter half of the third century BCE, Greek power was seriously
eroding, and much of the region was slipping from its grasp. This was largely
due to the rise of Rome, which conquered the Italian peninsula, the western
Mediterranean including Spain, eventually Carthage in northern Africa to
the south, and Macedonia to the east. At the beginning of the second century
BCE, the Seleucids were in control of Palestine and Asia Minor. However, they
suffered a crushing defeat at the hands of Rome in the battle of Magnesia
(Manisa in modern-day Turkey) in 190, thus losing Asia Minor, and they were
also required to pay a hefty tribute to their conquerors.

The Seleucids sought to reestablish their grip on their remaining realm and
initially gained some measure of stability. In 169–168, the Seleucid king Antiochus IV led semisuccessful campaigns against Egypt, acquiring significant
plunder. During this time, Rome also reaffirmed its support of Antiochus' claim
over Syria and Phoenicia. But then Antiochus engaged in a series of actions
against Jerusalem that would galvanize the Israelite people into a protracted
struggle for freedom and eventually contribute to the demise of the Seleucid
dynasty. While Antiochus was preoccupied with his campaigns in Egypt, a
false rumor of his death circulated in Judea. The former and disaffected high
priest, Jason, sought to take advantage of the apparent vacuum of power and
revolted, briefly retaking Jerusalem in 169. Before Antiochus could return,
Jason was expelled from the city. However, the Seleucid ruler used the turmoil
as an opportunity to reconquer Jerusalem, resulting in a series of extraordinary insults against the Israelite people. In addition to already controlling the
office of the high priest and leveling burdensome taxes, Antiochus invaded
Jerusalem, killing and enslaving tens of thousands, leveled its walls, stole from
the temple treasury, banned the worship of Yahweh, mandated the worship
of Greek gods and goddesses, turned the Jerusalem temple into a temple of
Zeus, and viciously persecuted those who resisted. His attack on Jerusalem
was a "reenactment of conquest" designed to legitimate his attempts to order
a widespread transformation of Judean culture and to establish himself as

its inhabitants' sole master and sovereign. As Anathea Portier-Young states: "Antiochus' methods of conquest were thus calculated to shatter the people's sense of autonomy and will to resist, so that all will and all freedom would derive from his own regime and own person."[1]

The Israelites revolted in 167 under the leadership of the Hasmonean family, leading to an extended rebellion known as the Maccabean Revolt. As recorded in 1 Maccabees, one of our primary sources for this period, the rebels used guerrilla tactics in a lengthy war of attrition and made slow progress toward independence. The Seleucids rescinded the ban on the worship of Yahweh in 164, shortly before Antiochus' death. Rome recognized Israelite independence in 161, making a treaty with the newly restored nation, and Israel eventually won its full freedom from the Seleucids in 142. Under the leadership of John Hyrcanus, who ruled as high priest from 134 to 104, Israel attained a significant measure of religious, political, and economic stability and regained most of the territory that it once held under David and Solomon. This political expansion continued under Hyrcanus' son, Alexander Jannaeus, and Alexander's wife, Salome (103–76). Yet the latter part of their reign and the years following it were marred by internal strife, culminating in the outbreak of civil war from 67 to 63 as the brothers Aristobulus II and Hyrcanus II vied for the rule of Israel. The Roman general Pompey intervened in 63 to settle the dispute. He seized Jerusalem from Aristobulus' partisans and named Hyrcanus II high priest, but stripped him of much of his political power and placed Judea under Roman tribute.

Pompey's intervention marked the start of Rome's interest in and control over the region of Palestine. It also marked the beginning of Israelite antipathy toward Rome. Following the treaty of 161, Israelite views of Rome were generally positive. But Pompey's siege of Jerusalem in 63 resulted in much suffering and death. Once the city was in his control, Pompey led a retinue into the temple, violating the Holy of Holies. As Josephus records, "Of all the calamities of that time none so deeply affected the nation as the exposure to alien eyes of the Holy Place, hitherto screened from view" (*War* 1.152).[2] From now on, "the damage that Pompey had caused would remain irreparable: henceforward the name of Rome became associated with the notion of sacrilege, and that notion began to be felt in the writings of that period."[3]

During its years of expansion in the first century BCE, Rome itself was plagued by internal strife and fought its own civil wars. As a republic for the

---

1. Anathea E. Portier-Young, *Apocalypse against Empire: Theologies of Resistance in Early Judaism* (Grand Rapids: Eerdmans, 2011), 138–39.
2. Translation from Mireille Hadas-Lebel, *Jerusalem against Rome*, trans. Robyn Fréchet, Interdisciplinary Studies in Ancient Culture and Religion 7 (Leuven; Dudley, MA: Peeters, 2006), 22.
3. Ibid.

better part of five hundred years, Rome had been ruled by the Senate, made up of elite landowners of leading families, in conjunction with magistrates (or consuls) who were elected by the citizenry. As Roman dominance expanded through military conquest leading up to the Common Era, powerful generals began to vie for control over the republic's affairs. At times, this control was pursued and practiced through alliances. The First Triumvirate included Pompey, Marcus Licinius Crassus, and Gaius Julius Caesar. But after Crassus died in battle, the triumvirate dissolved, and Pompey and Caesar fought each other for control of Rome. Caesar won control by defeating Pompey in 45 BCE. He was named dictator for life in 44, and his rule threatened to overshadow the influence of the Senate. Some senators, however, would not be so easily marginalized. Marcus Brutus and Gaius Cassius, former allies to Pompey, murdered Caesar in the Senate meeting hall. In the resulting struggle for power, consul Mark Antony, Octavian (Caesar's adopted heir), and exconsul Lepidus formed what was known as the Second Triumvirate. This triumvirate was also short-lived, leading to another bloody struggle. By 31, Octavian emerged from the fray victorious, assumed the name Caesar and the title "Augustus" (great, or worthy of honor), and became the first emperor of Rome. The office of emperor would continue to evolve over the ensuing decades, and the Senate would still hold some of its previous power, but with Octavian the transition to imperial rule in the form of an absolute monarch, or emperor, became complete. Octavian's victory marks Rome's transition from republic to empire.

The Pax Romana *and Rule of Rome*

Octavian's rule also ushered in the era known as the *pax Romana* (Roman peace), often described as a centuries-long period of relative stability and prosperity due to the strength of Roman rule. The *pax Romana* did indeed have many benefits. Warfare and regime change were destructive events, impacting all levels of society, and the economic prosperity enjoyed during this period facilitated better nutrition, increased life expectancy, higher population levels, and access to education. But the benefits of the *pax Romana* were not evenly distributed among Rome's subjects. Far from it. Most struggled under the burden of stifling economic oppression. Moreover, Rome's conquests continued, spreading north into Europe and reaching all the way to Britain and as far east as modern-day Iraq. Even into the Common Era, many lands came under the Roman peace only after the vanguard of Roman swords. Within Rome's provinces, including Palestine, challenges to Rome's power were effectively yet brutally suppressed by local elite loyal to the emperor.[4] When situations threatened to spin out of control, the response of the Roman military was inevitable and characteristically devastating for the rebels and many innocent bystanders alike.[5] In the case of the Israelite Revolt in Judea (67–70 CE), Roman fury resulted in the death or enslavement of thousands of Israelites, the sacking of Jerusalem, and the destruction of the temple.

The Many Heads of Roman Rule

Key to the maintenance of Roman control before, during, and after this period (as was true for the Greeks and Persians before them) was the use of client kings, governors, and other officials to rule the increasingly vast regions conquered by Rome. These rulers in turn appointed others to positions of authority, cultivating "a loyal clientele among local aristocrats by dispensing certain favors or benefits for them or their cities."[6] In exchange for the political and economic benefits attached to their positions, these client leaders were to assist in "keeping the peace," providing police support when needed, collecting taxes, maintaining important civic celebrations, offering sacrifices on behalf of the emperor and Rome, and encouraging allegiance to the empire. While many of these rulers were native to the areas under their charge, "these local elites, whose cooperation with the central power was so crucial to the smooth functioning of the empire, tended to adopt many Roman ways themselves."[7] Thus, along with the incursion of Roman power throughout the Mediterranean world and beyond, there arrived a second influx of Hellenistic culture, a reinforcing tide of Greco-Roman politics, religion, social structure, art, and architecture that profoundly shaped this region. For this era at least, the proverb "when in Rome, do as the Romans do" is seriously misleading, unless by "in Rome" one means the vast expanse of territory Rome came to control! Many were doing what the Romans did well beyond the city of Rome.

Palestine was no exception. Herod the Great ruled from 38 to 4 BCE. By Roman standards, his reign was impressive, albeit brutal, on many counts. He managed to navigate wisely his allegiances to Rome during its tumultuous years of civil war, and eventually secured the patronage of Octavian. He

4. See Ben Witherington III, *New Testament History: A Narrative Account* (Grand Rapids: Baker Academic, 2001), 60, 109.

5. See Richard A. Horsley, "High Priests and the Politics of Roman Palestine: A Contextual Analysis of Evidence in Josephus," *JSJ* 17 (1986): 435–63.

6. Richard A. Horsley, *Jesus and the Powers: Conflict, Covenant, and the Hope of the Poor* (Minneapolis: Fortress, 2011), 33.

7. James B. Rives, *Religion in the Roman Empire* (Malden, MA: Blackwell, 2007), 3.

hellenized the region in form and function, engaging in massive construction projects, including a major renovation to the temple in Jerusalem and the building of several cities that he dedicated to the emperor. He suppressed uprisings (real and perhaps imagined) and established a client network among the elite through both favors and threats. After Herod's death, the Roman distribution and exercise of power in Palestine came to be spread among three primary groups of agents. These included members of the Herodian family, who were assigned areas outside Judea; other officials appointed by Rome, such as the governor in Jerusalem, whose charge was to maintain peace and ensure the flow of resources to Rome; and the priestly aristocracy, who oversaw the maintenance of and raising of funds for the temple and governed most Israelite affairs. These leaders and the families closely allied with them controlled much of the arable land and also benefited from the revenues they gathered on behalf of Rome (more on this later). Thus, while several parties were involved in the rule of Palestine, the same sort of hierarchical pattern present in Rome and throughout the empire was in place here as well. As described by Richard Rohrbaugh,

> the urban elite made up about 2 percent of the total population. At its upper levels, the urban elite included the highest ranking military officers, ranking priestly families, and the Herodians and other ranking aristocratic families. They lived in the heavily fortified central areas of the cities . . . socially isolated from the rest of society. . . . The literacy rate among them was high, in some areas, even among women, and along with their retainers they maintained control of writing, coinage, taxation, and the military and judicial systems.[8]

To maintain their privileged stations and power, then, the Israelite elite in Palestine (like most elite everywhere in regions controlled by Rome) had to acquiesce to Roman rule. In practice if not in spirit, these Israelites signed on to the apparent truth that Caesar ruled the world. They also participated in the hierarchical socioeconomic structure that ensured their abundance at the expense of so many. Josephus, a contemporary of Luke, stands as one example of such acquiescence. An Israelite priest who transformed himself from a general leading the fight against Rome during the Judean Revolt (67–70 CE) into a chronicler of Israelite history criticizing his fellow revolutionaries—along with a few incompetent Roman appointees—and in turn receiving the generous patronage of Roman elite, he illustrates the malleable allegiance

---

8. Richard Rohrbaugh, "The Social Location of the Markan Audience," in *The Social World of the New Testament: Insights and Models*, ed. Jerome H. Neyrey and Eric C. Stewart (Peabody, MA: Hendrickson, 2008), 145–46.

of some socially ascendant Israelites. While numerous elements of Israelite sacred tradition speak against such partnering with foreign powers and the systemic neglect of the "alien, orphan, and widow," several of the Israelite heroes of old (e.g., Joseph, David, Ezra, Nehemiah, and Daniel) found a way to serve both Yahweh and gentile lords. Perhaps these figures provided some of the Israelite elite with a precedent that they saw as legitimating their own collusion with foreign rule. To drive this point home even further, consider this. The gate to the Israelite temple rebuilt by Herod was crowned with an eagle, the symbol of Roman rule, and sacrifices were offered daily by the priests on behalf of the emperor and Rome. Note the significance of these two realities! Even the institutional embodiment of Israel's covenantal relationship with Yahweh and the intimate, sacred ritual of sacrifice that helped to maintain that covenant bond were not spared from the hegemonic claim that all—at least in part—owed their place and continuation to the patronage of Rome.

The Social and Economic Landscape of Empire

Imagine this scene. A motley crew has gathered. Old and young. Some darkened from sun and labor, their skin a rough hide broken by an occasional sore. Others pale and sickly with vacant eyes. Some bent and shuffling with a limping gait. Several are thick-bodied, scarred and muscled—soldiers by the looks of them. At the front of the crowd stands a small clique of finer cloth. Erect and proud, they stiffen their faces with an air of contempt for the rabble with whom they are forced to wait. And wait they must, for their patron, Lucius, is a busy man. Or so he says. But the wait is more a message than a necessity. They are to wait *on* him. In their varying capacities they provide something he desires, and he in turn provides a token of his gracious patronage. It is never enough to satisfy. For most of them, especially those not at the front of the line, it is never enough to provide more than a brief respite of relief. Just enough to keep them coming back.

Scenes like this one replayed countless times in varying forms throughout the Roman world, and they represent well the social and economic structure of Luke's society. The crowd, themselves manifesting a diversity of social strata queued in hierarchical order outside Lucius' door, are there to petition one of greater rank and wealth in hopes of benefiting from his *patronage*. The function of patronage, as we shall discuss below, was not resource redistribution as much as it was the maintenance of the status quo. It was one of several mechanisms that kept folks like Lucius secure, very well heeled, and surrounded by needy devotees.

Perhaps another image will help: picture an imposing mansion of expertly laid stone alit with a golden glow and luxuriously appointed. Gardens and courtyards offer a tasteful accent to its fortress-like prominence. But stepping back and greatly widening your field of view, you note that this mansion sits atop a vast mountain, conical in shape. At the very bottom of the mountain, crammed together on the slopes of its lowest foothills, are the burrows, rudimentary lean-tos, and shacks of the poorest of the poor. Above these hovels, the bulk of the mountain is densely populated with mud-brick houses or cramped stone-block dwellings belonging to peasants, artisans, or slaves. Higher still, and now tapering severely toward the summit, is a narrow layer of what might be considered the "respectable" homes of fortunate merchants. Above them is yet another thin stratum of slightly-better-appointed homes belonging to higher-ranking soldiers, tax collectors, and police, whose task is to maintain the ordering of those beneath and above them. Finally, as the mountain crescendos to its peak, there are the dwellings of the elite, whose majesty and opulence are like in kind to that of the mansion that crowns the pinnacle. From the elite's vantage point—and few living on that mountain would disagree—life is far better at the top. Yet for those like Lucius' clients, the trudge upslope is tedious, and even after they have arrived at his mansion, gravity inevitably pulls them back down to where they belong.

Let us turn now from this image to the anthropological theory that informs it. To get us started, I offer the following diagram to depict the circulation of resources and the resulting power structure of the Roman world.

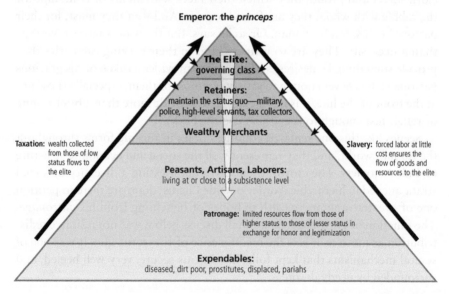

As the mountain metaphor I just provided suggests, the hierarchical stratification and resource distribution of the first-century Roman world—especially when these social and economic dimensions are in focus—could be usefully cast as pyramidal.[9] At the apex of Roman society was the emperor, father of the empire and its chief patron. To him was due the highest allegiance and honor, and he controlled the resources of the empire. Directly beneath him were other elites, the ruling class, likely composing no more than 2 to 3 percent of the population.[10] The elite, themselves divided into several levels, primarily consisted of properly pedigreed families who were longtime members of the aristocracy and had also established themselves as friends or clients of Roman leaders. The elite would also include recent entrants into their ranks, those few who through military prowess, political maneuvering, the acquisition of extraordinary wealth, or adoption by an elite family or patron managed to join the elite without being born into this social location.

Along a continuum from the lower levels of the elite down to the nonelite levels were retainers. This included "lower-level military officers, officials and bureaucrats such as clerks and bailiffs, personal retainers, high-ranking household servants, scholars, legal experts, and lower-level lay aristocracy. These worked primarily in the service of the elite and served to mediate both governmental and religious functions to the lower class and to village areas."[11] Retainers also played a crucial role in maintaining the flow of goods and services from producers, primarily the lower classes, to the elite. While a thin slice of the population enjoyed the good fortune of being wealthy merchants (a few of whom managed to join the ranks of the elite), the vast majority of the population were slaves and peasants, including urban merchants, artisans, day laborers, service workers, and rural peasants (those owning and farming small landholdings, tenant farmers, day laborers). Beneath them were those who were viewed by most as outcasts: the dirt poor, the diseased or severely handicapped, prostitutes, and other social pariahs.

The Circulation and Stagnation of Resources

The diagram above also seeks to convey Roman society's economic "circulatory system." The lower class produced nearly all the goods and services of the

9. Though see also the helpful diagram provided by David A. Fiensy (*The Social History of Palestine in the Herodian Period: The Land Is Mine*, Studies in the Bible and Early Christianity 20 [Lewiston, NY: Edwin Mellen, 1991], 158), which uses a vase-shaped image to focus on social stratification.

10. Fiensy (*Social History of Palestine*, 167), however, estimates that the Palestinian elite composed only 1 percent of the population.

11. Rohrbaugh, "Social Location," 148.

empire but retained very little of those resources for its members. Two primary mechanisms ensured the flow of wealth to the emperor and the elite: various modes of taxation, and cheap labor in the form of slavery and tenant farming.

Rome heavily taxed its subjects. Scholars estimate that between one-quarter and one-third of the goods harvested or produced by peasants, artisans, and tenant farmers were required for various taxes, tolls, and tithes.[12] A. Ben-David estimates the combined Roman and Israelite taxes for Roman Palestine at 33.1 percent.[13] Such heavy taxation on the underclass resulted in a precarious existence for peasants and artisans, with the vast majority of them living slightly above, at, or below a subsistence level. Speaking of Roman Palestine in particular, Rohrbaugh writes, "The wealth of the elite was based primarily on land ownership and taxation, which effectively drained the resources of the rural areas. The 'redistributive' economic system, as it is called in economic anthropology, served to expropriate peasant surplus and redistribute it among those in control."[14] Aggressive taxation also contributed to the high rate of debt suffered by peasant farmers. This debt, combined with onerous lending policies and unmercifully high rates of interest established by the elite, resulted in a massive foreclosure of ancestral landholdings in the years leading up to the Common Era.[15] Keith Hopkins estimates that from 80 to 8 BCE, about 1.5 million people, roughly half the peasant families of Roman Italy, were forced from their ancestral lands.[16] These figures are likely representative of conditions throughout the provinces of the empire, including Roman Palestine.[17]

Still another resource that greatly benefited the elite was their control of relatively cheap labor. Slavery was the engine that drove the economy, as Rome "created an institutionalized system of large-scale dependence on slave labor for the major portion of basic production."[18] Estimates on the number of

12. Gildas Hamel, "Poverty and Charity," in *The Oxford Handbook of Jewish Daily Life in Roman Palestine*, ed. Catherine Hezser (Oxford: Oxford University Press, 2010), 311; Phillip A. Harland, "The Economy of First-Century Palestine: State of the Scholarly Discussion," in *Handbook of Early Christianity: Social Science Approaches*, ed. Anthony J. Blasi, Jean Duhaime, and Paul-André Turcotte (Walnut Creek, CA: Alta Mira Press, 2002), 521.

13. A. Ben-David, *Talmudische Ökonomie: Die Wirtschaft des jüdischen Palästina zur Zeit der Mishna und des Talmud* (Hildesheim: Olms, 1974), 297–98, cited in Hamel, "Poverty and Charity," 311.

14. Rohrbaugh, "Social Location," 145–46.

15. See Douglas E. Oakman, *Jesus and the Peasants*, Matrix: The Bible in Mediterranean Context (Eugene, OR: Cascade, 2008), 11–22, 137–43.

16. Keith Hopkins, *Conquerors and Slaves*, Sociological Studies in Roman History (Cambridge: Cambridge University Press, 1978), 67.

17. Horsley, *Jesus and the Powers*, 30–31.

18. Richard Horsley, "The Slave Systems of Classical Antiquity and Their Reluctant Recognition by Modern Scholars," *Semeia* 83/84 (1998): 32.

slaves in the Roman Empire vary among anthropologists, ranging from 25 to 40 percent of the population. But the number of slaves could have easily swelled to the higher end of that range during the years surrounding the Common Era due to Rome's conquest of the Mediterranean (including Palestine) and beyond, augmenting the ranks of those enslaved because of debt.[19] As more and more arable land shifted to the elite, tenant farming, sharecropping, and day labor also became central to agricultural production throughout the empire. Along with many other peasants, these field laborers migrated at or below a subsistence existence, and sharecroppers were in perpetual danger of becoming slaves themselves. Gildas Hamel notes that "especially in the case of sharecropping, the factors of production provided by landowners (land, seeds, traction, tools) were set at a very high rate, usually amounting to half of the total value of the crop, a circumstance which, together with the smallness of the acreage under contract, guaranteed the fall into indebtedness."[20]

In sum, aggressive taxation, an elite-controlled market system that "nickeled and dimed" the underclass through rents and tariffs, lending policies that routinely resulted in the foreclosure of peasant landholdings, and the cheap labor of slaves, artisans, and agricultural workers all ensured the flow of wealth and resources from the underclass to the elite. This was, as declared by G. E. M. de Ste. Croix, "a massive system of exploitation of the great majority by the ruling class."[21]

Power through Patronage

Patronage, consisting of a relationship between a patron and clients, was a form of economic redistribution in which some resources were funneled to those of lower status. Returning to the diagram, note the white arrow that descends from the emperor downward. The emperor functioned as the chief patron for the entire empire, as he sanctioned the distribution of wealth to its various members. In turn, the elite would also serve as patrons to elites of lesser status and sometimes even to members of lower classes, and this would continue on down the social scale. What patrons offered their clients varied: financial or legal assistance during times of crisis, protection from

19. Hopkins (*Conquerors and Slaves*, 9) puts the number at the end of the first century BCE at 35 to 40 percent.

20. Hamel, "Poverty and Charity," 314.

21. G. E. M. de Ste. Croix, *The Class Struggle in the Ancient Greek World: From the Archaic Age to the Arab Conquests* (Ithaca, NY: Cornell University Press, 1980), 374, cited in Neil Elliott, *The Arrogance of the Nations: Reading Romans in the Shadow of Empire*, Paul in Critical Contexts (Minneapolis: Fortress, 2008), 7.

enemies, food, gifts, mentoring, appointments to an official post, among other favors or forms of assistance. In return, the patron could expect to receive honor, information, and political support from clients.[22] Often the relationship and exchanges between patron and client were face-to-face; at times, favors and requests were mediated through an intermediary or "broker." What the patron-client system amounted to for the peasantry was—to use a modern analogy—a rather meager form of "trickle down" economics. It "functioned as the means by which elites could increase honor and status, acquire and hold office, achieve power and influence, and increase wealth. In other words, it kept the social hierarchy intact."[23]

As the downward arrow in the diagram indicates, the farther patronage moved down the social scale, the smaller the dispersal of wealth. Through patronage, the greatest resources were disbursed to those already at or near the level of elite. For peasants, the resources received through patronage could be of significant temporary assistance but did not fundamentally alter their social and economic station. To put it differently, patronage among the upper classes was about favors, networking, and advancement. Patronage for the peasantry was about gaining resources that eased in varying degrees their struggle to stay out of insurmountable debt and even to survive. To put it more crassly, it simply took a lot less to buy the allegiance of a peasant than to buy that of a fellow elite.

Within Roman Palestine, elite who offered patronage to the underclass in order to gain their compliance or support included the temple establishment. The temple was the center of the Judean economy. It received tithes, offerings, and sacrifices from the populace, and also collected tribute for Rome, in exchange for its "brokerage" of divine forgiveness and blessing.[24] The economic benefits for the priesthood were significant, and members of the priestly aristocracy had acquired much of the arable land in the region through onerous lending policies and peasant foreclosure.[25] When it came to dealing with tenants and debtors, the priestly elite were expected to be just and kind to their tenants. But "they could also use the threat of short-term leases, eviction and physical violence (prison and torture)."[26] According to some Israelite sources, the priestly elites often opted for the latter: "Josephus and later rabbinic writings report the high priest's predatory practices of

22. K. C. Hanson and Douglas E. Oakman, *Palestine in the Time of Jesus: Social Structures and Social Conflicts*, 2nd ed. (Minneapolis: Fortress, 2008), 65.
23. Ibid., 66.
24. Horsley, *Jesus and the Powers*, 7.
25. Hamel, "Poverty and Charity," 314.
26. Ibid.

sending armed thugs and goon squads to the village threshing floors to seize the tithes intended for the ordinary priests and to intimidate the peasants in other ways (*Ant*. 20.9.2 §§206–7)."[27] While the temple establishment did collect offerings for the poor, it appears that the success of those offerings was inconsistent and the sums raised were dwarfed by the amounts set aside for personnel and the cult. As indicated by textual and archaeological evidence, more substantial and consistent assistance was provided to the poor on a community level and administered through synagogues. Synagogues served as hostels for transients and displaced persons, and funds were established for both long-term and emergency relief.[28]

Consequences for Elite and Peasant

As I noted above, it is likely that the Roman economy described above yielded consequences that varied regionally due to cultural, geographic, and climatic factors.[29] Moreover, in some circumstances resourceful and fortunate non-elite individuals could achieve a standard of living that approximated what we might call the "middle class."[30] It was also possible for high-level slaves within a prosperous household, by their own cunning and faithful service, to amass significant wealth, buy their freedom, and establish households for themselves. So not every member of Roman society was either extraordinarily well-heeled or struggling to survive. But according to most researchers, such disparity was the prevailing pattern, with the vast majority of the population (82–90 percent) living slightly above, at, or below the precarious edge of subsistence. The grossly inequitable distribution of resources described above fueled this disparity. Anthropologists commonly maintain that the top 2–5 percent of most agrarian societies likely controlled 50 to 65 percent of their territories' goods and services, leaving 95

27. Horsley, *Jesus and the Powers*, 76–77.
28. Hamel, "Poverty and Charity," 320.
29. Some researchers studying the economy of Roman Palestine argue for the recognition of regional variation, including the possibility that due to its fertility, Galilee may have been home to some relatively prosperous and small, family-owned farms. For a helpful review of perspectives, see Alexei Siverstev, "The Household Economy," in *The Oxford Handbook of Jewish Daily Life in Roman Palestine*, ed. Catherine Hezser (Oxford: Oxford University Press, 2010), 230–44; and Harland, "Economy of First-Century Palestine," 521–25.
30. A Roman-era economy scale as developed by Steven J. Friesen ("Poverty in Pauline Studies: Beyond the So-Called New Consensus," *JSNT* 26 [2004]: 323–61) and modified by Bruce W. Longenecker ("Exposing the Economic Middle: A Revised Economy Scale for the Study of Early Urban Christianity," *JSNT* 31 [2009]: 243–78) argues that 7–15 percent of urban populations possessed moderate resources that would have provided them a far more stable existence than most slaves and artisans.

percent of the population the remaining 35–50 percent.[31] Hanson and Oakman argue that documented tax rates corroborate these figures for Roman Palestine.[32] Assuming the middle ground for these estimates (5 percent controlling 57.5 percent of goods and services), the typical non-elite person would have access to less than 4 percent of the resources controlled by an elite person.

Elite Living

If you were to visit the first-century Mediterranean world, what would be immediately obvious about the elite is their access to relatively abundant material resources. Compared to the vast majority of the population, the elite lived a life of privilege and luxury. While some of the elite may have led busy lives overseeing their estates, managing their business affairs, and enhancing their social contacts, they probably had far more time for pursuing leisure activity and intellectual interests. To be sure, the elite were not removed from the vicissitudes of an agonist (competitive) society (see below). They likely encountered repeated challenges to their honor. If the elite held positions by appointment, their privileged station could suddenly change due to the whims of those above them. But much more than the vast majority, the elite avoided deficiencies and situations that dramatically shortened life expectancy. Their access to regular nutrition, superior shelter, rudimentary health care and hygiene, and clean(er) water; their avoidance of hard, manual labor; and the protection of cities made it far more likely for them to live into what we call "middle age" than the rest of society.

Peasant Struggle for Survival

In contrast, most of the lower class suffered irregular access to adequate nutrition, water, hygiene, and secure shelter. The consequences of perpetually living on the edge were debilitating.

> Obviously disease and high death rates were not evenly spread across all elements of the population but rather fell disproportionately upon the lower classes of both city and village. For most lower-class people who did make it to adulthood, their health would have been atrocious. By age thirty, the majority suffered from internal parasites, rotting teeth, and bad eyesight. Most had lived

31. See Gerhard E. Lenski, *Power and Privilege: A Theory of Social Stratification*, 2nd ed. (Chapel Hill: University of North Carolina Press, 1984), 228.

32. Hanson and Oakman, *Palestine in the Time of Jesus*, 105. See also Warren Carter, *The Roman Empire and the New Testament: An Essential Guide* (Nashville: Abingdon, 2006), 3.

with the debilitating results of protein deficiency since childhood. Parasites were especially prevalent, being carried to humans by sheep, goats, and dogs. Fifty percent of the hair combs from Qumran, Masada, and Murabbat were infected with lice and lice eggs, probably reflecting conditions elsewhere (Zias, 1991, 148). If infant mortality rates, the age structure of the population, and pathological evidence from skeletal remains can be taken as indicators, malnutrition was a constant threat as well (Fiensy, 1991, 98).[33]

As a result, the life expectancy of the urban peasantry was in the low twenties, and the rural peasantry in the low thirties. Infant mortality rates were about 30 percent, and over half of all peasants living past age one would fail to make it past age sixteen.[34] In short, many of the underclass were struggling to survive, their days filled with worry about the next harvest; the next tax, tribute, rent, or loan payment; and often the next meal.

The Legitimation of Elite Rule

Thus far we have examined the economic and social stratification governing the distribution of power and resources in the Roman world. As we have seen, the distribution of the empire's power and resources was characterized by extraordinary disparity, with the result that the vast majority of the population often wanted for life's basic necessities. How did the elite justify their privileged station in life? Perhaps most elite didn't spend much time thinking about it. Perhaps they assumed that this is just the way the world should be. But always in the background and sometimes at the forefront of the Roman worldview was the belief that the gods, and honor, have deemed it so.

The Inseparability of Religion, Politics, and Economics

Recall from the introduction that in Rome, as in most other premodern human societies, religion, politics, social stratification, and economics were inextricably intertwined. As Everett Ferguson rightly emphasizes, in the Roman world "human life was thoroughly permeated with religion"; religion infused nearly every political, intellectual, and civic activity.[35] Religion was

33. Rohrbaugh, "Social Location," 154. The two studies cited by Rohrbaugh are Joseph Zias, "Death and Disease in Ancient Israel," *BA* 54 (1991): 146–59; and Fiensy, *Social History of Palestine*.
34. Rohrbaugh, "Social Location," 150, 151.
35. Everett Ferguson, *Backgrounds of Early Christianity*, 2nd ed. (Grand Rapids: Eerdmans, 1993), 170–71.

also incorporated into most ancient persons' private lives. Though cultivating a bewildering diversity of beliefs, practices, and social forms, while unconcerned about integration and cohesion, most Romans viewed the workings of the world—natural and civic—as empowered and guided by the intersection of the divine and earthly realms.[36] As a polytheistic system, Roman religious tradition insisted "that gods existed, that they were many in number, that they could affect people's lives for good or ill, that it was necessary to win their favor through offerings and rituals, and that different contexts required different offerings and rituals."[37] Much of Roman religion, then, revolved around the proper civic and private practice of offerings and appeasements in order to ensure the gods' beneficent patronage of the Roman state and individuals.

Representatives of the Gods

Roman religion also presumed a cosmic order that paralleled the socioeconomic stratification and patterns of Roman society. The gods, themselves arranged in a loose hierarchy, were the patrons of the empire: to them was due honor in order to ensure their blessing upon the Roman people. Accordingly, allotments from the resources of the empire were to be placed at their feet in the forms of tithes, sacrifices, and offerings. The belief in divine patronage and the dutiful practice of making offerings to the gods by the Roman people (and most others) not only paralleled but normalized and implicitly justified the similar ordering of the Roman society and its economy. Just as the divine patrons deserve and require the honor and offerings of the Roman state, so the earthly patrons of Rome, who rule as representatives of the gods, require that offerings and honor be given them.

That the elite who ascended to prominent offices represented the divine is reflected in several features of their appointment. These rulers were installed and continually celebrated in a religious context, and prayers were regularly offered on their behalf. Moreover, by virtue of their office, nearly all public officials served in a cultic capacity as religious authorities.

> All those who held authority in public life, at whatever level, magistrate, promagistrate, legate, centurion, college president, or president of a local district, and so on—were also responsible for the cult of the community that they led. . . .

36. Rives (*Religion in the Roman Empire*, 52), among many others, emphasizes that Roman religion—apart from Judaism and Christianity—lacks a coherent and unified system of beliefs. In fact, "instead of 'a religion,' we can more usefully think of it as a group of loosely related but largely distinct ways of thinking about and interacting with the divine world."

37. Ibid., 86.

Every important decision involving religion, every innovation and disagreement relating to a religious problem that affected the public cult or other cults that were celebrated in public, fell within their domain.[38]

An important dimension, therefore, of the honor due to civic leaders was their role as cultic and religious leaders and their mediation of the nexus between human and divine spheres of reality. To put it rather baldly, the elite "used their wealth and influence to benefit the city in exchange for the social prestige and authority that their offices conferred upon them, including the implicit right to regulate the city's relations with its gods."[39] In short, the elite's role as mediators of the divine was contingent upon their social location and economic patronage. And their representative function as religious authorities, on whom the gods' favor rested, in turn legitimated their control of those positions and the means by which they achieved them.

The Roman tendency to associate political power with a divine mandate to rule is also manifested in what is often called the "imperial cult." The imperial cult is probably best described as a loosely connected and varied set of practices and perspectives that associate the emperor and even the imperial family with the divine realm.[40] With the elevation of the emperor as the sole head of the Roman Empire, to whom all political and economic allegiance was due, there also developed the tendency to regard him as a transcendent, divine-like figure. Since no other person held greater powers or honors than those of Augustus, "the emperor and his family were granted," by elite and many peasants alike, "honors equal to those enjoyed by the gods."[41] Such exaltation was manifested in various ways. Octavian initiated the practice of deifying deceased emperors by promoting the cult of the "Deified Julius," constructing a temple to honor the new god and appointing a priest as custodian. With Augustus' own death a formal procedure for deification of deceased emperors began to take shape, and temples to honor deceased emperors started springing up throughout the empire. Most Romans did not worship the emperors while the emperors were living, but many did worship the current emperor's *numen* (divine power) or *genius* (guardian spirit) in temples dedicated to those entities, a practice that Octavian himself no doubt encouraged by taking on the titles "Divi Filius" (Son of the Divine) and "Augustus" (great, or worthy of honor). However,

38. John Scheid, *An Introduction to Roman Religion*, trans. Janet Lloyd (Bloomington: Indiana University Press, 2003), 129.

39. Rives, *Religion in the Roman Empire*, 115.

40. Much of the present paragraph borrows from the helpful discussion of the imperial cult in ibid., 148–57.

41. Scheid, *Introduction to Roman Religion*, 164–65.

some provincial cults worshiped living emperors as gods, and the emperors Caligula and Domitian demanded that they be treated as gods while alive, while others such as Claudius more ambiguously portrayed themselves on coinage in the guise of specific deities. As mentioned earlier, sacrifices were regularly offered on behalf of living emperors, including in the Jerusalem temple, and the Roman cultic calendar came to include notable accomplishments and events in the lives of the emperors and other members of the imperial family. Despite the various forms and practices of the imperial cult, central to its mission was the notion that the emperor was to be "envisioned as the key point of intersection between the divine and human spheres."[42]

It is crucial to note the political, social, and economic significance of this religious belief. Roman power, social structure, and economy were extensions of the emperor's honor and authority. And the emperor was "the epiphany of divine power in the hands of a mortal."[43] He was the gods' steward to the Roman people. He himself ruled with the gods' authority and blessing. According to the various manifestations of the imperial cult, that reality was to be celebrated and cherished.

Honor, Pedigree, and Power

Much of ancient society revolved around the increase and loss of honor, and honor is commonly identified as one of the most important values in the Greco-Roman world.[44] Put simply and helpfully by Bruce Malina, "Honor is the value of a person in his or her own eyes (that is, one's claim to worth) *plus* that person's value in the eyes of his or her social group. Honor is a claim to worth along with the social acknowledgement of worth."[45] Honor could be either *ascribed* or *acquired*. "Ascribed honor" is honor claimed by and granted to a person due to their kinship group, or their authority within and perhaps outside that kinship group. For instance, if you were born into a prestigious and powerful family, you would likely be granted honor due to your membership in that family. Or, let's say all the pieces of your early life fell fortuitously in place and you found yourself a member of the emperor's court at a young age. You would also be ascribed honor due to your membership in that elite

42. Rives, *Religion in the Roman Empire*, 155.

43. Scheid, *Introduction to Roman Religion*, 165.

44. For a helpful and often-cited discussion of the values of honor and shame, see Bruce J. Malina, *The New Testament World: Insights from Cultural Anthropology*, rev. ed. (Louisville: Westminster John Knox, 2001), 27–57. The following summary of honor is indebted to Malina's discussion.

45. Ibid., 30.

group. Let's imagine again that your astute service caught the emperor's eye, and you were appointed as one of the emperor's trusted advisors. Here again you would gain honor not only by your gifted service but also by virtue of your association to another. The *emperor's* public recognition of you as a chief advisor would gain you honor in the eyes of the rest of the court and his loyal subjects (even if they were very jealous of you).

"Acquired honor" is honor that you gain by excelling over others. In other words, this is honor granted to you not simply because of your association with others but because you have demonstrated your mastery in the eyes of others. How could such mastery be displayed? Undoubtedly, many activities could potentially enhance a person's reputation: acts of heroism, the donation of funds to a public project, a distinguished military career or other service (as in the example above), eloquent oration, control of one's children, among others. Beyond these, a common form of social exchange often termed *challenge and response* also played a pivotal role in the gain and loss of honor. Challenge and response "is sort of a constant social tug of war, a game of social push and shove."[46] It typically contained the following elements and structure:

> Challenge-response within the context of honor is a sort of interaction in at least three phases: (1) the challenge in terms of some action (word, deed, or both) on the part of the challenger; (2) the perception of the message by both the individual to whom it is directed and the public at large; and (3) the reaction of the receiving individual and the evaluation of the reaction on the part of the public.[47]

Malina and others assume that this form of social exchange was exceedingly common—that it characterized, in fact, nearly all of one's interaction with those outside one's kinship group.[48] I suspect that some social interaction occurred that wasn't so conflicted, but the Gospels themselves reveal that challenge-response was indeed a frequent form of interaction in Mediterranean culture (see chap. 4). People were hungry for honor, and they often sought to outdo one another in obtaining it or to limit the amount of honor held by a perceived rival. In short, Greco-Roman society, especially among the elite and those wanting to achieve this social level, was highly competitive. Social jockeying to gain closer proximity to cherished patrons, generous benefaction in the form of monuments or public structures, challenge-and-riposte exchanges, the amassing and display of wealth—all such activities took place within an agonistic context in

46. Ibid., 33.
47. Ibid.
48. Malina, *New Testament World*, 36.

which the goal was to outdo one another in the acquisition of honor, and thus achieve the position and power to which honor provided access.

The agonistic pursuit of honor presumed and manifested a worldview in which all humans were not created equal. Most among the elite would have held an account of themselves and their kin that sharply distinguished them from most of the population. By virtue of their birth, kinship group (actual or "fictive"),[49] and place in society, by virtue of their ascribed and acquired honor, the elite saw themselves and their fellow elite as superior members of humanity. They embraced a worldview in which their pedigree, elevated sense of morality, and divine mandate included them as among a select few whose worth and potential for good was greater than that of those outside that group.[50] These perceptions of elevated worth—and the divine favor that the elite believed accompanied it—legitimated their near-exclusive access to and control of power and wealth. In other words, the elite made the laws, and rightly so, for they were the educated and virtuous. They established economic policy, for they knew how to best manage resources for the good of the empire and to honor the divine patrons of Rome. They spoke for the gods and goddesses, for they had the training and purity to access the divine mysteries and be the faithful guardians of sacred tradition. They ruled the empire, for their station was sanctioned by the emperor, who in turn was sanctioned by heaven and himself either a member of or closely connected to the divine realm.

Conclusion

Throughout the Roman Empire, including Roman Palestine, elite status meant access to the currency that ran and shaped the world. In sum, Roman society enacted as a fundamental doctrine that the exercise of political, economic, and religious power was the divinely mandated and socially recognized vocation of the elite. Yet this elite worldview—which was also embraced by many outside the elite's ranks—cultivated a social and economic hierarchy of extraordinary disparity, resulting in the concentration of incredible wealth in the hands of a few, and the experience of widespread deprivation and suffering by the many.

49. Fictive, or pseudo, kinship refers to groups of clients constituted by their commitment to a common patron; such groups are governed by the roles, obligations, and responsibilities between the patron and his or her clients, and by the clients' mutual calling to remain loyal to the patron and to some extent one another.

50. Neil Elliott (*Arrogance of the Nations*, 30–33) helpfully lists several examples of what he terms "the hidden transcript of the powerful," in which members of the ruling class express their contempt for and sense of superiority over the lower classes, and the need for brutal rule over them. See also Hamel, "Poverty and Charity," 316; and Fiensy, *Social History of Palestine*, 169–70.

2

Israelite Visions of the Kingdom

M ost Israelites in the years surrounding the turn of the Common Era commonly experienced the Roman world as a realm of disparity and want. Not surprisingly, many Israelites during this time were earnestly longing for the fulfillment of prophecies announcing that one day God would restore God's people to lasting peace, exalted prominence, and wondrous prosperity. Luke, like many Christians and some Israelites before him, frequently referred to this vision of Yahweh's coming restoration with the phrase "the Kingdom (or Reign) of God" (ἡ βασιλεία τοῦ θεοῦ).

Few topics related to the study of the NT and Christian origins have received more attention or been as vigorously debated as the meaning of "the Kingdom of God." Scholars have contended over multiple facets of the term's potential meaning for Israelites, Jesus, early Christians, and Christian communities today. Yet two relatively recent developments in the discussion of the term will greatly assist our exploration of how this concept was understood in the years leading up to the writing of Luke's narrative. The first is the tendency among many recent scholars to treat "the Kingdom of God" in late Israelite and early Christian thought as a richly variegated symbol, or narrative, that nevertheless revolved around a commonly held core of ideas. The second is a number of recent surveys on the various elements associated with God's sovereign rule among Israelites in Jesus' day.[1]

---

1. See, e.g., the various essays offered in Wendell Willis, ed., *The Kingdom of God in 20th-Century Interpretation* (Peabody, MA: Hendrickson, 1987). See also N. T. Wright, *The New Testament and the People of God* (Minneapolis: Fortress, 1992), 147–338; James Luther Mays,

The Kingdom of God: Variations on a Core Narrative

From the late nineteenth century through the first three-quarters of the twentieth century, scholars examining the meaning of "the Kingdom of God" were set on determining a distinct referent or concept for the expression in Israelite tradition, Jesus' teaching, and early Christianity. However, most scholars now recognize that the phrase pointed to a complex set of associations. Norman Perrin took the lead in steering scholarship away from the search for a single referent.[2] Borrowing from Philip Wheelwright's discussion on symbol, Perrin noted that certain symbols typically have a one-to-one association with the realities they represent.[3] These are termed "steno symbols" and function to convey a single, clearly defined concept. Other symbols, however, function not to identify a single referent but to invite reflection on a wide range of associations, experiences, and yearnings. Such "tensive symbols" are meant to engage the head and the heart, often evoking an entire myth, or story, and offering a multifaceted way of seeing the world. Perrin argued that the Kingdom of God is such a tensive symbol. Consequently, any attempts to define the singular meaning of the expression are misguided and doomed to frustration.

Many have found Perrin's treatment of the Kingdom of God as a myth-evoking symbol an extremely valuable one, while qualifying some features of his argument. For example, Perrin maintained that, as symbol, the Kingdom of God should not be regarded as an idea or conception—that its function was primarily to invite a response to the mythic account of God's engagement with Israel. Others, however, have argued that a tensive symbol need not be devoid of content that can be discerned and discussed, even one as variegated as the Kingdom of God. Accordingly, several recent studies have appreciated yet adapted Perrin's understanding of the Kingdom by arguing that while

---

"The Language of the Kingdom of God," *Int* 47 (1993): 117–26; John Paul Meier, *A Marginal Jew: Rethinking the Historical Jesus* (New York: Doubleday, 1994), 2:237–88; Darrell Bock, *Jesus according to the Scriptures: Restoring the Portrait from the Gospels* (Grand Rapids: Baker Academic, 2002), 566–93; H. Leroy Metts, "The Kingdom of God: Background and Development of a Complex Discourse Concept," *CTR* 2 (2004): 51–82; Alan Storkey, *Jesus and Politics: Confronting the Powers* (Grand Rapids: Baker Academic, 2006), 111–32; Mary Ann Beavis, *Jesus and Utopia: Looking for the Kingdom of God in the Roman World* (Minneapolis: Fortress, 2006); Ann Moore, *Moving beyond Symbol and Myth: Understanding the Kingship of God of the Hebrew Bible through Metaphor*, Studies in Biblical Literature 99 (New York: Peter Lang, 2009).

2. Norman Perrin, *Jesus and the Language of the Kingdom: Symbol and Metaphor in New Testament Interpretation* (Philadelphia: Fortress, 1980).

3. Ibid., 29–34. See also Philip Wheelwright, *Metaphor and Reality* (Bloomington: Indiana University Press, 1962), 45–69, 92–110.

the expression functions as a dynamic symbol inviting a myriad of responses and associations, it also likely conveyed a central core of ideas around which various other associations could potentially revolve. In addition, Perrin argued that the Kingdom of God, as a tensive symbol, is without temporal referent and thus provides no indication on the time of the Kingdom's arrival. John P. Meier, among others, also finds this unnecessary, arguing that "a time frame, however vague or mythic, was part of the underlying story of the Kingdom evoked by the tensive symbol. Thus it seems more reasonable to argue that the tensive symbol of the Kingdom would tend to evoke a number of possible time frames rather than none."[4]

These adaptations of Perrin's understanding of the Kingdom seem to fit very well with what the evidence suggests. As we encounter the term in Jesus' teaching and the literature of the NT, it is clear that the term does not identify a distinct concept but refers to a *story* about God and God's promised redemption of God's people.[5] Two features of this story are crucial for us to understand. First, the story to which "the Kingdom of God" refers, at least in its essential contours, predates the use of the specific term by centuries. The appearance of the expression in the years leading up to the Common Era did not signify a radically new way of conceiving reality. Rather, the expression labeled a well-worn, fundamental view of the world rooted in Israel's sacred traditions that framed and inspired ongoing ruminations about God's sovereignty, deliverance of Israel, and rule over creation. This core myth provided a "narrative substructure" for making sense of and articulating God's intentions for creation, Israel's identity as God's people, the current state of reality, and what the future would hold. This "kingdom story," in essence, was a story that proclaimed the following:

1. Yahweh is King of Israel and Ruler of the universe.
2. The current order of creation and state of God's people are not in alignment with God's will.
3. God will act to reorder creation into alignment with God's intentions.

Second, this was also a story that could be told very differently. The constituent elements of this mythic substructure were cast in various forms and supplemented by an array of secondary matters. We see in the years leading up to the time of Jesus a diverse plethora of kingdom stories.

4. Meier, *Marginal Jew*, 2:242.
5. I am using the terms "story" and "myth" here as they are commonly used in the study of religion to refer to a "foundational narrative," not to convey a negative judgment on the biblical narrative's historicity.

The Kingdom Story in Israel's Sacred Traditions

As mentioned above, the roots of Israelite kingdom stories emerging in late Second Temple Israelite thought are embedded in its ancient, sacred traditions. For these same story lines also serve as the basic narrative substructure of Israel's scriptures and of nearly all their constituent elements. Even the nonnarrative elements within the Israelite canon assume (such as the Psalms) or are contextualized within (such as the legal codes and wisdom traditions) this core narrative. The manifestation of these essential elements in Israel's canonical traditions is illustrated below.

Yahweh as King of Israel and Ruler of the Universe

The notion of God's kingly rule over Israel and all creation is well attested throughout the Israelite scriptures, indicating the prominence of this idea in Israel's ancient past and well into the exilic and postexilic periods, when many of its sacred traditions were being redacted and codified. Despite the ubiquity of the term "the Kingdom of God" throughout the NT, the phrase lacks a clear precedent in Israel's scriptural traditions. The closest parallel occurs in 1 Chronicles 28:5, which reads "Yahweh's kingdom" (מַלְכוּת יְהוָה). However, references to God's reign over Israel or all creation abound throughout these scriptures.[6] Numerous texts indicate God's rule over his "kingdom" (e.g., 1 Chron. 17:14; Pss. 103:19; 145:11, 12, 13; Dan. 4:3, 34).[7] While Israel is frequently characterized as Yahweh's realm of rule (e.g., Judg. 8:23; 1 Sam. 8:1–22; Ps. 114:2; Obad. 21), Isaiah's vision in the temple offers an exuberant celebration of Yahweh, the King of creation enthroned in the heavens (Isa. 6:1–5). Similarly, Zephaniah (late seventh century BCE) proclaims a coming time of deliverance for the righteous of Israel and the extension of God's rule over all creation. Yahweh will gather nations and assemble kingdoms, "that all of them may call on the name of Yahweh and serve him with one accord" (3:8–9, 15).[8] In traditions

6. In order to avoid the anachronistic use of "Old Testament," I will employ the terms "Israelite scriptures" and "Israelite tradition" to refer to those writings Luke and many of his fellow Israelites would have considered sacred. I realize, however, these two terms also lack precision, since those texts considered sacred and authoritative, or "canonical," by adherents of Israelite faith in Luke's day may have been somewhat variable from sect to sect and still in flux during Luke's time.

7. I owe these references to Dale Patrick, "The Kingdom of God in the Old Testament," in Willis, *Kingdom of God*, 72.

8. In Scripture quotations, I have replaced the NRSV's "the LORD" with a transliteration of the divine name ("Yahweh") to more accurately reflect the personal nature of the reference to God in the Hebrew text.

referencing the monarchy, the king was to rule under the authority of Yahweh, the universal Sovereign of all, and enact God's purposes for God's people (e.g., 1 Sam. 12:20–21; Pss. 2; 8; 72; 110). Two key texts conveying these notions are 2 Samuel 7 and 1 Chronicles 28, both of which record God's establishment of the Davidic dynasty. The sense of 2 Samuel 7:8–12 and its parallel in 1 Chronicles 28:4–8 is captured well in the following chapter of 1 Chronicles as David prays to God, "Yours, O Yahweh, are the greatness, the power, the glory, the victory, and the majesty; for all that is in the heavens and on earth is yours; yours is the kingdom, O Yahweh, and you are exalted as head above all" (29:11).

Perhaps the most passionate, and certainly the most concentrated, collection of testimonies to God's sovereignty over all is found in Psalms 93 and 95–99. These enthronement psalms jubilantly celebrate Yahweh as King over creation. For example, the psalmist exclaims,

> For Yahweh is a great God,
> and a great King above all gods.
> In his hand are the depths of the earth;
> the heights of the mountains are his also.
> The sea is his, for he made it,
> and the dry land, which his hands have formed.
> O come, let us worship and bow down,
> let us kneel before Yahweh, our Maker! (95:3–6)

God's sovereignty over creation is, of course, central to the later exilic and postexilic prophetic traditions as well. Because nearly all of these later prophetic traditions present God's kingly rule within an eschatological framework announcing the arrival of God's awaited redemption, I will address them below.

The Misalignment of the Status Quo with God's Will

Although Yahweh is Sovereign over the universe, creation has not gone as planned. The painful account of a creation warped by human infidelity is preserved in the Primeval History (Gen. 1–11). God's human creatures have refused to live in accord with God's intentions for creation, leading to the tragic consequence that the world has become degraded beyond imagination. Already by the start of Genesis 6, only a few chapters removed from the accounts of creation's origins, we learn of the tragic disaster that creation had become:

> Yahweh saw that the wickedness of humankind was great in the earth, and that every inclination of the thoughts of their hearts was only evil continually. And Yahweh was sorry that he had made humankind on the earth, and it grieved him

to his heart. So Yahweh said, "I will blot out from the earth the human beings I have created—people together with animals and creeping things and birds of the air, for I am sorry that I have made them." (Gen. 6:5–7)

Because of Yahweh's grace, the flood that follows becomes an act of cleansing and an opportunity for a new beginning, rather than a complete annihilation. This initiates a pattern of judgment and restoration that will continue throughout the rest of Israel's story, as marked by a series of covenants that Yahweh makes (and remakes) with Israel, most notably with Noah, Abraham, Moses, and David. This recurring pattern of Israel's "stiff-neckedness" and God's resulting rebuke, judgment, and forgiveness is featured prominently in the "summaries" scattered throughout scriptural narratives.[9] Yet despite Yahweh's care for Israel and repeated overtures of correction, mercy, and renewal, God's people have continually spurned God and God's instruction. They have habitually turned to other deities as sources of blessing, abused the poor, and embraced ways of relating that can only lead to enmity and strife.[10] Their infidelity to God and one another has repeatedly resulted in destructive consequences for Israel and others, including the annihilation of the northern kingdom (722 BCE) and ultimately the destruction of Jerusalem, extreme loss of life, and exile (586 BCE). Even though the destruction Israel suffers at the hands of the Assyrians and later the Babylonians is a result of God's judgment, prophetic texts also make it clear that God sees it as nothing less than tragic (e.g., Ps. 78:40–41; Isa. 1:2–3; 5:3–4; 63:10; 65:1–5; Jer. 2:1–3, 29–32; 3:11–14; 4:19–22; 8:18–9:3; Hos. 6:4–6; 11:1–7).

This sense of Israel's estrangement from God and the corruption of humankind in general continues in the postexilic era. Even though by the late sixth century BCE many Israelites have returned to Jerusalem, rebuilt the temple, and rededicated themselves to Yahweh's torah and the temple cult, the internal and external trials facing Israel as a people show that their return from exile and exaltation have yet to be achieved. According to the historical (Ezra–Nehemiah) and prophetic (Malachi, 3 Isaiah, Haggai, Zechariah) texts of this era, the people still fail to embrace God's torah in full measure,

9. E.g., Exod. 3:1–22; Lev. 26:1–46; Deut. 1:1–3:29; 6:20–24; 26:5–9; 28:1–68; Josh. 24:2–13; Judg. 2:11–23; 1 Kings 8:22–53; Pss. 78; 105; 106; 135:8–12; 136; Jer. 7:1–8:3; 30:1–31; Neh. 9. For a discussion of the prominence of these motifs in biblical summaries, see Karl Allen Kuhn, *Having Words with God: The Bible as Conversation* (Fortress: Minneapolis, 2008), 143–57.

10. On the abuse of the poor and marginalized as a common motif in prophetic rebuke, and on the reversal of fortune celebrated in Israelite visions of the new kingdom, see Ronald Clements, "Poverty and the Kingdom of God—An Old Testament View," in *The Kingdom of God and Human Society: Essays by Members of the Scripture, Theology and Society Group*, ed. Robin Barbour (Edinburgh: T&T Clark, 1993), 13–26.

the leaders are still acting corruptly, poverty is widespread, and surrounding nations frequently abuse God's people. In the years that follow, Israel's fidelity and identity are repeatedly tested by the temptation of assimilation and the threat of persecution under the Persians (Esther) and the Greeks (Daniel).

God's Intervention to Reorder Creation

Yahweh, King of creation, will intervene in the current order of things to return creation to a realm of peace and blessing, and to reestablish Israel's prominence among the nations. Of course, Yahweh's ongoing efforts to deliver the people from the threat of physical violence, the reality of social and economic oppression, and Israel's own waywardness are a constant refrain in Israel's scriptures. Among such traditions, the exodus story stands as the paradigmatic example of Yahweh as Savior. Time and time again, Israel's sacred traditions return to this story as a witness to Yahweh's character as one who has the will and the power to save God's people (e.g., Exod. 19:1–6; 20:2; 32:1–14; Num. 14:13; Ps. 77:16–20; Neh. 9:9–12). Accordingly, several of the prophetic promises of Israel's eventual renewal in the aftermath of Jerusalem's destruction and oppression portray Yahweh as fighting for Israel's deliverance and portray Israel's return from exile as a new exodus.[11] The writer of Isaiah 66 incorporates these motifs along with other striking imagery. The closing oracle of that chapter rehearses each of the three basic contours of the kingdom story as it proclaims the victory Yahweh, the King, will accomplish for his people. It opens with a declaration of the incomparable and insurmountable majesty of God:

> Thus says Yahweh:
> Heaven is my throne
>   and the earth is my footstool;
> What is the house you would build for me,
>   and what is my resting place? (v. 1)

The oracle then reviews the present state of Israel, focusing on the people's lack of faith as manifested in the hollow rituals of the present temple cult and a refusal to attend to God's instruction (vv. 3–4). But the prophet then turns to the awaited advent of God's deliverance of a faithful remnant from enemies and the unrighteous. As that announcement unfolds, the prophet presents

11. New-exodus imagery is particularly prevalent in the oracles of Isaiah: see 35:5–10; 40:1–5; 41:14–16, 18–20; 42:15–16; 43:19–20; 49:9–11; 52:11–12.

two striking, contrasting images of God's provision and power. The first is of a mother, tenderly nursing her child, whose flow of rich milk mirrors the blessing that God, the mother, will bestow on her children (vv. 10–13). This image of God as mother is immediately juxtaposed with the image of Yahweh the ruthless warrior. The enemies of God and the unfaithful among God's people will be utterly destroyed. With imagery and language reminiscent of the songs of Moses and Miriam after Yahweh's defeat of the Egyptians (Exod. 15:1–21), the prophet announces that the gathering of the faithful from far and wide—this new exodus—will come at a horrific cost to those who stand in the way (vv. 14–16).

Most prophetic texts speak of Yahweh as the one who calls the exiles to return home to a renewed Israel and makes it possible for them to do so (e.g., Jer. 31:1–14; Mic. 4:6–7; Joel 3:7–21; Zeph. 3:8–20; Zech. 14:1–21; Mal. 3:1–5). Other oracles of salvation announce the return of a faithful Davidic king to the throne to lead and govern the restored Israel (e.g., Amos 9:11; Jer. 23:5–6; Isa. 9:1–7; 11:1–9; Hag. 2:20–23). Daniel 7–12, dated by most to the second century BCE, depicts God, the ultimate Sovereign, forgiving the people, defeating Israel's enemies, and restoring Israel as a people of unmatched prominence and power. Yet it is the angels, Michael and another unnamed angelic figure, who lead God's forces into battle (10:1–21; 12:1–12), and Yahweh confers an eternal, universal kingdom upon a heavenly "one like a son of man" (7:13–14, 27).

God's rectification of the wrongs suffered by God's people is also likely in view in the final shaping of the Psalter. As mentioned earlier, the enthronement psalms, Psalms 93 and 95–99, celebrate Yahweh's reign as King over creation. Many have argued that the placement of these psalms at the start of book IV was meant as a response to the end of book III, which concludes with the despairing laments of Psalms 88–89. Unlike nearly all lament psalms, these two fail to move toward an expression of trust in or thanksgiving for God's eventual deliverance as they reflect upon the destruction of Jerusalem and exile. As a response to the pathos-laden close of book III, the enthronement psalms "explicitly affirm that the Lord is king or that the Lord reigns" and, in so doing, serve as the "theological heart of the psalter."[12] Moreover, because the final shaping of the Psalter proclaims this affirmation in response to the tragedy of destruction and exile, it takes on a thoroughly eschatological hue. The foundational profession that Yahweh reigns is brought to bear on the tragic past, the still-difficult present, and a far more blessed future: the King

12. J. Clinton McCann, *A Theological Introduction to the Book of Psalms: The Psalms as Torah* (Nashville: Abingdon, 1993), 44.

will save Israel once again. Psalm 96 explicitly invites the faithful into such an eschatological frame of view:

> Say among the nations, "Yahweh is king!
>> The world is firmly established; it shall never be moved.
>> He will judge the peoples with equity."
> Let the heavens be glad, and let the earth rejoice;
>> let the sea roar, and all that fills it;
>> let the field exult, and everything in it.
> Then shall all the trees of the forest sing for joy
>> before Yahweh; for he is coming,
>> for he is coming to judge the earth.
> He will judge the world with righteousness,
>> and the peoples with his truth. (vv. 10–13)

Among the various forces preventing God's people from experiencing the blessing God intends for them is, as we noted before, their own waywardness. Thus, the exilic and postexilic prophets announce that God's deliverance will include God's rescue of the people from their own inability to walk in God's ways. Jeremiah proclaims the forging of a new covenant between Yahweh and Yahweh's recalcitrant people, unlike "the . . . covenant that they broke, though I was their husband" (Jer. 31:32). God will write the new covenant "on their hearts," and so, Yahweh says, "I will be their God, and they shall be my people. . . . For they shall all know me, from the least of them to the greatest" (vv. 33–34). Similarly, Ezekiel announces that God's restoration of Israel will be so dramatic that the land will be transformed into an Eden-like utopia of abundant provision, bursting with life (36:33–38). Yet before Israel can attain that blessed state, the people themselves must be radically transformed with a new heart and a new spirit (36:25–30). This is an important point to appreciate, as it continues in the years to follow to be a fundamental dimension of God's salvation awaited by many Israelites (e.g., Mal. 3:1; 4:5–6; Dan. 9; 11:33–35; 12:3; *Pss. Sol.* 17:30, 32, 35, 36, 40–42; CD 6.7–11; 7.17; 4Q174). Israel was to be not only *reconstituted* as a people but also *re-created* into those who could and would finally devote themselves to Yahweh.

The Kingdom Stories of the Intertestamental Era

In the 150 years leading up to the Common Era, Israelites produced reams of literature reflecting an intense yearning for the arrival of God's rule. Several factors likely played a role in triggering this awakening of eschatological fervor, but chief among them was Israelite dissatisfaction with, and oppression by, both foreign and Israelite rulers. Early intertestamental traditions, such as those reflected in 1 Maccabees and 2 Maccabees, address the abuses of the Seleucids, including Antiochus IV among others. In the years following the Maccabean Revolt and Israelite independence, many Israelites became deeply dissatisfied with the Hasmonean leaders, protesting their abuse of power, acquisition of material wealth, oppression of the peasantry, illegitimate claim to the title of king and high priest (since the Hasmoneans were of neither Davidic nor Zadokite descent), and corruption of the temple and cult. After the Hasmoneans, Rome's violent subjugation of Palestine, violation of the temple, ongoing presence on Israelite soil, and economic exploitation of its subjects made Rome an object of loathing as well.[13]

The kingdom stories produced during this period continued to express their three constitutive elements. Let us review two traditions from this period to illustrate the continuing importance of these elements in Israelite tradition; then we will examine certain permutations of these stories that will help us better understand Luke's own account of the Kingdom's arrival.

The Psalms of Solomon

Though not in narrative form, the *Psalms of Solomon*, much like the Psalter, both assumes and frequently engages the core elements of the kingdom story. The psalms were written sometime after Pompey's entrance into Jerusalem in 63 BCE (e.g., *Pss. Sol.* 2:1–2, 19–24; 8:15–17; 17:11–13; 18:5). The collection as a whole celebrates God's kingship and sovereignty over creation (*Pss. Sol.* 2:30–32; 5:18–19), and *Psalm* 17 contains the closest linguistic equivalent to "the Kingdom of God" in literature predating the NT: "And the kingdom of our God is forever over the nations in judgment" (v. 3b).[14] Focusing in on this psalm, we see the three elemental story lines clearly conveyed. In the very first line of the psalm, God is extolled as sovereign King over creation: "Lord, you are our king forever more"; and with verse 46, this line forms an inclusio bracketing the entire psalm. Here too the state of God's people and creation is not in accord with God's intentions. Verses 4–25 offer a rich and dramatic account of Israel's story from the time of David onward, replete with biblical themes and imagery. God intended the Da-

13. On the emergence of Israelite apocalyptic and messianic thought in the second century CE and centuries following, see John J. Collins, *The Scepter and the Star: Messianism in the Light of the Dead Sea Scrolls*, 2nd ed. (Grand Rapids: Eerdmans, 2010), and Portier-Young, *Apocalypse against Empire*.

14. Translation is that of R. B. Wright in *The Old Testament Pseudepigrapha*, ed. James H. Charlesworth (New York: Doubleday, 1985), 2:665–66.

vidic monarchy to stand forever (v. 4); however, the psalmist says, "because of our sins, sinners rose up against us" (v. 5). The psalmist then laments the destruction and defilement of Jerusalem under illegitimate and foreign rule (vv. 5–18a), and even the corruption of creation (vv. 18b–19). To end this nightmare, the psalmist prays that God will raise up a Davidic king (v. 21). Through him, God will act to save the faithful, restore Jerusalem, return Israel to faithfulness, and transform creation to a place of peace and blessing (vv. 22–44).

War Rule *(1QM)*

The Dead Sea Scrolls (DSS) are a collection of writings and copies of Israelite scriptures written primarily during the intertestamental period. Found along the west side of the Dead Sea near a settlement called Qumran, this ancient cache of manuscripts was, according to most scholars, the work of a separatist Israelite sect called Essenes, which formed around 150 BCE in response to what it perceived to be the abuses and corruptions of the Hasmonean regime. Along with other like-minded (apocalyptic) texts of this era, many of the writings found at Qumran conceived of Israel's historic and present struggles against a broader, cosmic backdrop (more on this below). What the faithful were now experiencing was nothing less than the cataclysmic struggle between the forces of God (the sons of light) and those of Satan (the sons of darkness). Numerous texts found among the DSS join other intertestamental traditions in looking ahead to the victory that God the King will achieve on behalf of God's people over the evils oppressing them.[15] These traditions present "kingdom hope as a hope for a future divine intervention in history."[16] The results of God's intervention on behalf of the faithful would be a realm of justice (against oppressive enemies), peace (from injustice and war), and prosperity (as opposed to the pervasive reality of poverty). Illustrative of these common features is a hymn found in column 12 of the *War Scroll* or *War Rule* (1QM). The hymn opens by exclaiming,

> For Thou art [terrible], O God, in the glory of Thy kingdom,
> and the congregation of Thy Holy Ones is among us for everlasting
> succour.
> We will despise kings, we will mock and scorn the mighty;
> for our Lord is holy, and the King of Glory is with us together with the
> Holy Ones.[17]

---

15. For a helpful review of relevant DSS texts, see B. T. Viviano, "The Kingdom of God in the Qumran Literature," in Willis, *Kingdom of God*, 96–107.

16. Ibid., 105.

17. Translation from Geza Vermes, *The Complete Dead Sea Scrolls in English* (London: Penguin, 2004), 177, with versification borrowed from Viviano, "Kingdom of God," 105.

The hymn then shouts out a call to battle and announces God's victory over the enemies of the faithful and the rich plunder that will fill Israel. Earlier in the work, these enemies are labeled "the Kittim," likely referring broadly to those of Greek descent, or even gentiles in general, in light of Genesis 10:4. They are also described as "sons of Satan," the enemies of God's people whose rule has resulted in Israel's subjugation and misery. Then, in the closing section of column 12, the hymnist offers a jubilant call to praise in recognition that God's reign and Israel's dominion are at hand:

> O Zion, rejoice greatly!
> O Jerusalem, show thyself amidst jubilation!
> Rejoice, all you cities of Judah;
> Keep your gates ever open that the host of the nations may be brought in!
> Their kings shall serve you
>   and all your oppressors shall bow down before you;
>   [they shall lick] the dust [of your feet].
> Shout for joy, [O daughters of] my people!
> Deck yourselves with glorious jewels and rule over [the kingdom of the
>   nations!
> Sovereignty shall be to the Lord] and everlasting dominion to Israel.[18]

Variations on a Theme

While these three core dimensions (God is King; the world is misaligned; God will soon reorder creation) continued to undergird Israelite conceptions of God, of the present state of Israel and creation, and of hopes for a blessed future, they were cast in great variety in works of the intertestamental era. Scholars have tended to catalogue these variant castings of the kingdom story by identifying two major versions: one labeled as "prophetic" or "nationalistic," and the other as "apocalyptic."[19] Stated simply, the nationalistic vision of the Kingdom is a "this-worldly" hope set in the current world order, a vision of

18. Ibid., 178, with versification borrowed from Viviano, "Kingdom of God," 105.
19. Literature and perspectives labeled as "apocalyptic" are those that either correspond to the genre of an apocalypse or reflect the combination of ideas that are commonly associated with works of this genre. The following has become accepted by many as a standard definition for the genre of *apocalypse*: "A genre of revelatory literature with a narrative framework, in which a revelation is mediated by an otherworldly being to a human recipient, disclosing a transcendent reality which is both temporal, insofar as it envisages eschatological salvation, and spatial insofar as it involves another, supernatural world" (cited in John J. Collins, *The Apocalyptic Imagination: An Introduction to Jewish Apocalyptic Literature*, 2nd ed. [Grand Rapids: Eerdmans, 1998], 5).

salvation focusing (1) on Israel's restoration and reign as a sovereign socio-political entity possessing tremendous power and prosperity, and (2) on its return to covenant fidelity with Yahweh (e.g., 1 Maccabees). In some iterations of this vision, a Davidic king returns to the throne to defeat Israel's enemies and to guide the people (e.g., *Psalms of Solomon*). Apocalyptic visions of the Kingdom, in contrast, offer an "other-worldly" hope, in at least two senses. First, the struggle enjoined against Israel's enemies is cosmic in scope. The battle may include a terrestrial context and involve worldly realities and enti-ties, but that earthy conflict is intertwined with a heavenly conflict between the forces of God and the forces of evil as we saw in the *War Rule* above (see also Dan. 10–12; the "Animal Apocalypse" of *1 En.* 83–91; the *Community Rule* [1QS 4.8–11]). Second, in many apocalyptic traditions announcing God's victory over enemies, other agents from the heavenly realm fight on behalf of God's people—namely, angels or other transcendent beings, such as the "one like a son of man" in Daniel 7 and the Similitudes of *1 Enoch*, or the "Son of God" in the fragmentary *Aramaic Apocalypse* (4Q246).

Despite the usefulness of these two categories—nationalistic and apoca-lyptic—for identifying broad tendencies in intertestamental versions of the kingdom story, they run the risk of two shortcomings: (1) they may obscure points of similarity between so-called apocalyptic and nationalistic scenarios, and (2) they can project a false sense of uniformity upon the very diverse tra-ditions that are commonly labeled "apocalyptic." In what follows I continue to make use of the terms "nationalistic" and "apocalyptic" to refer to certain traditions and perspectives. But my main objective will be to explore five secondary elements often associated with intertestamental kingdom stories that were held in variant forms. The goal is to illustrate the diversity of these traditions and to foster an understanding of their permutations in order to help us see how they might be manifested and adapted in Luke's narrative.

Agents of Deliverance

We saw above that most prophetic traditions speak of Yahweh as the one who calls the exiles to return to a renewed Israel and a restored land, and who makes it possible for them to do so (e.g., Jer. 31:1–14; Mic. 4:6–7; Joel 3:7–21; Zeph. 3:8–20; Zech. 14:1–21; Mal. 3:1–5). Beyond the canonical tra-ditions, some intertestamental writings continue to focus on God alone as Israel's agent of deliverance. For example, the nonmessianic writings of 1 and 2 Maccabees (composed around 100 BCE) see the hand of God at work in the defeat of the Greeks by the Hasmoneans (e.g., 1 Macc. 3:16–27, 44–60; 4:55; 2 Macc. 1:1–17, 24–29; 3:22–28; 6:12–17; 15:20–24). The *Testament of Moses*, dated to the first half of the first century CE, announces the coming of God's Kingdom "throughout his whole creation . . . for the Heavenly One will arise from his kingly throne" (10:1, 3).[20] The evil one and Israel's enemies will be defeated (10:1, 7), and Israel itself will be enthroned in the stars of heaven to enjoy eternal bliss (10:8–10). Many other traditions from this period, both apocalyptic and nationalistic, testify to a wide array of redeemer figures that were on the minds and hearts of Israelites yearning for God's deliverance.

Davidic Messiah

As we noted above, God's awaited salvation was understood by some in the early postexilic period to include not only the advent of Yahweh to restore Israel but also the return of Yahweh's anointed one to the throne. Several among these traditions stress the messiah's overthrow of the nations responsible for subjugating Israel, and Israel's exaltation as the center of creation, with the Davidic king presiding as ruler and judge over all (e.g., Isa. 30:1–11; Hag. 2:21–24; 1QSb 5.27; 4Q285). Others associate God's anointed one with a reign of peace for Israel (Ezek. 34:23–31; 37:24–28) and even all the earth (Isa. 2:1–4; Zech. 9:9–10). Still others maintain that the restoration of God's people, and God's universal rule, can be accomplished in part through the reign of a non-Israelite monarch: Deutero-Isaiah celebrates the Persian king, Cyrus, as God's messiah, whose defeat of the Babylonians and whose patronage secure the return of God's people to Israel (e.g., Isa. 44:28; 45:1–17; see also Jer. 50:3).

The scarcity of Israelite traditions surviving from the mid-to-late Persian and early Greek periods (fourth to third centuries BCE) prevents us from tracking messianic conceptions during these centuries. But starting with the later Greek era and moving into the time of the Maccabees and Roman rule (second to first centuries BCE), several traditions testify to the persistence of these concepts among many Israelites.[21] As we saw, *Psalms of Solomon* 17 reflects numerous prophetic motifs, including the resounding defeat of Israel's foreign captors (vv. 22–24), the return of God's people to the land (vv. 26–31), the purging of all foreign peoples and abominations from Israel and Jerusalem (vv. 25, 28), and the embrace of righteousness among God's people (vv. 30, 32, 35, 36, 40–42), accomplished through the universal reign of a Davidic messiah who will rule justly over Israel and all the peoples of the earth (vv. 21–44). The covenanters of Qumran also looked ahead to the arrival of a Davidic

20. Translation is that of J. Priest in Charlesworth, *Old Testament Pseudepigrapha*, 1:931–32.

21. Collins (*Scepter and the Star*, 49–73) proposes that the resurgence of messianic hope among Israelites did not take place until the second century BCE, likely resulting from displeasure with the Hasmonean leaders following the Maccabean Revolt.

messiah among other redeemer figures (as we shall see below). Some of their texts speak of a Davidic king who will come at the end of days to restore the Davidic dynasty and inaugurate the long-awaited era of peace and justice.[22]

HEAVENLY REDEEMERS

Numerous apocalyptic and nonapocalyptic texts speak of the appearance of angelic figures who fulfill numerous roles. Among their duties, they serve as teachers and revealers of the divine mysteries (e.g., *Jub.* 1:27–29; 10:10–14; Dan. 7–12; *1 En.* 17–36) and emerge as heavenly warriors who will fight on behalf of God's people. In Daniel, Michael and a transcendent (nonhuman) "one like a son of man" contend with the demonic forces (10:18–11:1; 12:1).[23] The *War Scroll* (1QM) draws its inspiration from Daniel's account of the final battle against the Kittim (1QM 11.40–12.3; 14.4–8) and also presents Michael as God's appointed leader of the heavenly host (including Gabriel, Sariel, and Raphael) that defeats the forces of Satan.

Daniel's heavenly "one like a son of man" was also adopted and adapted in subsequent traditions as he became conflated with a Davidic messiah. Remarkably, this figure was also assigned attributes normally reserved for Yahweh in Israelite tradition. In short, it appears that a trajectory of tradition developed—as reflected in the *Aramaic Apocalypse* (4Q246), the Similitudes of *1 Enoch*, and *4 Ezra*—recasting Daniel's "one like a son of man" into one specially qualified and equipped to defeat the forces of evil.[24] Collectively, these traditions present Daniel's transcendent figure as preexistent Davidic king, universal ruler and judge, object of worship, and God's Son. Such portrayals show that the conception of an eschatological redeemer as transcendent and possessing characteristics normally predicated only of Yahweh in Hebrew tradition is not out of character for Israelite writings of this era. Moreover, the author of the *Aramaic Apocalypse* emphasizes the notion of divine sonship by using the titular forms "Son of God" and "Son of the Most High" in reference to its redeemer figure. Not only do these titles allude to Psalm 2:7 and 2 Samuel 7:14, and thus call to mind the Davidic monarchy; they also appear

22. See, e.g., 4QpIsa[a] on Isa. 11:1–5: "[Interpreted, this concerns the Branch] of David who shall arise at the end [of days]"; 4QpGen 5.3–4: ". . . [and the clans] of Israel are the divisions, until the Messiah of Righteousness comes, the Branch of David. For to him and his seed is granted the Covenant of kingship over his people for everlasting generations" (trans. Vermes, *Complete Dead Sea Scrolls*, 498, 494).

23. For a defense of the view that Daniel's "one like a son of man" should be viewed as an angelic figure, see Collins, *Apocalyptic Imagination*, 103–4.

24. For a more complete discussion of the "one like a son of man" tradition and its adaptation in 4Q246, see Karl A. Kuhn, "The 'One Like a Son of Man' Becomes the 'Son of God,'" *CBQ* 69 (2007): 22–42.

to underscore the unique character of that divine sonship attributed to the hero of the apocalypse. Thus in 4Q246 we find the first surviving combination of Davidic royal tradition; Daniel's heavenly, eschatological redeemer; *and* the concept of divine sonship emphasizing the unique and transcendent character of that redeemer.

PRIEST

As we have seen, the texts found among the DSS foretell the arrival of both a Davidic messiah and heavenly (divine-like) redeemers, and among them 4Q246 casts Daniel's heavenly "one like a son of man" in Davidic tones. But additional DSS texts tell of still other redeemer figures. Notable among these texts is the following one from the *Community Rule* that identifies two figures, "the Prophet" and "Messiah of Aaron," alongside a Davidic "Messiah of Israel," who arrive to usher in God's awaited reign: "They shall depart from none of the counsels of the Law to walk in all the stubbornness of their hearts, but shall be ruled by the primitive precepts in which the men of the Community were first instructed until there shall come the Prophet and the Messiahs of Aaron and Israel" (1QS 9.11).[25] The "Messiah of Aaron" referenced here and in other DSS texts is a priestly messiah. Some texts suggest that the authority of the priestly messiah will transcend that of the Davidic messiah (e.g., 1QSa 2.11–20).[26] While details on this priestly messiah are lacking, one could infer from these texts that his role within the restored Israel will be to ensure the purity of the people and the proper administration of the temple. Further adding to the complexity of the redeemers presented by the writings gathered at Qumran, the *Damascus Document* appears to speak repeatedly of a single messianic figure known as "the Messiah of Aaron and Israel" (CD 14.18–19; see also 14.9; 19.10). Thus, it is possible that at some point these two redeemer figures coalesced into one or, alternately, one divided into two.

ESCHATOLOGICAL PROPHET/TEACHER OF RIGHTEOUSNESS

We were introduced to the eschatological prophet of the DSS in the citation from the *Community Rule* above. Collins describes the eschatological prophet as "a shadowy figure not only in the Scrolls, but generally in Judaism of the time."[27] One of the vexing issues related to the prophetic figure indicated in 1QS is his relationship to another eschatological figure "who teaches righteousness

25. Translation from Vermes, *Complete Dead Sea Scrolls*, 110.
26. Collins (*Scepter and the Star*, 76) lists several other DSS texts indicating that the royal messiah must defer to priestly authority: 4QpIsaᵃ; 4Q285; 1QSb; *Florilegium* 1.11; CD 7.18.
27. Collins, *Scepter and the Star*, 116.

at the end of days" (CD 6.7–11; 7.17; 4Q174). It is also unclear to what extent
this eschatological teacher is to be linked with still another key figure in the
DSS: the oft-referenced Teacher of Righteousness, who was likely the sect's
founder and whose teachings are preserved in many of its documents. But what
does seem likely is that this figure "who teaches righteousness at the end of
days," whether the resurrected Teacher of Righteousness or not, is one whose
role will be to return the faithful to righteousness through his instruction.
Other testimony to an eschatological prophet is found, of course, in Malachi
3:1–4 and 4:5–6, which together identify Elijah as the messenger who shall
prepare the people for Yahweh's arrival, turning "the hearts of parents to their
children and the hearts of children to their parents" (4:6; see also Sir. 48:10).

The Realm of Future Blessing

One of the defining elements of apocalyptic perspectives is that they announce what Collins terms a "cosmic transformation" of the present world
order, resulting in a blessed realm in which God's faithful will dwell.[28] The
term "cosmic transformation," however, covers a variety of potential scenarios.
Some apocalyptic texts speak of the transformation of the current world order
leading to a new heaven for all (e.g., the "Apocalypse of Weeks" in *1 En.* 93;
91:11–17). Others speak of God constructing a new earth in which the faithful
will dwell (e.g., the "Animal Apocalypse" [see *1 En.* 90]; *Jub.* 1:23–29). Still others
announce the formation of a new heaven and new earth, presumably serving
as the dwellings for faithful creatures of the heavenly and terrestrial realms.

> On that day, I shall cause my Elect One to dwell among them,
> I shall transform heaven and make it a blessing of light forever.
> I shall (also) transform the earth and make it a blessing,
> and cause my Elect One to dwell in her. (Similitudes of *1 En.* 45:4–5)[29]

Others speak of an eternal life of blessing and joy for the faithful and
of eternal torment for the wicked, without specifying locale. Among these,
Daniel 12 presents resurrection as a vehicle to this life of blessing, while others announce an eternal life of bliss with no mention of resurrection (1QS
4.7–8; 1QM 1.5; 12.11–15). Still others proclaim that the faithful will enjoy
these blessings within the heavenly realms (e.g., *1 En.* 41:2; 51:4; 104:2, 4;

---

28. Collins, *Apocalyptic Imagination*, 7.
29. Translation is that of E. Isaac in Charlesworth, *Old Testament Pseudepigrapha*, 1:34.
The Similitudes also speak of the righteous dwelling with God and the holy angels in heaven
(*1 En.* 41:2; 51:4).

108:12) while leaving unaddressed the matter of how the faithful shall be delivered therein. Such cosmic transformation, however, is not strictly unique to apocalyptic thought but is anticipated already by the prophets, especially in postexilic prophecy. Numerous texts use the language of cosmic dissolution to describe the coming judgment of Yahweh upon the enemies of God's people (Isa. 13:4–13; 24:1–6; Ezek. 32:6–8; 38:17–23; Joel 2:30–31; 3:9–16), while others offer utopian visions of a cosmic renewal (see Ezek. 36:33–36; see also Isa. 2:1–4; 60:1–22; 61:1–7; 62:1–12; Jer. 31:10–17; Zech. 14:8–11).[30]

Israelite conceptions of who is to participate in the blessings of God's awaited Kingdom range from a select remnant of Israel (such as is found among some of the DSS writings) to the claims of certain Isaianic traditions (2:1–4; 42:6; 49:6; 56:1–8), Tobit (13:11; 14:7), 1 Enoch (10:21; 90:37–38), and the Sibylline Oracles (3:657–808 [second century BCE]) that gentiles will be included. Landing somewhere in between is the view that the gentiles who survive God's judgment will indeed come to know that Yahweh alone is sovereign (Ezek. 36:36; 37:28; 39:21–24), yet will be subservient to God's people (Zech. 8:20–23; 14:16–19; see also Isa. 61:5–6) and (according to Ezekiel) not allowed to worship in the temple precincts.

The Temple and the Kingdom

Another dimension of Israelite kingdom tradition we should review is the role of the temple in the coming age of God's rule. Several exilic and postexilic prophetic traditions (e.g., Ezekiel, Zechariah, Haggai) look ahead to the rebuilding of the temple, and this concern dominates the latter parts of Ezekiel. Mary Ann Beavis argues that "the vision of the new Jerusalem in Ezekiel 40–48 becomes the 'utopian blueprint' for an ideal, eschatological temple-state" that we find reflected in several subsequent traditions.[31] Ezekiel's vision of the new Israel with the temple at its center is governed by the concept of relative purity rather exclusively construed: "Ritual purity would be maintained by restricting Levites and non-Priestly Israelites to the outer court of the sanctuary; foreigners would be banned altogether (Ezek. 44:9)."[32] In this Ezekiel is

30. As M. C. de Boer ("Paul and Apocalyptic Eschatology," in The Continuum History of Apocalypticism, ed. Bernard J. McGinn, John J. Collins, and Stephen J. Stein [New York: Continuum, 2003], 170) states, "Post-exilic or 'late' prophecy (e.g., Ezekiel, Zechariah, Trito-Isaiah) tends to portray God's intervention in the affairs and history of Israel against a backdrop of cosmic upheaval and discontinuity, which gives this 'late' prophecy a proto-apocalyptic flavor."

31. Beavis, Jesus and Utopia, 42. Here Beavis is also drawing from John J. Collins, "Models of Utopia in the Biblical Tradition," in A Wise and Discerning Mind: Essays in Honor of Burke O. Long, ed. Saul M. Olyan and Robert Culley, Brown Judaic Studies 325 (Atlanta: Scholars Press, 2000), 55.

32. Beavis, Jesus and Utopia, 42.

followed by Ezra–Nehemiah (see Ezra 9–10; Neh. 13) but countered by the more inclusive vision of Isaiah 56:1–8, where the covenant and temple worship will be extended to all who obey Yahweh, including "foreigners" (vv. 3, 6).[33]

Some later traditions moderate the exclusivist vision of Ezekiel and are open to at least some level of non-Israelite involvement in the restored Israel, even if in a subordinate sense. As we saw above, the *Psalms of Solomon* laments that transgressions against the sanctuary are being committed by keepers of the temple and by the contaminating influence of gentiles, such as Pompey (see, e.g., *Pss. Sol.* 17:45; 18:5). Accordingly, among the many things God's messiah will accomplish as he reconstitutes the nationhood of Israel is the purification of Jerusalem and the temple so that the glory of Yahweh may return to the holy city: "The alien foreigner will no longer live near them." Even so, gentiles will serve God's messiah, and they will come from the ends of the earth to honor him and to escort exiles back to Jerusalem (*Pss. Sol.* 17:28–31).

Several apocalyptically oriented traditions awaited the arrival of a heavenly temple that will be unveiled as God's Kingdom reaches its fulfillment. According to R. G. Hamerton-Kelly, these traditions consistently present three emphases: (1) the present existence of the heavenly temple, (2) its centrality in the events and institutions of the eschatological age, and (3) hostility to the second temple because it suffered by comparison with the heavenly temple.[34] In some apocalyptic scenarios, the heavenly temple shall replace the earthly one, either by descending upon or being rebuilt on the earth (e.g., *Jub.* 1:17, 27, 29; *1 En.* 24:1–25:4; 90:28–29). Collins outlines three responses by the DSS community to the protracted crisis of the temple's mismanagement and their exile from it.[35] First, the sect regarded itself as a spiritual temple that embodied the true temple on earth (1QS 8.4–10; 4Q164 1–7). Second, the community celebrated the existence of a heavenly temple, and with devout imagination enacted the liturgy of the heavenly temple as a replacement for the corrupt temple cult in Jerusalem. For example, the Qumran *Songs of the Sabbath Sacrifice* constitutes "a quasi-mystical liturgy, designed to evoke the sense of being present in the heavenly temple."[36] Third, the community looked ahead to the coming day when a new temple would be established along with the

---

33. Collins, "Models of Utopia," 58.

34. R. G. Hamerton-Kelly, "The Temple and the Origins of Jewish Apocalyptic," *VT* 20 (1970): 4. See also Nicholas Perrin, *Jesus the Temple* (Grand Rapids: Baker Academic, 2010), 17–37, for a helpful review of Israelite perceptions of the present temple and its administration as contained in the *Psalms of Solomon* and the DSS.

35. John J. Collins, "Jerusalem and the Temple in Jewish Apocalyptic Literature of the Second Temple Period" (lecture, Bar-Ilan University, 1998), 13–24.

36. Carol A. Newsom, *Songs of the Sabbath Sacrifice* (Atlanta: Scholars Press, 1985), 59, cited in Collins, "Jerusalem and the Temple," 15.

new Jerusalem (see the *Temple Scroll* [11Q19–20] and the fragmentary *Vision of the New Jerusalem* [4Q544]). In varying degrees, these visions take up and recast Ezekiel's model of the new temple. The temple described in much of the *Temple Scroll* stands at the center of a restored Jerusalem and embodies God's presence among the people. However, this temple allows for a court of foreigners. At the same time, this new temple appears to be an interim one; it shall be replaced by a divinely constructed temple in the new creation.[37] The temple described in 4Q544 even more closely resembles Ezekiel's blueprint and yet is "an eschatological temple, created miraculously by God."[38]

Thus, for many Israelites of this era, the restoration of Israel and the arrival of God's Kingdom was inconceivable without a renewed or new temple playing a central role in God's new age. It remained, likely for most, a powerful symbol of God's presence among the people and of Yahweh's enduring invitation for them to be in intimate communion with their Lord and Creator.

The Bestowal of God's Spirit upon the Messiah and the Faithful

Israelite reflection on God's Spirit leading up to the turn of the era led to various conceptions of the Spirit's role and function. John R. Levison provides a useful guide through some of this material, examining the conceptions of the Spirit in the surviving writings of Philo, Josephus, and Pseudo-Philo.[39] He finds the Spirit described as a source of awesome and transforming power, manifested in the gifts of military prowess (Pseudo-Philo); prophetic inspiration (Pseudo-Philo); ideal rule, including beauty, poise, rhetorical skill, and virtue (Philo); and philosophical ascent—realizing the higher truths about the nature of reality (Philo). Borrowing from and endorsing the Stoic notion of a universal and unifying Spirit, Josephus seeks to counter Roman charges of Jewish misanthropy by celebrating the Spirit as God's overture of intimate relatedness to all humanity. Meanwhile, Philo takes up the same notion of the Spirit's universality as he discusses the Spirit's ability to inspire all humans, albeit temporarily (save for Moses, who possessed a permanent endowment). Borrowing from both Israelite and Greco-Roman thought (in this case, notably from Plutarch's writing on *daemons*), Philo also develops the notion of the Spirit as an angelic being who comes upon individuals either to confound, to control through charismatic utterance, to inspire, or to grant interpretive insight.

37. Collins, "Jerusalem and the Temple," 20.
38. Ibid., 24.
39. John R. Levison, *The Spirit in First Century Judaism* (New York: Brill, 1997). See especially the helpful summary Levison provides on pp. 217–36.

Among some eschatologically minded Israelites, the bestowal of the Spirit was celebrated as both sign and consequence of the arrival of God's Kingdom and was viewed in far less universalistic terms. According to Finny Philip, two primary strands of thought suggested by Israel's prophetic traditions came to characterize later Israelite reflection on the role of the Spirit in God's new age.[40] One was the idea that in the age to come God's Spirit would be bestowed upon a messianic figure (Isa. 11:2; 42:1; 61:1). Intertestamental traditions make frequent use of this motif (e.g., *1 En.* 49:2–3; 61:11–12; 62:2; *Pss. Sol.* 17:37; 18:7; CD 2.11–13; 11QMelch 2.18; 1QSb 5.24). Another was the hope that in God's awaited realm the redeemed house of Israel would be granted the gift of the Spirit. In some texts, the Spirit enlivens the community to partake in the blessings of God's new age (Isa. 44:3; Ezek. 37:1–14; 39:29). In others, the Spirit enables Israel to walk faithfully in God's ways and embody God's justice (Isa. 28:5–6; 32:15; 59:21; Ezek. 36:23–31; 37:1–14; 39:29; Zech. 12:10) or leads God's faithful to repentance (Ezek. 36:31). *Jubilees* 1:22–23 picks up on the motif of the transforming character of the Spirit, echoing the testimony of Ezekiel 36:25–27, among other traditions, to emphasize that "God's restorative activity begins with regathering the people, transforming their hearts . . . and purifying them" (see also *4 Ezra* 6:27–28).[41]

Likewise, numerous DSS texts speak of the present bestowal of the Spirit upon the community at Qumran. For them, however, the awaited gift of the Spirit is a present reality, since the community itself (and only this community) embodies the faithful ones of God living in the final days. The gift of the Spirit is granted to every member upon his or her entrance into the community (1QH 6.11–13; 7.6–7; 12.11–13; 13.18–14.13; 16.13–14). These texts also emphasize the purging and cleansing role of the Holy Spirit, which will bring the entrant near to God's will and into God's presence forever (1QH 8.20, 22).[42]

Identification with and Vindication of the Poor

The prophetic concern for the poor and marginalized contained in Israel's sacred traditions is also expressed in intertestamental texts longing for the arrival of God's new age. As noted above, some Israelites believed that due to the corruption of the present priesthood in Jerusalem, it was the duty of the faithful to establish an alternative temple community. Among them, the authors of the *Psalms of Solomon* call upon the faithful to identify with socially and

40. Finny Philip, *The Origins of Pauline Pneumatology*, WUNT 94 (Tübingen: Mohr Siebeck, 2005), 23–33.
41. Ibid., 82.
42. Ibid., 86.

economically oppressed members of society and even to become the poor themselves as they resist and distance themselves from the temple establishment (Pss.
Sol. 5:2, 11, 16; 10:6). Nicholas Perrin writes, "One of the distinctive marks of
this new priesthood—in contradiction to the regnant priesthood—was in its aversion to unnecessary wealth and a corresponding identification with the 'poor.'
Precisely as the suffering poor, this temple community would also help usher in
the longed-for day of vindication."[43] This call for resistance and identification
with the poor is also found among the DSS traditions (e.g., CD 3.17–21; 5.14–17;
19.9; 1QpHab 12.2–4; 1QHa 26.31–32). The covenanters of Qumran believed
that the arrival of God's deliverance would be preceded by the righteous suffering
of the faithful. In this vein, "poverty was not just a condition to be endured but
an eschatological reality to be embraced: God would honor the righteous who
gave freely, and God would deliver and save those who in their poverty 'take upon
themselves the period of affliction.'"[44] As again helpfully summarized by Perrin,

> For the authors of the DSS, part of what it means to be poor is to insist that
> those who belong to the true temple eschew the rapaciousness of the temple
> elite in Jerusalem. Part of what it means too, at least for those who had been
> fully admitted to the circle, is the transfer of a sizable portion of one's own
> resources to a collective pool of wealth. And finally, part of what this means is
> a distinctive orientation, involving association and practical care, towards the
> socio-economically marginalized of Jewish society.[45]

Summary: The Story of the Kingdom

This chapter has sought to illuminate the various ways in which the "story of
the kingdom" could be told by Israelites in the years preceding the writing of
Luke's narrative. Guided by others, we began with the assumption that "the
Kingdom of God" was not a distinct and fixed concept held by Israelite folk
in the centuries straddling the turn of the era. Rather, emerging in the late
intertestamental period, the expression signified a worldview in narrative form
proclaiming hope in God's restoring rule over a world gone awry. It signified
the long-told story that Yahweh's justice, righteousness, and peace would one
day reorder creation into a realm of abundant blessing.

The three core dimensions of this story are rooted in Israel's sacred scriptures, for they reflect Israel's fundamental confessions about the sovereignty of

43. Perrin, Jesus the Temple, 29. See, e.g., Psalm 5.
44. Perrin, Jesus the Temple, 34.
45. Ibid., 35.

God and God's will for creation, characteristic tendencies in God's response to human sin and tragedy, and the hopes of Israel's prophets and people following the destruction of Jerusalem and exile. In its most basic form, this core narrative announces that (1) Yahweh is in charge of this world; (2) despite God's sovereignty, the world and its human inhabitants have largely strayed from God's intentions for its peace and prosperity; and (3) God will act to reclaim and transform creation. This same worldview continues to be integral to Israelite traditions of the late Second Temple period, as many Israelites yearned for God's awaited reign to deliver them from the evils of this age and lead them to blessing once more.

As we discussed above, these three dimensions could be construed in different ways, and other elements were commonly integrated into this core narrative. In some traditions, Yahweh alone delivers Israel, while in others Yahweh acts through intermediary agents. Options include angelic warriors, a Davidic messiah, a divine-like Son of God, a transcendent one like a son of man, a priestly messiah, a prophet, a teacher of righteousness, or some combination of these. The wrongness of the world may be seen as some combination of Israel's defeat and exile, its subjugation to foreign powers, its lack of attentiveness to God's torah, its embattlement by Satan and his minions, the corruption of its own leaders, the defilement of the temple, and social and economic oppression. God's restoration may be in the form of a renewed Israel, elevated in prominence among all the nations, bursting with provision and secure in power and peace. Or it might involve the resurrection of the faithful to live with God in the heavenly realms, or the creation of a new heaven and a new earth in which the faithful will dwell, troubled no more by disease, violence, and unrighteousness. In many scenarios a restored or newly made temple is granted a central role in God's new age. In some visions of a renewed future, the Spirit of God empowers an awaited redeemer to conquer and to rule with justice or leads the people to walk in righteousness. A few expect non-Israelites to partake in the blessings of the faithful, while in most only a remnant of God's people are in view.

Knowing these fundamental elements of the kingdom story and its variant forms held by Israelites can help us recognize the ways in which Luke incorporated these core components and common variations and perhaps introduced some variations or emphases of his own. Yet our survey of Israelite conceptions of the Kingdom is not yet complete. We turn now to a version of the kingdom story preceding Luke-Acts that presents Jesus as its central actor: the Gospel of Mark. This narrative likely reflects the understanding of Jesus' identity and significance shared by most members of the early Christian movement. This includes Luke, who drew from Mark as a source for his own story of the Kingdom's arrival in Jesus.

Mark's Adaptation of the Kingdom Story

As is often noted, kingdom language dominates Mark's Gospel, and from beginning to end it is clear that Mark's narrative is a kingdom story. Already in the prologue, Mark titles his narrative as "the beginning of the good news of Jesus Christ, the Son of God," and characterizes the preaching of Jesus as "the good news of God" (1:14). He follows this with a representative overview of Jesus' message: "The time is fulfilled, and the kingdom of God has come near; repent, and believe in the good news" (1:15). In concert with the Gospel's opening line, Jesus' words here announce that with his baptism, ministry, crucifixion, and resurrection, the Kingdom is in the process of unfolding and awaits its consummation in Jesus' return (Mark 13).[46] As with our review of Israel's sacred tradition, we will use the three core elements of kingdom stories to structure a concise analysis of Mark's good news.

Yahweh as King of Israel and Ruler of the Universe

The "Kingdom of God" language that dominates Mark's account not only indicates the focus of Mark's narrative; it also repeatedly reminds Mark's audience that the story he presents is one that professes God's sovereignty over creation. Going a step further, we must also say that the ubiquity of "Kingdom of God" language contextualizes the narrative's focus on Jesus as one who inaugurates God's reign. Moreover, as David Rhoads points out,

> God is the force which drives the whole plot. God prophesied the powerful words through Isaiah (1:2–3). God sent John (1:2–4). God ripped apart the heavens (1:10). God anointed Jesus to usher in the realm of God. Jesus proclaims the good news about God (1:14, 15). It is God who empowers Jesus and the disciples to heal, drive out demons, control nature, pardon sins, raise the dead, cleanse the lepers. God has initiated God's realm, and God brings the increase of that realm. And it is God who will establish the realm in power when Jesus returns on God's right hand within a generation.[47]

Numerous passages emphasize God's rule while presenting Jesus as the Son of God whose life, death, and resurrection mark the Kingdom's arrival. For example, immediately before the transfiguration, Jesus refers to his return as the Son of Man "when he comes in the glory of his Father with the holy

---

46. Hence the use of the perfect tenses for both πληρόω, "fulfill," and ἐγγίζω, "come near," in v. 15, implying an action or reality whose effect is continuing on into the present.

47. David Rhoads, "Mission in the Gospel of Mark," *CurTM* 22 (1995): 343.

angels" (8:38), again underscoring both his exalted character as the divine Son who brings the Kingdom to its culmination and God's ultimate sovereignty (i.e., "glory of his Father"). Similarly, the final section of Mark's apocalypse (13:32–37) opens with Jesus' statement, "But about that day or hour no one knows, neither the angels in heaven, nor the Son, but only the Father" (v. 32; see also 12:35–37; 14:36). Of course, the very use of the concept of "divine sonship" to portray Jesus at once elevates Jesus' authority/identity while indicating his submission to God and enactment of God's will. Joel Marcus helpfully comments on the implications of 1:11 within the context of the Gospel's opening:

> Mark emphasizes the inseparable link between God and Jesus while at the same time maintaining the distinction between them. Jesus is God's *son*, not God himself. As son, however, he shares in God's βασιλεία, his kingly power, and becomes the instrument of its extension into every corner of the creation through his defeat of the demonic cosmic forces that twist and destroy human life.[48]

Mark's use of κύριος (Lord) for Jesus falls along these same lines. Larry Hurtado, among others, sees the designation of Jesus as κύριος throughout the NT as reflecting a confession widespread in early Christianity that in some sense regarded Jesus as on a level with Yahweh (cf. Phil. 2:5–11).[49] Mark does not use the title as frequently as Luke, and not as often in contexts that invite direct association between Jesus and Yahweh. However, the title occurs often enough to emphasize Jesus' exalted character, including two instances in which its ambiguous use invites recipients to see both Jesus and God as "Lord": the conflated quotation of Mark 1:2–3 from Malachi 3:1 and Isaiah 40:3 ("Prepare the way of the Lord"), and Jesus' instruction to the former demoniac in Mark 5:19 ("tell them how much the Lord has done for you"). Mark's portrait of Jesus emphasizes *both* Jesus' exalted, even transcendent, character as the divine Son and Lord *and* his calling to inaugurate God's reign among humanity.

The Misalignment of the Status Quo with God's Will

Mark shares with Israelite thought the basic conviction that the world in general, and humanity in particular, has gone incredibly awry. There are at least four broad strokes to Mark's portrait of the corrupted creation.

48. Joel Marcus, *The Way of the Lord: Christological Exegesis of the Old Testament in the Gospel of Mark* (Louisville: Westminster John Knox, 1992), 72.

49. Larry W. Hurtado, *One God, One Lord: Early Christian Devotion and Ancient Jewish Monotheism* (Philadelphia: Fortress, 1988), 108–9.

1. *Cosmic Corruption*. Along with other apocalyptic texts, Mark holds that forces beyond the terrestrial realm are actively degrading God's creation.[50] The Gospel's prologue and its opening scenes set the stage for this conflict, as Jesus is tempted by "the Satan" (1:12–13) and then immediately begins casting out demons (1:21–28). Demons and Satan remain in view throughout much of the narrative. Unclean spirits or demons torment humanity, and exorcism is one of the hallmarks of Jesus' ministry (1:34; 5:1–13; 6:7, 13; 7:29; 9:14–29). Jesus talks of binding Satan and plundering his house (3:27). Even so, for now Satan still has the power to oppose the word, snatching it away from the feeble-hearted (4:15) and leading even Jesus' own disciples astray (8:33; 14:38).

2. *Life-Defying Insults of This Age*. Perhaps the most apparent form of degradation manifest in Mark's narrative is that the world has become a painfully inhospitable place in which to (try to) live. I invite you to page through Mark's Gospel. Note that at nearly every turn disease, maladies, evil spirits, hunger, and enmity plague humanity.[51] Cursing, not blessing, is the norm. Satan and sin seem to be having their way, and the result is a people besieged with forces that defy life and spawn suffering. Mark's world, like the Roman world in general, is a world of desperate struggle and want.

3. *Misaligned Values and Darkened Minds*. The life-defying forces plaguing Mark's world are in large measure the result of the misaligned values most have come to embrace. Darkness clouds the thoughts and hearts of humanity. Fear pulls people away from trusting in God and God's instruction, leading them to entrust themselves to that which does not lead to blessing. Many have noted that Mark's narrative presents a contrast between two sets of values, two contrasting orientations to life: what God wills for people and what people will for themselves. Human sinfulness is reflected in the fact that people are self-oriented and self-serving. This becomes strikingly clear in the narrative and dialogue surrounding Jesus' three passion predictions (8:22–10:52): "People want to 'save their lives' (8:35), to 'acquire the world' (8:36), to 'be great' (9:35), and to 'exert authority over' or to 'lord over' people (10:43–44)."[52] In response

---

50. The apocalyptic character of Mark is commonly noted by interpreters. As Elizabeth Struthers Malbon (*Mark's Jesus: Characterization as Narrative Christology* [Waco: Baylor University Press, 2009], 45) summarizes: "The cosmic conflict of God and Satan is the deep background for all of Mark's Gospel and the immediate background for the opening of Jesus' ministry with his proclamation that '[t]he time is fulfilled, and the kingdom of God has come near' (1:15)." See also David Rhoads, Joanna Dewey, and Donald Michie, *Mark as Story: An Introduction to the Narrative of a Gospel*, 2nd ed. (Minneapolis: Fortress, 1999), 73–97.

51. See, e.g., 1:29–34, 40–45; 2:1–12; 3:1–6; 5:21–43; 6:30–44; 7:31–37; 8:1–10, 22–26; 10:46–52.

52. David Rhoads, "Losing Life for Others in the Face of Death: Mark's Standards of Judgment," in *Gospel Interpretation: Narrative-Critical and Social-Scientific Approaches*, ed. Jack Dean Kingsbury (Harrisburg, PA: Trinity Press, 1997), 85.

to the disciples, who frequently articulate the quest for self-preservation and gratification, Jesus explains "the values of the rule of God that underlie his actions and teachings."[53]

For Mark, it therefore follows that wealth is also an obstacle to entering the realm of God's rule. The pursuit and maintenance of wealth, especially in the agonistic, hierarchical world of Rome, is a quest for power, self-preservation, and gratification. It is an orientation, a deficiency of will and spirit, for which even near-perfect allegiance to torah cannot compensate (see 4:18–19; 10:17–27).

4. *Misaligned Rulers.* The fear of loss—loss of status, privilege, and even life—and the quest for blessing in all the wrong places are also reflected in the evangelist's depiction of the social elite. The misalignment of the elite's value system is repeatedly unmasked and attacked by Jesus. Their effort to maintain power and status is motivated by fear. Herod fears John the Baptist (6:20), but not more than he fears being shamed by his guests (6:26). Pilate fears the crowd, and so hands Jesus over to be flogged and crucified (15:15). The Israelite leaders fear having their status compromised by this itinerant healer and preacher, who challenges their system of piety (3:1–6; 7:1–23), the propriety of the temple cult (11:15–19), and their pursuit of wealth and honor (7:1–13). Thus, already by Mark 3:6 alliances are forged among the elite in opposition to their common enemy: "The Pharisees went out and immediately conspired with the Herodians against him, how to destroy him" (see also 11:18; 12:13; 14:43).

We saw in chapter 2 that criticism of the current religious elite and temple establishment was a common trend in apocalyptic thought. Here I will supplement the information we engaged in chapter 1 on the economic and political might of the temple as we assess Mark's views on that institution, its leaders, and other religious elite. The priestly aristocracy (Sadducees) regulated the maintenance of the temple cult in order to shape that institution into a major source of social, political, and economic capital. Drawing from their sacred tradition, which limited access to the temple via purity laws and also empowered them to administer its benefits of cleansing and atonement, the Sadducees legitimated their control of the temple cult, which—along with their more-often-than-not cozy alliance with the Herodians—eventually resulted in their control of a large share of the economic and judicial system of Judea. The mandatory temple tax they regulated provided a substantial revenue stream, as did their near monopoly on the supply of sacrificial animals. The temple tax also gave the Israelite elite a mechanism for ensuring widespread peasant indebtedness and access to peasant landholdings, which

---

53. Ibid., 84.

they routinely foreclosed.[54] This added loan interest and land rent to their income and gave them access to cheap labor in the form of tenant farmers, sharecroppers, and slaves.[55]

Accordingly, issues of wealth, purity, and authority stand at the forefront of Jesus' conflict with the religious elite in Mark. One section of the Gospel that plays a key part in characterizing this conflict is Mark 11–12, recording Jesus' entrance into Jerusalem and teaching in the temple precincts. Jesus' action in the temple unmasks and challenges the Sadducees' quest for control and perversion of God's house (11:15–19). Subsequent conflicts further emphasize their obduracy (11:27–33; 12:18–27), rejection of God's reign (12:1–12), collusion with Caesar (12:13–17), and quest for status and wealth at the expense of others (12:38–40). Karen J. Wenell helpfully writes of Jesus' engagement with the Sadducees and an assortment of other elite in this section of Mark:

> Wealth is a primary value associated with the opponents of Jesus in the temple conflict scenes in Mark 11–12. The λῃσται have, in a sense, stolen what belongs to God (12:13–17) and opposed his son (12:1–10). Jesus protests the values of power and wealth connected to the central temple which conflict with God's dominion and care for the least in society, such as the poor widow.[56]

God's Intervention to Reorder Creation

By Mark's account, the inauguration of the Kingdom in Jesus fulfills the prophetic dreams of deliverance (e.g., 1:1–3) and counters the depraved state of creation. As noted above, Jesus defies the wiles and forces of Satan, emerging victorious from his time of temptation, binding the strong man and his minions. His miracles undo life-sapping disease, ailment, the destructive forces of creation (4:35–5:34), and even death itself (5:35–43). Even though Jesus' reversal of evil is not yet complete, it anticipates the blessing that will commence when the Son of Man comes in God's glory (13:24–27). This hope in Jesus' return is founded upon the reality of Jesus' resurrection (see 8:31–38; 9:9–10).

Mark's Jesus also counters the depraved state of human hearts as he urges a radical realignment of values. Elizabeth Struthers Malbon concludes that Mark's depiction of Jesus as teacher, preacher, exorcist, healer, servant, and persecuted sufferer is presented within a plot that

54. Hamel, "Poverty and Charity," 314.
55. See Dennis E. Oakman, "Cursing Fig Trees and Robbers' Dens: Pronouncement Stories within Social-Systemic Perspective; Mark 11:12–15 and Parallels," *Semeia* 64 (1993): 260.
56. Karen J. Wenell, "Contested Temple Space and Visionary Kingdom Space in Mark 11–12," *BibInt* 15 (2007): 332.

consistently anticipates, insinuates and recapitulates its message: the Markan Jesus who proclaims and participates in the in-breaking of the rule of God, restoring health to the powerless ill and hungry, both within his group and beyond it, insists on continuing to serve those with the least status in society and teach whoever wishes to do the will of God to do the same, even at the clear risk of losing his life at the hands of the established powers, and accepts that risk as the will of God.[57]

Jesus' proclamation of "the word," especially in parables, enables those with "ears to listen" to leave behind the ignorance of this age and realign themselves with Jesus and the true values of God's reign (4:1–34).[58] Mark believed that the arrival of the Kingdom in Jesus subverts sacred traditions that circumscribe the domain of God's blessing, even those traditions established by Moses (recall 1:40–3:6; 7:19). True purity comes not from external conformity to law code but from the relinquishment of self-gratifying passions, self-sacrifice (e.g., 7:21–23; 8:31–38; 9:33–37; 10:17–31, 35–45), and trust in Jesus as the embodiment of God's reign (6:1–6; 7:24–29; 8:27–30, 38; 10:29). Above all else, love of God and one another defines the purity that leads one into God's realm (12:28–34; see also 10:2–12).

Forgiveness is another essential dimension of the restoration marked by the arrival of God's new age. John proclaims a "baptism of repentance for the forgiveness of sins" (1:4), while Jesus similarly urges repentance (1:15) in the face of the Kingdom's arrival and announces God's forgiveness of the faithful. However, such forgiveness is offered far from the temple courts and cult. And while agreeing with other apocalyptic writers on the current corruption of the temple and its leadership, Mark marginalized the future significance of the temple in God's designs for Israel. In fact, Mark foresaw (or witnessed) the destruction of the temple and understood its demise as part of the dissolution of the present age (13:1–2). The suffering, death, and resurrection of Jesus now accomplish what the temple and its sacrificial

57. Malbon, *Mark's Jesus*, 55. See also Rhoads, "Mission in the Gospel of Mark," 342–43; John R. Donahue and Daniel J. Harrington, *The Gospel of Mark*, Sacra Pagina (Collegeville, MN: Liturgical Press, 2002), 37–38; Adela Yarbro Collins, *Mark*, Hermeneia (Minneapolis: Fortress, 2007), 249.

58. For Mark, "the secret of the kingdom" (4:11) likely refers to the recognition that the reign of God is embodied in Jesus' teaching, miracles, suffering, and death; e.g., see Schuyler Brown, "'The Secret of the Kingdom of God' (Mark 4:11)," *JBL* 92 (1973): 73–74. From this and the parable of the sower, it follows that "insiders" are those inclined to see Jesus, his words, his actions, and the values they embody as the manifestation of God's reign. For these insiders, the parables awaken faith and understanding of the character of the Kingdom, especially when accompanied by the benefit of Jesus' additional instruction (4:8, 11, 13, 20, 25, 34). For the rest—"those outside" (v. 11)—the parables serve only to confound and condemn (4:4–7, 11–12, 14–19, 25).

offerings can no longer achieve: reconciliation between God and humanity and a renewal of human community (10:45; 14:24). What socioreligious form does that offer of reconciliation, release from evil, and genuine human community take? Faithful witness one household at a time, heartfelt repentance, and hospitality: these replace temple and cult (6:7–13).

Despite Mark's marginalization of the temple in God's Kingdom to come, his short apocalypse and other sections of his Gospel emphasize other common apocalyptic themes. Just as we saw with the inauguration of the Kingdom in Jesus, its culmination when Jesus returns is also cosmic in scope. The apocalyptic tendency to parallel the earthy and heavenly dimensions of the conflict that has already begun is reflected in the careful structuring of 13:3–27. The end of this age will be marked by terrestrial tumult, accompanied by the dissolution of terrestrial boundaries (vv. 3–8). On the positive side, the gospel is now to be preached to all kingdoms—the arrival of God's reign is to be "good news" for all humanity (v. 10). On the negative side, the chaos and strife of this eschatological age will even transgress kinship bonds, as "brother will betray brother to death, and a father his child, and children will rise against parents and have them put to death" (v. 12). Just as God's salvation is now open to all (see also 5:1–20; 7:24–30; 8:1–10), the faithful "will be hated by all because of my name" (13:13). Incredible depravity, suffering, and turmoil will characterize these days (vv. 14–23). These end-time upheavals of disorder and dissolution will also be suffered by the cosmic realm. The heavenly bodies that sustain the present world will be darkened, stars will be cast down, and the powers of heaven shaken (vv. 24–25). Then the gulf between heaven and earth will be breached, as the Son of Man descends with "great power and glory," gathering up the elect "from the ends of the earth to the ends of heaven" (vv. 26–27). In sum, tumult and the dissolution of boundaries shall occur (and are already occurring) on both the terrestrial and cosmic spheres. The current, corrupt age is passing away as God's realm advances.

Mark's apocalypse contains little description of the vindication to be experienced by the elect, apart from the gift of the Holy Spirit in moments of persecution (13:11) and the gathering of the elect by Jesus (v. 27). Mark's focus is on the faithful remaining steadfast in their trust and "keeping awake" until the final act of God's new age (vv. 32–36). Still, the Gospel as a whole testifies to the blessings that will be manifest in God's realm, blessings that we have addressed in the preceding section: realignment of values that will bring the faithful into right relationship with God and others, deliverance from Satan and the life-defying insults of this age, forgiveness apart from corrupt temple and cult, and a renewed community focused on the proclamation and living out of Jesus' instruction. In contrast, Mark gives far less attention to the fate of the wicked, who resist the ways of the Kingdom. Even so, he makes it clear that those who seek to save themselves at the expense of others shall find themselves on the "outside" (4:11–12), both as agents *and* as recipients of alienation and death (4:13–17, 25; 8:34–38; 12:9, 40).

Summary: Mark's Kingdom Story

Mark recasts the Israelite kingdom story with Jesus as its central actor. His narrative reflects an apocalyptic field of view, cosmic in scope. The treason of Satan and demonic powers is manifested in the waywardness of human hearts. Corruption exists in both the terrestrial and heavenly realms, and the evil that plagues both domains shall be overcome. Still, in Mark's Gospel the focus is on the need for human transformation in the here and now, as all humanity is called to resist the insanity of this age (as embodied in its values, institutions, and rulers) and embrace the ways of living and relating that reflect and manifest God's reign in the present. Mark also marginalizes the significance of the temple in the present and future movements of God's realm, for its destruction signals the advance of God's purpose and plan. The divine Son of God, Davidic messiah, Lord, and heavenly Son of Man, in both his exaltation and his suffering, his power and his vulnerability, reveals the power of God over all that ails humanity, including sin and death, and teaches humanity the ways of God. For Mark, this instruction occurs while believers meditate upon Jesus' actions and words about the Kingdom spoken to his disciples. Evil still resists God's intentions and shall continue to cause incredible injustice and suffering, especially for believers. But in the present the faithful are called to witness boldly to a different set of values, a different Lord, and a different realm. And in the end, Jesus will return to defeat evil in all its forms and gather the righteous to live in a new heaven and new earth. For Mark, the final act of the kingdom story has begun.

3

Luke's Place in Caesar's Kingdom

The Social Location of the Third Evangelist

One of the frustrating realities facing students of the Gospels is that we lack reliable data on the specific identities and settings of those who put these narratives in writing. The early church fathers attempted to identify the Gospels' authors using the best information available to them, but their informed speculation has failed to convince the majority of modern scholars. Moreover, the Gospels themselves are anonymous. Even though John's narrative identifies the beloved disciple as its writer (21:24), we know nothing about him except that he was one of Jesus' followers. Despite this unfortunate circumstance, readers of the Gospels have often found solace in the sage advice that the particular identity of the evangelists is of little consequence for understanding their writings. It is what they wrote about Jesus and the Kingdom of God that matters, and knowing this or that about features of their personhood would change little, if anything at all, about our understanding of their work. In Luke's case, for instance, does it really matter whether he was a physician, or a companion of Paul, or an Israelite, or just a really gifted gentile historian who gained access to a lot of good sources? Would it really help us better understand what he said and why he said it? Perhaps it is simply better for us to work with what we have before us, the text itself, and our general knowledge of the first-century Mediterranean world, than to chase after the ghostly contours of Luke's identity.

Perhaps. And yet there may very well be a feature of Luke's identity that is relatively accessible to us, and one that potentially sharpens our understanding of the two volumes on Christian origins he painstakingly composed. That feature is Luke's *social location*, by which I mean where Luke stood—socially and economically—relative to others in his society. But investigating Luke's social location entails more than just determining Luke's place on the social scale. It also includes determining Luke's proximity to those in power and the extent to which Luke shares in that power. It involves Luke's access to resources (food, shelter, health, leisure time) and his response to the culturally shared perspectives that would have legitimated his access to the resources that most in the Roman world possessed in only scant measure. This chapter will shed some light on this little-explored dimension of Luke's identity and reflect on how it helps us understand more fully the rhetorical edge of his writing.

Luke's Literacy and Social Location

In *Luke: The Elite Evangelist*, I argued that Luke was very likely a member of the elite. The primary index I employed for discerning Luke's social location was literacy—the ability to read and write.

Literacy and Social Location in the Roman World

Based on the most recent examinations of scholars engaging this subject, I argued that several features of literacy in the Roman world leading up to the Common Era are relevant for discerning Luke's social location. Below I distill the argument I offered in that earlier text.

1. *In Luke's day, literacy was restricted to a small minority of the population.* William V. Harris's landmark study, *Ancient Literacy*, has become the standard for assessing the rate of literacy in the Roman world.[1] Harris argues, based on investigations of increased literacy rates in early modern and modern Europe, that "writing ceases to be the arcane accomplishment of a small professional or social or religious elite *only* when certain preconditions are fulfilled and *only* when strong positive forces are present to bring the change about."[2] The chief precondition for mass literacy that Harris identifies is a *subsidized educational system*. Such a mechanism is needed to allow for widespread access to literacy training across a broad spectrum of the populace, including the peasant ma-

---

1. William V. Harris, *Ancient Literacy* (Cambridge, MA: Harvard University Press, 1989).
2. Ibid., 11–12.

jority.[3] Harris's volume also takes up a wide-ranging survey of epigraphic and literary material to provide data for estimating literacy rates in antiquity. The evidence Harris compiles confirms that the ability to read and write, beyond the rudimentary functions of signing one's name, recognizing the shape of some common words, or roughly scratching out a receipt (often called "semi-literacy"), was limited to a select few. Harris finds that in the Roman Empire of the first century BCE, it is "unlikely that the overall literacy of the western provinces even rose into the range of 5–10%,"[4] and the literacy rates of the empire as a whole were no greater than 10 percent.[5] For Egypt and other eastern provinces such as Judea, Harris suggests that rates of literacy may have been higher than was common in the west but still confined to a small proportion of the population.[6] Harris's conclusions on the limited extent of literacy in the ancient world have been largely adopted by subsequent treatments of the topic, including those examining Israelite literacy in Palestine.[7]

2. *In ancient Rome, higher levels of literacy and literary acumen were achieved by only a very select few.* Following Harris's study, another important exploration of the topic of literacy in ancient Greece and Rome was offered by Teresa Morgan in *Literate Education in the Hellenistic and Roman Worlds.*[8] Morgan's work examines surviving papyri "school texts" from Hellenistic Egypt, in tandem with discussions of education by Greek and Roman writers, to establish what subjects were being taught, to whom they were being taught, and for what purpose. While her study isn't chiefly concerned with rates of basic literacy, Morgan concurs with Harris's low estimation and additionally argues that only a very small minority went beyond a rudimentary literary education. Catherine Hezser finds the same to be typical of Roman Palestine, arguing that "the number of those who actually underwent years of rabbinic, rhetorical, or philosophical training and were subsequently accepted by their teachers as rabbis, orators, and philosophers in their own right will have been tiny indeed."[9]

3. See ibid., 11–24, 327.

4. Ibid., 272.

5. Ibid., 173.

6. Ibid., 276–82.

7. See, e.g., H. Gregory Snyder, *Teachers and Texts in the Ancient World: Philosophers, Israelites and Christians*, Religion in the First Christian Centuries (New York: Routledge, 2000); Martin Jaffee, *Torah in the Mouth: Writing and Oral Tradition in Palestinian Judaism, 200 BCE–400 CE* (New York: Oxford University Press, 2001), 15; Catherine Hezser, *Jewish Literacy in Roman Palestine*, Texts and Studies in Ancient Palestine 81 (Tübingen: Mohr Siebeck, 2001).

8. Teresa Morgan, *Literate Education in the Hellenistic and Roman Worlds*, Cambridge Classical Studies (Cambridge: Cambridge University Press, 1998).

9. Hezser, *Jewish Literacy*, 188.

3. *In Luke's world, literacy and especially advanced levels of literacy were primarily restricted to the social elite.* Coinciding with the view of researchers that literacy was relatively uncommon among the citizens of the Greco-Roman world is the attending claim that the ability to read and write was much more frequently held by members of the upper class than by peasants, artisans, and slaves. While some outside the elite may have gained a limited form of literacy, such as slaves serving as bookkeepers or military clerks, several factors would have prevented all but a very few of the non-elite from attaining literacy, *especially* higher levels of literacy that would have included some proficiency in grammar and rhetoric. Those factors were lack of access (the few schools that existed and tutors were generally restricted to the elite), lack of necessity (for most peasants and slaves literacy would not have had any tangible benefit), and cost (in terms of equipment, supplies, and time). Hezser similarly concludes that the rural and agricultural character of Roman Palestine would have resulted in little need for literate skills among the vast majority of the population.[10]

4. *In ancient Rome, literacy was used as a mechanism for enculturation, social stratification, and control.* Based on epigraphic data, Morgan observes that literacy skills in the Greco-Roman world were distributed through a "core and periphery" model of education. To summarize, Morgan argues that there was a typical set of skills, a select group of writers, and certain types of materials that students commonly engaged. More peripheral were the additional, highly variable writers that were read and the advanced subjects of grammar and rhetoric, which far fewer students explored. Morgan proposes that this core-and-periphery model served two important social functions. One was enculturation. Through the acquisition of literacy and familiarity with a select group of writers (e.g., Homer and Euripides) and collections of proverbial (gnomic) sayings, diverse peoples from across the Greco-Roman world, especially during the Roman era, became integrated into Hellenistic literary culture. However, while literacy and familiarity with revered writers provided an ethnically diverse matrix of folk with a sense of participation in Roman elite culture, these kinds of knowledge also led to differentiation among people as such acumen became a vehicle for pursuing honor and social status among the elite. The higher forms of literacy became markers of erudition and skill that elevated the social prestige of those who displayed them. As Keith Hopkins argues, those many years ago in ancient Rome, "it mattered to a surprising degree *how* you showed, and how much you showed, that you knew something of what was written in books."[11]

10. Ibid., 170–76.
11. Keith Hopkins, "Conquest by Book," in *Literacy in the Roman World*, ed. Mary Beard, Alan K. Bowman, and Mireille Corbier, Journal of Roman Archaeology Supplementary Series 3 (Ann Arbor, MI: Journal of Roman Archaeology, 1991), 144.

Beyond the two functions of enculturation and stratification, the increased use of writing in the Roman period also began to play a larger role in the maintenance and distribution of power.[12] One of the Roman state's primary instruments for implementing and safeguarding its control over its subjects was the written law, access to which was available only through the literate elite and their retainers.[13] Similarly, Mary Beard points out that as religious traditions became increasingly codified, this only reinforced the elite control of sacred traditions and practices.[14] In short, literacy served a pivotal role in the development of a religious elite and a proliferation of religious texts that they alone were deemed qualified to access.[15] Similarly, Israelite faith before and throughout the Roman period became heavily dependent upon written tradition for the preservation and dissemination of its religious doctrine.[16] Literacy, among other factors such as heredity, social standing, and purity, safeguarded access to sacred tradition, granting priests and scribes the authority to mediate revelation.

Luke's Level of Literacy and Social Location

Luke is commonly regarded as one of the most gifted and erudite writers of the NT, and his literary artistry is celebrated by many a reader. We will have occasion in part 2 of this work to explore Luke's literary talent and will find that he mastered and even adapted to his own ends a wide repertoire of narrative and rhetorical conventions found in other surviving works of his day. The inevitable conclusion required by Luke's remarkable literary acumen is that Luke was very likely among the social elite of his day. Other details from his writing could be marshaled to confirm this analysis. Luke reveals his familiarity with the formal proceedings involving the Roman elite (Acts 23:23–25:27), the reality of occasional enmity and alliance among the Roman hierarchy (Luke 23:6–12; Acts 25:13–27), and the types of appeals, pressures,

12. For a helpful discussion of the various social, economic, and political functions of writing in the Roman world, see Harris, *Ancient Literacy*, 196–231.

13. Hopkins, "Conquest by Book," 137.

14. Mary Beard, "Writing and Religion: Ancient Literacy and the Function of the Written Word in Roman Religion," in *Literacy in the Roman World*, ed. Mary Beard, Alan K. Bowman, and Mireille Corbier, Journal of Roman Archaeology Supplementary Series 3 (Ann Arbor, MI: Journal of Roman Archaeology, 1991), 39.

15. Beard, "Writing and Religion," 56–57. See also Richard Gordon, "From Republic to Principate: Priesthood, Religion and Ideology," in *Pagan Priests: Religion and Power in the Ancient World*, ed. M. Beard and J. North (Ithaca, NY: Cornell University Press, 1990), 179–98, esp. 184–91.

16. See Hezser, *Jewish Literacy*, 493–95.

or motivations that compelled their decisions (Luke 23:23–25; Acts 5:17–42; 16:35–40; 19:23–24; 22:22–29; 23:12–22; 23:23–25:27). The sense that emerges from Luke's portrayal of the Roman elite is that their world is one with which he is intimately acquainted.

Of course, it is not *impossible* that Luke was a mere scantily paid tutor or retainer with genius-like ability, and by some accident of fortune gained access to a wide range of texts and the time to study them diligently, leading to the acquisition of impressive literary talent, which, after yet another accident of fortune granting him extended periods of leisure, he was able to employ in the crafting of his lengthy two-volume work. Indeed, history is filled with exceptions, and stranger things have happened. But such an exception is not nearly as probable as the likelihood that it was Luke's membership in the upper echelon of society that facilitated his access to the education, literary texts, writing equipment, time, and resources he needed to develop the impressive repertoire of skills he came to possess and to compose the writing that has been admired by so many. From this it also follows that Theophilus, whom Luke addresses with the honorary appellation of "most excellent" (Luke 1:3), was among Luke's fellow elite (see also Acts 23:26; 24:2; 26:7) and may have held an even higher social rank than the evangelist.

Of the House of Israel

I think that a solid case can be made for Luke's social location as a member of the elite. Less certain is his ethnicity. Even so, I believe that the available evidence suggests that Luke was also an Israelite, though perhaps a slight majority of scholars believe him to be gentile.

The two strongest pieces of evidence in favor of Luke being gentile are church tradition, which considers Luke a "Syrian of Antioch," and the reference to Luke in Colossians 4. In Colossians 4:10–11, Paul refers to Aristarchus, Mark the cousin of Barnabas, and Jesus who is called Justus, as "the only ones of the circumcision among my co-workers for the kingdom of God." Paul then goes on to name others who also send along their greetings, including Epaphras, "who is one of yourselves," Luke, and Demas. The implication is that Epaphras, Luke, and Demas are not "ones of the circumcision," and thus not of the house of Israel.

Those arguing that Luke was most likely Israelite point above all else to his intimate knowledge of Israel's scriptures. This familiarity is exhibited in a number of ways: direct citation and widespread allusion to those scriptures throughout Luke-Acts; the patterning of characters in Luke-Acts after characters in the Israelite scriptures; the use of a Semitic, or Septuagintal, style of Greek in the infancy narrative and Peter's speeches; and the use of literary devices (such as direct and indirect discourse, widespread allusion to sacred tradition, the tendency to situate the events depicted within the larger story of God's dealings with Israel) that more closely parallel their use in Israelite tradition than in other Greco-Roman writings (see part 2).

In addition, Luke shows concern for the maintenance of at least some forms of torah piety. Luke presents Paul as more favorably disposed to Israelite law and practice than is reflected in Paul's Letters. Both Jesus and the witnesses of the early church honor the Sabbath by attending synagogue or the temple (Luke 4:16; Acts 2:46; 3:1; 5:20; 13:5; 17:2; 21:26). Also, leading characters of Luke's infancy narrative are presented as epitomes of torah observance. They serve in the temple (Luke 1:5–23; 2:25–38), circumcise their offspring (1:59; 2:21), and make the offerings required of new parents (2:22–24). Another telling piece of evidence that comes from Luke's Gospel is his handling of the tradition found in Mark 7:1–23. In this story, Jesus responds to the Pharisees' criticism of his disciples for not washing their hands before they ate by stating that it is not what goes into a person that renders the person unclean, but sinful actions and attitudes toward others (Mark 7:18–23). While reporting Jesus' response, lest the recipient miss the point of the story, Mark explains in a parenthetical aside, "Thus he declared all foods clean" (7:19). Matthew follows Mark's account closely, but omits the parenthetical comment declaring all foods clean. Luke, however, fails to mention the entire story! Accordingly, in Acts 15 Luke records the verdict of the Jerusalem conference that gentile Christians do not need to be circumcised but should participate in some of the dietary restrictions and abstain from certain foods (thus God's command for Peter to "kill and eat" unclean animals in the vision of Acts 10 is likely meant to be taken as a metaphor, not literally). While there are plenty of elements of Luke's narrative that challenge traditional Israelite notions of purity and piety, especially with respect to "unclean" and marginalized persons, it seems important to Luke that some of the dietary codes be maintained.

Still another important piece of evidence suggesting that Luke is Israelite, and one rarely considered in the debate, is the likelihood that Luke was also familiar with some of the writings found among the Dead Sea Scrolls. The Gospel contains a number of close parallels to DSS texts, including the "Son of God" text (4Q246; cf. Luke 1:32–35), the "Pierced Messiah" text (4Q285; cf. Luke 4:16–21), the "Resurrection Text" (4Q521; cf. Luke 4:18), and the Song of Miriam (4Q365 frag. 6; cf. Luke 1:46–55). George Brooke states that these parallels suggest "the place of Luke in preserving, in its special material and in its writer's handling of inherited traditions, the viewpoint of a strand of

Judaism which can be found in some fragmentary scroll texts."[17] In addition
to these parallels, Luke also makes distinctive use of introductory formulas
for scriptural citations that have almost exact Hebrew counterparts in Qumran texts: "as it is written" (καθὼς γέγραπται [Acts 7:42; 15:15]); "as also it
is written" (ὡς καί . . . γέγραπται [Acts 13:33]); "for it is written" (γέγραπται
γάρ [Acts 1:20; 23:5]); "as God spoke" (ἐλάλησεν δὲ οὕτως ὁ θεός [Acts 7:6]).[18]

In my view, the weight of the evidence falls in favor of Luke being of the
house of Israel. While it is not impossible that a gentile could immerse himself
in Israelite tradition to the extent that Luke clearly did, I think such intimate
knowledge of that tradition in Luke's day is far more likely to belong to an
Israelite person than to a gentile. Even if Luke were a gentile convert to Israel's
faith, one wonders whether he would have had the access to written texts and
instruction he would have needed to gain such a familiarity with these sacred
traditions. There is also the curious matter of Luke's familiarity with texts that
were also housed at Qumran. While copies of those texts could have existed
outside the Qumran community, I think it far more likely that Luke would
have had access to such writings, let alone even known about their existence,
if he were an Israelite and had Essene acquaintances than if he were gentile.

How then are we to account for the evidence suggesting that Luke was
gentile? First, I must point out that all of this evidence rests on the assumption that the author of Luke-Acts is indeed the "Luke" identified by ecclesial
tradition. This is less than certain. But even if it is the case that this Luke is
the author of Luke-Acts, the evidence suggesting he is a gentile is still not
very strong and can be read in more than one way. For instance, the description of this Luke as a "Syrian from Antioch" is provided in a single source,
the extratextual Prologue to the Gospel, which originated a hundred years
after the writing of Luke-Acts. Moreover, Luke's identification as a "Syrian"
does not necessarily entail that he is not Israelite, both religiously and ethnically. The term could be meant as a geographic marker (indicating Syrian
Antioch as opposed to Pisidian Antioch) rather than an ethnic marker (recall
that after 587 BCE, most Israelites lived outside Palestine). Or Luke could be
from a family of mixed ethnicity (also rather common) that has thoroughly
embraced its Israelite heritage. More problematic is the passage from Colossians 4, in which "Luke the physician" is not included among those who are
"of the circumcision." Rick Strelan argues, however, that the phrase need

17. George Brooke, "Luke-Acts and the Qumran Scrolls: The Case of the MMT," in *Luke's
Literary Achievement*, ed. C. M. Tuckett, JSNTSup 116 (Sheffield: Sheffield Academic Press,
1995), 77. On the parallels between Luke 1:32–35 and 4Q246, see Kuhn, "'One Like a Son of
Man,'" 22–42.

18. Joseph Fitzmyer, *The Acts of the Apostles*, AB 31 (New York: Doubleday, 1997), 93.

not be taken as referring to Israelites who were part of the Pauline mission as opposed to Paul's gentile associates. Instead, what the phrase may have in view is not differences in *ethnicity* but in *practice*. Thus, "those men 'of the circumcision' could refer to those Israelite followers of Christ who were ritually strict compared to the ritually lax Paul; it does not infer that those not 'of the circumcision' were not of Israel."[19]

Luke, the Elite Evangelist

In the introduction, I set forth my view of Luke as one who boldly proclaimed the coming of a Kingdom that would turn current sociopolitical realities on their heads. In this chapter I have argued that Luke was most likely a member of the elite, the 2–5 percent of the Roman world who benefited greatly from the status quo at the expense of others, and who were keenly interested in the current order of things being maintained. I have also presented, albeit less certainly, evidence that he was a member of the *Israelite* elite. Yet how could Luke be a member of the elite and yet advocate for the upside-down world of the Kingdom? It seems to me the best answer to this is the simplest one: inspired by the teaching and example of Jesus and his early followers, Luke was abandoning his allegiance to Rome and his privileged station as a member of the elite in order to embrace God's Kingdom and Jesus as his true Lord.

Consider this. As an elite, Luke was well positioned, socially and educationally, to reach out to his peers. His impressive literary talent would have also been a valuable asset, enabling him to cloak his bold rhetorical aims in the seductive ploy of storytelling. But what perhaps best equipped Luke as an evangelist to his fellow elite was that he was calling them to embark upon a journey that he himself had already begun to tread. Luke had already made the remarkable, world-defying commitment to give up his status as an elite. Compelled by the Israelite prophets and Jesus' own teaching, he chose the distribution of resources "as any had need" over the system that had granted him and his family access to so much at the expense of so many. He set aside the pretentious claim that his worth and authority as an elite transcended that of most other persons inhabiting the world, for a vision in which all people, especially the poor and marginalized, are called to take part in the bounty and stewardship of God's new age. Luke distanced himself from the daily pursuit of honor and replaced it with the call to take up daily the humiliation of the

19. Rick Strelan, *Luke the Priest: The Authority of the Author of the Third Gospel* (Burlington, VT: Ashgate, 2008), 105.

cross as he followed in the self-giving footsteps of Jesus, a crucified criminal of the state. Finally, Luke looked beyond the thrones of Caesar and his underlings and found another Lord and Kingdom to which all his allegiance was due.

I find it very likely that Luke hoped his two-volume work would eventually be read by diverse audiences and so would inspire many to seek the manifold blessings of God's Kingdom over the degrading practices and attitudes of Rome (which were embraced by many throughout the social spectrum). But in light of his and his patron's social location, Luke's target audience—at least initially—is most likely his fellow elites who would hopefully go on to share the work with others. Luke thus writes to Theophilus and others to call them to join him in leaving behind the kingdom of Rome, with all of its privileges, trappings, and inequities, to seek another, radically different realm, and to align themselves with another crowd and a much greater Lord.[20]

Precedents to Luke's Call for Reversal: Paul and Mark

Luke was not the only, or even first, early Christian writer who stressed the incompatibility of typically Roman pursuits and ways with the Kingdom of God. Recently, more and more scholars have found that such a critique is also present, albeit more subtly, in Paul's Letters and Mark's Gospel.

Paul's Opposition to Evil on an Imperial Scale

According to some readers of Paul, what seems to be lacking in Paul's version of a world gone awry, relative to the earlier Israelite traditions we reviewed in chapter 2, is much attention to concrete, earthly realities apart from the internal corruption of humanity that threatens the existence and righteousness of God's people. Beyond relatively small groups of detractors that oppose Paul's teaching in several locales (e.g., Galatia and Corinth), the "enemies" to be overcome are the vicissitudes of fleshly desire and the challenges of living together in community (e.g., Rom. 7:14–25; 12:1–13; Gal. 5:7–26; Phil. 3:17–4:1). Little

20. At the same time, it seems likely to me that Luke moved away from participation in the life of an elite gradually and probably didn't complete the move until shortly before or after writing Luke-Acts. Luke's own work as a historian—and the mastery of Greco-Roman (including Israelite) literary convention his writing displays—indicates that he must have possessed the resources needed to continue pursuing his literary craft in the years following his companionship with Paul. Though involved in the countercultural movement of the early church, Luke continued studying and writing and therefore needed access to large amounts of time and many texts. As we saw earlier in this chapter, the ability to engage in such technical and time-consuming work would be very unlikely for someone not among the elite.

attention, in other words, is given to the role of geopolitical entities in thwarting God's desire for God's people, such as we saw in the *Psalms of Solomon*, the Maccabean writings, and various apocalyptic traditions.

Many advocating this position would point to that key moment of transition in Paul's Letter to the Romans (12:1–2) as instructive. Here Paul shifts from proclaiming what God has accomplished in Jesus to exhorting the Roman church on how to live out its truth together in community: "I appeal to you, therefore, brothers and sisters, by the mercies of God, to present your bodies as a living sacrifice, holy and acceptable to God" (v. 1). Paul will go on to say, "Do not be conformed to this world" (v. 2). But his subsequent focus on community life (12:3–15:5) and his encouragement of acquiescence to the governing authorities (13:1–7) seem to reflect a spirit of accommodation toward the dominance of Rome. For Paul, some say, the battle to be joined is primarily a personal and communal one within the confines of the present political order. What likely motivated Paul's accommodating stance toward Roman rule and focus on community life was the expectation that Christ would soon return to right all wrongs (see 1 Thess. 4:13–5:11). In short, as apocalyptically shaded, Israelite traditions offering their own telling of the kingdom story in the first century CE, Paul's Letters are remarkable for their seeming lack of overt disdain for Roman rule and lack of hope for Rome's destruction.

More recently, however, an increasing number of readers of Paul's Letters, and Romans in particular, have emphasized that Paul subtly—yet clearly—counters Roman claims to sovereignty as he celebrates Jesus' exaltation as Lord over creation and the true savior of humankind.[21] Among them, Neil Elliott draws from the distinctions presented by James C. Scott between "public transcript," "hidden transcript of the dominant," and the "hidden transcript of the subordinate" to guide his reading of Romans.[22] Elliott endorses Scott's claim that most expressions of protest against domination in antiquity would

21. N. T. Wright's work reflects this shift in perspective. In 1991 ("Putting Paul Together Again: Toward a Synthesis of Paul's Theology," in *Pauline Theology*, vol. 1, *Thessalonians, Philippians, Galatians, Philemon*, ed. Jouette Bassler [Minneapolis: Fortress, 1991], 200), Wright argued that "the salvation Paul expects is not from an external enemy (namely, Rome or 'the Kittim') but from the wrath of God (1 Thess. 1:10, etc.). Evil is not 'out there' in the world beyond the pale of ethnic covenant membership, but a matter of the καρδία." A little more than a decade later, Wright (*The Resurrection of the Son of God* [Minneapolis: Fortress, 2003], 728–29) expressed the implications of Paul's proclamation of Jesus as resurrected son of god in relation to Rome in much different terms: "Calling Jesus 'son of god' within this context of meaning, [early Christian communities] constituted themselves by implication as a collection of rebel cells within Caesar's empire, loyal to a different monarch, a different *kyrios*. Saying 'Jesus has been raised from the dead' proved to be self-involving in that it gained its meaning within this counter-imperial worldview."

22. Elliott, *Arrogance of the Nations*, 30–57. See James C. Scott, *Domination and the Arts of Resistance: Hidden Transcripts* (New Haven: Yale University Press, 1992).

be introduced into the public transcript only in muted or veiled form for fear of swift and brutal reprisal: "Unable to express their resistance openly, subordinate groups must ordinarily rely on strategies of indirection and disguise, or seek the safety of anonymity."[23] Such indirection and disguise, Elliott among others argues, are precisely what occurs in the Letter to the Romans as Paul contrasts the justice of God with "the false claims of mortals who pretend at justice, but deserve God's wrath instead."[24]

As one key example, Elliott asks readers to consider the opening of Romans against a particular setting: the celebration of Nero's ascension to the Roman throne in the public transcript (54 CE), which included the acclamation of heaven and Nero's own deification. With these claims and attributions reverberating throughout the Roman Empire and especially within Rome, imagine now how Paul's preface (1:1–4) and what many consider the topic sentence, or thesis, of the letter (1:16–17) would have been heard by Paul's first recipients in Rome. In contrast and in resistance to the presentation of Nero as the king who arrives with proper pedigree and divine approval, Paul crafts a sender formula that "resonates with the weight of Roman diplomatic vocabulary"[25] and announces (following Elliott's translation):

> Paul, slave of the Messiah Jesus, called as an apostle set apart to the proclamation of God's triumph, which he proclaimed beforehand through his prophets in the holy scriptures, concerning his son, the descendant of the seed of David, according to the flesh, appointed God's son in power according to the spirit of holiness by resurrection from the dead: Jesus, the Messiah, our Lord . . . (1:1–4).[26]

Moreover, as the opening of the letter moves to its stated focus, Paul announces his "eagerness to proclaim the gospel to you also who are in Rome" (v. 15). He follows with a synopsis of the gospel's essential core in a chain of subordinating conjunctions (Elliott's translation):

> For I am not ashamed to announce God's imminent triumph [*euangelion*]; for his proclamation is the power of God for salvation to all who are faithful, to the Jew first and also to the Greek; for in it the justice of God is revealed, through faithfulness, to faithfulness; as it is written, "The one who is just shall live by faithfulness"; for the wrath of God is revealed from heaven against all impiety and injustice of those who by their injustice suppress truth (Rom 1:16–18).[27]

23. Scott, *Domination and the Arts of Resistance*, 5.
24. Elliott, *Arrogance of the Nations*, 62.
25. Ibid., 63.
26. Ibid., 62.
27. Ibid., 74.

Paul, according to Elliott, is announcing that God's triumph is unveiled in Jesus' triumph over all earthly lords and claims to sovereignty over creation. The one whose victory Paul exclaims in subtle though recognizable implication is Jesus, not Nero. The deification endorsed by heaven that rightly commands human devotion and faithfulness is not that of the emperor but that of Yahweh's messiah.[28]

Thus, when Paul calls upon the Roman believers in 12:1–2 to no longer be conformed to this world but be transformed by the renewing of their minds, he is urging them to set aside any allegiances they may still cultivate toward Rome and Roman ways. In place of that allegiance to Rome—and in contrast to Roman values—Paul exhorts believers to devote themselves to the "good and acceptable and perfect" way of God, as they live in humble fellowship with one another under the lordship of Christ (12:3–8). How then are we to understand the accommodating tone of Paul's instruction, shortly to follow in Romans 13, to be subject to the governing authorities? Those who find in the epistle subtle yet sharp polemic against Rome have generally adopted one of three ways of accounting for these verses. One is to point to recent disturbances in both Rome and the Diaspora (e.g., Suetonius' report of "tumults" or "riots" in 49 CE or Tacitus' report of a tax protest in Puteoli resulting in executions) that indicate the volatile situation in the capital city while the letter was being written. Paul's words of submission and accommodation are meant to avoid further bloodshed and reprisals as the Roman leadership seeks to reestablish its control.[29] Another, as promoted by Robert Jewett, is to make the case that Paul's language in Romans 13 actually presents a subtle yet recognizable critique of Roman rule in that it calls for a willing subordination rather than a forced obedience. It also challenges the hierarchy of Rome by calling for *all* persons to subject themselves to the authorities regardless of citizenship or social rank.[30] A third option is offered by T. L. Carter, who argues that Paul's use of such gratuitously deferential language would have clearly signaled to members of the Roman church that his remarks were meant to be understood as ironic or sarcastic.[31]

These three explanations need not be seen as mutually exclusive. Instead, one could argue that Paul calls for submission here in order to avoid devastating reprisal while using both subtle and sarcastic language that would nevertheless undermine Rome's own claim to sovereignty and divine acclamation. After all, in the immediately preceding verses, Paul refers to persecution and

28. So also Wright, *Resurrection*, 729.
29. See Elliott, *Arrogance of the Nations*, 154.
30. Robert Jewett, *Romans: A Commentary*, Hermeneia (Minneapolis: Fortress, 2007), 787–90.
31. T. L. Carter, "The Irony of Romans 13," *NovT* 46 (2004): 209–28.

suffering as one of the evils that believers presently experience under the reign of these very same authorities! The response he calls believers to adopt is to "bless those who persecute you . . . and do not curse them" (12:14) and to be those who "overcome evil with good" (12:21). Even so, Paul's instruction also betrays an edge of disdain and judgment: believers are to "leave room for the wrath of God; for it is written, 'Vengeance is mine, I will repay, says the Lord'" (12:19). Even the believers' irreproachable goodness "will heap burning coals on their heads" (12:20). By repeatedly—though indirectly and subtly—challenging the ideology of Rome, Paul calls upon believers and believing communities to adopt ways of thinking and relating that manifest *God's* way and rule. Believers are to resist as much as prudence allows, bearing witness to the true Lord and Kingdom. And as they do so, they are to hold on to the hope that ultimate vengeance belongs to God and that the final outcome for those in Christ is not in doubt.

In my view, Elliott, among others, helps us to appreciate Paul's implicit (though, to Paul's original recipients, likely obvious) challenge to Roman claims of sovereignty and divine approval and to many other Roman values. At the same time, one can push the pendulum too far to the other side, focusing only on Paul's anti-imperial agenda and neglecting Paul's equally fundamental concern for the way in which sin and death have taken up residence in human communities of any size *and* in individual human souls. The transformation Paul urges and celebrates is plural and singular in person; it is cosmic and personal in scope. The implications of the coming of God's reign for Rome and other embodiments of evil throughout the cosmos also bear upon the heart of every member of the human race. For Paul, *wherever* evil is found, there God's grace will be countering and transforming.

Mark's Hidden Transcript of the Subordinate

In our brief review of Mark's narrative in chapter 2, we saw that Mark counters values that were common in the Mediterranean world, especially among the elite. The extent to which Mark was not only challenging the elite of Palestine but also targeting the character and authority of Rome is debated among scholars.[32] Yet a careful reading of his narrative suggests that, like Paul in Romans, he is implicitly critiquing Roman rule. The subtle negation of Caesar's sovereignty in the controversy dialogue concerning taxes (12:13–17);

---

32. On the implicit and explicit conflict with Roman authorities in Mark, see Ched Myers, *Binding the Strong Man: A Political Reading of Mark's Story of Jesus* (Maryknoll, NY: Orbis, 1988), and Richard Horsley, *Hearing the Whole Story: The Politics of Plot in Mark's Gospel* (Louisville: Westminster John Knox, 2001).

the unflattering portraits of Herod (6:14–29; 8:15), the Herodians (3:6; 12:13), and Pilate (15:6–15); the account of the Gerasene demoniac afflicted with the demon named "Legion" (5:1–20); and the fact that the Sadducees would have likely been seen by most as an appendage of Roman rule all suggest that Mark, like Paul, conveys a "hidden transcript of the subordinate" in opposition to Rome.

Moreover, Adam Winn argues that Roman propaganda announcing the emperor Vespasian's "liberation" of Jerusalem from the Israelite rebels as the fulfillment of Israelite messianic prophecy significantly influences Mark's shaping of his account.[33] Writing to the church in Rome, Mark counters this propaganda by stressing Jesus' identity and superiority as Messiah, Son of God, and the true sovereign of all. I think that the evangelist had other equally prominent objectives and that Winn overstresses the extent to which Mark emphasizes Jesus' sovereignty at the expense of Mark's equal emphasis on Jesus' suffering and vulnerability. Nevertheless, if Mark's Gospel is to be dated after the fall of Jerusalem, it is hard to imagine that the Roman co-option of Israelite messianic prophecy was unknown to Mark and his audience. In this setting, to announce that Jesus, a crucified criminal of the state, was the true Messiah promised by the prophets is a bold—and not too subtle—counterclaim challenging Roman mastery. In short, Rome and Roman claims regarding Rome's authority as agent of the divine are part of the misalignment plaguing this corrupted world.

Summary

Having glanced ahead in the introduction to the counterimperial character of Luke's narrative, we see here the likelihood that Luke belonged to the elite helps to sharpen our appreciation for the rhetorical edge of his narrative. Through his kingdom story, Luke is calling Theophilus and other members of the controlling class to abandon their power and privilege in order to devote themselves to Jesus and the Kingdom of God. That Paul and Mark have already, albeit more subtly, stressed the disjunction between the claims and character of Rome, on the one hand, and the gospel they proclaim, on the other, is one more indication that Luke's narrative may indeed traverse similar ground as we follow Jesus to Jerusalem and Paul to Rome.

33. Adam Winn, *The Purpose of Mark's Gospel: An Early Christian Response to Roman Imperial Propaganda*, WUNT 245 (Tübingen: Mohr Siebeck, 2008). Josephus promoted Rome's stunningly brash co-option of Israelite prophecies announcing the deliverance of Jerusalem by God's messiah; Vespasian, he claimed, "who was proclaimed Emperor on Jewish soil," fulfilled them (*War* 6.312–13).

This view of Luke's identity and his primary aims in composing his two volumes needs, of course, to be substantiated by a careful assessment of the narrative itself. While we will engage several passages reflecting Luke's critique of Rome and elite values in part 2, the bulk of this analysis will come in part 3 as we more closely examine Luke's version of the kingdom story. In turning now to part 2, we will first explore Luke's literary tendencies and the techniques he employs in composing his engaging, poignant, and pointed account of God's reign arriving in the ministries of Jesus and the early church.

Luke's Narrative Artistry

P art 2 explores many of the techniques Luke employs to engage both the heads and the hearts of his audience. Chapters 4–7 summarize what many scholars have come to appreciate about Luke's narrative artistry, while also introducing my understanding of the large-scale plotting that drives and unifies his account. Chapter 8, however, invites readers into largely uncharted territory. Building on chapters 4–7, this chapter unveils some of the ways in which Luke marshals these and other literary techniques to infuse his narrative with pathos and to elicit an emotional response from his recipients. As a gifted writer, Luke knew that emotion was an effective, even subversive, means of drawing Theophilus and others into his narrative and compelling them to entertain the vision of the Kingdom it proclaims.

Part 2

Luke's Narrative Artistry

4

The Building Blocks
of Luke's Narrative

Most interpreters, including biblical scholars, engage the texts they study guided by certain convictions. My understanding of Luke's narrative is guided by the following assumptions. First, as stated previously, I perceive Luke to be a highly gifted and sophisticated writer. His telling of the kingdom story displays complex patterns of plotting and characterization and a host of narrative forms and literary techniques. Therefore, one's reading of his narrative needs to be informed by a familiarity with these conventions. Second, while I find value in various interpretive methods, including reader-response, deconstructionist, and ideological approaches such as feminist, womanist, and postcolonial among others, I also regard the pursuit of authorial intent as the chief aim of biblical interpretation. Third, and relatedly, I find that there are several scholarly tools one can and should use to pursue this objective. Accordingly, as will become evident in parts 2 and 3 of this work, my interpretive paradigm is an eclectic one, drawing from literary, historical-critical, social-scientific, and affective-rhetorical approaches as I seek to discern what the author of Luke-Acts was trying to accomplish by telling his kingdom story.

To get us started in our investigation of Luke's narrative artistry, this chapter aims to (1) introduce readers to how narratives in general typically function;

(2) review several of the "narrative forms" Luke commonly employs in Luke-Acts; and (3) begin exploring in more detail how Luke shapes his narrative in order to proclaim the arrival of God's Kingdom to Theophilus and others.

How Narratives Work

Much of what I address in this first section are features of narrative that most of us already know, at least implicitly. So commonly do we engage forms of narrative or story that the practice of reading, hearing, or viewing them is almost second nature to us. We give their constituent features hardly a thought, unless, of course, one of those elements happens to be missing (e.g., lack of a real ending), poorly crafted (e.g., stilted dialogue), or just plain strangely enacted (e.g., a narrator who keeps getting lost in digressions). Nevertheless, it may be helpful to review some fundamental elements of narrative so that we can all the more easily zero in on Luke's characteristic tendencies of storytelling.

1. *Most narratives follow a discernible structure or movement: a beginning, middle, and end.* Literary critics often claim that basic to narrative structure is a beginning, a middle, and an end. By this they mean a couple of things. First, narratives have some sense of linear progression; they are recording a series of interconnected events or occurrences that move through time. Second, narratives—though in varying ways—typically begin by introducing recipients to the setting and main circumstances of the story; then move to a "middle" section that contains the bulk of the narrative, in which the main actions and conflicts are engaged, eventually leading to a moment of climax and resolution of those conflicts; and then finally move to an ending that draws the action to a close and concludes the story. Take a moment and consider some of the narratives you know—for instance, a play, novel, film, biography, children's story. Note how easy it is to recognize this basic structure for most of them. Of course, writers can cast these basic elements of narrative in a variety of creative ways and may at times even subvert them. A modern novel may simply jump into the action of a story and delay informing the reader of basic elements of the setting and conflict until later in the narrative or even the very end.[1] Others may lack resolution of a main conflict, or allow other conflicts to linger, or introduce a new conflict or story line at the conclusion (especially

---

1. One hugely successful plotting strategy that reverses the typical ordering of narrative is the detective story, which begins with the end result of some action and then pieces together the setting and circumstances that led to that end result. At the same time, the major story line (i.e., how and why the crime transpired) is encased within a narrative that does proceed according to a beginning→middle→end trajectory.

if a sequel is intended). Still others may abruptly terminate the narrative at the point of climax, leaving readers to wonder how the story is to conclude. The important point here is that the structure of beginning→middle→end is a basic touchstone of narrative development that is followed in some fashion by most narratives and presumed by most readers. And so, even when authors try to subvert this basic structure, they are doing so for some sort of rhetorical effect that depends on the expectation that the story should be otherwise. As we investigate Luke's narrative, we will find several examples of Luke subverting the basic pattern of narrative.

2. *Authors and readers are guided by conventions and use a repertoire of techniques.* Beyond the expectation that narratives display a beginning, middle, and end, a host of other conventions and techniques are common to narrative. The particular form of a literary work, or its genre, is a conventional way of shaping an entire narrative. A literary form creates something of a loose contract, or shared understanding, between author and reader on what kind of story is going to be told and characteristic tendencies of how it is going to be presented (recall our discussion of the genre of Luke-Acts in the introduction). Within a literary work, those "characteristic tendencies" are literary conventions: typical and recognizable ways writers shape and present narrative material for particular purposes or effects. For example, the opening sections of many narratives not only establish the setting but often introduce important themes governing the work as a whole. First-person narration is often employed to facilitate readers' or viewers' sense of immediacy and of connection to a main character. Within drama, characters may offer a soliloquy, or even directly address the audience, in order to impart information essential to understanding the plot. Repetition is frequently employed in all forms of narrative to emphasize particular motifs or to show tendencies of characters. Some narratives, including the Gospels, use a host of forms. These forms each follow a particular pattern or structure and are geared toward relaying certain kinds of information. In fact, so important are a variety of forms to Luke-Acts that we will spend the bulk of this chapter exploring them.

3. *The sequencing of events, or plotting, is central to narrative artistry.* Plotting, which is basic to narrative, is the way in which a writer unfolds the narrative from its beginning, through its middle, and on to its end. On a macro-level, plotting includes such techniques as the sequencing of episodes within a narrative, drawing points of connection between different parts of the narrative (such as the beginning and end of a narrative), foreshadowing, and developing themes throughout the narrative via repetition or parallelism. These same techniques can also be applied on a micro-level within sections of a narrative and even individual episodes. In short, with narrative it is not

just *what* is said—the content of a narrative—that is important; it is *how* it is said that really matters.[2] How readers or viewers respond to a particular episode will depend in large measure on the episodes that have come before it and on the expectations and perspectives that have been cultivated thus far into the story. Context as much as content determines the meaning of episodes for readers and viewers. For this reason, an individual passage must be read with an eye attentive to its relationship to surrounding material and how its content may relate to still other episodes that come before and after. It is also important to assess how individual episodes and larger sections contribute to the rhetorical objectives of the work as a whole.

Luke, as we shall see, employs a host of techniques that contribute to the rather complex plotting of his two-volume work. He frequently emphasizes and develops themes through repetition, connects characters and events through parallelism and patterning, ties together major sections of his narrative through repetition and recapitulation (the retelling of events), and depicts the evolution of major themes in response to the central event of the narrative: the resurrection of Jesus.

4. *Characters and characterization are the life and power of a story.* Characterization includes the diverse ways in which authors cast and portray characters. Skilled authors do not simply record or compose what characters do and say. They often let us in on the thought processes, feelings, motivations, insecurities, vices, virtues, heroic attributes, and tragic flaws of their characters. In doing so, they create the potential for readers or viewers to relate to, sympathize with, or even empathize with characters. The affective attachment authors nurture between characters and recipients not only brings the story alive for their audience; it can also be a powerful rhetorical technique. An author can have admirable characters serve as spokespersons for perspectives or models of behavior the author wishes to promote. Conversely, authors can use despicable characters to manifest behaviors and perspectives that the author considers, well, despicable. More sophisticated characterization may present characters that are admirable save for one tragic flaw, perhaps to unveil the danger of that very same flaw the author sees in members of the audience or in humanity in general. Or the author may, with stealthy subtlety, invite readers or viewers to identify with a largely unadmirable character

2. Literary critics and their counterparts among biblical scholars ("narrative critics") speak of this distinction using the terms "discourse" (how the narrative is plotted) and "story" (the content of the narrative). See, e.g., Rhoads, Dewey, and Michie, *Mark as Story*, 6–7; Mark Allan Powell, *What Is Narrative Criticism?*, ed. Dan O. Via (Minneapolis: Fortress, 1990), 23. More helpful, it seems to me, is the use of the term "rhetoric" to indicate how the setting, plotting, and characterization are shaped by the writer in order to influence the recipients of a narrative.

in order to lead them to consider how their own actions or attitudes lack honor as well.

5. *Most compelling narratives challenge recipients to examine, and perhaps even alter, their worldviews.* Narratives are powerful. When we take the time to read a good book or see a well-conceived play, we find ourselves getting "caught up in the story," identifying with certain characters, imagining what we might do if we were one of them. With really engaging narrative, we yearn for the stories to be real, so that we too may live within the world they describe, become friends with leading characters, and join them in their brave and noble cause against evil and injustice. Even if we pick up a book or go to a play or movie simply to be entertained, what often takes place in our encounter with the tale depicted—at least the better ones—is an encounter with a way of seeing the world.

One reason that we find narratives so compelling is likely because narrative form is essential to the way in which most humans construe reality. With increasing frequency, psychologists, philosophers, neuroscientists, and literary critics are recognizing that we conceive of our lives as "storied," and that our emotions play an essential role in our narrative construals of ourselves and the world.[3] When we say to one another, "Tell me your life story," we are not merely using a figure of speech. We tend to see ourselves and others as characters in an unfolding life saga, moving toward what we hope to accomplish, experience, or become. This insight is commonly held alongside another: that well-composed narratives, because they have the power to engage us so deeply, also have the potential to mold our own story-formed perceptions of reality. Narratives gather us subtly, and at times subversively, into their storied world and call us to dwell there for a while. The more deeply we invest ourselves into that narrative world, and the more deeply that world captures us intellectually and emotionally, the more power that narrative has to alter our perceptions of the world we inhabit. Accordingly, one of the primary objectives of most worthwhile stories is to lead us to see something about the world or the human condition that the author wants us to see. Many narratives, in other words, are essentially *rhetorical* in character. They call their readers to grasp "certain urgent claims" about the nature of the world and their own selves.[4]

3. For a helpful introduction to this emerging consensus and a number of studies that support it, see Jonathan Gottschall, *The Storytelling Animal: How Stories Make Us Human* (New York: Mariner Books, 2013).

4. Carol S. Witherall, Hoan Tan Tran, and John Othus, "Narrative Landscapes and the Moral Imagination: Taking the Story to Heart," in *Literacy, Society and Schooling: A Reader*, ed. Suzanne De Castell, Allan Luke, and Kieran Egan (New York: Cambridge University Press, 1995), 40.

Many have found Luke-Acts to be such a compelling, rhetorically charged narrative. My sense is that many of Luke's first recipients, including Theophilus, found it so as well. In this chapter and the chapters to follow, we will explore Luke's narrative artistry, but not simply for the sake of aesthetic appreciation. Rather, we will engage Luke's artistry for the primary purpose of better understanding how he used his impressive literary acumen and creativity to compose a compelling kingdom story of his own.

Some Key Narrative Forms Employed in Luke-Acts

Several narrative forms appear frequently or play a critical role in Luke-Acts; most have ample precedent in Luke's literary milieu. I will describe each form, provide examples of where they appear in Luke's two-volume work, and indicate some of the characteristic ways Luke employs them. The chapter will then conclude with an exegesis of two passages illustrating how Luke marshals his literary artistry for his rhetorical ends.

Prefaces

Luke uses highly stylized prefaces at the beginning of both the Gospel and Acts (see Luke 1:1–4; Acts 1:1–2). Prefaces were commonly employed in ancient narratives to state the purpose and focus of the work to follow, and at times to indicate the credentials of the author, either directly or indirectly. They also occasionally identified the recipient or recipients of the work. So also with Luke's preface to his Gospel: it identifies Theophilus as the intended recipient (Luke 1:3) and states Luke's intention to lead Theophilus to the full truth of the gospel message he has begun to learn (v. 4). Luke's Gospel preface also states his qualifications in verse 3, noting the care with which he investigated "the matters fulfilled among us" (v. 1, τῶν πεπληροφορημένων ἐν ἡμῖν πραγμάτων) and his presentation of those matters in an "orderly fashion." The preface in Acts again addresses Theophilus and refers back to the "first book" while briefly summarizing its contents.

Less directly, Luke uses both prefaces to demonstrate his mastery of a more elevated Greek style and, in conjunction with the infancy narrative and several speeches in Acts, his stylistic range. Readers of Luke familiar with Greek commonly point out that Luke's proficiency with the language is the most advanced among the Gospel writers and perhaps even among the rest of the NT writers (with the possible exception of Hebrews). Assuming that Luke used Mark's Gospel as a source for his own, commentators note the many grammatical and syntactical improvements Luke makes to the material he borrows from the earlier Gospel.[5] Beyond his grammatical proficiency, Luke's vocabulary is wide ranging, and his writing shows many points of verbal and stylistic contact with the historians Josephus, Plutarch, and Lucian.[6] Fitzmyer argues that the prologue is an example of "stylistic excellence" that stands out for its formality.

The prologue also shows that had he wished, "Luke could have written the Jesus-story in cultivated, literary Greek."[7] Interestingly, however, Luke chose not to do so. Most of his Gospel and Acts are written in his "normal style" of elevated yet not overly formalized Greek. Yet, beginning already in 1:5, Luke switches to still another style of Greek containing phrasing and vocabulary that would have reminded readers of Greek translations of the Israelite scriptures (for a rough analogy, think of a modern writer suddenly launching into a "King James" style of English). Coupled with the focus of Luke's narrative, the intent of this stylistic creativity is clear. Luke wants his recipients to see his narrative of the "matters fulfilled among us" (1:1) as the continuation of the story recorded in Israel's sacred writings. Luke uses his impressive stylistic range for his rhetorical-theological ends: the stories of Elizabeth and Zechariah and Mary and Joseph and their respective children, John and Jesus, are of a piece with the story of God's dealings with God's people, Israel. Similarly, Luke returns to this Septuagintal style in the first part of Acts and Peter's missionary speeches, and throughout his second volume commonly "chooses the style which is suitable for the different periods, places, and persons he is describing."[8]

Infancy Narratives and Birth Announcement

In Greco-Roman biography, it was common for writers to include stories of the main figure's birth and early years, focusing on events and discourse that revealed the subject's character, special abilities, and calling.[9] Incorporating this form into his historical account, Luke significantly modifies the

5. For a detailed listing of the improvements Luke makes to Mark's style, see Fitzmyer, *Luke I–IX*, 107–8.

6. Hans Conzelmann, *Acts of the Apostles*, trans. James Limburg et al., Hermeneia (Philadelphia: Fortress, 1987), xxxv.

7. Fitzmyer, *Luke I–IX*, 109.

8. Charles H. Talbert, *Literary Patterns, Theological Themes and the Genre of Luke-Acts* (Atlanta: Scholars Press, 1974), 1.

9. Parallels in the Israelite tradition include the birth accounts of Jacob, Esau, Moses, and Samuel. Joseph B. Tyson ("The Birth Narratives and the Beginning of Luke's Gospel," *Semeia* 52 [1990]: 103) lists biographies of Plato, Alexander the Great, and Apollonius of Tyana as examples of Greco-Roman parallels.

convention by expanding its focus and function. He uses his infancy narrative (see Luke 1–2) to introduce us to the characters of both John and Jesus. In fact, Luke intertwines accounts of their annunciations and births (see Luke 1:5–25, 26–38) to compose a "step-parallelism" between the two characters (see chap. 5). Moreover, the infancy narrative includes several other prominent characters, and it is largely through their character speech that we learn the broad contours of the long-awaited salvation Luke announces and depicts in the pages to follow (see chap. 6). Thus, Luke broadens the typical purview of an infancy narrative, using it not only to shape our understanding of a single character but also to serve as a rich and compelling introduction to God's plan of deliverance portrayed in Luke-Acts as a whole, highlighting the main motifs that course throughout the rest of his two-volume work.

As found in Israel's scriptures (see Gen. 16:7–12 [Ishmael]; 17:1–8; 18:1–15 [Isaac]; and Judg. 13:1–23 [Samson]), birth announcements typically contain the following elements:[10]

1. The appearance of an angel of the Lord (or appearance of the Lord)
2. Fear or prostration of the visionary confronted by this supernatural appearance
3. The divine message:
   a. The visionary is addressed by name
   b. A qualifying phrase describes the visionary
   c. The visionary is urged not to be afraid
   d. A woman is with child or is about to be with child
   e. She will give birth to the (male) child
   f. The child is assigned a name
   g. An etymology interpreting the name is given
   h. The future accomplishments of the child are foretold (see below)
4. A response from the recipient
5. The giving of a sign to reassure the visionary

Beyond these formal elements, birth announcements sometimes indicate the child's identity and role with respect to God's people. Luke also employs his two annunciations for this purpose, using them to inform his recipients of how John and Jesus fit into the advent of God's Kingdom.

---

10. This list of elements is an adaptation of that provided by Raymond Brown, *The Birth of the Messiah: A Commentary on the Infancy Narratives in the Gospels of Matthew and Luke*, rev. ed. (New York: Doubleday, 1993), 156. I have reproduced his listing in its entirety while altering element 4, which Brown lists as "an objection by the visionary as to how this can be or a request for a sign."

Travel Accounts

Travel accounts in ancient narratives took several forms, though at times these forms were combined: the "march," or inland expedition, often recounted military campaigns (e.g., Herodotus, the Pentateuch); the "travel description" described land travel, taking an interest in geography and ethnography; the "sea travel account" focused on coastal voyages.[11] Luke, who makes use of both the march and sea travel forms, uses travel accounts to accomplish at least two rhetorical ends.

First, Luke employs travel sections and a "journey" theme to unify the otherwise episodic character of his Gospel, as well as to unify the narrative of Luke-Acts as a whole. Luke 9:51 is a key text in this regard. While the journey motif emerges before this pericope (see 9:1–6, 23–24, 31), it is here that Jesus' call to begin his journey to Jerusalem is explicitly noted: "When the days drew near for him to be taken up, he set his face to go to Jerusalem." Luke then repeatedly reminds his recipients in the narrative to follow (no less than fourteen times!) that Jesus is "on his way" (ἐν τῇ ὁδῷ). For it is in this sacred city that pivotal events of Jesus' ministry will take place: betrayal, arrest, crucifixion, and resurrection (see 9:51; 18:31–33). And it is *from* here, as depicted in Acts, that the message of salvation will spread to the ends of the earth as Jesus' followers take up his journey as their own (see Acts 1:8; 12:25–21:16; 27:1–28:6). Thus, the narrative as a whole is united by this movement toward and then away from the sacred city. In so presenting his two-volume work and shaping the travel narratives in this fashion, Luke provides a structure and plotting to his narrative that unifies his work while emphasizing the rootedness of God's deliverance of humankind in God's relationship with Israel.

Second, Luke uses the journey motif to emphasize the missionary character of discipleship. This is not a journey that Jesus intends to take alone: Jesus leads "the way" and calls those who consider themselves his disciples to fall in with him, to take up their own crosses daily, and to follow him to Jerusalem and beyond (e.g., Luke 9:23–27, 57–62; 10:1–12). And it is on this journey to Jerusalem, from Luke 9 onward, that the disciples repeatedly receive instruction on what it means both to embrace the Kingdom and to serve as its stewards.

Noting these two rhetorical objectives helps to explain a curious feature of Luke's use of the journey motif in his Gospel. Scholars debate the meaning of the phrase "his reception upwards" (ἀναλήμψεως αὐτοῦ) in Luke 9:51, along with "exodus" (ἔξοδος) in 9:31, commonly proposing either Jesus' crucifixion,

---

11. Aune, *New Testament in Its Literary Environment*, 122–23.

resurrection, or ascension, with most leaning toward the ascension. As I will argue in more detail in chapter 8, I believe that it is best to see the resurrection as the subject of these references. At the same time, it may be more important to recognize that Luke's Gospel is somewhat ambiguous as to the terminus of Jesus' journey. Most scholars locate the ending point of the travel narrative as Jesus' entrance into Jerusalem in 19:28–44. However, Luke, unlike the other evangelists, does not explicitly state that Jesus enters the city. In one episode, Jesus is near Jerusalem and laments its eventual destruction (19:41–44). In the next, Jesus is in the temple driving out the "robbers" (19:45–47). Luke may obscure Jesus' actual entrance into Jerusalem to prevent recipients from associating that moment with the journey's end. Yet we may do well to wonder whether Luke intends the journey motif, and even the travel narrative itself, to have an end. For after Jesus is resurrected, he continues to journey with the Emmaus disciples (24:13–32) and then directs the disciples to receive the Spirit and to journey in an ever-expanding arc away from Jerusalem, fulfilling their calling to be his "witnesses in Jerusalem, in all Judea and Samaria, and to the ends of the earth" (Acts 1:8; cf. Luke 24:46–48). Acts then records the preparations for and the undertaking of that journey, closing with Paul at his farthest destination yet, Rome, still sharing the good news. Appropriately, the church takes on the nickname "the Way" (ἡ ὁδός; Acts 9:2; 19:9, 23; 22:4; 24:14, 22). In essence, Jesus' journey has become the church's journey, and in light of Jesus' appearances and support of followers in Acts, we are likely meant to understand that Jerusalem was not Jesus' final destination, and that his journey with the church goes on.

Pronouncement Stories

Like the other Gospel writers, Luke uses pronouncement stories (see Luke 4:42–44; 5:33–39; 6:1–5; 10:38–42; 11:1–13, 27–28; 13:22–30; Acts 4:5–12; 11:1–18; 13:4–12, 44–49) more often than any other form. This form is closely related, and often identical, to the *chreia*, a form well represented throughout Greco-Roman literature. Theon's *Progymnasmata*, an ancient rhetorical handbook dating back sometime before the Common Era, defines the *chreia* as "a concise statement or action which is attributed with aptness to some specified character or to something analogous to a character."[12] Some *chreiai* simply present the action or saying along with an identification of the actor, but many also provide a setting that portrays the action or saying as a response to

---

12. Ronald F. Hock and Edward N. O'Neil, *The Chreia in Ancient Rhetoric: Volume 1: The Progymnasmata* (Atlanta: Scholars Press, 1986), 83.

a particular situation. This fuller manifestation of the *chreia* form is essentially identical to the pronouncement story form found throughout the Gospels:

1. Setting
2. Action or statement that addresses or challenges Jesus or his disciples
3. Pronouncement by Jesus/disciples

So, for example:

> Then his mother and his brothers came to him, but they could not reach him because of the crowd. And he was told, "Your mother and your brothers are standing outside, wanting to see you." But he said to them, "My mother and my brothers are those who hear the word of God and do it." (Luke 8:19–21)

In addition to corresponding to the *chreia* form, pronouncement stories that include a challenge against Jesus or the disciples (sometimes called "controversy dialogues") also typically manifest a common form of social exchange known as a "challenge-riposte (response)" sequence. As I discussed in chapter 1, the Mediterranean world was a competitive culture, with its members frequently seeking to elevate their own honor at the expense of others. The challenge-riposte exchange was a form of social interaction through which this honor game was played.[13] The intent on the part of the challenger was to display the inadequacy of the one being challenged, thereby lessening the opponent's honor in the eyes of observers and increasing one's own. The one challenged was then expected to offer a "riposte," and onlookers were left to judge the effectiveness of the response and its resulting impact upon the participants' honor (see, e.g., Luke 5:27–32, 33–39; 6:1–5, 6–11; 7:36–50; 10:25–37; 20:20–26). Since Luke frequently portrays Jesus participating in the challenge-response exchange, some may be led to conclude that he means to present Jesus as a willing, if not eager, participant in the honor game of his time. Yet so frequently does the evangelist use controversy dialogues to show Jesus upending contemporary conceptions of honor that his objectives must be otherwise. Jesus does indeed respond to the challenges of his detractors with penetrating pronouncements, but not to elevate his status at their expense. Luke simply presents Jesus as operating according to a different set of standards, ones that lead him to share table with people across the social spectrum, including those whom the Pharisees would place at the lowest rung. More than anything, Jesus' pronouncements are prophetic and didactic in character, designed to lead even his opponents to recognize the emergence and character of the Kingdom in their midst.

13. See Malina, *New Testament World*, 32–36.

Longer Dialogues and Speeches

It was common in Greco-Roman and especially Israelite historiography to devote significant attention and space to direct discourse. The evangelist makes copious use of this convention, providing many extended dialogues and speeches throughout Luke-Acts. Within the Gospel, dialogues gather together a multitude of Jesus' sayings (e.g., Luke 6:17–49; 7:18–35; 8:4–21; 11:14–36, 37–53; 12:1–13:9; 15:1–17:10). The dialogues are mostly composed of independent, episodic traditions taken over from other sources, such as Mark, Q, and other materials unique to Luke. They also include a variety of forms, such as pronouncement stories, parables, and even miracles that serve as a stimulus for challenge or conversation. But what sets them apart as dialogues is that each of them is composed of a relatively lengthy course of Jesus' instruction within a particular narrative moment or setting. These dialogues may lack the polished unity we find in the direct discourse of Luke 1–2, 24, and the numerous speeches of Acts. Nevertheless, their arrangement and placement are not haphazard. Shaped by Luke's own redaction and sequencing, the dialogues emphasize motifs integral to Luke's vision of the Kingdom and what it means to take part in it. The direct discourse of Luke 1–2 and 24 and the speeches in Acts, being extraordinarily important to Luke's plotting and his telling of the kingdom story, will receive focused attention in chapter 7.

Miracle Stories

One of the primary means Luke employs to demonstrate the in-breaking of God's reign in Jesus and his disciples is miracle stories (see Luke 4:38–39; 5:12–16; 9:37–43; Acts 9:32–35, 36–43; 16:16–18; 20:7–12; 28:7–10). In them, the inauguration of God's Kingdom comes to life as Jesus begins to unleash God's blessings, thwart the powers of disease and death, and overtake the dominion of Satan. Like pronouncement stories, miracle stories have a relatively consistent form:

1. Description of need
2. Act of healing, often accompanied by a touch or statement
3. Indication of the results
4. Response from onlookers

The need presented in the Gospels can be quite variable: illness, condition, threat from natural forces, lack of provision. Exorcisms are a type of miracle story that has a closely related form:

1. Demon recognizes exorcist and resists
2. Exorcist threatens and commands
3. Demon emerges, making a demonstration
4. Spectators react

It is also not uncommon for the evangelists to create hybrid miracle-pronouncement stories, with the miracle sometimes serving as the setting that leads to Jesus or the disciples being questioned, challenged, or misunderstood (e.g., Luke 5:1–11, 17–26; 6:6–11; 8:22–25; Acts 14:8–19). Along with several other elements, miracle stories bear witness to the "inaugurated eschatology" that characterizes Luke's account. As we will discuss in some detail in part 3, Luke understood that the Kingdom arrived in Jesus' person and ministry, and continued to be embodied in the community and ministry of Jesus' followers, even as they awaited its full manifestation.

Parables

Parables form the heart of much of Jesus' teaching on the Kingdom of God. Frequently occurring within dialogues and pronouncement stories, and in response to challenges raised by Jesus' detractors, the parables often serve notice to Luke's recipients that the true Kingdom subverts long-held assumptions about God and what it means to be God's people.

Two basic features of the parables enable them to serve this purpose. First, the parables—on a literal level—frequently tell short stories making use of everyday, mundane kinds of activities that lead to unexpected, if not downright extraordinary, outcomes. Their puzzling plotting grabs the attention of recipients and perhaps even leads them into cognitive dissonance. "What? You've got to be kidding!" was likely a common response to many of Jesus' parables, and the Gospel writers continue to make use of parables' counterintuitive character to energize audience interest and reflection. Second, the parables are *analogical*, meaning that they present metaphorical scenarios that in some fashion are analogous to certain dimensions of the Kingdom of God or what it means for believers to be part of it. They aren't just interesting, odd tales but are spoken by Jesus and scribed by the Gospel writers in order to help them tell the kingdom story.

How the parables function as analogies or metaphors has been vigorously debated among scholars.[14] For some time, modern scholarship has countered the tendency among earlier readers to treat the parables as allegories with

14. For a helpful review of the debate on parable interpretation, see Craig L. Blomberg, *Interpreting the Parables*, 2nd ed. (Downers Grove, IL: IVP Academic, 2012), 17–32.

multiple points of connection to the realities they depict. Instead, some modern scholars have argued that parables—at least as they were used by Jesus and other sages of his time—were almost always focused on a single referent or analogous reality. However, in the last quarter century more and more readers have argued that such an aversion to the allegorical interpretation of the parables simply fails to account for their true literary character and commonly results in exegetes forcing parables into a single referent when there is clearly more than one.

Craig Blomberg is one such scholar who has argued that many parables are meant to function in an "allegorical-like" manner. They are not—typically at least—full allegories, where nearly every detail of the story has a corresponding referent (as in the parable of the sower). But the main actors in the parables are meant to represent certain dispositional, and often contrasting, responses to the Kingdom. The structures of the parables themselves betray this analogical function, as they present action gravitating around one, two, or three sets of characters. The most common form is a triadic structure, comprising about two-thirds of the parables in the Gospels.

The triadic form has three principle character sets, from which three analogues may be discerned. In nearly all cases, the three characters include a master who symbolizes God and two contrasting subordinates symbolizing those who embrace the ways of the Kingdom and those who reject them.[15] By way of example, consider the three-point form of the parable of the prodigal

15. Blomberg further distinguishes between simple and complex three-point forms. Complex forms are those which at first glance may seem to include additional character sets or a more complicated structure, but which can usually be seen as disclosing these same three main points based on the actions of characters or groups of characters: e.g., the good Samaritan (Luke 10:25–37); the great supper (14:15–24); the unjust steward (16:1–13); the minas (19:12–27).

son and his brother in Luke 15:11–32. Though of significant length, the parable has the simple form of a compassionate father representing God, a son who loses his way but then repents, and a jealous, straitlaced brother who resents his father's forgiving heart.

Many of the shorter parables and similitudes have only one or two main characters and corresponding points of emphasis. Those with two points of emphasis are termed dyadic parables. They often depict a contrast between a character set that welcomes God and one that opposes God, without a character set representing God, such as the example story of the tax collector and the Pharisee (18:9–14). Parables or similitudes with one point of emphasis or comparison to the Kingdom are called monadic parables. Lukan examples include the parables of the mustard seed and the leaven (13:18–21) and the parable of the tower builder (14:28–33).

Keeping these different forms of parables straight can be a bit challenging at first, but they can give a reader a leg up on discerning the function of a parable in Luke, as well as in Matthew and Mark. Yet here are two additional, and important, points to keep in mind when working with the parables. First, while knowing the different types of parables employed by the Gospel writers can greatly assist your attempts to determine how a parable is intended to function, these are only meant to be guides and starting points for interpretation. These categories will work well with most parables, but other parables may resist easy classification.[16] So keep an open mind as you engage the parables and be ready for exceptions. Another reason that these types and forms should be used as a starting and not an ending point for interpretation is that readers also need to take into account how the evangelist uses a particular parable within its narrative context. Each parable is part of a larger whole, and Luke may be using it alongside other elements of the narrative to emphasize an important motif, draw attention to or foreshadow a specific event, or provide commentary on an event (e.g., Luke 12:41–48; 20:9–19). An essential point to appreciate is that the parables in the Gospels are not meant to be read in isola-

16. For example, Blomberg labels the parable of the lost sheep in Luke 15:3–7 as triadic in form, yet the parable seems to present four character sets: shepherd, lost sheep, the ninety-nine remaining sheep, and the friends and neighbors. Moreover, there doesn't seem to be, on the face of it at least, a character set opposed to the ways of God. It seems to me that the intent of this parable as well as that of the lost coin, which follows it (Luke 15:8–10), is likely dyadic: emphasizing God's earnest desire to restore the wayward and the need for sinners to be found. Consider again the parable of the prodigal son. What of those who refuse to give the son anything to eat (15:16), especially in light of Luke's description of the Pharisees as "lovers of money" (16:14) and the parable of the rich man and Lazarus to follow (16:19–31)? Could the structure of the parable—at least as it appears in Luke—be "quadratic," or are we to see these callous characters as part of the same character set as the frustrated brother?

tion from the rest of the narrative, but are to be read as commentary on the Kingdom that nearly always intersects with prominent themes and sometimes illuminates what is going on in the immediate context.

Meal Scenes: Symposia

Literary portraits of the Greco-Roman symposium recounted the second stage of a formal meal, during which those present would drink and debate matters of interest. Typically, these literary depictions included a common cast of characters: the host, usually noted for his wealth or wisdom; the chief guest, notable for his wit and wisdom; and other participants.[17] The typical structure of symposium accounts moved from an identification of the guests, to an action or event that determines or introduces the topic under discussion, and to the discourse itself. Such accounts also frequently exhibited the social norms that governed such meals: guests (especially the chief guest) were those whose presence would enhance the status of the host, and they were typically seated in proximity to the host in a way that indicated their relative status. Luke's Gospel contains several such meal scenes (see Luke 5:27–32; 7:36–50; 11:37–54; 14:1–24; 19:1–10; 22:10–38; 24:28–32), which also correspond to the form of a pronouncement story.

Noting the commonality of symposia in Luke's day and their characteristic tendencies helps us to see all the more clearly how Luke steers this particular version of a pronouncement story to his own rhetorical ends. These scenes contain striking contrasts to the typical features of symposia and emphasize three features of Jesus' ministry. First, Jesus' table fellowship is radically inclusive, as Jesus shares table with characters of wildly varied backgrounds and social locations, including those whom many label as "sinners" (e.g., 5:30; 7:34, 37; 19:1–10). Second, and related, Jesus uses these meal scenes as occasions to teach about the Kingdom and about the radical reorientation of perspective that life in the Kingdom demands. Frequently, Jesus challenges the honor and status concerns that were the "unwritten rules" governing such meals, and instead unveils actions and dispositions more in keeping with the Kingdom, such as humility and repentance (e.g., 7:36–50; 11:37–54; 14:1–24; 19:1–10). Accordingly, the practice of table fellowship in the Gospel is itself an expression of God's new age, which challenges the rules of the current age. Finally, throughout the Gospel, table fellowship presents Jesus as a provider,

17. For this review of the symposium form, I am indebted to Paul J. Achtemeier, Joel B. Green, and Marianne Meye Thompson, *Introducing the New Testament: Its Literature and Theology* (Grand Rapids: Eerdmans, 2001), 76–77.

or savior, either as one presiding over the meal or as one who offers God's salvation to others. As did Mark before him, Luke incorporates the traditions of the feeding of the five thousand (9:10–17) and the Lord's Supper (22:10–38) to present Jesus as the one who feeds the multitudes and gives his very "body and blood" to inaugurate a new covenant between God and God's people. In addition, Luke alone records two other episodes in which Jesus' role as a provider/savior is emphasized in the context of a meal scene. In 7:36–50, Jesus announces God's forgiveness of a "sinful woman" while dining at the home of a Pharisee. Luke's emphasis on Jesus' role as a provider/savior within the context of table fellowship is confirmed in the Emmaus meal scene, where Luke has Jesus, the guest, host the meal (24:28–32). In short, Luke's meal scenes present Jesus as the host or provider of the kind of fare and community that lead to true blessing.

Summaries

Luke employs summaries to characterize events he records and to transition between episodes. Several of these summaries he takes from Mark (see Luke 4:37, 40–41; 6:17–19; 9:6), but he adds several of his own in the Gospel (Luke 1:80; 2:19–20, 40, 52; 7:21) and throughout Acts, including longer (Acts 2:43–47; 4:32–35; 5:11–16; 13:13–41) and shorter (1:14; 8:1b–4; 9:31; 11:19–21; 19:11–12; 28:30–31) varieties. While some summaries are primarily transitional in purpose, many of them play an important role in guiding the recipients' understanding of the events Luke portrays. In other words, not only do they function as reviews of what has just taken place in the narrative or provide additional information that needs to be relayed; they also serve as "interpretive disclosures" of how Luke wants these events to be understood. This is also true of the shorter summaries. Consider, for example, Luke 2:39–40, occurring immediately following Jesus' presentation in the temple (vv. 21–38) and just before his visit to Jerusalem at the age of twelve (vv. 41–51). This summary, in stating that Jesus' parents "finished everything required by the law of the Lord," again emphasizes their character as upstanding, pious Israelite folk faithful to the law (see also 2:22, 41). It also reminds recipients of Jesus' hometown of Nazareth, which will play an important role near the beginning of Jesus' public ministry in 4:16–30 and may also be intended to signal Jesus' social location as a peasant far removed from the power centers of Jerusalem and the temple. Finally, the summary also stresses Jesus' character as strong, filled with wisdom, and blessed with the favor of the Lord (see also 2:52), continuing to present him in terms reminiscent of Israel's heroes of old despite the division and heartache his mission shall cause for Israel. This is a lot of information packed into two short verses! In sum, pay attention to the summaries. They function like spotlights illuminating aspects of Jesus' person or ministry, or that of the disciples, or portions of the narrative that come before and after.

Dramatic Episodes

Scholars frequently use the term "dramatic episodes," "longer narrative sequences," or "legends" to indicate sections of narrative that are longer and more complex than shorter narrative forms. One common characteristic of dramatic episodes in the works of Greco-Roman historians is that they are employed to "heighten the dramatic conflict just before a resolution."[18] Another is that they are often used to frame narratives or sections of a narrative. A third function is that they often introduce or reinforce major themes within the narrative.

Luke employs dramatic episodes for these same ends. The infancy narrative, while including other narrative forms, is really a series of dramatic episodes that play a major role in introducing basic motifs in Luke's story of the Kingdom. Those opening chapters also form an inclusio with the three resurrection stories in Luke 24, which themselves take up and rehearse those very same motifs announcing the arrival of God's salvation. Together, these chapters frame the Gospel with a consistent proclamation, even celebration, of Luke's vision of salvation (I will say more about this in chaps. 6–7). The dramatic episode of Acts 10:1–11:18 shows how the mission to the gentiles is a key element in God's plan of salvation and locates the origin of this ministry in the Jerusalem community, thereby reinforcing the programmatic theme announced in Acts 1:8 that the proclamation of the Kingdom would emerge from Jerusalem and eventually reach to the ends of the earth. Acts 27:1–28:16 is a storm scene, a common form of dramatic episode in Greco-Roman writing. It presents Paul in a manner reminiscent of Jesus while at the same time underscoring the blessings now made manifest in the Kingdom's arrival: Paul provides comfort and announces deliverance to the crew (Acts 27:33–35), just as Jesus did during a storm at sea (Luke 8:22–25); he provides nourishment by breaking bread and giving thanks (Acts 27:35–38), echoing Jesus' feeding of the five thousand (Luke 9:10–17) and his last meal with the disciples (22:14–23); he is imbued with God's power and shares it freely with others by healing many (Acts 28:3–10), just as Jesus did throughout his ministry. To be sure, a function of these dramatic episodes is to stimulate interest

18. Aune, *New Testament in Its Literary Environment*, 128.

and draw recipients more deeply into the narrative, but exegetes also need to be aware that Luke often employs these stories to animate and underscore key dimensions of his vision of the Kingdom.

Forms of Narrative Artistry: Some Examples from Luke-Acts

To further our investigation into how Luke employs his narrative artistry for his rhetorical ends, we now engage two texts that manifest some of the forms and techniques described above. Our aim is twofold: to offer more detailed examples of how Luke uses these devices and to begin exploring some of the main emphases in Luke's telling of the kingdom story. In my discussion of these passages, I will also be pointing out how Luke employs characterization and pathos, a topic we will be addressing in more detail in chapter 9.

Conception of a Savior and God's Salvation: Luke 1:26–38

Luke 1:26–38 and the passage that comes before it correspond to the birth announcement, or annunciation form, we discussed above. It is also one of the many instances of direct discourse that Luke weaves into his infancy narrative (see also 1:13–20, 42–56, 67–79; 2:10–14, 28–35). As noted above, annunciations in the Israelite scriptures typically introduce key elements of the child's character and role with respect to God's people. This is clearly the case with Gabriel's announcements of John's (1:5–25) and Jesus' births. This also corresponds to the overriding purpose of the infancy narrative, which is to disclose the main features of God's salvation and how it is to be accomplished in the ministries of John and Jesus. Similarly, character speech in Luke-Acts often serves the role of interpretive disclosure, helping recipients to understand the significance of the events reported by the narrative (in this case, the conception and birth of Jesus).

The brief introduction of the scene establishes important points of continuity and difference between the two birth announcements (1:26). The mention of the "sixth month" of Elizabeth's pregnancy ties the two episodes together (see also v. 36) and provides initial indication that the events announced by the first annunciation are closely related to what now takes place. Similarly, the repeated occurrence of an angelic visit by one who is again identified as Gabriel implies that the eschatological tenor that characterized the first episode is to be seen as continuing in these verses. The description of Gabriel as "sent by God" (v. 26) reminds us that God is the originator of these events and reaffirms the truthfulness of Gabriel's testimony. Moreover, the mention of

Joseph as "of the house of David" (v. 27) strengthens the connection of these events to Israelite tradition and paves the way for Jesus to be portrayed as the Davidic messiah (see also 1:69; 2:4). Finally, the passages, both of which follow the annunciation form, unfold in a remarkably similar manner and contain numerous verbal parallels.[19]

Despite these points of continuity, the narrative context of the present episode differs from that of the previous one by being far removed from the piety and status often associated with Jerusalem, the temple, and the priesthood. The locale of Nazareth places the annunciation in an obscure town with no known significance in Jewish tradition.[20] Moreover, the character of Mary, a betrothed virgin of as-yet-unmentioned family origin, contrasts sharply with Zechariah, a priest serving in the temple and of the house of Aaron. As stated by Joel Green, "Mary's insignificance seems to be Luke's primary point in his introduction of her."[21]

Yet the insignificance shrouding Mary's character is then dramatically contrasted by Gabriel's greeting. The expression in verse 28, "the Lord is with you,"[22] and the clarifying statement "for you have found favor with God" (εὗρες γάρ χάριν παρά τῷ θεῷ [1:30]), which parallels "favored one" (κεχαριτωμένη [1:28]), both suggest that Mary is to be viewed as one who will play a key part in forwarding God's covenant relationship with Israel. Of the many instances of the several forms of the expression "the Lord is with you" in the Septuagint, the overwhelming majority are predicated of individuals whom God calls to serve an essential role in fulfilling God's covenant promises to Abraham and all Israel: Isaac (Gen. 26:3, 24, 28), Jacob (28:15; 31:3), Joseph (39:2, 21), Moses (Exod. 3:12), Joshua (Josh. 1:5, 9, 17; 3:7; 6:27), the tribe of Judah (Judg. 1:19), Gideon (Judg. 6:12, 16), Samuel (1 Sam. 2:26), David (1 Sam. 18:12; 2 Sam 7:3), Solomon (1 Kings 11:38), Jehoshaphat (2 Chron. 17:3), Jeremiah (Jer. 1:8, 19; 15:20). Similarly, forms of the statement "for you have found favor with God" also occur with respect to individuals at key moments in the history of the relationship between God and God's people: Noah (Gen. 6:8); Abraham (18:3); Gideon (Judg. 6:17). The use of this terminology for Mary places the young virgin in exalted company: she is to be counted among

19. For a helpful presentation of these verbal parallels, see Green, *Gospel of Luke*, 83.

20. Fitzmyer (*Luke I–IX*, 343) observes: "Nazareth is not mentioned in the OT, Josephus, or rabbinical writings."

21. Joel B. Green, "The Social Status of Mary in Luke 1,5–2,52: A Plea for Methodological Integration," *Bib* 73 (1992): 465; so also Darrell L. Bock, *Luke 1:1–9:50*, BECNT 3a (Grand Rapids: Baker Academic, 1994), 107.

22. In light of the context of this episode in which God's favor upon Mary and her role in the unfolding of God's plan are emphasized, ὁ κύριος μετὰ σοῦ is here best rendered in a declarative sense as in Judg. 6:12, rather than as a wish, "May the Lord be with you."

the leading figures in Israel's history called to serve God's designs for God's people. Given the implications of Gabriel's greeting, it is surely understandable that this otherwise insignificant Mary is "much perplexed" (NRSV) or "utterly confused"[23] by this address (Luke 1:29). But she has little time to ponder "what sort of greeting this might be." Gabriel again affirms her favor before God and then presents a most unexpected announcement: "And now, you will conceive in your womb and bear a son, and you will name him Jesus" (v. 31).

Scholars have long noted that the annunciations of John's and Jesus' births are to be seen in parallel relationship, with the result that Jesus emerges as the (much) greater child than John. We will be examining this important feature of Luke's infancy narrative in the following chapter. For now, let us focus on the remarkable things Gabriel says about Jesus in the birth announcement. To begin, we must note the name that is to be given to Mary's child: "Jesus" (1:31). "Jesus" is the Greek equivalent of the Hebrew "Joshua," which means "Yahweh saves." Jesus/Joshua was a common Israelite name. But appearing here in a birth announcement that has as its primary purpose to introduce recipients to the significance and character of this child, those recipients would be expected to make an immediate connection between the literal meaning of the name and what this child would become: God's long-awaited savior.[24] Moreover, in the words of Gabriel, Luke assigns to Jesus features of mission and person that are typically predicated only of God in Israelite tradition. Jesus is, without qualification, "great" (v. 32) and "holy" (v. 35). Absolute greatness is a trait reserved for Yahweh in the Israelite scriptures (e.g., Pss. 48:1; 86:10; 135:5; 145:3); where greatness is attributed to humans (e.g., Lev. 19:15; 2 Sam. 19:32; Sir. 48:22), it is always qualified in some sense (e.g., "great before God" or "great before humans").[25] Similarly, "holy" is also typically predicated of God in the Israelite scriptures. Although it is also attributed to others in numerous instances (see also Luke 2:23), it is not so used in the titular, absolute sense that appears here.[26]

Gabriel also twice applies the designation "Son of the Most High/Son of God" to Jesus (1:32, 35). Used here as a title for Jesus, its emphasis on Jesus' unique relation to God incorporates but goes beyond the nontitular descriptions of the Israelite king as God's son (e.g., Ps. 2:7). Reinforcing this

23. Luke Timothy Johnson, *The Gospel of Luke*, Sacra Pagina 3 (Collegeville, MN: Liturgical Press, 1991), 37.

24. In Matthew, of course, the angelic visitor makes explicit to Joseph what is implicit here in Luke: "She will bear a son, and you are to name him Jesus, for he will save his people from their sins" (Matt. 1:21).

25. René Laurentin, *Structure et Théologie de Luc I–II* (Paris: Gabalda, 1957), 360–67, 122. So also Fitzmyer, *Luke I–IX*, 325.

26. Laurentin, *Luc I–II*, 122.

exalted sense of the titles, Luke also draws a direct connection between Jesus' designation as the holy one, Son of God, and his conception via a creative act of the Holy Spirit: "The Holy Spirit will come upon you, and the power of the Most High will overshadow you; *therefore* the child to be born will be holy; he will be called Son of God" (Luke 1:35). As Brown aptly puts it, "We are not dealing with the adoption of a Davidid by coronation as God's son or representative; we are dealing with the begetting of God's Son through God's creative Spirit."[27]

What sets Jesus apart from someone as great as John is what sets him apart from all others: he is the Spirit-conceived, divine Son, called into existence not by a human union but by the very Spirit of God. Luke is portraying Jesus here in the guise of an apocalyptic "divine agent," one commissioned by God who possesses attributes normally reserved for God in Israelite tradition.[28] But for the evangelist, it may go further than this. Luke, it seems, is already inviting his recipients to sense a "convergence" in the characters of Jesus and God, as his frequent use of "Lord" for God and Jesus throughout Luke-Acts will also accomplish. Here, this merging of their characters is expressed both in terms of Jesus' accomplishment of God's promised salvation as God's messianic divine agent who will reign on Jacob's throne forever *and* in terms of his very person as the uniquely great, holy, and Spirit-conceived divine Son. In sum, Mary's child, Jesus, participates in the power, purpose, and person of Yahweh.[29]

While Luke's disclosure of Jesus' person and mission is an essential element of the passage, so too is Mary's response to her encounter with Gabriel and his extraordinary announcement. Mary's interaction with the annunciation is conveyed at the beginning, middle, and end of the passage: her puzzlement (1:29), her question of Gabriel (v. 34), and her response of devotion (v. 38). The characterization that emerges in Luke's shaping of the pericope is of a girl initially overwhelmed by this most unexpected (good?) news, who struggles to comprehend it, and then impressively overcomes that fear and confusion to embrace boldly what God has in store for her: "Behold ['Ιδού], I am the servant of the Lord; let it be with me according to your word" (my translation).[30] Coming on the heels of John's birth announcement and opening with the conspicuous "Behold!," Mary's faithful response stands in sharp contrast to the doubting of Zechariah. Thus, the step-parallelism that exists

---

27. Brown, *Birth of the Messiah*, 312.

28. Recall our discussion of divine-like redeemer figures of Israelite tradition in chap. 2.

29. We will explore this feature of Luke's Christology further in chap. 9.

30. Luke commonly uses "behold" (ἰδού) throughout Luke-Acts to attract attention to an event and/or to indicate that what is to be said next is of special importance (e.g., 1:20, 31, 36, 48; 2:10, 34).

between these two passages is not only between Jesus and John. It exists between Mary and Zechariah as well, with the Israelite girl embracing her even more incredible call with a humble trust that far outstrips the trembling doubt of the righteous priest (1:18–20).

One of the key interpretive issues confronting recipients of this text is Mary's question of Gabriel in Luke 1:34: "How can this be, since I do not know a man?" (my translation). Mary's query presents two problems for interpreters. Why is Mary's question, unlike that of Zechariah, not regarded by Gabriel as an instance of unfaithful doubt? The second is more difficult. Why does Mary ask the question in the first place? As one who was betrothed and awaiting marriage, shouldn't she assume that her conception of Jesus would result from her union with Joseph? The view that has won the support of most recent commentators is that Luke uses the question as a literary device to set up the further disclosure of Jesus' person and mission in verse 35, including his conception by the Holy Spirit.[31] This solution is indeed plausible, but it fails to explain how Luke intended the confused question itself to be handled by a recipient. When one recognizes that Luke is a skilled rhetorician who would have invited recipients to identify or even sympathize with characters in his narrative (more on this in chap. 8), another, perhaps more satisfying answer presents itself.

What were Luke's rhetorical aims in this passage? It seems to me that Luke sets out in this story to present some pretty extraordinary claims about the mission and person of Jesus, even beyond his identity as the Messiah. Luke's notions of Jesus' divine sonship, eternal reign, and conception by the Holy Spirit were likely matters of heated contention between Christian and non-Christian Israelites[32] and were perhaps even debated among Christians, with some holding to an adoptionist notion of Jesus' sonship that was more consistent with Israelite tradition.[33] Mark L. Strauss suggests that "Luke seems to be consciously opposing the view that Jesus' sonship is merely 'functional'—a special relationship with God by virtue of his role as king."[34] Luke, in other words, through his paradoxical portrait of Jesus, would be seen by many

---

31. E.g., Brown, *Birth of the Messiah*, 307–9; Fitzmyer, *Luke I–IX*, 350; Green, *Gospel of Luke*, 90; Carroll, *Luke*, 42.

32. See Larry Hurtado, *Lord Jesus Christ: Devotion to Jesus in Earliest Christianity* (Grand Rapids: Eerdmans, 2003), 349–407.

33. Mark's lack of the virgin birth tradition and his commissioning scene of Jesus at his baptism (1:9–11), in which the heavenly voice cites the enthronement psalm, Psalm 2, suggest that some Christians adapted the "adoptionist sonship" concept commonly applied to Jewish kings as a means of understanding Jesus' divine sonship, rather than employing the "divinely begotten" model promoted by Luke, Matthew, and John.

34. Mark L. Strauss, *The Davidic Messiah in Luke-Acts: The Promise and Its Fulfillment in Lukan Christology*, JSNTSup 110 (Sheffield: Sheffield Academic Press, 1995), 93.

of his potential recipients (including, perhaps, Theophilus) as pushing the
christological envelope, even confusing the boundaries between Jesus and
God, the human and the divine.

This is where Mary's befuddlement comes into play. As a means of leading recipients to at least entertain the portrait of Jesus he presents despite
the dissonance it creates, Luke invites them to identify with Mary and her
own perplexity. He presents Mary as an admirable character who nevertheless
responds to Gabriel's very first words with confusion. Luke employs the emphatic "to be much perplexed" or "to be greatly confused" (διαταράσσομαι) to
underscore Mary's bewilderment with the angelic greeting implying Mary's
exalted role in God's designs for Israel. In addition, he diverges from the
typical annunciation form by portraying Mary's reaction not as fear directed
at the sudden appearance of the angelic visitor (as is standard; cf. 1:12) but as
intense puzzlement at this greeting. Note too the redundancy, via parallelism,
that Luke employs in verse 29 lest the recipient miss this point:

> But she was much perplexed by his words
> and pondered what sort of greeting this might be.

For Mary, unlike Zechariah, the problem is cognitive dissonance, not doubt.
Accordingly, after learning more from Gabriel about the role she is to serve
as the mother of God's awaited messiah (1:30–33), she does not ask for a sign
as a test of God's faithfulness. Rather, confronted by this earthshaking news,
she confusedly asks, "How is this going to happen?" The question, in all its
oddity, also reflects Mary's sense that something completely at variance with
the normal course of reality as she understands it is about to take place. And
then Gabriel's response, with its startling disclosure regarding the son she will
bear and the manner of his conception, confirms that this is indeed the case!

Understood in these terms, we see how Mary's confusion can fit into the
flow of the narrative and serves Luke's rhetorical ends. Luke invites recipients
to identify with Mary's confusion and claim her as an ally, for these notions
about Jesus and his manner of conception are just too strange to grasp. But
then, when she hears what God has done for Elizabeth and hears the angel's
profession about what is possible for God (1:36–37), Mary remarkably pulls
out of her befuddlement and embraces Gabriel's words. Or, better said, perhaps we are meant to see her as putting faith in God despite her lingering
uncertainty about the details concerning Jesus and his conception.[35] And in

---

35. This is also suggested, perhaps, by the repeated notices throughout the infancy narrative
that Mary continued to ponder the significance of the child she would bear: 2:19, 51.

this Luke intends her to serve as an example for those who sympathize with her and perhaps even identify with her confusion.[36] For the assurance Gabriel provides seems directed at doubting or confused recipients as much as it is at Mary. Yes, this really is amazing, hard-to-believe stuff about Jesus and how he came to be, Luke admits. But recall what God has already done for Elizabeth, he reminds Theophilus. Then comes the poignant profession: "For *nothing* will be impossible with God" (v. 37). And Theophilus is invited to respond in a way that matches Mary's admirable trust and devotion: "Behold, I am the servant of the Lord; let it be with me according to your word" (v. 38, my translation). Insofar as recipients relate to Mary via the sympathy or reader identity that Luke invites for her as one who is understandably unprepared for the wondrous announcement she receives, and as they admire her for the courageous trust she nevertheless exhibits at the end, they are also prodded to join Mary in responding to these extraordinary claims with their own bold devotion.

Community Mission and Resistance: Acts 4:32–37

At first glance, the summary of the early believers' ministry in Acts 4:32–37 may strike readers as somewhat benign, even quaint. But when we read it in conjunction with the dramatic episodes leading up to and following this passage, we see that the passage participates in and amplifies the intense conflict coming to the fore. This series of dramatic episodes is a good example of how the sequencing of narrative can affect the reception of a passage. Set in its context, Luke's description of the believers' testimony and economics—perhaps even more so than its counterpart in 2:42–47—signals the believers' radical resistance to both the culture of the elite and the wiles of Satan and their intent to embrace the kind of Kingdom community constituted by Jesus.

The immediately preceding section of Acts presents the bold witness of Peter and other apostles to Jesus and the gospel in the face of virulent resistance by the Israelite elite. Peter heals a lame man (3:1–10) and then uses the occasion to proclaim the essentials of the gospel to mesmerized crowds. Peter's speech emphasizes the exalted character of Jesus, describing him as the "Holy and Righteous One" (3:14), the "Author of life" (3:15), God's resurrected Messiah (3:15, 18, 20), and the awaited prophet whose arrival had been proclaimed by "all the prophets, and as many as have spoken, from Samuel and those after

---

36. So also John Nolland, *Luke 1:1–9:20*, WBC 35a (Dallas: Word, 1989), 57. In fact, as we shall see, this same pattern characterizes the response of many throughout Luke-Acts when confronted with the salvation God is inaugurating among them (e.g., Luke 24).

him" (3:22–25). Tragically, God's people of this holy city, acting in ignorance and sinfulness, rejected and murdered Jesus (3:13–19). Despite all this, Peter announces an astounding offer of grace and reconciliation: their wicked rejection of God's Holy and Righteous One, their murder of the Author of life—all that can be forgiven, if they just turn back to God and embrace Jesus as Messiah (3:19–26). Instead, the Israelite elite, very much annoyed with the apostles and their testimony, have them arrested. When the prisoners are brought the next day, Peter and John proclaim Jesus as Lord and Savior of all creation (4:10–12). Yet the elite continue in their stubborn ignorance, refusing to see God's hand at work in the healing of the lame man, and demanding that the disciples refrain from speaking or teaching in Jesus' name (4:13–22). Upon being released, the apostles return to the community, which then erupts in praise of God, citing Psalm 2 and celebrating the victory of God and God's messiah over the kings of the earth. Echoing and further empowering their bold witness, the place where they were gathered was shaken, and all were filled with the Holy Spirit (4:23–31).

In relaying this story of bold, Spirit-compelled resistance, Luke unveils manifestations of God's power that are just as countercultural as they are ultimately unassailable. Consider this: (1) Peter and John, unlearned, common men, speak with Spirit-inspired boldness and effectiveness (Acts 4:13); (2) the silent witness of the formerly lame man thwarts the authorities' attempt to denounce the apostles' testimony (v. 14); (3) the common folks' reception of the sign prevents the elite from punishing Peter and John (v. 21); and (4) all of this commotion, conversion, and healing is done in the name of a crucified criminal of Rome. In drawing attention to these details, Luke challenges the Roman sense of where true power and authority reside. He is calling Theophilus to join the common folk in choosing a perception of the world and of power completely at odds with that zealously guarded by the elite.

As I said earlier, key to understanding Luke's summary of community life in 4:32–37 is to view it in connection with and *as an instance of* the early believers' bold resistance to embodiments of power that characterize their Roman world. The plotting of the passage itself also encourages recipients to see it as of a piece with the preceding narrative. Luke begins the account with the connective δέ, best translated as "now," for the transition Luke intends is "from the empowerment of the apostles to the demonstration of power within the community of believers."[37] The structuring of the passage reinforces this connection. At the center of the passage is Luke's notice that "with great

37. Luke Timothy Johnson, *The Acts of the Apostles*, Sacra Pagina 5 (Collegeville, MN: Liturgical Press, 1992), 85.

power the apostles gave their testimony to the resurrection of the Lord Jesus" (v. 33a), emphasizing once again the sovereignty of Jesus as "Lord" and the power that enables the bold witness of the apostles *and* the entire community: "and great grace was upon them all" (v. 33b). Enveloping this notice of the community's bold witness is Luke's account of how the believers shaped their economy (vv. 32, 34–35). It is clear from this plotting that the economy of the community is inextricably linked to their powerful testimony to Jesus and the manifestation of the Kingdom in their midst.

As to the character of that economy, several features of the passage emphasize the holding of community resources in a common trust: (1) the repetitive nature of the passage as a whole, serving as a doublet with Acts 2:44–45, which emphasizes the same; (2) the synonymous parallelism composed by the near-twin phrases of 4:32bc: "and no one claimed private ownership of any possessions, but everything they owned was held in common"; (3) the connection Luke draws between the social and spiritual unity of the community, on the one hand ("the whole group of those who believed were of one heart and soul" [v. 32a]), and their economic solidarity, on the other (v. 32bc); and (4) the repetition of the community's common sharing of goods on the back end of the bracketing Luke composes (v. 34). In sum, the early believers' sharing of resources is a feature of their testimony that Luke wants Theophilus to understand as essential to their mission and as a manifestation of the "great power" and "great grace" that rest upon them.

The sharing of resources among friends is, according to Luke Timothy Johnson, "an unmistakable allusion to the Hellenistic *topos* concerning friendship," echoing the widely distributed proverb that "friends hold all things in common" (see, e.g., Plato, *Republic* 449C; Aristotle, *Nicomachean Ethics* 1168B; *Politics* 1263A; Plutarch, *The Dialogue on Love* 21 [*Mor.* 767E]; Philo, *On Abraham* 235).[38] Yet this Greco-Roman ideal is more *refracted* than *reflected* in the early believers' economy. "Friendship," either between equals or between patrons and clients, and the sharing of resources that took place within the bounds of that relationship, were governed by the practice of reciprocity. The gifting of resources demanded a countergift of equal value, "for in reality there are no free gifts, just gifts that mark the initiation or continuance of an ongoing reciprocal relationship."[39] But this summary, like its counterpart in Acts 2:43–47, makes no mention of reciprocal gifting. The community acts as family, as kin, rather than as friends.[40]

38. Johnson, *Acts of the Apostles*, 58–59. See also Witherington, *Acts of the Apostles*, 205–6.
39. Malina, *New Testament World*, 95.
40. See Witherington, *Acts of the Apostles*, 205.

Two additional aspects of Luke's account of the early church's common life make clear the radically countercultural character of the community's economic resistance to Rome and Jerusalem. First is Luke's insistence that "there was not a needy person among them" (Acts 4:34) and that the resources of the believers were "distributed to each as any had need" (v. 35; see also 2:45). As we saw in chapter 1, resources in the Roman world were typically meted out not according to need but according to social rank, with the lion's share distributed among the elite and their retainers. So entrenched was this form of economic distribution, in fact, that members of the early community themselves were not immune to falling back into this socially scripted pattern of resource allocation. In Acts 6 we learn that the widows of the "Hellenists" (likely Greek-speaking Israelites) "were being neglected in the daily distribution of food" (6:1) and that the widows of the "Hebrews" (Hebrew-speaking Israelites) were being favored. Guided by the intervention of the apostles, the community promptly resolves the issue by appointing members to ensure the equitable distribution of resources (6:2–6). Second, the resources of the community are "laid . . . at the apostles' feet," seemingly indicating the apostles' elevated social status within the community and their role as patrons (vv. 35, 37). But they are patrons of a most unusual sort. Their social location within the community was based on their companionship with Jesus before and after he was raised (see Acts 1:21–22) and on their bold, Spirit-inspired testimony to God's Kingdom. On this level, their reception of honor and authority bears some similarity to the divine mandate claimed by the elite.[41] But unlike the Roman and Israelite elite, the apostles were "uneducated and ordinary men" (4:13), lacking the family pedigree or any other characteristics that would have distinguished them from the ranks of commoners. There is also no intimation that the apostles expected favors in return for their patronage. Just as remarkably, the apostles readily set aside their roles as patrons when it becomes clear to them that they are not able to devote adequate attention to the task. Moreover, the ones taking up the charge in their place are not appointed by the apostles—they are not, in other words, brokers. They are selected from among the people by the people (6:3–4).

Following this summary, Luke relays two stories of believers participating in the community's radical departure from Greco-Roman economy. The first is about Joseph, a native of Cyprus, whom the apostles name "Barnabas." This is likely the same Barnabas who introduces the newly converted Saul to the apostles and later accompanies Paul on some of his missions (9:26–27; 13:1–14:28). He sells a field that belongs to him and faithfully lays the proceeds

41. Recall our discussion in chap. 1 concerning the elite's divine mandate to rule over community and cult.

at the apostles' feet (4:36–37). Yet in the next account the married couple Ananias and Sapphira struggle to embrace the mode of economy that characterizes Kingdom living. Ananias and Sapphira, like Barnabas, sell a piece of property; they, however, keep some of the proceeds for themselves. Peter's rebuke unmasks the deception that accompanies their offering (5:3–4, 8–9). Not only do their actions violate the economy of the community, in which all things are to be held in common trust (4:32b); they also violate the "one heart and soul" that binds the community together in common grace and witness (4:32a). Because God's very own Spirit dwells within that community and empowers its testimony in word and deed (4:31), Ananias and Sapphira's actions are in essence an act of defiance against the Spirit, a choice to follow the lead of Satan rather than the lead of God (5:3–4). The consequences are dire. Upon hearing Peter's rebuke, Ananias falls dead (5:5). Sapphira does the same when she arrives later and repeats her husband's sin (5:7–10).[42]

Two vexing issues confront interpreters of these passages, raised in part by the story of Ananias and Sapphira: the extent to which resources were actually held in common, and whether or not the forfeiture of personal resources was voluntary or required. Acts 4:32 and 34 seem to indicate communal ownership of all goods and that *all* members of the community with such resources did place them in common trust. Yet Peter's statement to Ananias in 5:4 suggests to some that the liquidation and dispersal of property occurred gradually, and that it was not necessary for believers to turn over all their resources to the community: "While it remained unsold, did it not remain your own? And after it was sold, were not the proceeds at your disposal?"[43] In my view, however, the clear sense of 4:32–34—which is that believers did and were expected to transfer all their holdings over for the welfare of the community and its members—is to govern our understanding of the two stories following the summary. The idea that the faithful are to forfeit worldly possessions for the sake of the Kingdom is certainly not unique to this passage (see Luke 9:23–25, 58; 12:21; 14:33). Moreover, a disjunction occurs between 4:32–34 and 5:4 only if one assumes that Ananias was already an established member of the community and not a recent convert who had yet to offer his resources to the apostles. Peter's statement in 5:4, in other words, does not acknowledge Ananias' right to withhold some of the proceeds from the community as one of its members but highlights the

---

42. Note the somewhat similar story of Simon the magician, who offers Peter and John money in the hopes of receiving the power to grant the Holy Spirit (8:9–24). Peter's rebuke also makes clear the egregious and even life-threatening nature of Simon's depravity and offense against God (vv. 20–23).

43. This view is maintained by Johnson, *Acts of the Apostles*, 88; Witherington, *Acts of the Apostles*, 215–16; Fitzmyer, *Acts of the Apostles*, 323; F. Scott Spencer, *Journeying through Acts: A Literary-Cultural Reading* (Peabody, MA: Hendrickson, 2004), 66.

freedom Ananias has to choose whether or not to belong to the community at all. Finally, Peter's rebuke in 5:3 clearly indicates that Ananias and Sapphira's sin against God and collusion with Satan (5:3a) consists of both their misrepresenting the extent of their generosity toward the community (5:3b) and their refusal to give all the proceeds to the community as was expected of them (5:3c): "'Ananias,' Peter asked, 'why has Satan filled your heart to lie to the Holy Spirit and to keep back for yourselves [νοσφίσασθαι] part of the proceeds of the land?'" (my translation). [44] The lie *and* the withholding of funds were both demonic acts. As noted well by Spencer, recipients of Luke's narrative "will recognize a pattern of diabolical efforts to infiltrate and sabotage the Jesus movement by appealing to human greed. . . . Satan cleverly manipulates property and profit to ensnare Jesus' followers."[45]

This story does, understandably, strike modern readers as extreme; perhaps it struck Luke's original recipients the same way. But if recipients, ancient or modern, find the story of Ananias and Sapphira shocking and strange, it is likely because they have failed to appreciate the radical reorientation and resistance of the church already signaled in the narrative leading up to this tale, including 4:32–37, and failed to appreciate the necessity of that form of resistance, at least in that time and place. In Luke's eyes, for members of the early Christian community to violate their unified testimony to the Kingdom in order to maintain some level of economic fidelity to the ways of Rome is tantamount to choosing Caesar as Lord over God's messiah (recall 4:12, 24–30). It is tantamount to resisting God's insistence that the provision of creation be made accessible to all people, especially those in need. The choice the community and the recipients face is essentially between the way of Satan and death and the way of Jesus and life.

Conclusion

Narrative is a deeply compelling form of human discourse, especially narrative that skillfully and passionately unveils profound implications for how we conceive the world and our place within it. Through his use of various narrative forms and literary techniques that we have only begun to explore, Luke unmasks unfaithful patterns of relating that enslave humanity to demonic degradation. He calls Theophilus and others to leave the collapsing regime of Rome and Satan and their lies behind, to embrace the realm of the true Lord whose reign and provision will never fail.

44. The NRSV fails to capture the middle voice of the infinitive of νοσφίζω here in v. 3.
45. Spencer, *Journeying through Acts*, 66–67. See also Acts 8:9–24; Luke 8:14; 22:3–6.

5

Plotting through Parallels

In the preceding chapter I noted that one of the most basic conventions of narrative form is plotting—the way a writer presents the setting and unfolds the action and tensions of the narrative from its beginning, through its middle, and on to its end. Luke, as already mentioned, employs numerous techniques to enact the rather complex plotting of his two-volume work. Among the more significant of Luke's plotting techniques are the connections he draws between characters, events, and historical developments through patterning and parallelism. In modes both apparent and subtle, Luke uses these techniques to impress upon his recipients that the matters he records, along with matters recorded by faithful Israelites before him, are threads of the same narrative tapestry.

Parallelism through Patterns

Ancient historians frequently composed patterns in their narration of both characters and events. They cast episodes or sections of a narrative in clearly defined structures, often consisting of alternating (ABAB) or chiastic (ABCBA) patterns. They also depicted the actions of characters in formulaic cadences of common elements. Clear examples are found in Homer's *Iliad* and *Odyssey*, in the plays of Aeschylus and Euripides, in the histories of Herodotus and Thucydides, and in Vergil's *Aeneid*, *Eclogues*, and *Georgics*, among others.[1]

---

1. Talbert, *Literary Patterns, Theological Themes*, 67.

According to Charles Talbert, who has offered one of the more detailed surveys of this technique in ancient historiography and Luke-Acts, such patterns could function as "(a) an assist to the memory of the recipients/hearers, that is, a mnemonic device; (b) an assist to the meaning of the whole or of a section; or (c) as an abstract architectonic principle, a convention, used solely for aesthetic purposes."[2] While not precluding the possibility that Luke used the device to assist recipients' memories and for aesthetic reasons, we can affirm that Luke's primary aim in using patterns was "as an assist to the meaning of the whole or of a section." More specifically, Luke uses patterns to cast the characters, actions, and events he narrates as integral parts of his overarching kingdom story, and to draw comparisons and connections between characters and between their actions, in order to advance his rhetorical ends.

Luke and His Patterns

Luke is known as an author with a penchant for patterns.[3] Most occur on a small scale within a passage and serve as an important structuring feature for the pericope, such as the alternating or chiastic patterns discussed above, those typical of the various generic forms Luke employs, or other patterns unique to Luke. Some of these patterns, especially those unique to Luke, draw connections among a series of passages or between episodes and characters spaced throughout the narrative. For example, many have identified parallel elements in John's and Jesus' birth narratives and in the accounts of Jesus', Stephen's, Peter's, and Paul's ministries. Other patterns appear to tie together and structure larger sections of Luke's kingdom story. In fact, a few scholars have proposed detailed chiastic structures for Luke's travel narrative[4] as well as for Luke's account of Paul's ministry in Acts 15:1–21:6.[5] Talbert also proposes complex, interlocking parallel sections and chiastic structures for Luke-Acts as a whole.[6]

2. Ibid., 81.
3. On Luke's frequent use of patterns and parallelism throughout Luke-Acts, see Talbert, *Literary Patterns, Theological Themes*; P. Boyd Mather, "Paul in Acts as 'Servant' and 'Witness,'" *Journal of the Chicago Society of Biblical Research* 30 (1985): 23–44; Tannehill, *Narrative Unity*, 1:1–9, 15–20; Andrew C. Clark, "The Role of the Apostles," in *Witness to the Gospel: The Theology of Acts*, ed. I. Howard Marshall and David Peterson (Grand Rapids: Eerdmans, 1998), 185–89.
4. See Michael D. Goulder, "The Chiastic Structure of the Lucan Journey," in *Studia Evangelica*, 2 vols., ed. F. L. Cross (Berlin: Akademie Verlag, 1964), 2:195–202; R. Morgenthaler, *Die lukanische Geschichtsschreibung als Zeugnis*, ATANT (Zurich: Zwingli, 1948), 1:156–57; Talbert, *Literary Patterns, Theological Themes*, 51–55.
5. Ibid., 56–61.
6. Ibid., 62–63.

Most modern readers of Luke-Acts, however, have not found these detailed, large-scale, chiastic structures for major portions of Luke and Acts compelling and useful. Indeed, many do find that Luke employs broad narrative patterns to structure large sections of his account, and even his work as a whole, and I will be discussing this feature of his plotting in what follows. But the "macro-patterns" identified by most are much less complex than the highly detailed structures proposed by Talbert and others, and reflect broader and more easily discernible elements of Luke's narrative rhetoric. Moreover, readers tend to focus more attention on the readily discernible, smaller-scale patterns Luke employs to characterize and draw connections between characters, events, and different parts of his narrative. This use of parallelism does much of the heavy lifting when it comes to advancing the plotting and thematic development of Luke-Acts.

Patterns and Parallels

When I speak of "pattern" and "parallel" with respect to Luke's plotting, I am referring to particular things. By "pattern" I mean the structuring of an episode or larger section so that its elements conform to a mode of sequencing common to Luke's literary milieu or occurring elsewhere in Luke's narrative. In short, a pattern in this respect has multiple iterations in Luke's narrative or is present in other literary works of his day. Regarding patterns present in other literary works, recall by way of example Luke's use of generic forms within his narrative, or recall the use of chiastic or alternating structures by Greco-Roman writers mentioned above. By "parallel" I mean to indicate the use of patterning or other devices for the primary purpose of drawing a connection between characters or developments within the narrative (what some call "intratextuality") or between these characters or developments and Israel's sacred traditions (what some call "intertextuality"). In Luke-Acts, many of the patterns Luke employs compose these intratextual parallels, while citation and allusion to Israel's sacred traditions are the main mechanisms for the intertextual parallels he composes.

Patterns and Parallels Employed by Luke

The following discussion of Lukan patterning and parallelism aims at both breadth and depth. I will first briefly overview a number of different narrative patterns creating textual parallels throughout Luke-Acts. The purpose of this survey is to give readers an informed sense of how parallelism is manifested in

specific ways throughout Luke's two-volume work and to give some suggestions of how these parallels serve specific rhetorical ends. I will then overview
Luke's practice of composing parallels, through citation or allusion, to earlier
Israelite tradition in order to infuse the characters and the events he portrays
with additional layers of meaning.

Prophecy Leading to Fulfillment

Luke announces in his prologue that the narrative to follow will give an
account "of the matters fulfilled among us." True to this overview, Luke
frequently—and immediately—employs a pattern of "prophecy leading to
fulfillment" as he relays his story of Jesus and the early church.[7] Repeatedly, predictions made by divinely sent or Spirit-filled characters are shown
to be fulfilled. These include statements that are programmatic for the
narrative to follow, such as Gabriel's birth announcements (Luke 1:13–17,
30–37), Jesus' inaugural sermon in Nazareth (4:16–30), the passion predictions (9:21–22, 44; 18:32–33), Jesus' call for followers to bear witness to "all
nations" (Luke 24:44–49; Acts 1:8), and Jesus' predictions of his followers'
own sufferings (Luke 21:12–15). Others pertain to more immediate plot
developments, such as Stephen's characterization of Israel as those who reject and kill God's prophets, a characterization fulfilled as stones then rain
down on this Spirit-filled prophet (Acts 6:8–8:1), and the prophet Agabus'
prediction of Paul's sufferings (Acts 21:10–14), which soon after comes true
(21:30–35).

The repetitive manifestation of this prophecy-fulfillment pattern throughout Luke-Acts underscores at least two key elements of Luke's kingdom story
that are emphasized in a number of ways. First, the instigation of the pattern
in the words of divinely sent or Spirit-filled characters makes clear that the
events Luke records unfold in fulfillment of *God's* plan to redeem Israel and
all humanity. In this we again encounter Luke's insistence that the conception, planning, and inauguration of the Kingdom come forth from the heart,
mind, and instrumentality of God. Second, the prophecy-fulfillment pattern,
both in terms of its *form* as prophecy fulfilled and in terms of the allusions
to Israelite tradition contained in many of its instances (more on this below),
joins with numerous other intertextual echoes to underscore that the essential
backdrop to Luke's kingdom story includes Israelite hopes and expectations
for the dawn of a new age.

7. For a helpful review of this Lukan feature, see Johnson, *Gospel of Luke*, 15–20.

Revelation Leading to Faithful Testimony

Luke also uses patterns to characterize and draw connections between the actions of characters. One such prominent pattern, and one that often "piggybacks" on the prophecy-fulfillment pattern, governs Luke's portrayal of faithful witnessing activity throughout Luke-Acts. Having been called to eyewitness the arrival of God's salvation, characters typically embrace the revelation they receive and then erupt in praise once it becomes manifest (though often in a penultimate sense) in their midst. This becomes evident early in Luke's narrative as each announcement to the characters in the infancy narrative concerning the advent of God's salvation in John and Jesus, along with the immediate manifestation of what was just announced, is followed by a corresponding act of celebratory witness that praises God and testifies to God's redeeming activity among them. The annunciation to Zechariah and the birth of his son, John, lead to Zechariah's (albeit delayed) canticle (Luke 1:68–79) proclaiming the coming of God's messianic redeemer, whose way John will prepare; the Spirit-led leaping of John in the womb results in Elizabeth's greeting to Mary (1:41–45), in which Elizabeth recognizes Mary's newly conceived offspring as "my lord"; Mary answers Gabriel's annunciation and Elizabeth's greeting with a jubilant song (1:46–55) celebrating Mary's conception of a son (vv. 48–49) and proclaiming its inauguration of God's deliverance of Israel in fulfillment of God's promises (vv. 50–55); the announcement of the angel and the proclamation of the heavenly host lead to the shepherds' "ma[king] known what had been told them about this child" to those gathered around the manger (2:17); and in response to Jesus' presentation in the temple, Simeon and Anna erupt in thanksgiving to God and prophesy about Jesus as the embodiment of God's long-awaited salvation (2:25–38). As characters respond to the revelation and manifestation of God's redemption among them, praise takes the form of testimony that witnesses to what God has accomplished and will yet accomplish in Jesus. The role of the Holy Spirit in empowering the witnessing activity of these characters is also a common feature throughout the infancy narrative: Elizabeth (1:41), Zechariah (1:67), and Simeon (2:27) are all moved by the Holy Spirit to announce the saving significance of the events taking place before them.[8]

These very same elements in Luke's portrayal of the figures in his infancy narrative mirror his casting of witnesses throughout his two-volume work, as individuals are chosen to behold and then called to proclaim the reality of God's

---

8. While the Spirit's inspiration is not expressly indicated for Mary, her blessed state as one chosen by God and having conceived by the Holy Spirit, and the biblical (Septuagintal) style of her hymn, seem to imply the inspired nature of her praise to God as well. So also Ju Hur, *A Dynamic Reading of the Holy Spirit in Luke-Acts* (London: T&T Clark, 2004), 200.

awaited salvation in their midst. For instance, in the first call story of the Gospel (Luke 5:1–11), Jesus provides a bountiful catch of fish for a certain group of fishermen and then commissions them as his disciples, telling them, "From now on you will be catching people" (v. 10).[9] The twelve and later the seventy are then chosen by Jesus (6:12–16; 9:1–6; 10:1–24), given power over demons and disease, and sent out "to proclaim the kingdom of God and to heal" (9:2; cf. 10:9). The Gerasene demoniac is released from his bondage to Satan (8:26–39) and, sent forth by Jesus, proclaims "how much Jesus [has] done for him" (v. 39). After encountering the risen Jesus, the disciples are commissioned as witnesses (Luke 24:48–49; Acts 1:6–8). Accordingly, those who witness the revelatory events of Jesus' life, death, and resurrection are allotted the apostolic ministry of proclaiming the good news (Acts 1:17; 10:41; 13:31), while others such as Stephen, Philip, Barnabas, and Paul are also called to be instruments of the gospel.

The evangelist draws the same connection between such testimony and the ministry of the Spirit throughout Luke-Acts as he does in the infancy narrative. This is readily evident in the programmatic commissioning of Luke 24:48–49 and Acts 1:6–8, in which Jesus presents the "power from on high" (Luke 24:49), later specified as the Spirit (Acts 1:5, 8), as the guiding and empowering force behind the disciples' witness. Moreover, like characters in the infancy narrative, individuals in Acts are also commonly said to be filled with the Holy Spirit when bearing witness to the good news (Peter [4:8]; Stephen [7:55]; Paul [9:17; 13:9]) or to be variously directed/inspired by the Spirit in their witnessing activity (Stephen [6:10]; Peter [10:19; 11:12]; Philip [8:29]; Barnabas [11:24]; Paul and his companions [16:6, 7]). A number of recent studies focusing on the character of the Holy Spirit in Luke-Acts emphasize these correspondences, finding that the Spirit's role with respect to the characters in the infancy narrative is the same as that found throughout the narrative and especially in Acts: to empower believers to bear witness to what God has accomplished in Jesus.[10]

The Kerygma

In addition to composing parallel patterns in the witnessing activity of characters throughout the narrative, Luke draws clear parallels in what the characters proclaim about the arrival of God's Kingdom in Jesus. The major (Acts 2:14–36;

9. Note that the bountiful catch of fish and the resulting astonishment of Peter and the others are present only in Luke's account of this episode (cf. Mark 1:16–20; Matt. 4:18–22).

10. See, e.g., Robert P. Menzies, *Empowered for Witness: The Spirit in Luke-Acts*, Journal of Pentecostal Theology Supplement Series 6 (Sheffield: Sheffield Academic Press, 1994), 106–22; W. H. Shepherd Jr., *The Narrative Function of the Holy Spirit as a Character in Luke-Acts*, SBLDS 147 (Atlanta: Scholars Press, 1994), 112–26.

3:12–26; 10:28–43) and shorter (4:8–12; 5:30–33) speeches of Peter, Stephen's speech (7:1–53), and others of Paul (13:16–41; 17:22–31; 22:1–21; 24:10–21; 26:2–29; 28:17–29) are frequently cited as clear instances of the early Christian *kerygma*: that early, core narrative of Jesus and his significance proclaimed by Jesus' followers. For our purposes it is also important to note that most elements of the kerygma are already voiced or implied by the characters of Luke 1–2.

Kerygmatic Speeches in Acts	Characters of Luke 1–2
Jesus attested to by miracles and signs (2:22; 10:38)	1:44, 49 (implied); 2:12
Jesus delivered up according to God's plan (2:23; 10:39; 13:29)	2:34–35
Jesus rejected by the Jews (2:23; 3:13–14, 17; 7:52; 10:39)	2:34 (implied)
and crucified (2:23; 3:15; 4:10; 7:52; 10:39; 13:28)	
Jesus raised from the dead (2:25; 3:15; 4:10; 10:40; 13:30; 22:8; 24:21; 26:15–18, 22–23)	
Jesus as Lord (2:36; 10:36), Christ (2:36; 3:18, 20; 4:10, 26; 10:36; 13:34; 26:23), Son of God (9:20; 13:33), and Savior (5:31; 13:23)	1:32, 35, 43, 69, 76; 2:11
According to the Scriptures (2:25, 29–30; 3:18, 22–26; 10:43; 13:33; 26:22; 28:23)	1:70; 2:32
According to God's promise/covenant (2:39; 3:25)	1:54–55, 72–75
Christ, agent of God's salvation (2:38; 3:19, 26; 4:12)	1:51–54, 68–71; 2:29–32
for Israel (2:38–39; 3:18–25; 5:31)	1:51–54, 68–71; 2:31–32
for gentiles (3:25; 10:34)	2:31–32
For the forgiveness of sins (2:38; 3:19; 5:31; 10:43; 13:38; 22:16; 26:18)	1:77
Jesus grants the promise/power of the Holy Spirit (2:33; 10:38)	
and its bestowal upon believers (2:14–21, 33, 38; 5:32)	
The disciples as witnesses of resurrection (2:32; 3:15; 10:39; 13:31; 22:15; 26:16)	

The only kerygmatic elements fully missing from the testimony of human characters in the infancy account (Jesus raised from the dead; Jesus grants the promise/power of the Holy Spirit and its bestowal upon believers; the disciples as witnesses to the resurrection) are those that are naturally the focus of the narrative following Luke 24, when they become dominant threads of Luke's plot. Despite these omissions, the preponderance of shared elements is remarkable. In light of these striking correspondences, it is difficult to avoid the conclusion that Luke intends to portray the characters of the infancy narrative as already bearing witness to "the word" that he sets out to narrate. Note also that Luke depicts Jesus proclaiming "the word of God" (ὁ λόγος τοῦ θεοῦ) before his crucifixion and resurrection and even before the passion predictions (see Luke 5:1; 8:11, 21). If by "the word" (Luke 1:2) the evangelist has in mind "the message about Jesus and the divine events,"[11] then it would seem that the testimony of the characters in the birth accounts meets this description just as well as the apostolic testimony recorded in Acts.[12]

The Ministries of Jesus and Others

Luke also composes numerous parallels between characters in Luke and Acts, and within Acts. Luke's accounts of Jesus and Paul have notable structural similarities. Luke has us follow both to various locales as they proclaim the arrival of the Kingdom, leading to a lengthy travel narrative (Luke 9:51–19:44; Acts 19:21–28:31), in which both are repeatedly resisted, offer passion predictions (Luke 9:21–22, 44; 18:31–33; Acts 20:22–23), and suffer trials and persecution at the hands of the elite. Both of these accounts have Jesus and Paul perform similar miracles: exorcisms (e.g., Luke 4:33–37, 41; 8:26–39; 11:20; cf. Acts 10:38); healing of a lame man (Luke 5:17–26; Acts 14:8–14); healing of other sick persons (Luke 4:38–40; 6:17–19; cf. Acts 28:7–10); even raising the dead (Luke 7:11–17; 8:40–42, 49–56; cf. Acts 20:9–12).[13] Luke also composes parallels between Jesus and Stephen: Stephen's similar view of Israel's rejection of the prophets (Acts 7:1–53; cf. Luke 11:45–52; 19:41–44; 20:9–19); faithful martyrdom, including the statements "receive my Spirit" and "Lord, do not hold this sin against them" (Acts 7:59, 60; cf. Luke 23:34, 46); and affirmation that Jesus does indeed sit at the right hand of God (Acts 7:56; Luke 22:69). Luke also has Peter and Paul (and thus also Peter and Jesus) perform similar miracles of healing: Peter also heals a lame person (Acts 3:1–10) and raises a dead woman to life (Acts 9:36–43), and both receive visions that compel them to reach out to gentiles (Acts 9:1–19; 10:9–16).

Taken together, the four patterns we have just discussed—prophecy leading to fulfillment, revelation leading to faithful testimony, the kerygma, and the ministries of Jesus and others—which appear in the witnessing activity of Luke's characters, help to underscore four critical features of Luke's kingdom story. First, the connections—or parallels—Luke draws between these

---

11. Bock, *Luke 1:1–9:50*, 58.

12. See Karl Allen Kuhn, "Beginning the Witness: The αὐτόπται καὶ ὑπηρέται of Luke's Infancy Narrative," *NTS* 49 (2003): 237–55.

13. For additional parallels between Jesus and Paul, see A. J. Mattill Jr., "The Jesus-Paul Parallels and the Purpose of Luke-Acts: H. H. Evans Reconsidered," *NovT* 27 (1975): 15–46.

characters through the patterning of their witnessing activity demonstrate, once again, that the Spirit-inspired mission of Jesus begun in the Gospel is now continuing in the ministry of his followers in Acts. Second, these parallels amplify the unity of the early church's mission, especially that of Paul and Peter. Third, Luke's patterning of this testimony makes it clear that the testimony is unified by a consistent content. Luke's version of the kerygma embodies a consistent narrative of the arrival of God's Kingdom in Jesus' ministry and its ongoing emergence in the life of the church. Finally, the parallels emphasize that the witnessing activity of Jesus' followers and the *authority* to bear normative testimony are not limited to a select few. Rather, the troop of evangelists Luke portrays is characterized not only by a consistent witness and authorization but also by an eclectic mix of folk representing a broad spectrum of society, including priests, a young maiden, shepherds, temple prophets, fishermen, tax collectors, women, leading citizens, former demoniacs, a well-connected, zealous Pharisee, and a learned, eloquent Jew of Alexandria. We saw earlier that in both Greco-Roman and Israelite society of the first century CE, the authority to practice and proclaim the cult was typically limited to the social elite. Luke's kingdom story clearly transcends this exclusive, hierarchical religiosity. While the apostles do play a central role in the transition of the Kingdom's emergence from the life of Jesus to the ministry of the church, their significance does not lessen the relevance and authority of those whose witness came before (such as that provided by characters in the infancy narrative) or that of those who later joined the ministry of the early church. As one of the many gifts the followers of Jesus are inspired to share, kerygmatic testimony is authorized not according to social rank but by the Holy Spirit.

The Step-Parallelism between John and Jesus

Scholars have long noted that the annunciations of John's and Jesus' births are to be seen in parallel relationship. Conceptual and verbal correspondences between the accounts draw direct connections between the two figures and reveal Jesus as the superior of the two, resulting in a "step-parallelism."

The instances of step-parallelism created by these correspondences are commonly considered to consist of the following:

1. John the Baptist is great before the Lord (Luke 1:15a), but Jesus is "great" without qualification (1:32).
2. John the Baptist is filled with the Holy Spirit even from his mother's womb (1:15c), but the very conception of Jesus involves a creative act of God through the Holy Spirit (1:35b).

3. John the Baptist will make ready for the Lord a prepared people (1:17e), but Jesus will actually rule over the house of Jacob/Israel and possess a kingdom without end (1:33).

In addition to these, John Nolland adds:

4. John is consecrated to Nazarite abstinence, but Jesus' holiness as the divine Son extends to the very basis of his existence.[14]

Many commentators are simply content to indicate that the step-parallelism presents Jesus as superior to John without providing any further explanation for Luke's motivation. Raymond Brown, however, argues that Luke's concern to present Jesus as greater than John stems from the presence of a messianic sect proclaiming John as the Christ.[15] Others follow Hans Conzelmann's lead in claiming that John represents the Period of Israel, which Luke shows as superseded by the Period of Jesus' Ministry.[16] However, two features of Luke's portrayal of Jesus and John indicate that the primary point of the step-parallelism was not to compare Jesus to John, but Jesus to God.

First, the correspondences in Luke's portrayal of John and Jesus in the paired annunciations and throughout the infancy narrative not only reveal the differences between the two prophets but also emphasize their common mission as well as the exalted significance of *both* of them: both are "great," and both are empowered by God's Spirit. Second, throughout the infancy narrative Luke avoids directly stating that John prepares the way for Jesus. Instead, John is presented as the eschatological Elijah who prepares the way of the Lord *God* (Luke 1:15–17, 76–77). It is only by implication that members of Luke's audience are able to discern that Jesus is the one for whom John prepares. An adequate explanation of the step-parallelism must account for these two features.[17]

In my view, Luke's emphasis on both John and Jesus as persons essential to the accomplishment of God's awaited advent, and the fact that Luke presents John as readying Israel for the advent of Yahweh *and* Jesus, together suggest that Luke is primarily concerned to portray the greatness of Jesus not vis-à-vis John, who some have thought is the Messiah, nor vis-à-vis John as the representative of

14. Nolland, *Luke 1:1–9:20*, 40–41.
15. Brown, *Birth of the Messiah*, 283–84.
16. Hans Conzelmann, *The Theology of St. Luke*, trans. Geoffrey Buswell (New York: Harper & Row, 1961). So also H. H. Oliver, "The Lucan Birth Stories and the Purpose of Luke-Acts," *NTS* 10 (1963–64): 202–26; John Drury, *Tradition and Design in Luke's Gospel: A Study in Early Christian Historiography* (Atlanta: John Knox, 1976), 63–64; Strauss, *Davidic Messiah*, 83–84.
17. For a fuller articulation of this argument, see Karl A. Kuhn, "The Point of the Step-Parallelism in Luke 1–2," *NTS* 47 (2001): 38–49.

the Period of Israel, but vis-à-vis John as one who *prepares the way of the Lord*. This proposal helps us grasp two important functions of the step-parallelism Luke composes between John and Jesus. First, it is Jesus' superior greatness and significance with respect to John as revealed in the step-parallelism Luke employs that sets Jesus apart as the one for whom John prepares. Otherwise Jesus' role in the unfolding of God's salvation becomes unclear: that is, if John prepares the way of the Lord God—and not that (also) of Jesus—then how does Jesus, who is greater than John and hailed Messiah and Son of God, fit into God's restoration? By his portrayal of Jesus as greater than John, Luke implies that Jesus must be the one whose way John readies, an implication that becomes more and more clear as the narrative unfolds.[18] At the same time, the seeming contradiction that this implication creates (how can John be directly said to prepare the way of the Lord God, while it is clearly indicated by the narrative that it is also Jesus for whom John prepares?) invites Luke's audience to consider that Yahweh's awaited advent and Jesus' coming are somehow one and the same. It also invites Luke's audience to reflect upon the nature of the relationship between Jesus and God.

From Revelation to Proclamation in Luke 24

Above, we discussed the pattern, evident throughout Luke-Acts, of revelation leading to the acceptance of that good news and Spirit-guided, faithful witness. A similar, though slightly adjusted, pattern is also manifested in the three episodes of Luke 24: revelation → misunderstanding → corrective instruction → understanding → proclamation. Here is an account of how each instance of the pattern is manifested:

24:1–11

Revelation:	the stone is rolled away, the tomb is empty (vv. 1–3)
Misunderstanding:	the women are perplexed (v. 4a)
Corrective Instruction:	the angelic attendants remind the women of Jesus' passion predictions (vv. 5–7)
Understanding:	the women remember (v. 8)
Proclamation:	and return to the disciples to tell "all this" (v. 9)

18. Luke continues to imply that John prepares the way for Jesus: the unborn John leaps upon the arrival of Mary (1:41); Zechariah proclaims the significance of his son in a canticle that is largely devoted to celebrating the arrival of God's promised salvation in the person of the Messiah (1:67–79); finally, John answers those who were wondering whether he was the Messiah, stating, "I baptize you with water; but one who is more powerful than I is coming; I am not worthy to untie the thong of his sandals. He will baptize you with the Holy Spirit and fire" (Luke 3:16; cf. Mark 1:7–8).

24:13–27

Revelation:	the kerygmatic details prophesied by Jesus and the women's account of the empty tomb
Misunderstanding:	"A prophet mighty in deed and word . . . but they did not see him" (vv. 19–24)
Corrective Instruction:	Jesus' rebuke and teaching (vv. 25–27), breaking of the bread (v. 30)
Understanding:	recognition of Jesus and indication that the Scriptures have been opened to the disciples (vv. 31–32)
Proclamation:	returning to Jerusalem and sharing the good news (vv. 33, 35)

24:36–53

Revelation:	Jesus appears among the disciples (v. 36)
Misunderstanding:	the disciples are frightened and think they are seeing a ghost (v. 37)
Corrective Instruction:	Jesus assures them that he is not a ghost, opens the Scriptures to them, commissions them as his witnesses, blesses them, and ascends before them (vv. 38–51)
Understanding:	the disciples respond with joy (v. 52)
Proclamation:	and continually praise God in the temple (v. 53)

Attending to this adjusted pattern enables us to recognize that Luke is interested in depicting a process by which the disciples come to understand the events taking place in their midst as good news. What would be the point of this? The pattern common to each episode in Luke 24 portrays how the disciples' bewilderment and lack of faith were finally resolved: by repeated acts of corrective instruction emphasizing the divine and scriptural necessity of Jesus' suffering and resurrection and, above all else, by the reality of the resurrection itself. Second, and as we shall discuss in chapter 7, the threefold iteration of this pattern creates a parallel series of "threshold moments" that heighten the tension recipients experience as they wonder whether the disciples, as assisted by the angels and Jesus, will finally overthrow their misunderstanding and doubt to embrace the good news of Jesus' resurrection from the dead.

To and from Jerusalem, to and from Resurrection

Near the start of this chapter I indicated the aversion of many readers to highly detailed, large-scale patterns some suggest for major sections of Luke's narrative, while also stating that many point instead to the evangelist's employment of more general, large-scale patterning in the plotting of Luke-Acts. One such pattern—representing a rudimentary chiastic structure—is the movement of the bulk of Luke's narrative first toward and then away from Jerusalem (as we noted in chap. 4). This movement underscores the centrality of Jerusalem in God's plan of salvation: Jerusalem is to be the place of Jesus' suffering, rejection, death (Luke 9:22, 44), and resurrection (9:22, 31). It is from that sacred city that the message of God's salvation is to spill out to the rest of the world (Luke 24:45–49; Acts 1:8). In so presenting his two-volume work, Luke provides a parallel plotting to his narrative that unifies it while emphasizing the rootedness of God's deliverance of humankind in God's relationship with Israel (see also chap. 10).

But it seems to me that the movement to and from Jerusalem is not the only pivot point Luke provides as he transitions from the narrative of the Gospel to that of Acts. Equally important as a structuring pattern is Luke's focus on the resurrection as a transitional hinge for his two-volume work. I will have more to say about this feature in the next chapter as we examine Luke's use of character speech and its role in the thematic development in Luke-Acts. For now, let me preview that discussion by adding that Luke presents the resurrection as essential to the realization of God's reign within the ongoing ministry of the risen Jesus, the Spirit, and believers. Just as the narrative purview throughout much of the Gospel gazes ahead to Jerusalem, it also gazes ahead to the cross and the resurrection (see Luke 9:21–22, 51; 18:31–33). It is because of the resurrection that the tragic news of Jesus' passion becomes the good news of the kerygma. Because of the resurrection, the disciples are transformed from those who cannot grasp the significance of the events taking place around them to those who become bold champions of the kingdom story. Because of the resurrection, the saving reign of the risen Jesus is enacted in the ministry of his followers, and the journey continues in their lives of witness and service.

Parallels to Israelite Tradition

As stated in the introduction to this chapter, not only does Luke compose parallels between characters, actions, and developments within his narrative through his use of patterns; he also frequently draws comparisons between the matters he records and the hopes, expectations, and sacred stories of Israelite tradition. This technique is, of course, common to all the NT writers, but Luke's use of it is especially pronounced. While most of the Israelite traditions Luke engaged were contained in his sacred scriptures, some were among the rich mix of ideas and formulations that had developed during the intertestamental period. This section will overview Luke's use of intertextual parallels. First I will say a word about how such parallels are manifested in Luke's kingdom story. Then I will discuss the various, though often overlapping, functions this intertextuality serves in Luke's narrative, and provide some specific examples along the way.

The Character of Luke's Parallels to Israelite Tradition

The forms in which parallels to preceding Israelite tradition appear in the NT writings, and Luke-Acts in particular, are somewhat variable. Commentators will commonly speak of two main types: citations and allusions. *Citations* are instances in which the NT author directly cites from Israelite tradition, most often the Israelite scriptures. Citations are often introduced with some sort of introductory formula, such as (to use two Lukan examples) "for it stands written" or "as it is written" (e.g., Luke 3:4; 19:46; 22:37; Acts 1:20; 13:33). Alternatively, in Acts 2, Peter states, "This is what was spoken through the prophet Joel" to introduce his citation of Joel 2:28–32 (Acts 2:16). In Luke 4, we are told that Jesus entered the synagogue, received the scroll of Isaiah, unrolled it, "and found the place where it was written" before reading from the prophet (4:17). Citations may also be used without an introductory formula, such as in Acts 4:11, when Peter proclaims, "This Jesus is 'the stone that was rejected by you, the builders; it has become the cornerstone,'" quoting from Psalm 118:22.

What separates citations from allusions is that citations are more often than not introduced, and they closely approximate if not directly follow the original wording of the tradition being cited (most often from the Septuagint or other Greek translation). But note that I said "closely approximate." It is not uncommon for NT authors, including Luke, to alter slightly the wording of a citation to make its connection to the matters they are presenting more apparent. New Testament authors will also create or cite preexisting "composite quotations," in which two or more Israelite texts have been spliced together. For instance, if we carefully examine Jesus' citation of Isaiah in Luke 4, we find that it is very close to the Septuagint's rendering of Isaiah 61:1–2. But when we turn to that Isaian text, we discover that the line "to let the oppressed go free" is not there. That line is taken from Isaiah 58:6. Moreover, we also find that a couple of lines from Isaiah 61:1–2 have not been included in Jesus' citation, such as "the day of vengeance of our God" and "to comfort all who mourn" (Isa. 61:2). An important task for the interpreter, then, is to reflect on why certain phrases were added, and others omitted.[19]

---

19. It is of course possible that Luke is drawing on a preexisting, conflated quotation here. Nevertheless, the question of why Luke chose to follow along with these additions and deletions is still relevant.

Allusions are typically understood as references to particular characters or events of Israelite tradition, or the use of wording, phrasing, or even forms that recall certain traditions. Allusions can range from the obvious to the extremely subtle, and when appearing on the subtle end of the spectrum, perceived allusions can be a point of contention among scholars. Indeed, subtle allusions may be no more than faint echoes resulting from the evangelist simply being influenced by the language or phrasing of a preceding tradition (and perhaps unconsciously so).[20] What often helps to make the case for an *intended* allusion, one that the evangelist wanted his recipients to recognize, is finding references to that same text or broader tradition in the surrounding context of the supposed allusion.

To take an example—and a not-too-subtle one—many scholars find an allusion to Abraham and Sarah in Luke's description of Zechariah and Elizabeth as a barren, elderly couple longing for a son (Luke 1:5–7). The fact that God's covenant with Abraham is mentioned repeatedly in the context (1:33, 55, 73) affirms the likelihood that Luke intended his audience to perceive that allusion. Another useful indicator is when there are multiple points of verbal or conceptual parallels between the Gospel passage and the preceding tradition. In the case of Zechariah and Elizabeth, the additional details of their obvious piety and the claim that their promised offspring will play a key role in the fortunes of God's people (vv. 13–17) add to the recipients' sense that an allusion to Sarah and Abraham is clearly intended. The next step for interpreters, then, is to discern why Luke used this parallel in this pericope. In the case of Luke 1:5–7, most argue that the parallel amplifies the sense that an event critical to the fortunes of Israel and intimately connected to their covenantal relationship with God is about to unfold.

A more subtle allusion, but one that many scholars recognize, occurs in Luke 2:4 as Luke tells us that "Joseph also went from the town of Nazareth in Galilee to Judea, to the city of David called Bethlehem, because he was descended from the house and family of David." The reference to Bethlehem points recipients to Micah 5:2, which identifies the town as the place from which a future, and righteous, Davidic king shall come who will restore Israel. The attractiveness of this proposed allusion is that it helps to create a startling and compelling irony (at least for fans of the peasant infant soon to be born): Caesar's imperial edict that all shall be registered is a blatant manifestation of his power and majesty as emperor of Rome, and yet in giving that bold command Caesar unwittingly fulfills the necessary conditions for the birth of the true Messiah, Lord, and Savior!

20. Those of you who have done a significant amount of writing may have found yourselves occasionally using phrasing from a favorite book or author, and perhaps didn't recognize that you were doing so until you later reread your work.

There is still another type of parallel Luke frequently composes between the events he narrates and Israelite tradition: certain events fulfill "all the prophets" or the entirety of Israel's scriptures (e.g., Luke 24:44–49; Acts 3:18, 24, 43; 17:2–3; 18:28; 24:14; 26:22).[21] Perhaps these could be usefully termed "general affirmations," since they are generalized statements emphasizing the intimate connection between the events Luke records and God's revelation to Israel.

The Purpose of Luke's Parallels to Israelite Tradition

The functions of the parallels to Israelite tradition Luke constructs are also variable, though often overlapping. You may recall that we reviewed the various perspectives characterizing Israelite versions of the kingdom story back in chapters 2–3. We will be leaning on that discussion here as we consider how Luke integrated elements of those kingdom stories into his own through his use of citation and allusion.

LUKE'S STORY AS A CONTINUATION OF ISRAEL'S STORY

One of the more basic, yet important, functions of Luke's citation of and allusion to Israel's sacred traditions is to make clear that the story he tells is the next chapter of Israel's story. The "general affirmations" we noted above clearly serve this purpose, and one could rightly claim that all the intertextual parallels Luke employs contribute to, even presume, this essential claim. Moreover, three types of allusions Luke employs also seem to have this objective as one of their primary functions.

1. *Style.* As noted in chapter 4, starting with Luke 1:5 and lasting through the infancy narrative, the evangelist employs a style containing phrasing and vocabulary that would have reminded recipients of Greek translations of the Israelite scriptures. When this stylistic allusion is coupled with the focus of his narrative, the intent of the allusion is clear. Luke wants his recipients to see his narrative as the continuation of the story recorded in his sacred writings.

2. *Genre.* Most of the literary forms Luke utilizes, in light of his literary milieu, may strike us as natural choices to structure the scenes of his narrative. But Luke includes several generic forms that are not necessitated by the historiographical form of his work. These include annunciations, hymns, genealogies, and prayers. As with Luke's use of a Septuagintal style in his infancy narrative, the function of these generic forms—in addition to serving as useful vehicles for the information that Luke wants to relay—is to score the narrative in tones that remind Luke's recipients of Israel's sacred traditions.

---

21. Fitzmyer, *Acts of the Apostles*, 91.

3. *Character Parallels.* We noted above the parallels Luke draws between major characters within his narrative. Luke also draws parallels between John, Mary, and Jesus, on the one hand, and Israelite heroes of old, on the other. Luke makes explicit connections between John and Elijah in Luke 1:17; 7:27; and 9:8. As mentioned above, Gabriel's greeting of Mary in 1:28–30 associates the girl with characters who played a key part in forwarding God's covenant relationship with Israel (see under "Revelation Leading to Faithful Testimony," p. 107). In his inaugural sermon at Nazareth (also unique to Luke), Jesus proclaims that Isaiah's prophetic vocation announcing good news is now fulfilled in his own arrival (4:16–21), and he compares his ministry to those of Elijah and Elisha (vv. 25–27). Jesus' raising of the widow's son at Nain (Luke 7:11–17, also unique to Luke) recalls Elijah's similar miracle at Zarephath (1 Kings 17:8–24). Luke also draws parallels between Jesus and Moses. In Acts 2:22–24, Peter describes Jesus as "a man attested to you by God with deeds of power, wonders, and signs," clearly echoing the similar description of Moses in Deuteronomy 34:10–12. Then, in his next speech, as recorded in Acts 3, Peter makes the connection even more explicit, here through direct citation: "Moses said, 'The Lord your God will raise up for you from your own people a prophet like me. You must listen to whatever he tells you'" (v. 22). While some of these parallels serve additional functions that I shall comment on below, they also help to underscore that the inauguration of the Kingdom through the characters of Luke's narrative is consistent with God's past acts of deliverance through heroes of old.

THE MATTERS FULFILLED AMONG US

A second basic function of the intertextual parallels Luke employs is to draw more specific connections between key features of the kingdom story he tells and the hopes announced in Israelite traditions leading up to the birth of Jesus. In fact, Luke presents nearly every facet of the emergence of God's Kingdom in Jesus and the ministry of the early believers with parallels to preceding Israelite tradition. By drawing such connections, Luke further stresses that "the matters fulfilled among us" are the continuation of Israel's sacred story. But more than this, he also affirms that the specific contours of these matters were anticipated by the prophets of old. Such parallels are far too numerous to treat comprehensively here. Below are an overview and representative sample that will enable readers to recognize more easily this important feature of Luke's narrative. The bulk of the examples are parallels Luke composes between features of his kingdom story and the Israelite scriptures, though I will also identify a few parallels to Israelite intertestamental traditions.

1. *God's Deliverance and Mercy through Jesus*. A host of texts, in variable fashion, draw from Israelite sacred tradition as they announce the arrival of God's salvation of Israel and humanity in Jesus from both enemies and sin. Here are a few examples. Gabriel tells Mary that her son shall reclaim the throne of David (Luke 1:32–35), and his given name, "Jesus" (v. 31), implies his role as savior. Mary's and Zechariah's hymns—themselves patch-quilt pastiches of biblical citations and allusions—celebrate God's messiah and one who will deliver Israel from its enemies and grant mercy to Israel in ful- fillment of the promises of old (vv. 50, 72, 78). In addition, Simeon's canticle cites Isaiah 42:6 and 49:6 as it extends God's mercy ("a light of revelation") to the gentiles (Luke 2:32).

We noted above Jesus' sermon in Nazareth announcing that he has come to fulfill Isaiah's oracle of salvation, stressing Jesus' deliverance of the mar- ginalized and oppressed. This passage serves as a representative sample of his preaching of "the good news of the kingdom of God" (4:43) throughout Galilee. The narrative to follow includes recurring reminders that the dawn of the Kingdom in Jesus fulfills Israel's long-awaited deliverance in a manner that recalls God's promises and saving ways of the past. The raising of the widow's son at Nain (7:11–17) alludes to Elijah's similar miracle in Zarephath (1 Kings 17:17–24). Moses and Elijah appear with the transfigured Jesus, speaking with him about his "departure" to be accomplished in Jerusalem (Luke 9:30–31). The mission of the seventy-two likely alludes to the seventy-two nations of the world in the Septuagint version of Genesis 10 (and/or to *3 En.* 17:8; 18:2–3) and "can be understood as prefiguring the universal mission in Acts."[22] After the seventy-two return with joy and proclaim the success of their mission, even over the demonic realm, Jesus turns to his disciples and proclaims, "Blessed are the eyes that see what you see! For I tell you that many prophets and kings desired to see what you see, but did not see it, and to hear what you hear, but did not hear it" (Luke 10:23–24).

Adapted from Q and Mark, respectively, the apocalyptic traditions of Luke 17:20–37 and 21:7–36 contain numerous allusions to Israelite scriptures and echo apocalyptic versions of the kingdom story reviewed in chapter 2. In Luke 17, Jesus compares the lack of attentiveness that will characterize humanity on the day of his arrival with the similar lack of awareness prior to the flood and the destruction of Sodom and Gomorrah (vv. 26–32). In Luke 21, a mix of cataclysmic events (vv. 10–11), persecution of the faithful (vv. 12–18), the destruction of Jerusalem, and cosmic upheaval will occur before the arrival of Daniel's Son of Man, "'coming in a cloud' with power and great glory" (v. 27)

22. Green, *Gospel of Luke*, 412.

to redeem the faithful (vv. 25–28). It is difficult to discern whether Luke or the compilers of these traditions before him had any specific intertestamental traditions in view besides Daniel 7 (and possibly the Similitudes of *1 Enoch*) or simply intended to reflect commonly known apocalyptic themes in their presentation of Jesus' teaching. Yet the description of cosmic upheaval in 21:25–28 is replete with allusions to Israel's scriptures.[23]

Luke also draws from preceding Israelite tradition to emphasize the importance of repentance and forgiveness as part of the mercy God now extends to Israel and the rest of humanity. Gabriel's description of John as one who will minister in "the spirit and power of Elijah" includes Israel's return to righteousness (1:17). Zechariah's canticle includes forgiveness of sins as one of the manifestations of divine grace (1:77). Luke follows Mark in characterizing John's ministry as "proclaiming a baptism of repentance for the forgiveness of sins" (3:3) in fulfillment of Isaiah 40:3–5. That Luke sees forgiveness as a basic dimension of God's salvation foretold by the prophets is also evident in the programmatic statement of Luke 24:45–49 and many of the speeches in Acts (see Acts 2:37–42; 3:11–26; 7:1–53; 8:31–35; 13:16–43, 44–52). Even to those responsible for killing the "Author of life," Peter calls for them to "repent therefore, and turn to God so that your sins may be wiped out" (Acts 3:19). For even their acts of rebellion were "foretold through all the prophets" (3:18) and now they can join in the "universal restoration that God announced long ago through his holy prophets" (3:21). Later, Peter will come to understand and proclaim that the good news of God's forgiving mercy in Jesus is meant even for those outside Israel: "All the prophets testify about him that everyone who believes in him receives forgiveness of sins through his name" (10:43).

2. *Jesus: Messiah, Son of God, Savior, Lord, and Son of Man.* We will discuss Luke's exalted portrayal of Jesus in more detail in chapter 9. Here I simply want to establish that another key dimension of Luke's kingdom story for which he employs parallels to Israelite tradition is his characterization of Jesus as Messiah, Son of God, Savior, Lord, and Son of Man. We have already noted the Danielic, and possibly Enochic, background for "Son of Man" above (see "Heavenly Redeemers" in chap. 2, p. 37). So prevalent is the notion in Israelite thought that God would return a faithful Davidic king to the throne of Israel in fulfillment of God's covenant with David (2 Sam. 7:11–16), that the mere mention of "Messiah" (Χριστός) in any Israelite text of Luke's era would certainly recall these associations. The title "Son of God" lacks widespread precedent in Israelite tradition as a designation for an awaited redeemer figure.

---

23. See Darrell L. Bock, *Luke 9:51–24:53*, BECNT 3b (Grand Rapids: Baker Academic, 1996), 1682, for an extensive list of potential allusions to Israelite traditions.

But it does occur twice in the fragmentary *Aramaic Apocalypse* (4Q246) in reference to a messianic figure, and as I argue elsewhere, Luke was likely drawing from 4Q246 text when composing Gabriel's announcement in which Jesus is twice declared "Son of God" (1:32, 35).[24] Luke also follows Mark's lead in reporting the heavenly voice that refers to Jesus as the divine Son during his baptism (3:22), alluding to Psalm 2:7, and during the transfiguration (9:35), alluding to Isaiah 42:1 (see also Acts 13:33).

The angelic host in Luke 2:11 identifies Jesus using two terms that were normally predicated of God in Israelite tradition: "savior" (σωτήρ) and "Lord" (κύριος). Κύριος would have been used by Greek-speaking Israelites and Greek translations of their scriptures as an equivalent of the divine name, Yahweh (יהוה), and the word frequently conveys that sense in many Lukan passages. Σωτήρ is used along with κύριος by Mary in 1:46–47 in reference to Yahweh. Within the context of that hymn, filled with numerous scriptural allusions to God's long-standing relationship with Israel and celebrating the arrival of God's long-awaited salvation promised to Abraham and his posterity, the two titles call to mind Yahweh's character—repeatedly demonstrated but paradigmatically so in the exodus story—as entailing both the will and power to save God's people. In Luke 2:10–11, the terms are, remarkably, both used of Jesus, appearing with "Messiah," as Luke here forges the composite title "Messiah Lord" (Χριστὸς κύριος) for Jesus (see also Acts 2:36). The upshot of this is that the ideas associated with Yahweh within Israelite tradition through the titles Savior and Lord, which Luke has already awakened in Mary's Song, are now applied to Jesus. This is yet another way in which we find Luke drawing points of comparison, even convergence, between the characters of God and Jesus. Somehow, Jesus Messiah is also Savior and Lord. To put it another way, Yahweh's character as Lord and Savior, as that has been revealed in the past and now in the present, is held up by Luke as a lens through which to view Jesus. Peter's use of the title σωτήρ in Acts 5:31 suggests this exalted sense as well: "God exalted him at his right hand as Leader [ἀρχηγός] and Savior that he might give repentance to Israel and forgiveness of sins" (see also Acts 13:23).

3. *Bestowal of the Spirit.* We noted in chapter 2 that a common feature in Israelite visions of the Kingdom's arrival was the bestowal of the Spirit upon the Messiah and/or the redeemed and purified Israel (see "The Bestowal of God's Spirit upon the Messiah and the Faithful," p. 42). These motifs are also important to Luke and are frequently amplified by the evangelist with attending citations or allusions to Israel's sacred traditions. As noted above, Luke takes over Mark's casting of the baptismal scene (Luke 3:21–22; cf. Mark 1:9–11),

24. Kuhn, "'One Like a Son of Man,'" 22–42.

in which the Spirit descends upon Jesus, and God declares Jesus God's "beloved Son," recalling the enthronement and anointing of the king envisioned in Psalm 2:7. Luke then describes Jesus as "full of the Holy Spirit" as he is led into the wilderness by the same Spirit to square off with Satan (4:1). Following the temptation, Jesus returns "in the power of the Spirit" to Galilee (4:14) and subsequently enters the synagogue of Nazareth. There he stands up to teach those gathered and reads from the prophet Isaiah (61:1–2), beginning with the words "The Spirit of the Lord is upon me" (4:18).

First the twelve (9:1–6) and then the seventy-two (10:1–12, 17–20) are sent out with the power to heal and cast out demons. As noted earlier, their numbers—through their allusion to Genesis—likely symbolize the reconstitution of Israel and humanity as a whole. In Luke 24:46–47, Jesus includes the disciples' Spirit-empowered testimony as among the events foreordained by the Scriptures. Then, at Pentecost, Peter explains to the amazed, perplexed, and sneering members of the crowd the source behind the believers' linguistic genius and bold testimony, rooting this event in expectations from of old by citing from the prophet Joel (Acts 2:14–21; Joel 2:28–32). Peter's statement regarding the significance of the Spirit's bestowal continues to reverberate throughout the rest of Acts as recipients are continually reminded of the Spirit's role in empowering believers and their ministry of healing and testimony (e.g., 4:31; 5:32; 6:5; 8:15–17, 29, 39; 9:17; 10:38, 45, 47; 11:12, 16, 24; 13:4, 9, 52; 15:8; 16:6–7; 19:1–7; 20:22–23, 28; 21:4).

4. *The Passion, Death, and Resurrection of Jesus.* Basic to Luke's narrative is the notion that all the features of Jesus' ministry emerge from God's plan to redeem humanity, including especially Jesus' suffering, death, and resurrection. In the first passion prediction, Jesus stresses that "the Son of Man *must* [δεῖ] undergo great suffering, and be rejected by the elders, chief priests, and scribes, and be killed, and on the third day be raised" (Luke 9:22). The same note of certainty occurs in 9:44: "Let these words sink into your ears: the Son of Man is going to be betrayed into human hands." Then, in 18:31, Jesus prefaces yet another passion prediction with the statement, "See, we are going up to Jerusalem, and everything that is written about the Son of Man by the prophets will be accomplished."

Following his resurrection, Jesus continues to teach his disciples that these events fulfill "Moses, the prophets, and the psalms" (Luke 24:44). Now, with the atrocity of The Skull (23:33) and the seeming finality of the tomb overcome, the disciples are ready to understand as Jesus "open[s] the scriptures" to them (24:25–27, 32, 44–48). The essential claim that these pivotal events of Jesus' ministry were foretold by the Scriptures is often repeated in the preaching of the early believers: in Peter's speeches (Acts 2:23–36; 3:17–26;

4:11; 10:34–43), Stephen's defense (7:51–53), Philip's teaching (8:32–35), Paul's witness to the gospel (9:22; 13:16–47; 17:11; 24:14; 26:19–23, 27; 28:23–28), James' judgment regarding Paul and Barnabas' ministry (15:15–18), and Apollos' ministry (18:24–28). Much of their testimony also cites from the Scriptures to validate their claims (2:25–35; 3:22–25; 4:11; 8:32–33; 13:17–41, 46–47; 15:15–18; 28:23–28).

CHARACTERIZATION

Above, I noted the role of intertextual parallels in comparing characters in Luke's narrative to those in Israel's scriptures. One function of such parallels is to stress that the story Luke records is the continuation of Israel's sacred story. At the same time, these parallels may also indicate or affirm key dimensions of a person's or group's role or character. As noted above, the importance of Elizabeth and Zechariah and their crucial place in the arrival of God's Kingdom are suggested by the similarities Luke draws between their circumstances as an elderly, barren couple and Abraham and Sarah's circumstances. The additional allusions to Hannah and Elkanah (1 Sam. 1) that emerge as Elizabeth and Zechariah's story unfolds further prepare recipients to recognize that, like Hannah and Elkanah, they too are called to give their child to the Lord, and to sense the pathos that accompanies Luke's account of John's birth (more on this in chap. 7). We have already noted the elevation of Mary in Gabriel's greeting—which helps recipients appreciate the authoritative character of her testimony after she conceives (vv. 47–55)—and her faithful rumination about her son's role in the fulfillment of God's plan (2:19, 51). The parallels Luke draws between John and Elijah affirm John's role as one who faithfully prepares the way for both Yahweh and Jesus at this pivotal moment in Israel's history.

Meanwhile, the parallels Luke composes between Jesus, on the one hand, and Elijah, Elisha, and Moses, on the other, lead recipients to recognize Jesus' role as a prophetic figure teaching Israel how to be rightly related to God and one another and calling Israel to repentance. They also affirm Jesus' significance by comparing him to these major figures of old, especially in Acts 3 and 7, where Jesus is described by Peter as the "prophet like Moses" who was to come (3:22; 7:37). Yet such parallels can also be used by Luke to indicate that Jesus' authority and teaching ultimately supersede that of these heroes of Israel. On some occasions, recipients discover that Jesus is not, in this instance at least, like Elijah—he does not condone divine violence as a response to these Samaritans' faithlessness (Luke 9:51–56; cf. 2 Kings 1:1–16), and he regards the request to bid farewell to family as inconsistent with the devotion required to serve the Kingdom (9:57–62; cf. 1 Kings 19:19–21). Accordingly, the transfiguration scene emphasizes Jesus' unique identity as God's beloved Son as he appears with Elijah and Moses (Luke 9:28–36). The point of this scene is not in any way to lessen the stature of Moses and Elijah. Far from it. It upholds their remarkable, even unparalleled significance in Israel's past *and* present! But Luke has already revealed to his recipients—through the testimony of Gabriel, the angelic host, God, and even Satan (4:9–10) and demons (e.g., 4:33–34, 41)—that as Messiah, Lord, and Son of God, Jesus has no equal. And thus it is Jesus who is declared the beloved Son and to whom the disciples are called to listen (9:35).

Conclusion

I stated at the start of this chapter that Luke has a penchant for patterns. While his cultural milieu may have placed this literary technique at his disposal, Luke utilized it not simply for aesthetic ends or to aspire to the standards of his literary peers. Instead, he composed these patterns to amplify the central events, themes, and characteristic responses (good and bad) to the arrival of God's salvation, and to present his kingdom story as the next and greatest chapter (at least so far) in the history of God's relationship with Israel and humanity. These parallels, along with the thematic development they facilitate, also weave into Luke's account unifying threads that help to gather all its elements into one complex and compelling narrative tapestry. We turn now to yet another technique Luke employs to shape his story into a consistent and rhetorically effective testimony to the patterns of God's saving activity.

6

The Kingdom Story through Speech and Theme in Luke's Infancy Narrative

Characters freeze. Lights dim. A lone figure steps downstage and pauses. Spotlights illumine him in an almost fiery glow, casting everything else in shadow. The cadence and intensity of his voice parallel his movements as he sweeps, strokes, even grasps the air. But more than anything else, the audience hangs on his every word. For the words, not so much the actor himself, hold center stage. The words gather the characters, their actions, and settings together into a storied witness to the world.

Not unlike a soliloquy in a theatrical performance, character speech in Luke-Acts often provides a rich and engaging testimony to the essential claims of Luke's storied witness to his world. This and the following chapter introduce Luke's use of character speech and the crucial role it plays in the repetition, amplification, and transformation of motifs that define his kingdom story.

Luke's Use of Character Speech

The use of direct and indirect discourse was a common feature of ancient historiography, both Greco-Roman and Israelite. It was employed for a variety of purposes: to dramatize the motivations leading to a moment of decision, to entertain, to characterize key figures, to inform the recipient of details not expressed in the third-person narration, to display rhetorical artistry, or any combination of these. In addition to these functions, character speech in ancient historical narrative often served to focus audience members' attention on specific events portrayed in the narrative and to help them understand why those events were central to the story unfolding before them. In doing so, such discourse also presented those events in ways that drew out themes central to the unity and plotting of the narrative.[1]

Luke likely employs character speech for all of these diverse functions. Yet Luke is particularly interested in shaping the words of his characters to interpret the significance of key events or situations and to propel his narrative along a trajectory of interlacing motifs. Marion Soards, among others, argues that the evangelist shapes the speeches in Acts to cast the events he narrates within a consistent vision of God's intervention in history.[2] According to Soards, Luke used the repetition of speech to unify what was otherwise a diverse collection of materials into "a history that was coherent, and moreover, ideologically pointed."[3] In addition, "Luke weaves speeches into the narrative of Acts and creates emphasis so that the speeches articulate a distinct worldview."[4] Thus, Luke employs the speeches not only to interpret the significance of particular events but also to consistently repeat particular themes, constructing a conceptual framework within which the narrative as a whole is to be understood.

In other words, Luke employs character speech to construct an "ideological context" for his narrative not only in Acts but in the Gospel as well.[5] This is especially apparent in sections of his first volume where he is less constrained by his sources, such as in the infancy narrative and Luke 24. In

1. For an overview of the use of direct discourse in Greco-Roman and Israelite historiography, see Kuhn, *Luke: The Elite Evangelist*, 51–55.

2. Marion Soards, *The Speeches in Acts: Their Content, Context, and Concerns* (Louisville: Westminster John Knox, 1994); for a helpful overview of the study of the speeches of Acts, see pp. 1–11. See also the bibliography on the subject in Joel B. Green and Michael C. McKeever, *Luke-Acts and New Testament Historiography* (Grand Rapids: Baker, 1994), 123–30.

3. Soards, *Speeches in Acts*, 12. According to Soards (161), the distinctiveness of Luke's shaping of speeches is most evident in their "sheer repetitiveness," in terms of the number of speeches as well as their content. Such repetition in character speech is found in both Greco-Roman and Israelite precedents to emphasize particular motifs. Luke, it appears, is further developing this already well-known use of direct and indirect discourse.

4. Ibid., 183.

5. I am using the terms "ideological context" and "ideological framework" as synonyms of "worldview." I don't mean them to convey the negative connotations that are sometimes associated with the word *ideology*, such as "inflexible" and "myopic."

these chapters we find a preponderance of speech that is either unique to or heavily redacted by Luke. These chapters also serve crucial narratological roles that make them obvious candidates for the same kind of ideologically pointed character speech that we find in Acts. The infancy narrative lays the interpretive grid for understanding the significance of the kingdom story to follow, and Luke 24 engages in the complex exercise of drawing the narrative of the Gospel to a close, recapitulating and in some cases redrawing its major themes, while also transitioning recipients into the evangelist's second volume. In both of these sections of the Gospel, the character speech composed by Luke plays an essential part in fulfilling these important functions.

Here I will analyze three of several instances of direct discourse the evangelist employs to introduce the vision of the Kingdom that governs the entirety of his two volumes: Elizabeth's greeting, Mary's Magnificat, and Zechariah's Benedictus. My aim will be to illustrate how Luke employs character speech along with other literary techniques in his infancy narrative to weave prominent motifs into a unified vision of his kingdom story. To prepare for the discussion to follow, the chapter will conclude by reviewing the dominant themes of Luke's Gospel narrative. Chapter 7 will provide a similar analysis of Luke's use of direct discourse in Luke 24, focusing on how its episodes—largely through character dialogue—gather up and recast the dominant themes of the Gospel in light of Jesus' resurrection while also rehearsing the vision of salvation announced in the infancy narrative. Finally, I will discuss how the recast themes and vision of salvation emerging from Luke 24 are taken up in the character speech of Acts.

Character Speech in Luke 1–2

In our discussion of patterns and parallels in the preceding chapter, I pointed out the preponderance of kerygmatic elements in the character speech of Luke 1–2. I also noted that the witnessing activity of characters in the infancy narrative has strong parallels to the witnessing activity of the disciples in Acts. Already by this we should suspect that the instances of character speech that are the source of these kerygmatic details in the infancy narrative function in a manner similar to how the speeches in Acts function. As we look more closely, we find that through the consistent repetition of five dimensions or motifs in the words of his characters at the beginning of the Gospel, the evangelist introduces a distinct ideological context, or "kerygmatic worldview," which is to guide his audience's understanding of his kingdom story.

Five Primary Contours of Luke's Kingdom Story

1. *God Reigns and Brings These Things to Pass.* Fundamental to Luke's interpretation of the events he records in Luke 1–2 is the claim that the saving events that have come to pass are all rooted in the plan, power, and will of God.

2. *Fulfillment of God's Promises to Save.* In conjunction with settings (such as the temple), his description of characters as among the faithful of Israel, and other parallels to Israelite tradition, Luke shapes the words of his characters in the infancy narrative to underscore that the present events mark the fulfill- ment of God's promises to visit and save God's people and even all humanity.

3. *Faithful Response: Believing and Rejoicing in the Good News.* Through- out the infancy narrative, Luke stresses the importance of a faithful response to the in-breaking of God's redemption by contrasting characters (Zechariah vs. Elizabeth and Mary) and by portraying them as responding to the good news of God's salvation with jubilation, praise, and witness.

4. *God's Visitation of God's People in Jesus, the Messiah, Divine Son, and Lord.* Central to Luke's kingdom story is the claim that the awaited coming of Yahweh to restore Israel is accomplished in the advent of Jesus. Moreover, several aspects of Luke's presentation in the infancy narrative cast Jesus as an exalted, even divine, figure and point to the very close relation between Jesus and Yahweh (e.g., 1:26–38). He is the Spirit-conceived Messiah, divine Son, and Lord.

5. *Reversal.* Luke emphasizes that the arrival of God's salvation in Jesus will manifest itself in various ways that upend the prevailing realities of piety and power and expectations concerning God's messiah, as well as human at- tempts to thwart God's saving plan.

Let us turn now to Elizabeth's greeting (1:41–45), Mary's Song of Praise (1:46–56), and Zechariah's Canticle (1:67–80) to see how Luke integrates these motifs through the use of character speech and other features of his narrative.

Elizabeth's Greeting (Luke 1:41–45)

Due to Zechariah's lack of trust and her own faithful perception, Elizabeth holds the honor of being the first human character in Luke's narrative to bear witness to the inauguration of the Kingdom among Israel. Spurred by John's leaping in the womb, she greets Mary's arrival by pronouncing Mary and her offspring blessed and proclaims Mary as "mother of my Lord," who "believed that there would be a fulfillment of what was spoken to her by the Lord" (vv. 42–45). In this brief act of character speech, Elizabeth addresses most of the several dimensions of the ideological context Luke establishes in these opening chapters. God is clearly the one orchestrating and accomplishing these events: God has looked favorably upon Elizabeth, and Mary's conception marks the fulfillment of what Gabriel proclaimed "by the Lord." Elizabeth's beatitude also emphasizes Mary's faithful regard for Gabriel's testimony. Her identification of Mary as "mother of *my Lord*" (v. 43) reminds recipients of the exalted identity of Jesus just introduced in verses 32–35 and also marks the first use of κύριος for Jesus in Luke's narrative. Similarly, her reference to John's leaping in the womb indicates to us that John is already engaged in his mission of preparing the way of the Lord. Elizabeth's greeting also contains a note of reversal, as the elder kinswoman now acknowledges the exalted significance of the younger.

Mary's Song of Praise (Luke 1:46–56)

Following Elizabeth's economical though richly expressive instance of character speech, the Magnificat marks one of the more lengthy testimonies in the infancy narrative to the inauguration of God's reign in Jesus. Whether composed by Luke or adapted from a preexisting tradition, Mary's hymn of praise harmonizes well with the other voices that ring out in the evangelist's celebration of the Kingdom's arrival. Due to the greater level of detail in Mary's and Zechariah's hymns, I will address each of the primary motifs identified above separately as I engage these accounts.

God Reigns and Brings These Things to Pass. From beginning to end, the Magnificat exclaims that the saving event at hand—the conception of Jesus—and the blessings this event brings to Mary and Israel emerge from God's sovereignty and will. So clearly and intentionally does the canticle burst forth with this proclamation that this point hardly needs further elaboration. Yet along with the hymn's celebration of what God has accomplished, the hymn also amplifies certain features of God's character. At the start, Mary rejoices in "God my Savior," an appellation that not only indicates that what God has done for Mary and Israel is a redeeming act but also reverberates with allusion to Israel's sacred story. God's role as savior in preceding Israelite tradition, including the intertestamental kingdom stories we considered in chapter 2, is typically associated with both God's merciful keeping of the convent and his victory over Israel's enemies.[6] Accordingly, Mary repeatedly references God's "mercy" (vv. 50, 54b), and her closing lines announce God's fulfillment of the

---

6. These associations are also represented in the four passages of the LXX that offer the closest parallels to the expression "the Lord my Savior." Each connects the idea of God as savior with God's forgiveness and triumph over Israel's enemies. See the surrounding context of Hab. 3:18; Ps. 24:6–7; Isa. 12:2; Mic. 7:7.

covenantal promises (vv. 54–55). Mary's hymn also celebrates God as "Mighty One" (ὁ δυνατός, v. 49), emphasizing God's sovereignty both absolutely and with respect to "the powerful" (δυνάσται) whom God brings down from their thrones (v. 52). The title casts God as the divine Warrior who overthrows the enemies of Israel (see Deut. 10:17; Ps. 23:8 [LXX]; Jer. 39:18; Isa. 10:21; 42:13; Zeph. 3:17).

Fulfillment of God's Promises to Save. The claim that Jesus' conception marks the restoration of God's people is central to the hymn. As the song develops, Mary's rejoicing in the salvation and blessedness she herself has experienced (vv. 47–49) gives way to a celebration of her son's significance for all of Israel (vv. 50–55). As noted in the previous chapter, allusions to the Israelite scriptures abound in every line of the hymn, so much so that many have characterized the Magnificat as a pastiche of scriptural allusions and quotations.[7] Similarly, Mary's concluding statement in verses 54–55 casts the entire song as a celebration of the fulfillment of God's promises to redeem God's people: God's current act of helping Israel (v. 54a) and remembering God's mercy (v. 54b) fulfills God's promise (v. 55a) to forever extend mercy to Abraham and his descendants (v. 55b). In short, the concluding pronouncement confirms Luke's intent to portray God's mighty intervention through the advent of Jesus as the long-awaited and ultimate fulfillment of God's promise to Abraham and his offspring. Accordingly, the rather awkward placement of "forever" (εἰς τὸν αἰῶνα) at the end of the hymn is probably best explained "by the desire to end the poem with reference to the eternal dimensions of God's accomplishment now being celebrated."[8] Likewise, Robert Tannehill concludes: "The gift of the child is the act of mercy which fulfills the promise given to Israel at the beginning of its history. Thus this gift is placed within the context of Israel's long history of hope and is celebrated as its fulfillment, which makes explicit the significance of the poem's extensive use of traditional biblical language."[9] As Gabriel's announcement has informed Theophilus (see 1:31–35), Jesus is conceived as one who ushers in the fulfillment of the Davidic covenant, for he will rule on the throne of David forever. Here it is announced by Mary that Jesus' birth also marks a culmination of the covenant that called Israel into being (cf. Gen. 12:1–3).

---

7. It has been common for scholars to see Hannah's Song (1 Sam. 2:1–10), which similarly celebrates God's deliverance of Hannah and Israel, as the primary model for the Magnificat. However, others have pointed out that while Hannah's Song may provide a paradigm for the general shape of the hymn, nearly every allusion to the Israelite scriptures, with the exception of v. 48a, finds a closer parallel elsewhere. For a listing of the more obvious allusions contained in the Magnificat, see the helpful chart provided by Brown, *Birth of the Messiah*, 358–60.

8. Nolland, *Luke 1:1–9:20*, 73.

9. Robert C. Tannehill, "The Magnificat as Poem," *JBL* 93 (1974): 274.

Faithful Response: Believing and Rejoicing in the Good News. In her greeting, Elizabeth pronounced Mary blessed because Mary believed the word from God delivered through Gabriel. Now Mary herself erupts in praise befitting one who earlier said, "Let it be with me according to your word" (v. 38). The redundancy provided by the synonymous parallelism of the opening lines and the terminology Mary employs, "My soul magnifies" (μεγαλύνω) / "my spirit rejoices" (ἀγαλλιάω), emphasizes the earnest and heartfelt nature of her celebration of what God has done for her and for all of Israel. Her rejoicing thus matches the joy (ἀγαλλίασις, v. 44) that has already erupted within John and that others shall come to know (1:14).

God's Visitation of God's People in Jesus, the Messiah, Divine Son, and Lord. As a response to her elder relative's greeting, Mary's hymn adds depth to Elizabeth's confession of Jesus as "my Lord" and John's joyful leaping in the womb. The notion that Jesus' coming fulfills God's promised visitation is again put before Theophilus. It is Jesus' conception that leads to Mary's praise of God as Savior, and that same event constitutes God's definitive act of steadfast love and mighty deliverance on behalf of Abraham and his descendants. God's visitation, in fulfillment of God's promises to Israel, is once more extraordinarily localized in the advent of Jesus.

Reversal. In the previous episodes, Luke presented the dimension of reversal through his portrayal of the characters who were first to receive the announcement of God's coming salvation. Zechariah, the faithful priest, proves faithless when confronted with the wondrous news of John's birth and all that it shall entail, while Mary, the peasant girl, embraces even more astounding news with trust, if not complete understanding. Moreover, she and her kinswoman Elizabeth now "speak with a prophet's voice."[10] Yet the reversal magnified in Mary's hymn takes on another form of manifestation as the faithful of Israel are set in opposition to the elite of the Roman world. Representative of God's people, the "lowly" and the "hungry" shall be exalted, while the "powerful" and the "rich" will be brought low. As we noted in chapter 2, the association of God's deliverance of the faithful with reversal of fortune is well represented in Israel's scriptures and intertestamental traditions, as is God's favor upon and exaltation of the lowly or poor, especially in the Psalms (see Pss. 9:9; 12:5; 67:11; 81:1b–4; 108:31; 112:7–8; 139:13; 144:14–16; 146:3 [all LXX]; Isa. 25:4). Moreover, Stephen Farris points out that the typical characteristics of the poor as portrayed in the Psalter are present in the Magnificat.[11] The poor are those

10. Carroll, *Luke*, 46.
11. Stephen Farris, *The Hymns of Luke's Infancy Narrative: Their Origin, Meaning, and Significance*, JSNTSup 9 (Sheffield: JSOT Press, 1985), 122.

who are socially and economically "lowly" (vv. 48a, 52b), and they are "hungry" (v. 53a). In contrast to the "proud" (v. 51), the "powerful" (v. 52a), and the "rich" (v. 53b), the poor are those "who fear [God]" (v. 50). It is these who shall be exalted to share in God's glory (v. 52) and whose impoverished bodies shall be filled with all good things (v. 53a). As John Carroll notes, "Jesus, in carrying out his ministry—with its vision of radical social transformation that elevates the poor and powerless and demotes the wealthy and powerful—will not be an innovator. . . . The social revolution of God's realm continues an ancient story."[12] Here in the Magnificat, however, the typical presentation of the poor undergoes a significant development: "that rescue of the poor which is so characteristic of God" is now on the cusp of being definitively achieved.[13]

In light of the association of the poor with God's deliverance in the Psalter and throughout the Israelite scriptures and intertestamental traditions, some have argued that the presence of this motif here in the Magnificat simply functions as another general expression of God's eschatological deliverance of Israel and should not be read as referring to political or economic realities. This view suffers from two serious oversights. First, as most recent commentators recognize, the terminology Mary employs indicates that the salvation she announces has just as much to do with the basic necessities of life (which the elite had in abundance and the rest in scarcity) as it does with "spiritual" poverty and richness.[14] Accordingly, Joel Green points out that the verbs of verses 51–53, which "sponsor images of God's salvific work that are so concrete and this-worldly," and their setting "within a larger narrative world of foreign occupation and religio-political oppression," together "[require] that we not relegate Mary's vision of redemption to some distant future or spiritualize it as though it were not concerned with the social realities of daily existence."[15] Just as relevant is the fact that (as we discussed in the introduction and chapter 1) religion, economics, politics, and social stratification were all inextricably intertwined in the ancient world (and for most of human history). It simply would not have dawned on Mary, Luke, Theophilus, and other recipients of Luke-Acts, as well as those earlier writers of Israelite texts yearning for the advent of God's eschatological deliverance, to view God's awaited reversal as anything other than "political," "economic," "social," and "religious" all at the same time.

12. Carroll, *Luke*, 52.

13. Farris, *Hymns*, 122.

14. See especially Edouard Hamel, "Le Magnificat et le Renversement des Situations," *Greg* 60 (1975): 55–58, 76–77. See also Brown, *Birth of the Messiah*, 363; I. Howard Marshall, *The Gospel of Luke: A Commentary on the Greek Text*, NIGTC 3 (Grand Rapids: Eerdmans, 1978), 84; Nolland, *Luke 1:1–9:20*, 72, 76; Farris, *Hymns*, 124.

15. Green, *Gospel of Luke*, 100. See also Hamel, "Magnificat," 72.

Summary. Elizabeth's spirit-inspired and joyful greeting is met by Mary's equally jubilant hymn of praise. The Magnificat takes up but then moves beyond the celebration of Jesus' conception as an event that God has accomplished for Mary, to its celebration as a saving act that the Merciful and Mighty One has worked on behalf of all Israel. As the eschatological context established by the preceding episodes has prepared us to see, this saving act is not to be counted merely as one among many that God has performed for God's people. Rather, it puts into motion the decisive, long-awaited era of restoration that marks the culmination of God's promise to restore Israel once and for all. Thus, again, the advent of God's awaited salvation is strikingly particularized in the advent of Jesus. Moreover, the announcement of the Kingdom's arrival in Jesus' conception is already manifested in the exaltation of Mary, God's servant, for the radical reversal of human society that is to mark God's saving reign is already revealed in the blessing that God has bestowed on her as one of the lowly.

Zechariah's Canticle (Luke 1:67–80)

Zechariah's hymn emerges from the story of John's birth and the ensuing controversy over what he is to be named (vv. 57–66). I will have more to say about this poignant scene in chapter 9. Remarkably, even though the setting of the episode clearly indicates that the canticle is a response to the birth of John, only two of its twelve verses (vv. 76–77) actually speak of John and address the question of the people: "What then will this child become?" (v. 66). As a whole, the canticle focuses not upon the Baptist but upon God's visitation and redemption made manifest among the people in the advent of the Messiah.

God Reigns and Brings These Things to Pass. As with the Magnificat, this dimension of the ideological context established by the infancy narrative is so clearly expressed throughout Zechariah's song that it hardly needs discussion. From its opening to its end, the canticle celebrates the accomplishment of salvation as that which stems from God's will to redeem God's people. And yet, as we shall discuss below, God's "horn" or "power of salvation" is embodied in the ministry of God's messiah.

Fulfillment of God's Promises to Save. Similar to previous episodes of character speech in the infancy narrative, Zechariah's canticle draws from a variety of Israelite traditions expressing the promise of God's awaited salvation. At the canticle's start, the visitation and redemption of God is described as God's act of raising up a "horn of salvation for us in the house of his servant David" (v. 69 RSV). By itself, the image of a "horn of salvation" (κέρας σωτηρίας) may not imply a messianic figure: it can serve simply as a reference to God's mighty rule.[16] Yet its coupling with "in the house of his servant David" clearly casts it against a background of messianic expectation. Precedents for the use of "horn" imagery in a messianic context are found at the conclusion of Hannah's Song in 1 Samuel 2:10, in Psalms 88:25 (LXX) and 131:17 (LXX), and in Ezekiel 29:21. It is also important to note that, with the exception of 1 Samuel 2:10, each of these parallel texts not only refers to the Messiah as a "horn" but also provides a description of the messianic figure as a "shoot" or that which "shoots forth."[17] Elsewhere in the Septuagint, the noun "shoot" (ἀνατολή) also refers to an awaited messianic redeemer (Isa. 11:1; Zech. 3:8; 6:12), while the verbal form "to arise" (ἀνατέλλω) is used of a rising sun or star in Numbers 24:17 and Malachi 4:2. Both of these images, that of a shoot/branch (ἀνατολή) and that of a rising (ἀνατέλλω) sun or star, were also common messianic designations in the intertestamental period. Among the DSS, the "Branch" of Isaiah 11:1–10 and the rising Star (and Scepter) of Numbers 24:17 frequently occur in expressions of messianic expectation.[18] The common pairing of these concepts (horn, shoot/shooting forth) in relation to an awaited messiah figure in various Israelite traditions strengthens the claim of many that messianic imagery is again being invoked in verse 78b: literally, "that which springs up from on high will visit us" (ἐπισκέψεται ἡμᾶς ἀνατολή ἐξ ὕψους).

This messianic imagery is presented by Zechariah as a manifestation of God's visitation and redemption of Israel. In the Septuagint, ἐπισκέπτομαι (to visit) most commonly renders the Hebrew פָּקַד and when used of God refers both to God's judgment and to his gracious intervention on behalf of Israel.[19] Similar notions are again in view here—as in the Magnificat—as the song celebrates God's imminent salvation in the form of deliverance from enemies (vv. 71, 74) and manifestations of God's mercy: forgiveness of sins (v. 77); "light to those who sit in darkness and in the shadow of death" (v. 79a); and guidance in the way of peace (v. 79b). For Luke, forgiveness and revelation leading to illumination are especially crucial markers of the Kingdom's arrival and are associated with God's mercy manifest in Jesus throughout Luke's narrative.

16. The closest parallels come from 2 Sam. 22:3 and Ps. 18:2, each of which applies the designation to God in a nonmessianic context.

17. Psalm 131:17 reads: "There I will cause a horn to sprout up [ἐξανατέλλω (LXX)] for David," and Ezek. 29:21 states, "On that day I will cause a horn to sprout up [ἀνατέλλω (LXX)] for the house of Israel."

18. See Collins, Scepter and the Star, 49–73. References to an awaited messiah as "Branch" or "Shoot" include CD 7.18–19; 1QM 11.6; 4Q175 (=4QTest) 12; 4Q161 (=4QIsaᵃ); 4Q252 (=4QPatriarchal Blessings) 3; 4Q285. References to a messianic "Star" include CD 7.14–21; 1QM 11.6; 4QTest 12; cf. T. Levi 18:3.

19. E.g., Gen. 21:1; 50:24; Exod. 4:31; Ruth 1:6; Pss. 80:14 (LXX); 105:4 (LXX); Jer. 15:15; Jud. 13:20; Pss. Sol. 11:2.

Faithful Response: Believing and Rejoicing in the Good News. The Benedictus models the call to respond to the good news of God's salvation with faith and rejoicing. Because of his lack of faith, Zechariah was silenced. Now, as he acts in accord with Gabriel's words concerning the naming of his son (v. 63; cf. 1:13), Zechariah's tongue is loosed and he erupts in a manner befitting his character as a righteous and now inspired one of God. Filled with the Holy Spirit, he becomes God's sentinel, weaving together an extraordinarily rich and sophisticated celebration of God's victory.

Yet the canticle not only models such faith and rejoicing but also directly addresses this dimension in verses 74–75, where a faithful response is presented as an intended result of God's salvation: "that we, being rescued from the hands of our enemies, might serve him without fear, in holiness and righteousness before him all our days." Here the dimensions of God's restoration and call to devotion overlap. Moreover, the terminology employed in the expression adds depth to what it means to believe and rejoice in the good news. In many contexts, to "serve" or "worship" (λατρεύω) carries a cultic sense. However, Zechariah's praise echoes God's revelation on Sinai that the Israelites have been saved in order that they may be a people set apart for Yahweh, a people called to service that "embraces the whole way of communal life" (Exod. 19:3–6; cf. Josh. 24:14–15; Eph. 4:24).[20] The concluding phrase, "all our days," not only testifies to the definitive nature of God's deliverance but also emphasizes the expansiveness of this call to serve God: it is to define one's existence.

God's Visitation of God's People in Jesus, the Messiah, Divine Son, and Lord. As noted above, the setting of the song (vv. 57–67, 80) is clearly focused on the significance of John, as the song follows the people's question, "What then will this child become?" (v. 66). Yet with the exception of vv. 76–77, Zechariah's hymn centers on the redemption to be won by the messianic "horn of salvation" (v. 69). The stark contrast between the setting of the canticle and its actual contents indicates that the person and significance of John are to be wholly understood with respect to the arrival of God's promised deliverance in the person of the Messiah. The few verses that actually focus on John's role confirm this perception. Although John himself will give knowledge of salvation for the forgiveness of sins (v. 77), such granting of knowledge is explicitly cast as preparatory (v. 76) for the salvation that comes in the visitation of the messianic "dawn from on high" (vv. 78–79).

Other features of the canticle add to the convergence of mission and person between Jesus and God that we saw in preceding episodes. At the very start of the hymn, the visitation of God (v. 68b) is made equivalent to the raising

20. Green, *Gospel of Luke*, 117.

up of the Davidic messiah (v. 69), who in the context of the infancy narratives can only be Jesus (1:32–35). Furthermore, at the conclusion of the hymn, the event that embodies the salvation stemming from the tender mercy of God is the advent of the messianic dawn from on high (v. 78). Thus, as further indicated by a key terminological parallel bracketing Zechariah's praise and prophecy, the visitation (ἐπισκέπτομαι, v. 68) of God, as already suggested by verse 69, is fully encompassed by the visitation (ἐπισκέπτομαι, v. 78) of the Messiah. The close relation between Jesus and God is also suggested as John is proclaimed as one who will prepare the way of "the Lord" (v. 76). That κύριος should here be taken as referring to Yahweh is suggested by the fact that in the previous description of John's mission (1:15–17, esp. v. 16), it was clearly God for whom John was to prepare. Also, the expression "his people" in verse 77 would likewise seem to indicate that Yahweh is in view. But because Luke has repeatedly indicated—including here in this canticle—that the Messiah is the one for whom John prepares, and because he has already employed "Lord" (κύριος) for Jesus in verse 43, many see the use of "Lord" in verse 76 as a direct reference to Jesus.[21] Yet perhaps John Nolland is closest to the mark when he refers to the occurrence of "Lord" here as a "happy ambiguity."[22] For even an ambiguous appearance of the title in the present episode invites consideration of the relationship between Jesus and Yahweh. Luke has set all the pieces in place for us to make the connection that Jesus is the one who comes after John—*in fulfillment of God's coming*. The ambiguity of verse 76 further leads Luke's audience to see that somehow both Jesus and Yahweh are the κύριος whose way John readies.

Summary. With the loosing of Zechariah's tongue, this righteous one of God belatedly erupts with praise and witness celebrating the good news manifest in his midst. The awaited arrival of God's deliverance is once more cast against a backdrop of eschatological fulfillment. Just as Israel's ancient traditions foretell, Yahweh's salvation encompasses the restoration of the faithful from threat within and without. Even the call to respond to God's redemption with rejoicing and devotion is portrayed as a benefit of the salvation that God works among God's people. The convergence of mission and person between Jesus and God that has characterized the previous episodes continues here. In the hymn's opening lines, God's visitation and redemption of Israel is presented as God raising up a messianic horn of salvation. Then, at the psalm's end, God's redemption and visitation is presented as the visitation of the messianic "dawn

---

21. E.g., H. Schürmann, *Das Lukasevangelium I. Kommentatar zur Kap 1,1–9,50*, HTKNT 3 (Freiburg: Herder, 1969), 90–91; Fitzmyer, *Luke I–IX*, 85–86, 379; Farris, *Hymns*, 139; Green, *Gospel of Luke*, 118.

22. Nolland, *Luke 1:1–9:20*, 89.

from on high." Once more, Luke designates the Coming One as κύριος, inviting his audience to ponder the mystery that the one for whom John prepares should, like Yahweh, be called Lord.

Speech and Theme in the Gospel Narrative

The preceding discussion has endeavored to illustrate how Luke weaves through the words of his characters in the infancy narrative a conceptual frame of reference, or kerygmatic worldview, for his narrative to follow. If space would allow, we could also explore how the vision of salvation announced in Luke's opening chapters is re-presented in several instances of character speech throughout the Gospel that are unique to or heavily redacted by Luke, such as the summary of John's preaching (Luke 3:7–17); Jesus' sermon in Nazareth (4:18–21); his announcement of blessings and woes (6:20–26); the parable of the rich man and Lazarus (16:19–31); the paired parables of the unjust judge (18:1–8) and the Pharisee and tax collector (18:9–14); and the coming of the Son of Man (21:7–36). Through these instances of direct discourse as the Gospel continues to unfold, Luke reminds Theophilus and others of the prominent contours of his kingdom story introduced in the opening chapters. However, it is also important for us to recognize that Luke's story is even more richly variegated than indicated by these five fundamental dimensions. As we move into the body of the Gospel, we find these five essential contours of Luke's narrative taken up by several prominent motifs that emerge as he now incorporates the traditional material from Q and Mark with several episodes from his own sources.

I will review each of these motifs below, illustrating how they are repeatedly manifested in the Gospel narrative. But first let us consider how these themes from the body of the Gospel take up and advance elements of Luke's worldview introduced in his infancy narrative. (1) The divine and scriptural necessity of Jesus' suffering, death, and resurrection not only emphasizes the theocentric character of Luke's kingdom story; it also characterizes Jesus' ministry as fulfilling Israelite hopes for deliverance. (2) Rejection of Jesus largely arises because of Jesus' challenge to the notions of righteousness, power, and economy prevalent in his society and because of his proclamation of God's imminent reversal. This rejection also displays the antithesis of faithful witness as many of Jesus' fellow Israelites tragically fail to recognize the arrival of the Kingdom in his ministry. (3) Discipleship as a journey of witness and sacrifice likewise includes clear points of connection to the dimension of faithful witness, as Jesus urges his multitude of disciples to take up their own crosses while following him to Jerusalem. (4) Relatedly, misunderstanding illuminates the struggle of the disciples (not unlike Zechariah) to embrace and embody the full reality of the Kingdom. (5) Jesus' ministry in the power of the Spirit further develops the confession that Jesus is the divine Messiah, Son of God, and Lord, as Jesus is portrayed as engaging in ministry and enacting God's will in ways that no mere mortal could achieve, and in ways that bear witness to the world-defying character of the Kingdom. (6) Finally, table fellowship with Jesus as a manifestation of life in the Kingdom includes multiple points of contact with the core elements of Luke's narrative introduced in the infancy stories. It is often during meal scenes that the world-defying character of the Kingdom is unveiled, and sometimes resisted. Jesus is also depicted in these scenes as host and Lord who mediates the reality of the God's reign in the midst of his companions and calls them to join him in embracing it.

1. The Necessity of Jesus' Suffering, Death, and Resurrection

Throughout the Gospel, particularly in Jesus' passion predictions, Jesus' suffering, death, and resurrection are presented as the fulfillment of God's will and scriptural prophecy. These events are spoken of as a divine "must" (δεῖ, 9:22; 13:33; 17:25; 22:37), "preordained" (ὁρίζω, 22:22), and "in fulfillment of what is written in the prophets" (18:31; see also 22:37: "this scripture must [δεῖ] be fulfilled in me"). Markan and Matthean passion predictions contain similar expressions of divine necessity (though less commonly: Matt. 16:21; 26:54; Mark 8:31) and scriptural fulfillment (Matt. 26:54; Mark 9:12; 14:21, 27). However, only Luke includes the fulfillment formula found in 18:31 as well as the prediction recorded in 22:37.

Luke's emphasis on the divine and scriptural necessity of Jesus' rejection, suffering, and crucifixion can already be discerned toward the end of the infancy narrative as Jesus is taken to Jerusalem by his parents "to present him to the Lord" (2:22). Guided by the Spirit, the prophet Simeon comes into the temple, takes the infant into his arms, and proclaims Jesus as the embodiment of God's salvation (2:25–32), "a light for revelation to the Gentiles and for glory to your people Israel" (v. 32). In saying this, Simeon offers the first direct indication that the arrival of the Kingdom is indeed good news "for all the people" (2:10), Israelite and gentile alike. But then Simeon leaves Mary and Joseph (and Luke's audience) with these ominous words: "This child is destined for the falling and the rising of many in Israel, and to be a sign that will be opposed (and the soul of you yourself will also be pierced by a sword) so that the wayward thoughts of many will be exposed" (vv. 34–35, my translation).

Scholars commonly identify Simeon's description of Jesus as "a sign to be spoken against" (σημεῖον ἀντιλεγόμενον) and the reference to the "rising and falling of many" as an allusion to the "stone texts" tradition. Consisting of a conflation of Isaiah 8:14–15; 28:16; and Psalm 118:22, these texts had been combined in early Christian tradition (see Rom. 9:32–22; 1 Pet. 2:6–8) into a messianic prophecy to help explain Jesus' rejection by his fellow Israelites. Even though Simeon speaks these words near the front end of Luke's narrative, it seems likely that Luke would have intended for his recipients to immediately connect this opposition with Jesus' passion. The parable of the tenants in the vineyard (Luke 20:9–19) is the only other place in the Gospel where the evangelist employs the stone tradition. There he also uses it to speak of Jesus' rejection—in a parable that rather transparently addresses Jesus' impending death at the hands of the unfaithful of Israel. Similarly, in Acts 4:10–11 Luke again uses the image in connection to Jesus' rejection and crucifixion. Moreover, Simeon's parenthetical yet emphatic remark to Mary in verse 35a—"and the soul of you yourself will also be pierced by a sword" (my translation)—also suggests that Jesus' arrest and crucifixion are in view.[23] According to Marshall, "the thought is of the anguish that Mary would share at the general rejection of her Son, culminating in the passion."[24]

How would an allusion to Jesus' death here serve Luke's rhetorical interests? By foreshadowing Jesus' rejection at the start of the narrative in the words of Simeon, a faithful Israelite filled by the Holy Spirit, Luke reveals here what he will also repeat throughout the Gospel and especially in the passion predictions: namely, Jesus' death was no accident. Rather, it was from the beginning a part of God's plan to redeem God's people. Thus, here in the confines of this episode, the wondrous news of God's saving embrace of all nations collides with the tragic truth that many of those whom God has called God's own will turn their backs upon the one begotten as Son of God and Lord.

2. Rejection of Jesus as the Embodiment of the Kingdom

The rejection of Jesus by many of his fellow Israelites is certainly a major plotline of each of the Gospels. That Luke himself presents it as a central motif throughout the body of his Gospel is clear not only from its foreshadowing by Simeon and its essential role in the plotting of the Gospel but also by its frequent appearance in material unique to or heavily redacted by Luke: Jesus' rejection by his fellow Nazarenes (4:22–30); his announcement of blessings and

---

23. For a review of the many interpretations of this statement, see Brown, *Birth of the Messiah*, 462–63, and Bock, *Luke 1:1–9:50*, 248–50.

24. Marshall, *Gospel of Luke*, 123. So also Nolland, *Luke 1:1–9:20*, 121–22.

woes (6:20–26); Jesus' laments over Jerusalem (13:31–35; 19:41–44); and the parable of the ten minas (19:11–27). As evidenced in many scenes of conflict and challenge, Jesus' rejection by some of his fellow Israelites is primarily a result of his alternative understandings of righteousness and the reversal he advocates as a sign of the Kingdom's arrival: for example, the controversies over the call of Levi (5:27–32), fasting (5:33–39), gleaning wheat on the Sabbath (6:1–5), healing the man on the Sabbath (6:6–11), welcoming the "sinful woman" in Simon's home (7:36–50), eating with unwashed hands (11:37–54), and the use of money (16:14–15; 21:1–4).

3. The Disciples' Misunderstanding

Throughout the Gospel, Jesus' teaching concerning his impending passion and resurrection is routinely not understood by his disciples. In two instances, such lack of understanding is expressed in both the active and passive voice:

> And they did not know/understand this matter, and it was concealed from them in order that they may not perceive it. (Luke 9:45, my translation)

> But they did not understand any of these things, and this matter was concealed from them and they did not grasp the things being said. (Luke 18:34, my translation)

It is likely that the passive forms of these constructions reflect the use of the "theological passive," with the implication that the disciples' lack of comprehension is by divine design. Some commentators dispute this and instead argue that the disciples alone are to bear the responsibility for their obtuseness.[25] However, the use of the passive voice in these passages is unique to Luke (cf. Mark 9:30–32), and the redundancy of the expressions in 9:45 and 18:34 seems to be Luke's way of saying, "The disciples did not understand, and the reason they did not understand was that it was kept from them (by God)."

Another indication of the disciples' lack of understanding occurs in comments made by the disciples immediately after Jesus' predictions of his suffering. Following Jesus' second passion prediction (9:44–45), the disciples argue among themselves as to which of them is the greatest (9:46). Jesus responds with instruction meant to correct their perceptions of greatness (9:47–48). During the Passover meal, Jesus' statements concerning his betrayal and suffering (22:21–22) are once again followed by the disciples' dispute about greatness (v. 24) and Jesus' corrective instruction (vv. 25–27). The scene concludes

---

25. E.g., Green, *Gospel of Luke*, 390, 845.

with Jesus' final passion prediction (v. 37), followed by yet another instance of the disciples' misunderstanding ("Lord, look, here are two swords") and Jesus' correction (v. 38). The juxtaposition of Jesus' comments concerning his betrayal and suffering with the disciples' clearly inappropriate comments (dispute about greatness, possession of swords) reveals the disciples' inability to comprehend how Jesus shall accomplish God's salvation and that the Lord whose example they are to follow is one who shall submit to the suffering of the cross. This state of affairs is also dramatically illuminated by the fact that the clearest references to the disciples' lack of understanding (9:45; 18:34) are in response to the passion predictions that occur in immediate proximity to the start (9:51) and conclusion (18:31–33) of the travel narrative. In effect, the disciples follow Jesus all the way to Jerusalem, from beginning to end, without ever grasping the real reason for the journey!

4. Discipleship as a Journey of Witness and Sacrifice

As we discussed in chapter 5, Luke uses the journey theme and travel section as one means of unifying the otherwise episodic character of the pericopes it contains. Yet as already noted, the journey on which Jesus embarks in 9:51 is not one that he intends to take alone. Before and throughout the travel section, Luke portrays Jesus' journey as a model for the mission that the disciples are to embrace as their own. In anticipation of his turn toward Jerusalem, Jesus requires, "If any want to become my followers, let them deny themselves and take up their cross daily and follow me. For those who want to save their life will lose it, and those who lose their life for my sake will save it" (9:23–24). Immediately after Jesus sets his face toward Jerusalem, he instructs his potential followers on the demands of journeying after him (9:57–62) and then sends out the seventy(-two), empowering them, as he previously did the twelve (9:1–6), to cast out demons and heal in his name (10:17), while at the same time warning them about the rejection they will encounter (10:10). Among the starkest, even if hyperbolic, of Jesus' instructions to "count the cost" of this journey occurs in 14:25–33. All commitments—familial, political, and economic—are to be subordinated to one's devotion to Jesus and the Kingdom (see also 12:4–34, 41–53; 14:15–24; 16:19–31; 18:18–30). While several of the journey references focus exclusively on Jesus (13:22, 33; 17:11; 19:1, 11, 28), others refer to both Jesus and his disciples (9:52, 56; 10:38). Jesus also prefaces his third passion prediction by stating, "See, *we* are going up to Jerusalem . . ." (18:31). In short, Jesus calls his disciples to follow after him by embracing their own journey of power, rejection, and suffering, with the expectation that their humble and devoted embrace of this mission will also lead to their exaltation as members of God's Kingdom (see especially 18:28–30; 22:24–30).

5. The Ministry of Jesus, Exalted One, in the Power of the Spirit

That Jesus would be specially endowed with the power of the Holy Spirit is already strongly suggested in Gabriel's annunciation to Mary. Whereas John shall be filled with the Holy Spirit "even before his birth" (1:15), Jesus' very conception will be a creative act of the Holy Spirit, resulting in a child that is "holy," set apart as the very "Son of God" (1:35). This suggests a level of pneumatic endowment for Jesus that transcends that of John. John will later confirm this to be true. In response to his admiring followers wondering whether he might be the Messiah, John proclaims, "I baptize you with water; but one who is more powerful than I is coming; I am not worthy to untie the thong of his sandals. He will baptize you with the Holy Spirit and fire" (Luke 3:16–17). John's response to the crowds provides a fitting overview of Jesus' ministry to follow. As one who baptizes with the Holy Spirit and fire, Jesus will manifest the in-breaking of God's reign among them. His ministry shall mark the healing of creation and the call to repentance and righteousness arriving with God's new age.[26] Thus, this motif takes up and advances the convergence of mission and person between Jesus and God that we discerned in Luke's infancy narrative. Jesus, filled with the Spirit, is the Messiah, divine Son, and Lord who inaugurates God's world-defying Kingdom.

Luke's portrayal of Jesus as empowered and guided by the Spirit is affirmed immediately and repeatedly following John's testimony. As Jesus is baptized, the Spirit descends upon him, and God pronounces, "You are my Son, the Beloved; with you I am well pleased" (3:21–22). Then "Jesus, full of the Holy Spirit, returned from the Jordan and was led by the Spirit in the wilderness" (4:1). Following the temptation, "Jesus, filled with the power of the Spirit, returned to Galilee" (4:14). Returning to Nazareth, Jesus reads from the scroll of Isaiah, beginning with, "The Spirit of the Lord is upon me" (4:18). These obtrusively redundant references to Jesus' possession of (by?) the Holy Spirit within the context of eschatological expectation at the start of his ministry cast all his proclamation, teaching, and healing to come as a manifestation of the Spirit's power and the Kingdom's advent. Accordingly, in a summary statement regarding Jesus' ministry of teaching and healing, Luke writes, "They had come to hear him and be healed of their diseases; and those who

26. Recall that these were features commonly associated with God's awaited Kingdom during the intertestamental period; see pp. 32–45.

were troubled with unclean spirits were cured. And all in the crowd were trying to touch him, for power came out from him and healed all of them" (Luke 6:18–19; see also 8:25; 9:43). As we shall discuss in more detail in chapter 9, Luke also frequently employs "Lord" for Jesus in an absolute sense throughout the Gospel to indicate Jesus' exalted, authoritative identity as he goes about his ministry of teaching and healing.

The attention Luke gives to Jesus' frequent engagement in prayer is also likely connected to his portrayal of Jesus as filled with the Holy Spirit. When Jesus is praying during his baptism, the Holy Spirit descends upon him (3:21), implying that prayer serves for Jesus as a means of accessing the Spirit's power or inspiration. Accordingly, Luke repeatedly—and more so than the other evangelists—shows Jesus in prayer (5:16; 9:28–29; 10:21–22; 11:1), including at pivotal moments in his ministry when he is facing some sort of trial or choice (6:12; 9:28–36; 22:41–44). In addition, Luke prefaces a prayer of praise by Jesus with the phrase "At that same hour Jesus rejoiced in the Holy Spirit" (10:21–22), thus identifying the Spirit as the empowering impetus for the prayer (see also 1:67; 2:27; Acts 4:31). Moreover, Jesus also teaches or encourages his disciples how to pray that they too may be filled with the Spirit (Luke 11:13) and be led in ways consistent with God's will or be empowered to resist temptation (e.g., 11:2–13; 18:1–8; 22:46).

6. Table Fellowship with Jesus as a Manifestation of Life in the Kingdom

In chapter 5 we discussed Luke's use of meal scenes to emphasize three features of Jesus' ministry. First, Jesus' table fellowship is radically inclusive, as Jesus shares table with characters of wildly varied backgrounds and social locations, including those whom many label as "sinners" (e.g., 5:30; 7:34, 37; 19:1–10). Second, Jesus uses these meal scenes as occasions to teach about the Kingdom and the radical reorientation of perspective that life in the Kingdom demands. Frequently, Jesus challenges the honor and status concerns that were the "unwritten rules" governing such meals, and instead he unveils actions and dispositions more in keeping with the Kingdom, such as humility, repentance, and compassion (e.g., 7:36–50; 11:37–54; 14:1–24; 19:1–10). Finally, throughout the Gospel, table fellowship presents Jesus as a provider or savior, either as one presiding over the meal or as one who offers God's salvation to others. In sum, Luke's meal scenes present Jesus as the host or provider of the kind of fare and community that truly lead to blessing. Accordingly, in the Gospel, the practice of table fellowship with Jesus is itself a manifestation of God's new age.

Conclusion

Essential to the story that Luke tells is the speech of his characters as well as the thematic tapestry that these characters weave though their witnesses to the Kingdom. Already by the end of Luke 2, Theophilus and other recipients of Luke's narrative know the fundamental contours of the salvation the evangelist proclaims in the narrative to follow. By the persistent yet engaging cadence of themes amplified by spirited testimony and beautiful orations rejoicing in the arrival of God's salvation in John and Jesus, recipients cannot help but be drawn into the hopes, expectations, and challenges of this new world unveiled before them. These motifs go on to provide the conceptual framework for the rest of Luke-Acts, the rudiments of Luke's kingdom story, within which he knits still other story lines and features of the Kingdom of God.

7

The Kingdom Story
through Speech and Theme
in Luke 24 and Acts of the Apostles

This chapter will continue where the previous one left off, focusing now on the crucial role that character speech serves in Luke 24 and Acts.

Speech and Theme in Luke 24

In my view, Luke 24 is an impressive literary and rhetorical achievement. In these closing scenes, Luke artfully composes three episodes filled with drama, irony, humor, intensifying suspense, and joyful resolution. But the final chapter is noteworthy not only for its dramatic appeal. Here Luke draws his preceding narrative to a close with an incredible combination of sophistication and seemingly unobtrusive ease.

First of all, Luke shapes these stories, and especially the character speech they feature, to rehearse in concentrated fashion the vision of salvation presented in Luke 1–2. In fact, all the dimensions of the worldview that Luke presents in his opening chapters are recapitulated here in Luke 24. Luke's focused re-presentation of the worldview introduced in the infancy narrative leads his audience to discern that the salvation proclaimed at the Gospel's beginning is brought to fruition in Jesus' ministry, his death, and, above all, his rising from the dead. Thus, Luke 1–2 and 24 provide an interpretive frame for understanding the Gospel as a whole.

However, in Luke 24 the evangelist not only reasserts each of the main elements of the ideological context he establishes in the Gospel's opening chapters; he also integrates the major themes that dominate the Gospel narrative following the infancy narrative. In bringing his Gospel to its dramatic conclusion, Luke portrays the convergence and transformation of these motifs in light of Jesus' resurrection, and he does this primarily through character speech. As noted above, the motifs that dominate Luke's kingdom story following Luke 1–2 continue to reflect the multiform vision of salvation introduced in the infancy narrative. But here in his final chapter Luke shows how the major story lines of the Gospel are recast or resolved, and how the Kingdom advances, once Jesus rises from the dead.

Here I want to offer the reader a word of encouragement. I realize that it may be a bit of a chore to keep straight all the motifs we have been considering and to follow this somewhat complicated discussion of how Luke converges and recasts his major themes here in Luke 24. If the terminology and preponderance of motifs prove overly onerous, I suggest you focus on those motifs that seem to you most significant and interesting as you read through the following discussion. The basic lesson on Luke-Acts that this chapter offers is that Luke 24 plays a very important role in bringing the narrative of the Gospel to a close and transitioning to the narrative of Acts, and Luke does this while emphasizing the centrality of the resurrection to *everything*. If you come away from this chapter with that firmly in mind and catch some of the details of how Luke accomplishes this, I will be satisfied that you have given it the old "college try" and confident that your understanding of Luke's kingdom story will be the better for it. At the same time, to assist readers with terminology and help them understand how the primary motifs of the Gospel take up and advance the dimensions of Luke's kerygmatic worldview (as I just overviewed on pp. 129–30), and how these same motifs are then recast in light of the reality of the resurrection in Luke 24, I have charted a "CliffsNotes" version of my discussion in figure 7.1.

So the ambitious aim of the following section is to illustrate the rehearsal, convergence, and recasting of motifs that Luke composes in the final chapter of his Gospel. I will attempt to do this as economically as possible by providing a summary of each of the three episodes Luke presents in Luke 24.

Figure 7.1. The Thematic Plotting of Luke-Acts

Vision of Salvation Introduced in Luke 1–2	Major Themes of the Gospel	Major Themes Recast in Light of the Resurrection
In his infancy narrative, Luke unveils the essential dimensions of his kerygmatic worldview, which governs the entirety of Luke-Acts.	*In the body of his Gospel, Luke amplifies a number of key motifs that take up and advance elements of the vision of salvation introduced in his infancy narrative.*	*Luke converges and recasts the major themes of the Gospel in light of the resurrection, bringing them into further alignment with Luke's vision of salvation.*
God Reigns and Brings These Things to Pass *The saving events that have come to pass are all rooted in the plan, power, and will of God to save.*	**The Divine and Scriptural Necessity of Jesus' Suffering, Death, and Resurrection** *In various ways, and especially through the passion predictions, Luke emphasizes that the events of Jesus' ministry will fulfill God's promises and plan to establish God's Kingdom.*	*Prediction becomes proclamation: all this has occurred in fulfillment of the Scriptures and the plan of God.*
Fulfillment of God's Promises to Save *The present events mark the fulfillment of God's promises to visit and save God's people and even all humanity.*		
Faithful Response: Believing and Rejoicing in the Good News *Recipients of God's revelation are called to respond to the good news of God's salvation with trust, praise, and witness.*	**Rejection of Jesus as the Embodiment of the Kingdom** **The Misunderstanding of the Disciples** **Discipleship as a Journey of Witness and Sacrifice** *These three motifs underscore, via negative and positive examples, the importance of faithfully responding to the Kingdom's arrival and the radical form of righteousness it demands.*	*Ignorance and faithlessness must end: the time for forgiveness and blessing is at hand for all who repent and trust in Jesus as resurrected Lord.* *The disciples take up their own ministry in the power of the Spirit, a journey of witness and sacrifice as they shape the new community of the Kingdom.*

God Visits God's People in Jesus, the Messiah, Divine Son, and Lord	Jesus, Exalted One, Ministers in the Power of the Spirit: Urging Repentance, Teaching the Ways of the Kingdom, Healing, and Prayer	*The resurrection of Jesus—the Exalted One—reverses human rejection and is the pivotal event in the advancement of God's awaited Kingdom.*
The awaited coming of Yahweh to restore Israel is accomplished in the advent of Jesus, the Spirit-conceived Messiah, Divine Son, and Lord.	Table Fellowship with Jesus as a Manifestation of Life in the Kingdom	
Reversal *God's salvation arrives in Jesus in ways that upend the prevailing realities of piety and power, expectations concerning God's messiah, and human attempts to thwart God's saving plan.*	*These two motifs continue to emphasize Jesus' exalted identity and the world-defying character of the Kingdom.*	

The Angels' Announcement and the Women's Report (Luke 24:1–12)

On the first day of the week, at early dawn, Mary Magdalene, Joanna, Mary the mother of James, and others with them came to the tomb, bringing the spices they had prepared. But when they went into the tomb, no body was to be found! These women were planning to honor their memory of Jesus by preparing his body for burial. Little did they realize that Jesus had already prepared their memories to honor the resurrection of his body as the manifestation of the Kingdom in their midst. Angels arrive to rebuke and remind: "Why do you look for the living among the dead? He is not here, but has risen. Remember how he told you, while he was still in Galilee, that the Son of Man must be handed over to sinners, and be crucified, and on the third day rise again" (vv. 5–7).

Rehearsing and Recasting Themes from the Gospel

In reciting Jesus' passion predictions, the two angelic figures continue the Gospel's claim that Jesus' rejection, suffering, death, and resurrection are all in accord with God's plan to redeem God's people: "the Son of Man must [δεῖ] be handed over to sinners" (v. 7). With Jesus' resurrection, however, what was once prediction has now become proclamation. Rather than prophecy of a future event, Jesus' words recited by the angels and remembered by the women now interpret the significance of the empty tomb: he is risen. Accordingly, the message that Jesus is alive envelops the angels' announcement (vv. 5, 7c) and indicates the reason that Jesus' earlier words now become kerygma.

Emerging alongside the Gospel themes of rejection and the divine necessity of Jesus' passion and resurrection is the disciples' misunderstanding. The women (and Peter?) are both perplexed by the revelatory reality of the empty tomb (24:4, 12).[1] However, the rebuking tone of the angels' address to the women and the angels' command to "remember" Jesus' words reveal that Luke is also recasting this motif. Jesus' instructions should have prepared them to understand the significance of his missing body. In fact, those instructions should have made a trip to the tomb itself unnecessary: "Why do you look for the living among the dead?" (v. 5). Because the events that Jesus predicted have now come to pass, culminating in Jesus' resurrection, more is now expected of his followers. The messengers of heaven indicate that with Jesus' resurrection the understanding that before had been kept from them (9:45; 18:34) is now to be grasped and proclaimed.[2] Yet where human faith fails, heaven's grace provides. Prompted by the angels' rebuke and instruction to recall Jesus' words, the women remember and return from the tomb to tell "all this" to the eleven and "all the rest" (v. 9). Thus, we see here the first instance of the threefold pattern characterizing each episode of Luke 24 that we discussed in chapter 5:

> revelation (empty tomb) →
> misunderstanding (women perplexed) →
> corrective instruction (angels' rebuke) →
> understanding (the women remember) →
> proclamation (they tell all this to the eleven and all the rest).

Recalling the Vision of Salvation Introduced in Luke 1–2

It will not be until the final episode of Luke 24 that the vision of salvation established in the birth narrative will be expressed with a fullness matching its portrayal in the episodes of Luke 1–2. Nevertheless, at least four dimensions

---

1. An important text-critical issue related to Luke 24 concerns the so-called Western noninterpolations or omissions in Luke 24:3, 6, 12, 36, 40, 51, 52 found in Codex Beza (Codex D). Westcott and Hort's Greek Text (1881) considered these "omissions" genuine, and their assessment was commonly adopted by interpreters. However, with the discovery of the Bodmer Papyrus 75 (P[75]), which contains the longer readings and is the earliest known witness by two hundred years (ca. 175–225 CE), many recent commentators and text critics accept most of the longer readings as genuine. Carroll (*Luke*, 479–80), however, considers the account of Peter in v. 12 a later addition, and I am inclined to agree.

2. Additional support for this point is provided by the speeches in Acts, in which leading characters identify the period preceding Jesus' resurrection as a period of ignorance that both Israelites and gentiles are now called to leave behind (see Acts 3:17; 13:27; 14:16; 17:23).

of the worldview Luke establishes in his opening chapters are represented in
the angels' announcement as Luke begins to recast the main story lines of the
preceding narrative in light of the resurrection.

The motif that God reigns and brings these saving events to pass is clearly
manifested in divine necessity expressed by the angels (v. 7). In addition, the
angels' announcement of fulfillment recalls and confirms the confidence expressed in the infancy narrative that God will indeed accomplish God's plan of
salvation. Another dimension of the ideological context that receives attention
in the angels' words, in tandem with the third-person narration, is that the
good news of God's coming salvation is to be met with trust and rejoicing.
The obtuseness of these women disciples finally intersects with, and now is
overcome by, the necessity that the good news of God's salvation in Jesus be
embraced with comprehension, faith, and witness. A fourth dimension engaged here is reversal, manifested in several ways. Women are the first human
characters to learn of, comprehend, and proclaim the reality of the resurrection. Reversal is also inherent in the notion that the Messiah is to be rejected,
suffer, and be crucified. Yet still another form of reversal is also expressed: a
"reversal of the human *no* to Jesus."[3] Jesus has undergone one of the most
extreme acts of violent rejection and humiliation, but now he has been raised
and exalted in accordance with God's plan (v. 7).

Summary

The angels' rebuke, announcement, and charge to remember reveals to the
women disciples the significance of the empty tomb. These words begin the
convergence of major Lukan themes taking place in this chapter as they recall
Jesus' rejection and the divine necessity of Jesus' suffering, death, and resurrection, and as they confront the seemingly impenetrable misunderstanding of
the disciples. At the same time, this instance of character speech serves notice
that with the rising of the Messiah things are no longer as they were: prediction that confounds has now become proclamation that yields understanding.
Dimensions of Luke's vision of salvation introduced in Luke 1–2 are also
signaled by the angels' words. Once again, as always with Luke, what takes
place is the result of the will and sovereignty of God. These extraordinary
events fulfill God's intention to save while reversing human expectations and
faithless deeds, calling for faith and joyful witness.

3. Charles H. Talbert, "The Place of the Resurrection in the Theology of Luke," *Int* 46 (1992):
22. So also Bock, *Luke 9:51–24:53*, 1900; Charles H. Cosgrove, "The Divine ΔΕΙ in Luke-Acts:
Investigations into the Lukan Understanding of God's Providence," *NovT* 26 (1984): 188–89.

The Journey to Emmaus (Luke 24:13–35)

It has been commonplace for scholars investigating the Emmaus story to preface their commentary with high praise for its artistry, complexity, and depth of insight, and with good reason. In this account, the author so skillfully weaves together a host of his most prominent motifs—and in the guise of a tale so engaging—that one must look carefully to notice and grasp the profound associations and thematic development. It is thus not surprising that some hail it as a "gem of literary art."[4] Because Luke's engagement of these motifs in this episode is more detailed, I will treat them each separately.

Recasting of Major Lukan Themes

1. *The Divine Necessity and Scriptural Fulfillment of Jesus' Death and Resurrection.* The divine necessity of Jesus' rejection, death, and resurrection is again expressed in the character speech of the Emmaus story. Hints of it occur in the disciples' description of the "things that have taken place" (v. 18), which echoes Jesus' own predictions concerning his passion and resurrection: that he would be condemned to death (cf. 9:22, 44; 18:33) and raised to life on the third day (cf. 9:22; 18:33). The clearest manifestation of the motif takes place in Jesus' instruction to his disciples: "Was it not necessary [δεῖ] that the Messiah should suffer these things and then enter into his glory?" (v. 26). Luke's emphatic summation of Jesus' instruction to his disciples ("beginning with Moses and *all* the prophets, he interpreted to them the things about himself *in all the scriptures*" [v. 27]) also expresses the closely related notion of scriptural testimony to Jesus' passion and resurrection. In this episode, as in the previous, what was previously misunderstood prophecy becomes the heart of the kerygma: Jesus suffered, died, and was raised, in fulfillment of the Scriptures and in accordance with God's will.

2. *Rejection.* The rejection motif is implied in the statements acknowledging Jesus' suffering and death.

3. *The Misunderstanding of the Disciples.* The misunderstanding of the disciples is made apparent in the highly ironic, even comical scene in which the Emmaus pilgrims report to their fellow traveler (vv. 18–24) the "things that have taken place there in these days" (v. 18): the disciples narrate to the unrecognized Jesus the rudiments of the kerygma, without realizing that it is *kerygmatic*. They also rebuke Jesus, stating, "Are you the only stranger in

---

4. As pronounced by Reginald H. Fuller, *The Formation of the Resurrection Narratives* (New York: Macmillan, 1971), 104.

Jerusalem who does not know the things that have taken place there in these days?" (v. 18b), when Jesus is quite intimately acquainted with those events! Two other features of the disciples' report also reveal their failure to grasp the significance of the events that have transpired. First, their reference to Jesus as "a prophet mighty in deed and word" (v. 19b) shows that they have understood essential dimensions of Jesus' identity and mission. Yet Jesus has also repeatedly indicated to them that as a prophet he would suffer the same fate as other prophets before him (Luke 4:24–30; 13:31–35; 20:9–18; see also Acts 7:52). A second is still another highly ironic statement: "But we had hoped that he was the one to redeem Israel" (v. 21). This scene manifests a clear instance of what William S. Kurz calls "implicit commentary."[5] Through his use of irony, Luke implicitly—yet dramatically and clearly—reveals the thickheadedness of the disciples.[6]

Luke's portrayal of the misunderstanding of the disciples in light of the reality of the resurrection also reflects the development discerned in the previous episode. In the exchange between the travelers and Jesus, the disciples' culpability is made especially evident as Luke's skill in building pathos is impressively displayed. After hearing the disciples report all the things that correspond precisely to what Jesus had told the disciples to expect, culminating in the women's report that Jesus is alive, Luke's audience is left asking, "What more do they require to believe?" Yet instead of putting the pieces together, the disciples then report a visit to the tomb by some of their group. They found it exactly as the women had said. But this still has not penetrated the stupor clouding their hearts and minds! Almost casually, they dismiss what they have heard from the women and the obvious manifestation of its truth before them: "but they did not see him" (v. 24). Jesus' ensuing rebuke (echoing the frustration welling up in Luke's audience) could not be clearer in naming the shortcoming of the disciples: "Oh, how foolish you are, and how slow of heart to believe!" (v. 25).

Even though Jesus' words to his disciples throughout the Gospel, now confirmed by the events taking place before them, should have been sufficient to lead the disciples to rejoicing, more is needed. It is only through Jesus' explanation of the divine and scriptural necessity of the passion that the disciples come to comprehend the significance of what has taken place (vv. 25–27).

5. William S. Kurz, *Reading Luke-Acts: Dynamics of Biblical Narrative* (Louisville: Westminster John Knox, 1993), 143–44, 151.

6. Kurz (ibid., 136) explains that "the key to irony in Luke-Acts is to approach the narrative on two levels: on a higher level, the readers share with the implied author and his narrator insight and information lacking to dramatis personae on the lower level of the plot line within the account."

This development is not only indicated by third-person narration but is also emphasized by the character speech of the episode. After Jesus had been made known to them in the breaking of the bread, the disciples exclaim to themselves, "Were not our hearts burning within us while he was talking to us on the road, while he was opening the scriptures to us?" (v. 32). The fact that the disciples have transitioned from those who neither understand nor believe to those who now grasp *and* proclaim the good news also finds expression in verse 34: "the Lord has risen indeed!"[7] As revealed through character speech, the disciples' seemingly impenetrable lack of comprehension is giving way to Easter faith. The resurrection and the revealing word of the risen Jesus pave the way for this transformation.

4. *Discipleship as a Journey of Witness and Sacrifice.* Residing subtly yet notably in the third-person narration and character speech of the Emmaus pericope is the evangelist's recasting of the journey motif.[8] The prevalence of terminology that characterizes the well-known travel section of the Gospel (9:51–19:44) reveals Luke's use of the motif here in recounting Jesus and his disciples' journey to Emmaus: "to go" (πορεύομαι; 24:13, 15, 28 [2x]); "to walk" (περιπατέω; v. 17); "to come near" (ἐγγίζω; vv. 15, 28); "the way" (ὁδός; vv. 32, 35). The occurrence of "the way" in the character speech of the Emmaus disciples (v. 32) and the evangelist's summary statement (v. 35) is especially telling, given the repeated use of the term by the evangelist during the travel section to remind his audience that Jesus is "on his way."[9] The disciples are once again "journeying" with Jesus.

---

7. I suspect, in light of the most awkward phrasing and switch of subjects between v. 33 and v. 34, that the participial form of λέγω ("said") was originally in the nominative plural and not the accusative, with the result that it is the *Emmaus disciples* who announce that "the Lord has risen indeed" and not the "eleven and their companions." The use of the nominative plural in Codex D—while by itself not strong evidence of the nominative as the original wording—at least bears witness to the fact that some early scribes also found the accusative problematic. Why would someone have changed the participle from the nominative to the accusative? Together with the equally awkward and likely secondary phrase "and has appeared to Simon!," this redaction realigns the pericope with the early tradition that the risen Jesus first appeared to Simon (see 1 Cor. 15:5). If my speculation is correct, the original text likely read something like this:

Καὶ ἀναστάντες αὐτῇ τῇ ὥρᾳ ὑπέστρεψαν εἰς Ἰερουσαλήμ καὶ εὖρον ἠθροισμένους τοὺς ἕνδεκα καὶ τοὺς σὺν αὐτοῖς, λέγοντες ὅτι ὄντως ἠγέρθη ὁ κύριος.

And rising that same hour they returned to Jerusalem, found the eleven gathered together and those with them, and said, "The Lord is risen indeed!"

8. As Joseph A. Fitzmyer (*Luke X–XXIV*, AB 28a [New York: Doubleday, 1985], 1558) states, "The subtle yet highly deliberate use of this Lukan motif is not to be missed." So also B. P. Robinson, "The Place of the Emmaus Story in Luke-Acts," *NTS* 30 (1984): 481; David H. Gill, "Observations on the Lukan Travel Narrative and Some Related Passages," *HTR* 63 (1970): 216–17.

9. Luke 9:52, 53, 56, 57; 10:1, 38; 13:22, 33; 14:25; 17:11; 18:31, 35; 19:1, 11, 28.

The reappearance of the journey motif in the Emmaus story suggests that Luke is drawing on the associations he assigned to this theme throughout the Gospel, and that he is also interested in recasting that motif in light of the resurrection. In elucidating this point, I stray from the view of most interpreters that Jesus' journey culminates in his ascension. The primary impetus for the majority perspective is the reference to Jesus' ascension in Acts 1:2, 11, 22 using the verb "take up" (ἀναλαμβάνω). Since the noun "upward reception/elevation" (ἀνάλημψις) is used in Luke 9:51 to refer to the event that will bring Jesus' journey to its culmination, it is likewise taken as referring to Jesus' departure in 24:50–53, or at least to a series of events that culminate in his ascension.[10] While this is an attractive position in light of the verbal parallels between Luke 9:51 and Acts 1:2, 11, and 22, five factors suggest that the term should instead be seen as referring to the passion events that culminate in the resurrection.

First is the simple fact that Luke places the ascension outside Jerusalem. References in the Gospel to the end result of Jesus' journey ("exodus," 9:31; "reception," 9:51; "everything that is written about the Son of Man by the prophets," 18:31) are explicit in naming Jerusalem as the place where that culminating accomplishment is to occur. Second, and building on the first point, Jesus' prediction in 18:31–34 names the passion events *and* the resurrection as that which Jesus is to accomplish *in Jerusalem*. Third, Jesus' proclamation of the fulfillment of the scriptural prophecies takes place before, and does not refer to, Jesus' ascension. Rather, it is focused on the accomplishment of the events culminating in the resurrection (24:6–7, 46). Fourth, as Gerard Mussies observes, in comparison to Luke's account in Acts, the ascension is described rather matter-of-factly in Luke 24:50–51.[11] Rather than the culmination of the narrative, it seems to serve simply as a departure scene, with its setting outside Jerusalem further indicating that what Jesus had set out to accomplish in 9:51 has already been completed. Finally, in 24:44, Jesus says to his disciples, "These are my words that I spoke to you *while I was still with you* . . . ," indicating that with the resurrection Jesus' predictions of his upcoming "exodus," or "reception," have already come to pass. Therefore, despite the references in Acts 1:2, 11, 22 to Jesus being taken up using the verb ἀναλαμβάνω, the evidence weighs in favor of seeing Jesus' journey as reaching its culmination in the resurrection.

10. See Richard J. Dillon, *From Eye-Witnesses to Ministers of the Word: Tradition and Composition in Luke 24*, AnBib 82 (Rome: Biblical Institute Press, 1978), 278; Fitzmyer, *Luke I–IX*, 828; Tannehill, *Narrative Unity*, 1:229; Johnson, *Gospel of Luke*, 162; Green, *Gospel of Luke*, 403–4; Bock, *Luke 9:51–24:53*, 968.

11. Gerard Mussies, "Variation in the Book of Acts," *Filologia Neotestamentaria* 4 (1991): 165–82.

The completion of the journey initiated in 9:51 helps us discern why Jesus and his disciples are once again journeying. Luke is preparing his audience to perceive that with the resurrection, not only has the Gospel's journey reached its end but a new journey is now begun. This journey has been anticipated in the preceding narrative by Jesus' repeated commands to his disciples to follow and by the two separate occasions on which the disciples were sent out to heal, cast out demons, and proclaim the good news (9:1–10; 10:1–12, 17–20). It will be more explicitly indicated in the very next episode and serve as the program for Luke's second volume.[12] Consistent with the appearance of the motif in this passage, it is a journey that will be primarily the disciples' own, but one not without the accompaniment and guidance of their risen Lord.

5. *The Ministry of Jesus, the Exalted One, in the Power of the Spirit: Urging Repentance, Teaching the Ways of the Kingdom, Healing, and Prayer.* Throughout the Gospel, Jesus' ministry in the power of the Spirit was manifested in his miracles, his spoken witness to the arrival of the Kingdom and what it means to take part in it, and prayer. Here in this episode, the Emmaus disciples describe Jesus as "a prophet mighty in deed and word before God and all the people" (v. 19). We also see Jesus' power of word and deed in practice as he interacts with the disciples: rebuking them for their foolishness and slowness to believe (v. 25), calling them to repentance, opening their eyes in the breaking and blessing of the bread (vv. 31, 35), and burning their hearts and minds while opening the Scriptures (vv. 26, 32). Above all else, Jesus' power in the Spirit is most dramatically revealed in his resurrection from the dead.

6. *Table Fellowship with Jesus as a Manifestation of Life in the Kingdom.* We noted above that Luke typically uses meal scenes in his Gospel as occasions to teach about the Kingdom, to emphasize its radical inclusivity, and to present Jesus as the host or provider of the kind of fare and community that truly leads to blessing. Each of these functions is represented here. The meal scene at Emmaus serves as that moment of recognition finally awakening the disciples' grasp of the Kingdom unveiled before their very eyes. Jesus also functions as the host of this meal: in language clearly echoing the Last Supper (22:19), Jesus "took bread, blessed and broke it, and gave it to them" (v. 30). The inclusive character of this meal is more subtly expressed, signaled by the fact that the Emmaus disciples are traveling away from Jerusalem and are not

12. Arthur A. Just (*The Ongoing Feast: Table Fellowship and Eschatology at Emmaus* [Collegeville, MN: Liturgical Press, 1993], 51) has also suggested that the geographical locale of the Emmaus meal foreshadows the spread of the gospel (and thus God's redemption) beyond Jerusalem: "If the Emmaus meal is proleptic of the meal fellowship of early Christian communities, then the location of the Emmaus meal is also proleptic of the primary geographical location where meal fellowship will be celebrated in the Church, i.e., outside of Jerusalem."

part of "the eleven" (v. 33), and in that those who have failed to comprehend the signs of the Kingdom nevertheless receive the grace of understanding.

Along with these obvious affinities to the use of the table fellowship motif in the body of the Gospel, its appearance here with the *risen* Christ now presiding over the meal recasts that motif significantly. After reflecting on the parallels between this scene and Acts 2:42, Arthur A. Just rightly concludes that "the Emmaus meal is the pivotal meal in the table fellowship matrix because it continues Jesus' pre-resurrection table fellowship and is paradigmatic for the table fellowship of the emerging church."[13] As we shall see, table fellowship in Acts continues to manifest the radical inclusivity of Jesus' provision, welcome, and proclamation of the Kingdom. It also becomes an integral dimension of the new community being formed by the ministry of the early believers. But more than this, Jesus' meal with the Emmaus disciples reveals the centrality of his resurrection in making this sacred meal and others to follow possible. For in Acts, it is the reality of God's victory over the oppressive and death-dealing forces of this world, as well as the ongoing ministry of Jesus in the Spirit, that empowers and emboldens believers as they shape themselves into a different kind of community, sharing a different kind of table, beholden to a different kind of Lord.

Manifestation of Luke's Vision of the Kingdom

In the Emmaus story we find the ideological context introduced in Luke 1–2 more fully represented than in the previous episode. Each dimension of Luke's vision of salvation is manifested in the character speech of this passage.

1. *God's Reign, Which Brings These Things to Pass.* The action and sovereignty of God are again encased in the notion of divine necessity and scriptural fulfillment (vv. 26–27, 32). His action and sovereignty are also expressed in the description of Jesus as a prophet mighty in word and deed *before God* (v. 19), which implies that Jesus' power and actions are an extension of divine will. The report of a vision of angels (v. 23) further presumes God's hand at work in the events that have come to pass.

2. *Fulfillment of God's Promises to Save.* Luke's concern to present these events as fulfilling God's promise to restore Israel is evident in the report of the Emmaus disciples: "But we had hoped that he was the one to redeem [λυτρόω] Israel" (v. 21). This is the only occurrence of the verb in Luke's Gospel, while the noun form appears only twice, both times in the infancy narrative to speak of God's redemption of Israel inaugurated in Jesus' birth

13. Ibid., 260–61.

(1:68; 2:38). The irony dominating the disciples' report implies that Jesus is indeed the one who has come to fulfill this awaited restoration. Jesus' rebuke and corrective instruction affirm this sense: "beginning with Moses and all the prophets," Jesus interprets to the disciples the things concerning himself in all the Scriptures (v. 27).

3. *Faithful Response: Believing and Rejoicing in the Good News.* The call to respond to the good news with faith, rejoicing, and witness is well represented by the character speech of the episode. As we have seen, the misunderstanding of the disciples is now cast as lack of faith, both by the implicit commentary in Luke's portrayal of their report and by Jesus' rebuke ("Oh, how foolish you are, and how slow of heart to believe . . ." [v. 25]), and thus it provides a negative instance of the dimension. The remarkable transition depicted in the story offers two positive manifestations of the motif in the character speech of the episode. The disciples' reflection in verse 32 reveals that the disciples now "get it," since the Scriptures have been opened to them by Jesus. Their proclamation that follows also embodies this transition ("The Lord has risen indeed" [v. 34]) and serves to portray the disciples as those who are believing, rejoicing in, and witnessing to the good news of Jesus' resurrection. Finally, the indirect discourse of verse 35 restates and thus emphasizes the jubilant witness of the disciples who have returned from Emmaus.

4. *God's Visitation of God's People in Jesus, the Messiah, Divine Son, and Lord.* We saw in Luke 1–2 that Luke presents a convergence of mission and person between Jesus and Yahweh. This dimension is again manifested by several features of the Emmaus pericope. First, we saw in the infancy narrative that one of the ways Luke suggests this close relation between Jesus and Yahweh is in his use of the title "Lord" for both characters. Here we again find κύριος used in reference to Jesus (v. 34), which, like the many uses of the title throughout Luke, reflects early Christian devotion to Jesus. Moreover, Jesus describes his exaltation as Messiah as "enter[ing] into . . . glory" (v. 26). What one would instead expect to find here in light of Jesus' previous passion predictions and the angels' call to remember (vv. 6–7) is a reference to the Messiah being raised from the dead. This has led some commentators to understand the statement as referring primarily to the resurrection.[14] This view is consistent with my argument above that Jesus' journey culminates in the resurrection. At the same time, Jesus' entrance into δόξα ("glory") also likely designates Jesus' authority and power as one exalted to share in the reign of

14. E.g., Fitzmyer, *Luke X–XXIV*, 1566; Dillon, *Eye-Witnesses*, 141–43. Others (e.g., Tannehill, *Narrative Unity*, 1:284; Nolland, *Luke 18:35–24:53*, WBC 35c [Dallas: Word, 1989], 1204) see it as also including Jesus' ascension, so that the resurrection and ascension are viewed as together embodying Jesus' entrance into glory.

God. During the scene of the transfiguration (9:28–36), which culminates in the pronouncement of the heavenly voice saying, "This is my Son, my chosen; listen to him!," Luke alone among the Gospels describes Jesus as appearing with Elijah and Moses "in his glory" (9:32). In the previous episode, Jesus speaks of the Son of Man coming "in his glory and the glory of his Father and of the holy angels" (9:26). Later in the Gospel, Jesus again refers to the Son of Man "coming in a cloud with power and great glory" (δόξης πολλῆς, 21:27). As Robert Tannehill summarizes, "the interest is not just in resurrection but in Jesus' entry into a new status, which involves becoming 'head of the corner' (20:17) or 'sitting at the right hand' of God (20:42–43; 22:69), thereby sharing in God's power and glory as messianic king."[15] The implications of transcendence that Luke evokes by this reference to δόξα—especially in light of the connections he makes in the preceding narrative between Jesus' glory and divine sonship—invite Theophilus to consider Jesus' relation to God as one who embodies God's power and authority.

5. *Reversal*. In my discussion of the previous episode, I noted that the proclamation that Jesus, the messianic divine Son, was to suffer recalled the reversal announced by Simeon in the infancy narrative, while the attending claim that Jesus is alive constituted God's reversal of the "human no" to Jesus. These two notions of reversal are presented again in the Emmaus story. The disciples report that Jesus, a prophet mighty in word and deed, suffered rejection and death at the hands of the chief priests and leaders of Israel (v. 20). But this report is then followed by the incredible news that Jesus is alive (v. 23b) and by Jesus' explanation of the divine origins of both forms of reversal (vv. 25–31).

At least two other elements of reversal are presented by the character speech of this episode. Previously I noted that the women at the tomb also needed an interpretive word "from above" in order to grasp the significance of the events that had taken place. However, through the implicit commentary unveiled in their report to their fellow traveler, the Emmaus pilgrims are presented as much more blameworthy in their failure to understand than the women. Accordingly, they are also presented as much more needy in terms of what it takes to rescue them from their stupor. These disciples have not only the evidence of the empty tomb but also the women's report of all that transpired. Yet they still do not believe, and for this reason Jesus sharply rebukes them (in contrast to the angels' mild rebuke of the women). Moreover, it is only when the risen Jesus himself instructs the Emmaus disciples through the opening of the Scriptures and the breaking of the bread that they are able to recognize

---

15. Tannehill, *Narrative Unity*, 1:284. So also Bock, *Luke 9:51–24:53*, 1917: "The emphasis here is on his entering glory, so that the exalted nature of his current position is stressed."

him and accept what has transpired (vv. 32, 34). Coupled with the fact that the women are the first to believe and proclaim the good news of Jesus' resurrection, it seems that Luke is once again elevating those whom his society regards as of inferior status. Another possible instance of status reversal, which I mentioned above, resides in the fact that the Emmaus disciples are not part of the original eleven. It is remarkable that the first resurrection appearance Luke records should be to these two obscure disciples, one of whom goes unnamed. For this reason, Jacques Dupont proposes that Luke's inclusion of the Emmaus meal reflects the evangelist's affinity for traditions "existing on the fringe of apostolic tradition."[16]

Summary. In my brief treatment of this wonderfully crafted story, I hope that I have been able to draw attention to its main contours and its important narratological role. Here in this episode, each dimension of Luke's vision of salvation unveiled in Luke 1–2 is represented. Moreover, four major motifs from the preceding narrative are recast in light of the reality of the resurrection. As in the previous episode, this story serves notice that with the rising of the Messiah, things are no longer as they were: prediction that confounds has now become proclamation that yields understanding and faithful witness to God's reversal of human rejection. Luke also now prepares his audience to perceive that with the resurrection the Gospel's journey may have reached its end; but as these disciples trek with Jesus to Emmaus, a new journey now begins.

The Risen Jesus and the Disciples (Luke 24:36–53)[17]

In his discussion of the final episode of Luke's Gospel, Tannehill comments:

> We have seen that the narrator helps recipients to recognize and interpret major developments within the plot through key scenes which reveal the nature of God's purpose that is being realized in the story. I previously suggested that we are likely to find such keys to the plot in scenes which provide a preview or review of central events in the story, state the commission which important characters must fulfill, appeal to Scripture to interpret events in the story, and give weight to an interpretation of major developments by placing it in the mouth of an authoritative character. Luke 24:44–49 fulfills all of these criteria.[18]

16. Jacques Dupont, "The Meal at Emmaus," in *The Eucharist in the New Testament: A Symposium,* ed. J. Delorme (Baltimore: Helicon Press, 1964), 114.

17. While vv. 36–49 are frequently treated separately from vv. 50–53 by interpreters, the framing provided by "he stood among them" (v. 36) and "he withdrew from them" (v. 51) suggests that vv. 36–53 are best taken as a unit.

18. Tannehill, *Narrative Unity,* 1:294.

Tannehill's statement provides a wonderfully clear and succinct summation of the crucial narratological role served by this account, along with Luke 24 as a whole. As the evangelist closes his narrative and anticipates his second volume, he again shapes the narration, and especially the words of the characters, to recast major Lukan themes in light of the resurrection, while at the same time amplifying the vision of the Kingdom he established at the Gospel's beginning.

Recasting of Major Lukan Themes

1. *The Divine Necessity and Scriptural Fulfillment of Jesus' Death and Resurrection.* For the third time in this chapter, Luke uses character speech to underscore the profession that Jesus' suffering, death, and resurrection on the third day were necessitated by God's will (v. 44). Jesus' instruction also repeats two closely related notions from the previous episode: (1) the connection between divine necessity and scriptural fulfillment ("everything written about me . . . must [δεῖ] be fulfilled [πληρόω—v. 44]"), and (2) a description of Scripture that emphasizes that its witness to Jesus involves the entire corpus: "the law of Moses, the prophets, and the psalms" (v. 44).

Unique to this expression of divine necessity and scriptural fulfillment is its inclusion of elements other than the suffering, death, and resurrection of Jesus. Jesus' exposition of the Scriptures includes three subordinate clauses, each beginning with an infinitive (in the Greek):

> Thus it is written, that
> 1. the Messiah is to suffer
> 2. and to rise from the dead on the third day,
> 3. and that repentance and forgiveness of sins is to be proclaimed in his name to all nations beginning from Jerusalem. (vv. 46–47)

The structure of the sentence indicates that all three clauses are to be seen as describing the fulfillment of God's will and scriptural testimony.[19] Consequently, the final kerygmatic statement offered in the Gospel is also the most complete, including as divinely determined the proclamation of repentance and forgiveness of sins in Jesus' name to all nations, beginning in Jerusalem. Moreover, the transformation of these statements from passion prediction to kerygma in light of the resurrection is also here *explicitly* relayed. It is Jesus' rising "from the dead on the third day" that both makes possible and neces-

---

19. Jacques Dupont, "La portée christologique de l'évangélisation des nations d'après Luc 24,47," in *Neues Testament und Kirche*, ed. J. Gnilka (Freiburg: Herder, 1974), 127; Dillon, *Eye-Witnesses*, 208.

sitates the proclamation of this astounding truth and its blessed consequences for humanity. Integral to these events' fulfillment is the divinely determined result that they and their significance will be proclaimed to all people.

2. *Rejection*. As in the rest of Luke 24, rejection is implied in the statements acknowledging Jesus' suffering and death.

3. *Misunderstanding*. As with each of the preceding episodes, the misunderstanding of the disciples once again emerges in response to the revelation of Jesus' resurrection. However, in light of the disciples' apparent acceptance of Jesus' resurrection in the previous episode (v. 34), many interpreters of Luke find this rather difficult to untangle. Simply stated, the reemergence of the disciples' doubt at the start of the episode appears to contradict their expressions of understanding in the immediately preceding verses. While their being startled at the sudden appearance of the risen Jesus does not necessarily present a problem (v. 37a), their ensuing terror (v. 37b), their mistaken impression that they were seeing a ghost (v. 37c), and especially Jesus' characterization of their response as "doubts aris[ing] in your hearts" (v. 38) suggest the reappearance of the disciples' lack of comprehension. This incongruity is dealt with in various ways by interpreters. It can be easily resolved, however, if one considers—as I argued above—that the original text of verse 34 attributed the proclamation "The Lord has risen indeed" to the Emmaus disciples and not to the eleven gathered in Jerusalem, and did not include the statement "he has appeared to Simon." If this is indeed the case, then the present episode begins in the very same fashion as the previous. The disciples journeying to Emmaus had been provided with the women's testimony to Jesus' resurrection, but they refused to believe. Similarly, the eleven and all the rest have been provided with the testimony to Jesus' resurrection by the women *and* the Emmaus disciples, but they also persist in fear and doubt: "Why are you frightened, and why do doubts arise in your hearts?" (v. 38).

Jesus' rebuke defines the disciples' response as yet another instance of misunderstanding and lack of faith. Accordingly, Jesus follows his rebuke of the disciples with corrective instruction that includes several proofs of his physicality (vv. 39–43) and the interpretation of his passion and resurrection according to the Scriptures (vv. 44–47). In this episode, however, the disciples' fear and doubts are finally resolved.[20] Jesus stands before them all, not only offering his presence but again opening the Scriptures for them to understand why it all had to be so. The disciples are commissioned as "witnesses of these things," upon whom Jesus will send "what [his] Father promised . . . power from on high" (vv. 48–49; see Acts 1:8), anticipating their faithful proclamation of the gospel

20. Contra Matt. 28:17 and Mark 16:8.

as recorded in Acts. Moreover, after witnessing Jesus' ascension to heaven, the disciples return to Jerusalem with "great joy" (replacing the disbelieving joy of v. 41) and "were *continually* in the temple blessing God" (v. 53).

A final point with regard to this motif should be addressed. At the end of this thrice-repeated pattern of revelation → misunderstanding → corrective instruction → understanding → proclamation, we are in position to recognize the extent to which Luke sees this resolution of doubt as a consequence of God's grace. Richard J. Dillon rightly emphasizes this point throughout his analysis of Luke 24, and after his treatment of this final scene, he jubilantly concludes: "Between the αὐτὸν δὲ οὐκ εἶδον of 24:24 and τότε διήνοιξεν αὐτῶν τὸν νοῦν in 24:45 the determining factor is *not* what human senses could perceive, but the gracious gift of God that is imparted with the *complete self-disclosure* of the risen One: *living presence, illuminating word!*"[21] Above I argued that in light of the reality of the resurrection, the disciples *should* have understood the significance of the events that have taken place, as indicated by the rebuke that consistently counters the disciples' lack of faith. Nevertheless, Dillon's emphasis on the gracious nature of Jesus' disclosure still holds true, and perhaps even more so. The risen Jesus continues to instill within his unbelieving disciples the understanding and faith they need to grasp the awesome significance of what has taken place. That gift of faith, repeatedly offered, is indeed a gift of grace.

4. *Discipleship as a Journey of Witness and Sacrifice.* The words "to all nations, beginning from Jerusalem" (v. 47) present the journey motif as fundamental to Luke's portrayal of the disciples' anticipated mission. As the manifestation of the motif in the Emmaus story prepared us to see, as the Gospel's journey reaches its conclusion, another is just beginning. In light of the resurrection and their newfound understanding, the disciples are now called to go forth to testify to the fulfillment of God's plan of salvation in Jesus, announcing in his name a message of repentance and forgiveness of sins to all people, "in Jerusalem, and in all Judea and Samaria, and to the ends of the earth" (Acts 1:8). The disciples have been called to mission before. Moreover, Jesus' instructions concerning discipleship (Luke 9:23–27, 57–62; 14:25–33) and the mission that the disciples were to take up as their own (9:1–6; 10:1–20) lead us to anticipate that, like Jesus' journey to Jerusalem, their ministry will be one of saving power, suffering, and exaltation.

5. *Ministry of Jesus, Exalted One, in the Power of the Spirit: Urging Repentance, Teaching the Ways of the Kingdom, Healing, and Prayer.* As in the previous episode, Jesus' call to repentance and his instruction continue as his

21. Dillon, *Eye-Witnesses*, 200.

words enable the disciples to move beyond the stupor of doubt and embrace the astounding truth of his resurrection and all that it sets in motion. Here Luke's narrative begins to transition from focusing simply on the power of the Spirit made manifest in Jesus to the reality that this power shall shortly become manifest in his disciples. Jesus announces that he will send the "power from on high" upon them, as was promised by the God through the prophets of old (v. 49). In short, Jesus' ministry of the Spirit will from now on be conducted through his disciples, as the sending of the twelve (9:1–6) and the seventy (10:1–12) led us to anticipate.

Manifestation of Luke's Vision of the Kingdom

This final episode of the Gospel expresses the prevailing vision of the Kingdom's arrival that governs Luke's entire narrative. In fact, Luke here recasts his vision of salvation with a richness of detail matching its expression by the character speech of the infancy narrative. All the dimensions of the ideological context established in Luke 1–2, including many of its more specific features (repentance, forgiveness of sins, inclusion of all nations, gift of the Spirit, divine sonship), are re-presented in this episode.

1. *God's Reign, Which Brings These Things to Pass.* That God is ultimately responsible for the accomplishment of the saving events that have come to pass is again expressed through the notions of divine necessity (δεῖ) and scriptural fulfillment (v. 44). However, as the character speech shifts its focus from the events that have been accomplished (vv. 44–46) to those anticipated (vv. 47–49), God's ordination and empowerment of what is yet to take place are also emphasized. In commissioning his disciples to be his witnesses, Jesus tells them, "I am sending upon you what *my Father* promised" (v. 49), while his description of the Spirit as "power from on high" further points to the source that will empower their ministry in Christ's name. Relatedly, Charles Talbert observes, "Another reason the disciples are to remain in Jerusalem until they receive the gift of the Spirit has to do with the Lukan conviction that God has the initiative in salvation history, so that what human beings do must be done in response to divine leading and empowering."[22] Consistent with the worldview he presents in Luke 1–2, the evangelist again underscores his fundamental claim that all "the things fulfilled among us" (1:1) usher forth from the will and power of God to save.

2. *Fulfillment of God's Promises to Save.* As already noted, a central component of Jesus' instruction is that his rejection, death, and resurrection fulfill

---

22. Talbert, "Place of the Resurrection," 29. So also Bock, *Luke 9:51–24:53*, 1938.

the Scriptures (v. 44). Yet now the evangelist also provides specific details about the Kingdom's fulfillment of Israelite hopes, details that echo the celebration of this salvation offered in the infancy narrative. Just as the opening chapters of the Gospel led to a climactic expression of God's restoration as including not only Israel but all humanity (see 2:1–13, 29–35), so too does the Gospel close with the announcement that God's salvation in Jesus will extend to "all nations" (v. 47). As similarly announced in the infancy narrative, this salvation will consist of the people's embrace of repentance and God's forgiveness of their sins (v. 47; cf. 1:16–17, 54, 76–77). Moreover, in having God's saving reign spread "from Jerusalem," Luke once again underscores that God's culminating act of restoration for the world is rooted in the relationship between God and God's people, Israel. It is from among them, in fulfillment of their hopes and dreams, from the center of their nation, and *by them* that the good news that saves will be offered to all. Thus, it is fitting that as we anticipate the journey to come, the Gospel ends where it began: in the temple (v. 53).

3. *Faithful Response: Believing and Rejoicing in the Good News.* The pattern of narrative development repeated in this episode, focusing on the resolution of the disciples' misunderstanding, again manifests the ideal of a faithful response to the good news. As in the previous episodes, the passage begins with the nega-tive example of the disciples, who once again react with bewilderment when confronted with the reality of the resurrection. Jesus' rebuke (v. 38) challenges this lack of faith by casting it in language ("doubts" [διαλογισμοί]) employed throughout the Gospel to refer to the doubts of Jesus' followers or the thoughts of his opponents (2:35; 5:22; 6:8; 9:46–47). However, Jesus' commission to the disciples to undertake another journey of mission (vv. 48–49) presumes and indicates that their doubt shall now be decisively overcome, and underscores the Lukan conception that those who faithfully follow Jesus are to witness to the salvation that God has accomplished through him. The third-person narration and indirect discourse at the Gospel's close further confirm the disciples' em-brace of the reality of the resurrection and their calling to celebrate with praise and rejoicing. Employing terminology used throughout the infancy narrative to express a faithful response to God's good news, Luke presents the disciples returning to Jerusalem with "great joy" (χαρᾶς μεγάλης [v. 52; cf. 2:10]) and being continually in the temple "blessing (εὐλογέω) God" (v. 53; cf. 1:64; 2:28).

4. *God's Visitation of God's People in Jesus, the Messiah, Divine Son, and Lord.* Several features of Jesus' address to his disciples continue the claim that Jesus' ministry fulfills God's awaited visitation. In a manner similar to previous episodes of character speech, Luke expresses this dimension by once again portraying the very close relation between Jesus and God in terms of both Jesus' advancement of God's plan and his very person. Perhaps one of

the most noteworthy manifestations of this dimension in all the Gospel comes in Jesus' brief statement, "And see, I am sending upon you what my Father promised" (v. 49). The phrase recalls divine sonship as an essential category for understanding Jesus' identity and relation to Yahweh. Moreover, the very notion that Jesus himself would oversee the granting of the "power from on high" echoes John the Baptist's proclamation concerning Jesus' power in 3:16 ("he will baptize you with the Holy Spirit") and further speaks to Jesus' integral role in the accomplishment of God's salvation and the exalted nature of his person.[23] Again, Jesus is presented as the one who carries out God's salvation and whose relation to God is of such an intimate nature that he himself refers to Yahweh as "my Father" and wields God's Spirit.

Still another aspect of the passage that manifests this dimension is the statement that "repentance and forgiveness of sins is to be proclaimed *in his name*" (v. 47). Larry Hurtado notes the traditional use of the expression "in his name" in the baptismal rites of the early church, and describes its function as that which identifies Jesus as the exclusive agent of God's redemption. In comparing the phenomenon to other portrayals of divine agents in Israelite tradition, Hurtado adds, "I know of no comparable use of the name of any redeemer figure in other Israelite groups of the time."[24] He concludes, stating, "Thus, baptism 'into the name' of Jesus is another example of the Jewish-Christian modification of Jewish monotheism constituted by the prominence given to the risen Christ in their devotional and cultic life."[25] Luke's continued use of this and similar phrasing in relation to baptism throughout Acts (2:38; 8:16; 10:48; 19:5; 22:19) suggests this very same conception here in verse 47 as it is associated with repentance and forgiveness of sins. Similarly, both in the Gospel and throughout Acts, the disciples heal and teach in Jesus' name (Luke 9:49; 10:17; Acts 3:6, 16; 4:10, 17; 5:28, 40). In these instances, the expression also testifies to Jesus as the one through whom God's saving reign is bestowed upon humanity, and it presents Jesus himself as the source of the disciples' power and authority. Therefore, at the close of his first volume, Luke again emphasizes the exalted nature of Jesus' person, his accomplishment of God's saving reign, and the very close relation between Jesus and God to a degree suggesting the convergence of their identities.

23. See also the similar expression contained in Peter's Pentecost sermon in Acts 2:33: "Being therefore exalted at the right hand of God, and having received from the Father the promise of the Holy Spirit, he has poured out this that you both see and hear."
24. Hurtado, *One God, One Lord*, 108.
25. Ibid. As stated earlier (p. 47), Hurtado argues that the early Christian modification of Jewish monotheism consisted of a cultic binitarianism that exalted Jesus alongside God as a recipient of devotion and worship.

5. *Reversal.* The increased emphasis on Jesus as the divine Son and transcendent agent of divine redemption correspondingly heightens the notion of reversal also presented in this passage: the paradoxical truth that this same Exalted One was destined for suffering and the cross is cast in even sharper relief. Similarly, this emphasis also underscores the astounding reversal embodied in God's raising of Jesus, for the one who was killed has become the source of salvation for all humanity. As Luke portrays the decisive resolution of the disciples' bewilderment and lack of faith, still another aspect of reversal appears to be manifested. Those who earlier this same day rejected the women's report as nonsense, who failed to grasp the significance of the empty tomb because "they did not see him" (Luke 24:24b), and who did not recognize the risen Lord even though he stood right before them are those now commissioned to proclaim and interpret the significance of these events for others. Luke gives the impression that the reversal of the disciples' doubt and fear is no less a miraculous act of God's power and paradoxical, restoring grace—a perception further suggested by Luke's shaping of the kerygma to include the proclamation of the gospel itself as part of the accomplishment of God's salvation (v. 47).

Summary of Episode and Luke 24

Located at the juncture between Luke's two volumes, the character speech contained in Jesus' final appearance to his followers again converges and recasts Luke's major motifs in light of Jesus' resurrection. At the same time that the evangelist skillfully morphs and interlaces major themes from the preceding narrative, he also shapes his character speech to recall the vision of the Kingdom he established in the opening chapters. As the preceding analysis of Luke 24 has led us to see, however, Luke does not obtrusively reintroduce the elements of this ideological context. Rather, it is *through* his recasting of the motifs of the preceding narrative that Luke reemphasizes this worldview. Stated differently, in his final chapter Luke brings the major story lines of the Gospel into complete alignment with the vision of salvation introduced in the infancy narrative, and it is the resurrection that makes this alignment possible. Thus, Luke 1–2 and 24 provide an interpretive frame for understanding the Gospel as a whole and at the same time reveal how the intervening narrative reaches its culmination in Jesus' resurrection.

Speech and Theme in Acts

Even so, the evangelist does not bring the major story lines of the Gospel to a resolution in Luke 24. For the purview of the Gospel's end not only includes what has come before; it also anticipates the central story lines of the evangelist's next volume (see Acts 1:8). From the vantage point of the Gospel's final chapter, Luke's use of character speech unites the narrative of both Luke and Acts under the same complex vision of God's salvation in Jesus. This becomes even clearer as one attends to the numerous speeches in Acts.

In recognition of Luke's recasting of the motifs of his Gospel while aligning them with the essential elements of his vision of salvation in Luke 24, and by drawing from the preceding discussion, I recast here my own description of these motifs accordingly as we prepare to review the direct discourse of Acts (again, see fig. 7.1, pp. 149–50).

> The disciples take up their own ministry in the power of the Spirit, a journey of witness and sacrifice as they shape the new community of the Kingdom.
>
> The resurrection of Jesus—the Exalted One—reverses human rejection and is the pivotal event in the advancement of God's awaited Kingdom.
>
> Ignorance and faithlessness must end: the time for forgiveness and blessing is at hand for all who repent and trust in Jesus.
>
> Prediction becomes proclamation: all this has occurred in fulfillment of the Scriptures and the plan of God.

The speeches of Acts, as mentioned at the start of chapter 6, function as a repeating chorus giving voice to Luke's account of the Kingdom. The recast motifs I listed above, now transformed in light of the resurrection, are the score to that chorus. These recast motifs are, of course, manifested in much of Luke's third- and first-person narration, but they are repeatedly amplified in the words of Luke's characters.

Peter's Pentecost Sermon

A detailed examination of Luke's use of character speech in Acts is well beyond the scope of this chapter. However, Peter's Pentecost sermon, by virtue of its length, impressive crafting, and strategic position in the narrative (standing as the first major speech), ably serves as a representative example of how the vision of the Kingdom and the transformed themes emerging from Luke 24 continue to be amplified in the character speech of Acts. For this reason I first discuss how Peter's Pentecost sermon and his conversation with its recipients in Acts 2, in conjunction with the scene's context, manifest these recast themes. Then I will overview the ongoing prevalence of these motifs in other instances of direct discourse in Acts.

A Familiar Structure. One readily notable feature of the Pentecost story, and one that further encourages us to look for the recast motifs of Luke 24 in this episode, is that it unfolds in exactly the same fashion as the three accounts of the Gospel's final chapter:

Disclosure:	the Spirit descends upon the believers (vv. 2–4)
Misunderstanding:	the onlookers are bewildered, amazed, astonished, perplexed, and skeptical (vv. 5–13)
Corrective Instruction:	Peter's Pentecost sermon (vv. 14–40)
Understanding:	the crowds are "cut to the heart" (cf. Luke 24:32), ask how they should proceed (v. 37), and then become baptized members of the community (vv. 41–42)
Proclamation:	as members of this community, they praise God and bear witness to the Kingdom made manifest in their midst (vv. 46–47)

The transformation of the disciples, who in such short order go from those in need of radical transformation of mind and heart to those who now shepherd that same transformation in others, is extraordinary. Jesus had said it would happen (Luke 24:48–49; Acts 1:4–8), but the change is profound. Now filled with the promised "power from on high," the once bewildered and faithless disciples take over where Jesus left off, offering Spirit-inspired testimony to the Kingdom's inauguration that dispels doubt and misunderstanding and fosters a new community.

The Disciples' Spirit-Empowered Witness Cultivates a New Community. Accordingly, the ministry of the disciples in the Spirit, who empowers them to witness, is clearly one of the main focuses in the passage. Luke unveils the setting for Peter's sermon in dramatic detail:

> When the day of Pentecost had come, they were all together in one place. And suddenly from heaven there came a sound like the rush of a violent wind, and it filled the entire house where they were sitting. Divided tongues, as of fire, appeared among them, and a tongue rested on each of them. All of them were filled with the Holy Spirit and began to speak in other languages, as the Spirit gave them ability. (Acts 2:1–4)

The direct discourse of the Israelite pilgrims (vv. 7–12) underscores the astounding character of this divine disclosure, leading to their amazed and perplexed query, "What does this mean?" (v. 12). Peter, standing with the eleven, lifts up his voice. He informs the bystanders that this incredible linguistic feat has nothing to do with wine! Rather, it is none other than the manifestation of the Spirit's arrival as promised by the prophet Joel (vv. 16–21).[26] Then toward the end of the sermon, Peter calls the Israelite pilgrims to repentance and baptism, that they may receive the Spirit themselves (v. 38). Peter's words also speak to the new community that will be shaped as a result of the Kingdom's arrival and the Spirit's anointing. People from near and far will be gathered in response to God's invitation (v. 39; cf. Luke 14:23). Then, through third-person narration, we receive additional details on the inclusive, countercultural community that forms in response to the apostles' witness and "the Lord's" call, with table fellowship, learning, and sharing of resources "as any had need" as the fundamental features of this community (vv. 41–47).

The Resurrection of Jesus—the Exalted One—Reverses Human Rejection and Is the Pivotal Event in the Advancement of God's Awaited Kingdom. After explaining the dramatic display of the Spirit's bestowal, citing from Joel 2 (vv. 17–21) and other scriptural texts, Peter turns his attention to unveiling the central act around which everything else that God is now accomplishing revolves, reciting the basic elements of the kerygma, which climax in the resurrection of Jesus (vv. 22–24), whom Peter's listeners "crucified and killed by the hands of those outside the law" (v. 23). Peter then offers an extended midrash on verses from Psalms 16, 18, 132, and 110, marshaling all of them to demonstrate that Jesus' resurrection fulfills these prophecies of old and God's preordained plan. Then, like a symphony performance gradually crescendoing to its climax, Peter's Pentecost sermon reaches its apex in his jubilant proclamation of Jesus' resurrection and exaltation to "the right hand of God" (vv. 32–33). "Therefore," Peter goes on to announce (echoing the composite title "Messiah Lord" in Luke 2:11), "let the entire house of Israel know with certainty that God has made him both Lord and Messiah, this Jesus whom you crucified" (v. 36). As we saw already in the infancy narrative, the "Lord," to whom the faithful are to look for salvation, is not only the Lord Yahweh (see Acts 2:39–40) but also the Lord Jesus (see 2:36, 47). Moreover, Peter's call to the crowd to be baptized in "the name of Jesus Christ" (v. 38), as we discussed above, likely reflects the binitarian devotion of the early church.

Ignorance and Faithlessness Must End: Forgiveness and Blessing for All Who Repent and Trust. Peter concludes his citation of Joel 2 with the words, "Everyone who calls on the name of the Lord shall be saved" (2:21). Then, in response to the heart-struck query of the crowd, "Brothers, what should we

---

26. As Spencer (*Journeying through Acts*, 45) notes regarding the citation from Joel: "Given its length and strategic placement at the beginning of a major introductory discourse, the Joel citation serves a programmatic function within Acts: what Joel announced sets the agenda for the entire Acts journey."

do?" (v. 37), he calls the crowd to repent of their faithless rejection of Jesus and the Kingdom. He urges them to be baptized for the forgiveness of sins and the blessing of the Spirit (vv. 38–39). Against the larger backdrop of Israel's sacred story, invited into view though Peter's copious use of Israelite tradition, the bestowal of the Spirit at Pentecost undoes the evil forged at Babel (Gen. 11:1–9).[27] There the pride of humankind led to the confusion of its language and alienation between God and humanity, and between one human being and another. In the aftermath of that tragic event, God called Abram and covenanted with him and his offspring, so that ultimately "all the families of the earth shall be blessed" (Gen. 12:3; see Acts 3:25). Now, the one who fulfills that covenant with Abraham, the Messiah Lord Jesus, sends the Spirit (Luke 24:49) to *everyone* who seeks God's salvation—no matter their social class, gender (2:17–18), or ethnicity—gathering all humankind from exile and proclaiming a word intelligible to all, for "the promise is for you, for your children, and for all who are far away" (v. 39).[28]

Prediction Becomes Proclamation: All This Has Occurred in Fulfillment of the Scriptures and the Plan of God. As already noted in each of the above sections, Peter proclaims that all that has taken place fulfills Israelite hopes and expectations—as foreshadowed in the Scriptures—that God's promise to deliver his people, and indeed all humanity, is now coming to pass.

The Sermons and Narrative to Follow

These very same themes continue to dominate and interweave throughout the narrative of Acts. They are highlighted particularly in the remaining speeches of Peter (3:12–26; 4:8–12; 10:34–43; 11:4–18), Stephen (7:1–53), James (15:13–21), and Paul (13:16–41; 15:7–12; 17:22–31; 20:18–35; 22:1–21; 24:10–21; 26:2–29; 28:17–29), but are also commonly featured in shorter instances of direct discourse and third-person narration.

The Disciples' Spirit-Empowered Witness Cultivates a New Community. The commission of the early believers to bear witness to the arrival of God's reign in Jesus is a common motif in the character speech of Acts beyond 1:8 and Peter's Pentecost sermon. Not only is this motif implied by the simple reality that in offering these speeches the disciples are bearing witness; it also is directly cited in the following passages.

27. So also ibid., 42–43.
28. Fitzmyer (*Acts of the Apostles*, 266) states, "'Those still far off' could conceivably mean other Jews not present for the Assembly, but still in the diaspora; but from the thrust of the narrative of Acts it becomes clear that Luke is already hinting at the reconstitution of Israel as the people of God, which will incorporate the Gentiles."

3:15	Peter:	"To this we are witnesses"
4:29	Community:	"to speak your word with all boldness"
10:37, 39, 41–42	Peter:	"That message spread throughout Judea, beginning in Galilee. . . . We are witnesses . . . chosen by God as witnesses. . . . He commanded us to preach to the people and to testify . . ."
11:1–14	Peter:	recounts his call from Jesus to preach to Cornelius and his household
13:26, 32	Paul:	"To us the message of this salvation has been sent . . . and we bring you the good news"
15:7	Paul:	"that I should be the one through whom the Gentiles would hear the message of the good news"
20:18–25	Paul:	summarizes his witness and trials on behalf of the Kingdom
22:6–21	Paul:	recounts his conversion and call to proclaim the gospel to the gentiles
26:12–22	Paul:	recounts his conversion and call to proclaim the gospel to the gentiles
28:17–28	Paul:	refers to his calling to bear witness to the "hope of Israel" as he speaks with Israelites in Rome

Frequently in Acts, these displays of testimony interweave with indications that communities of believers are both constituted by and integral to this witnessing ministry. In the aftermath of Peter and John's bold testimony (3:12–26) and appearance before the Sanhedrin (4:5–22), the community itself erupts in celebration of God's and Jesus' sovereignty over the rulers of the world and in celebration of the community's calling to proclaim this good news to others (4:24–30). Luke's conclusion to the scene underscores that such bold witness and empowerment by the Holy Spirit are constituent elements of the new people God is calling into being: "When they had prayed, the place in which they were gathered together was shaken; and they were all filled with the Holy Spirit and spoke the word of God with boldness" (v. 31). A summary of community life similar to 2:41–47 follows in 4:32–35, again revealing that faithful life in community is one of the key manifestations of the Kingdom's arrival.

Later in the narrative, God's testimony to Peter leads him to understand and proclaim that "God shows no partiality, but in every nation anyone who fears him and does what is right is acceptable to him" (10:34–35). Peter's testimony to Cornelius and his household results in their embrace of the gospel and their own reception of God's promised Spirit and forgiveness. Though astounded that even gentiles should receive the Spirit, Peter orders that Cornelius and his household should be baptized "in the name of Jesus Christ" (v. 48). Just as notably, Peter stays with them for several days (v. 48), sharing table with them and underscoring that the community of the faithful, gathered around the apostles, has now expanded to include those not of Israel. The ensuing debate among the Israelite followers of Jesus in Jerusalem regarding the inclusion of gentiles into their community, Peter's response, and the disciples' decision to welcome gentile believers reveal how radical a development this is, even if it has been foreshadowed (11:1–18).

Moving forward, the ministry of Paul and Barnabas to both Israelites and gentiles swells the mixed ranks of the community considerably. As with the other apostles, their witness leads many to embrace the good news, and these in turn create communities of their own in a widening arc away from Jerusalem (e.g., 11:19–30; 14:21–23; 18:1–17, 18–23; 19:1–10; 28:13–14). The tensions and questions created by the massive influx of gentiles into the community revolve around what it means for these bodies of mixed believers to worship and share table together. The amount of attention Luke devotes to this conflict and its resolution in 15:1–32 (much of it relayed through indirect and direct discourse) further underscores how central community life is to Luke's conception of the Kingdom. In sum, Luke portrays such fellowship, in both third-person narration and character speech, as manifesting the best of Kingdom living (Acts 2:41–47; 4:29–30, 32–35; 11:17–18, 19–30; 12:5, 12–17; 13:1–3; 18:8–11, 26–28; 20:1, 17–36; 21:17–26; 27:33–36; 28:13–15), being threatened (5:1–11; 6:1; 15:36–41), and in the process of being figured out (6:2–7; 8:26–28; 11:1–18; 15:1–21).

The Resurrection of Jesus—the Exalted One—Reverses Human Rejection and Is the Pivotal Event in the Advancement of God's Awaited Kingdom. The proclamation of the disciples in Luke 24, "The Lord has risen indeed!," signals the centrality of the Easter message to everything that follows. Accordingly, as we saw already in Peter's Pentecost sermon, this fundamental motif—along with its accompanying refrain proclaiming the exalted character of Jesus—is basic to the preaching of the early believers throughout Acts. Not only does the proclamation of Jesus rising from the dead repeatedly occur in the character speech of Acts; Luke's characters also frequently amplify its centrality in God's plan of salvation by the amount of attention given to this event and its attending consequences (e.g., Acts 10:40–43) or through the climactic plotting of their testimony (e.g., 4:9–12; 24:21), or both (e.g., 13:26–39; 26:15–18, 22–23). For instance, Paul's speech in Acts 13 parallels that offered by Peter at Pentecost in terms of its length, development, and content. Like Peter, Paul emphasizes Jesus' rejection by his own people (vv. 26–29). But also like Peter, Paul uses a developed midrash on several psalm texts (including Ps. 16) relating to David to demonstrate the scriptural necessity of Jesus' resurrection. This comprises the heart of Paul's testimony to the Kingdom's arrival and its blessed benefits for those who embrace it: "By this Jesus everyone who believes is set free from all those sins from which you could not be freed by the law of Moses" (13:39).

Still another way in which Luke presents the resurrection of Jesus as central to the advancement of the Kingdom in both character speech and third-person narration is the repeated indications that the risen Jesus is actively engaged in and supporting the ministry of the early believers.[29] Jesus appears to Stephen (7:55), confronts Saul (9:1–7), instructs Ananias (9:10–17), and again appears to Paul (22:17–21). Additionally, Dillon notes that the many references to acts of healing accomplished in the "name of Jesus" suggest that the power and authority of the disciples to perform these ministrations comes from Jesus, and in their exercise "Jesus is himself present."[30] In Acts, the risen Jesus is still actively at work bringing to fruition God's plan and salvation. Moreover, Paul's own life—his transformation from one hell-bent on destroying "the Way" to one who becomes one of its leading champions—is another dramatic witness to the power of Jesus' resurrection and ongoing ministry to effect incredible reversal in human hearts. Beyond the depiction of his transformation in third-person narration, Paul himself highlights it in his own character speech (see 22:6–21; 26:12–18).

In Acts, as in the Gospel, the risen Jesus is repeatedly exalted as "Messiah" (3:18, 20; 4:10, 26; 10:36; 13:34; 26:23) and is also revealed as the prophet like Moses (3:22) who was to come. Moreover, the same convergence of mission and also of person between Jesus and Yahweh that we find in the Gospel is also present in Acts. Here too Luke frequently employs κύριος for Jesus (e.g., 2:36; 10:36; 14:3) and again frequently uses the term in contexts where it is not clear whether it refers to Jesus or God (e.g., 2:47; 8:25; 14:3; 18:9–10; 23:11).[31] As in the Gospel, the ambiguous uses of the title are intentional and lead Theophilus and others to view both Jesus and God as "Lord." An additional indication that Luke intends the title to signal the exalted supremacy of Jesus' character occurs in 10:36, where Jesus is described as "Lord of all." Still other titles or descriptors are employed to cast Jesus as divine and converge his identity with God. Jesus is boldly hailed by the characters of Acts as the Author of life (3:15), Son of God (9:20; 13:33), "judge of the living and the dead" (10:42), and Savior (5:31; 13:23).

29. See Robert F. O'Toole, "Activity of the Risen Jesus in Luke-Acts," *Bib* 63 (1981): 471–98.
30. Dillon, *Eye-Witnesses*, 210.
31. As Witherington (*Acts of the Apostles*, 148) reports, of the 104 appearances of κύριος in Acts, 18 clearly refer to God, 47 clearly refer to Jesus, 4 to secular rulers or masters, and the remaining 35 refer to either Jesus or God, but the context does not make it clear which is in view.

Ignorance and Faithlessness Must End: Forgiveness and Blessing for All Who Repent and Trust. Often accompanying the proclamation of Jesus' resurrection are celebrations of its blessed consequences for those who accept this good news as their own. Repeatedly, the faithful in Acts announce that Jesus' death and resurrection mark a new age in the relationship between God and humanity. As Robert W. Wall summarizes, "the epicenter of Luke's theological conception of Israel's restoration is a God who forgives every person who names Jesus as their Lord and confesses him as God's messiah."[32] As he did in the Gospel, Luke continues to unveil the various ministrations of the Kingdom's power and salvation, though now offered through Jesus' followers: healings, deliverance from oppression and danger, forgiveness, reconciliation, the reception of the Spirit, and a new kind of community life. As Wall goes on to note, "Even as his conception of God's salvation is international in scope it is also holistic in consequence."[33] The bestowal of these same gifts, as indicated already in Peter's citation of Joel 2 in his Pentecost sermon, also continues to transcend social location and gender: for example, portfolios are liquidated and the resources are shared by all (2:45; 4:32; 6:1); the sick and diseased are healed (e.g., 5:12–16); a widow named Dorcas is raised from the dead (9:36–42); Peter is received into the home of Simon, a tanner (9:43), and then Cornelius, a centurion (10:48); a widow-merchant named Lydia receives the good news (16:11–15); Paul bears testimony to God and the good news before Governor Felix (23:23–35) and Agrippa and Bernice (26:1–29), and then to fellow shipmates and prisoners (27:21–26, 33–35). As always, Luke insists that the arrival of the Kingdom will upend prevailing notions of privilege and power.

Accordingly, the speeches in Acts are also filled with calls for hearers to turn from ignorance and wickedness so that they too make take hold of God's Kingdom and the blessings it provides (e.g., 3:22–23; 10:43; 14:15–17; 17:30–31; 26:20). Paul relays most elegantly the commission he received on the road to Damascus: Jesus sends him to both Jews and gentiles, "to open their eyes so that they may turn from darkness to light and from the power of Satan to God, so that they may receive forgiveness of sins and a place among those who are sanctified by faith in me" (26:18; see also 2:39; 3:19; 4:12; 5:31; 10:43; 13:38; 17:31; 22:16). On occasion, however, these calls to repentance take the form of harsh rebuke in response to the virulent rejection and hostility that believers frequently encounter. In this we see another parallel between the plotting of Luke's Gospel and that of the story of Acts. Just as in the Gospel Jesus was the cause of division and the

---

32. Robert W. Wall, "The Acts of the Apostles," in *The New Interpreter's Bible*, ed. Leander E. Keck (Nashville: Abingdon, 2002), 10:65.

33. Ibid.

object of derision and responded with castigation and warning, so too is this pattern manifested in the ministry of Acts' leading characters. Their character speech both highlights and responds to this resistance, helping Theophilus and others to see that what God has done in Jesus compels a response, either faithful or faithless, and to recognize the utter seriousness of what is at stake.

Among the most intense and pathos-filled of such warnings, and certainly the most developed, is Stephen's speech to those who are about to murder him (7:2–53). After a lengthy review of key events in Israel's history, much of it focusing on Moses and his faithful resolve to stick it out with a stiff-necked, abusive people (vv. 23–43), Stephen erupts with this scathing invective:

> You stiff-necked people, uncircumcised in heart and ears, you are forever op-posing the Holy Spirit, just as your ancestors used to do. Which of the prophets did your ancestors not persecute? They killed those who foretold the coming of the Righteous One, and now you have become his betrayers and murderers. You are the ones that received the law as ordained by angels, and yet you have not kept it. (vv. 51–53; see also 13:36–41; 28:23–29)

Tragically, but not surprisingly, those gathered are enraged, and Israel kills yet another prophet of God.

Prediction Becomes Proclamation: All This Has Occurred in Fulfillment of the Scriptures and the Plan of God. As indicated by the examples cited above, Luke's characters frequently claim that the events surrounding the life of Jesus and the ministry of the faithful occur in accordance with the Scriptures (Acts 3:18, 22–26; 4:24–30; 10:43; 13:33; 26:22; 28:23) and with God's plan or promise (3:25; 10:38–43; 13:29). We also saw that these statements are supplemented by repeated notices in third-person narration and direct discourse regarding the ongoing direction provided by Jesus and the Holy Spirit. All together, the speeches in Acts articulate "a view of the world characterized by the convic-tion that God intervenes in life in this world to initiate relationships, to give directions for present or future actions, and to reverse the course of events by undoing certain effects which result from particular humanly initiated causes that are inconsistent with God's own purposes."[34]

Conclusion

The goal of these two chapters has been to help readers recognize the essential function that character speech plays in the plotting, thematic development,

---

34. Soards, *Speeches in Acts*, 184.

and rhetoric of Luke-Acts. Through the words of his characters, Luke reveals to Theophilus and others the fundamental contours of the kingdom story he proclaims as well as the crucial role of the resurrection in making all of it possible. We turn now to still another important feature of Luke's narrative artistry: his use of pathos to draw readers more deeply into his narrative and to experience—not only intellectually but also affectively—what is at stake in the choices they make about which Lord to serve and which Kingdom to call home.

8

The Power and Prominence
of Luke's Pathos

I n the introductory chapter I stressed that Luke not only portrays characters responding to the arrival of the Kingdom in Jesus with intense emotion; he also skillfully uses pathos to shape the way in which Theophilus
and others engage his claims about the world. Indeed, without its use of
emotional appeal, Luke's narrative would have very little rhetorical power
at all. It certainly would not have become the admired and cherished work
that it is, and chances are that you and I (and most others) would have
never read it!

The Crucial Role of Affect in Narrative Rhetoric

On one level, this should be quite obvious. Emotion is basic to our experience
of nearly all forms of narrative expression. When we read a novel or a dramatic
work of nonfiction or view a play or movie, our affective faculties are often
deeply engaged. Narratives cause us to feel—we all know that. Many scholars of narrative know it as well. In fields such as literary theory, psychology,
philosophy, social science, and educational theory, it is widely recognized that
emotion is integral to the experience of narrative, and the affective impact of

literature is a subject of widespread attention.[1] It is also widely recognized in these fields, as I discussed in chapter 4, that affect is essential to the rhetorical function and force of narrative. To summarize, emotion plays a crucial role in our reading of a narrative, in our consideration of its claims about the world, and in our willingness or not to recast our own storied worldviews in response to that encounter. Good authors know this, either consciously or implicitly: *affective appeal in varying forms is the means by which narratives compel us to enter their storied world and entertain the version of reality they present.* Such recognition of the essential role of emotion in narrative rhetoric is also not limited to authors of the modern era; it was recognized by writers and rhetoricians from at least the time of Aristotle, and pathos was frequently employed by Greco-Roman historians.[2] Strangely, however, Scripture scholars have generally shown very little interest in getting in touch with the affective dimension of biblical narrative.

How Luke Employs Pathos

In what follows, I identify specific modes of plotting and characterization, and other features of narrative artistry, that strike me as geared toward engaging the affective faculties of recipients. I will describe each of these features of biblical narrative and then illustrate them by offering some specific examples of how these techniques are employed by Luke.[3]

Plotting

Plotting, the sequencing and presentation of events and actions, as we discussed in chapter 5, is one of the defining elements of narrative. It is, in most worthwhile stories at least, carefully composed and rhetorically charged. Not only does such sequencing typically indicate some sort of temporal, causal, or teleological relationship in the events depicted and the challenges that must be overcome; it also draws recipients into the narrative and makes them vulnerable to the interests of the author. In ways that are often subtle yet compelling, stories sequence and "set up" the events they narrate in order to compose in

---

1. See Karl A. Kuhn, *The Heart of Biblical Narrative: Rediscovering Biblical Appeal to the Emotions* (Minneapolis: Fortress, 2009), 1–5.
2. See ibid., 6–10. For a helpful discussion and demonstration of the use of affect by Greco-Roman historians preceding Luke, see Doohee Lee, *Luke-Acts and "Tragic History,"* WUNT 346 (Tübingen: Mohr Siebeck, 2013), 34–201.
3. For a more detailed discussion and illustration of these affective techniques, see Kuhn, *Heart of Biblical Narrative*, 29–59.

us an experience that moves both our minds and our hearts. Following are five "rhetorically affective" plotting techniques that writers of biblical narrative commonly employ.

LEADING READERS TO THRESHOLD MOMENTS

Narratives are, of course, filled with "threshold moments," those liminal states when what is sought by leading characters stands on the edge of achievement or failure. In certain instances, however, it is clear that a writer tries hard to shape the story so that such a moment captures his or her recipients' attention, leaving them teetering on the brink as they eagerly await climactic resolution, whether for good or ill.

As we saw in Luke 24, for instance, the evangelist composes a series of three accounts in which disciples cross the threshold from misunderstanding to understanding and become witnesses to God's salvation in Jesus: the women's visit to the tomb (24:1–12), Jesus' fellowship with the Emmaus disciples (vv. 13–35), and Jesus' appearance to the eleven and other disciples (vv. 36–49). The threefold repetition of this pattern creates an extended threshold moment, or series of threshold moments, leading to a third iteration in which doubt is finally resolved and the disciples are sent forth by Jesus as witnesses. Why extend the threshold moment to this degree? One of the evangelist's motivations was likely to emphasize that the death and resurrection of Jesus could be grasped only after these extraordinary events had taken place, and their significance fully understood only when explained to the disciples by the risen Jesus himself. It was one more way Luke could underscore the pivotal role of Jesus' resurrection and ongoing ministry in God's designs for humanity.

Yet another reason also seems likely. In so extending the threshold moment, Luke also leads his recipients to participate more fully in the frustration evoked by the disciples' repeated inability to grasp the reality of Jesus' resurrection: the women are perplexed at the empty tomb (24:4); the disciples disregard the women's witness as "an idle tale" (v. 11); the disciples heading to Emmaus— ironically, and even comically—fail to recognize the significance of the events they narrate (vv. 18–24); and despite being told by the Emmaus disciples (or others) that "the Lord has risen indeed," when Jesus appears to them the disciples think they are seeing a ghost (vv. 36–37)! By having his audience dwell on the disciples' slowness to understand and believe, Luke cultivates within his audience an affectively amplified reaction (along with that of Jesus—see 24:25!) to the disciples' foolishness for not believing sooner. This encourages Theophilus and others (perhaps without them even realizing it) to regard any doubt they may have about this extraordinary event as similarly foolish in light of the testimony that these characters in the narrative—and other Christians

they know—have provided. It further prods them to embrace the rather paradoxical and counterintuitive claim that God's messiah really did need to suffer
the humiliation of the cross in order to fulfill God's plan to save, and it also
pushes them to join the disciples in living lives of joyous praise and witness
(vv. 44–49, 50–53). In sum, the affective dimensions of Luke's portrayal serve
his rhetorical and pastoral ends.

SEQUENCING THAT CONNECTS AND COMPARES

In chapter 5 we saw how Luke employs patterning and parallelism to compare and connect characters, events, and portions of his narrative. Bracketing, framing, or enveloping is one such common arrangement used to help
the recipient see connections between sections of the narrative. The narrator
constructs this device by placing similar material at the beginning and end of
a narrative unit, large or small, creating an ABA or chiastic pattern. Its specific
narratological effect varies. In some cases, the effect may be to connect the
beginning and end of a lengthy section or of a work as a whole. For example,
we saw that the bracketing provided by the concentrated portrayal of Luke's
vision of salvation in Luke 1–2 and 24 directs his recipients to perceive that
the Kingdom announced in Luke 1–2 has significantly advanced in the death
and resurrection of Jesus.

Another bracketing technique that some call "sandwiching" or "intercalation"
leads the recipient to see two stories in close relation to each other. Mark is well
known for these sandwich constructions, in which he (or his source) has seemingly taken one story, pulled it apart, and inserted another story within it. Luke
preserves a number of those constructions that he borrows from Mark. Consider,
for instance, the intercalated stories of Jairus' daughter and the woman suffering
from hemorrhaging in Luke 8:40–56 (Mark 5:21–43). While Jesus is on his way
to heal Jairus' daughter, the woman approaches, touches Jesus, is healed, and
is commended by Jesus for her faith. Then Jesus resumes his course to Jairus'
house and heals the young girl. There are other details in these accounts that
also invite the recipient to draw comparisons between them: the girl is twelve
years old (Luke 8:42), and the woman has been suffering from her ailment for
twelve years (v. 43); both are regarded as beloved daughters, the girl by Jairus
(v. 42) and the woman by Jesus (v. 48); both are restored because of faith, the
woman by her own (v. 48) and the daughter by that of her father (v. 50).

Still another way biblical authors draw a connection between different parts
of a narrative is by sequencing episodes in such a manner that the recipients'
perception of one event is colored by those preceding it. Of course, this commonly takes place when there is a clear causal relationship between events or
when a particular event has been foreshadowed in some fashion. But what I

am referring to here are connections more subtly drawn by the author in order to cast an event or situation in a particular light, leading to a more highly charged response from recipients than would normally be the case. Consider, for example, the account of Ananias and Sapphira in Acts 5. The couple's reluctance to part with all the proceeds of the sale of their field appears particularly egregious in light of the episodes immediately preceding this pericope. The Christian community is dramatically infused with the power of the Spirit (see Acts 4:31). As we saw above, one manifestation of the Spirit's empowerment of the community, as indicated by the juxtaposition of 4:23–31 with Luke's summary of the early believers' blessed life together in 4:32–37, is the community's bold and countercultural commitment to holding possessions in common and distributing to each as any has need (vv. 32–37). This information helps recipients understand the gravity of Ananias and Sapphira's selfishness and dishonesty. They have done nothing less than resist the presence of the Spirit and have instead—unwittingly or not—colluded with Satan.

Commentators frequently point out Luke's use of these plotting techniques to shape his recipients' responses to the matters he records. But note too that these sequencing strategies are likely to increase the dramatic effect of the stories. This certainly seems to be the case with the examples just provided, in which the sequencing joins with other dramatic elements to provoke both thought and feeling in Luke's recipients. In Luke 24, the evangelist again impresses upon his recipients the vision of salvation he unveiled in the infancy narrative. This instance of bracketing accentuates their frustration and relief as they simultaneously encounter in dramatic fashion the three threshold moments depicting the disciples' struggle to believe these events, which cry out for their embrace. With the stories of the two daughters joined together, recipients are led to consider that the healing power of God's Kingdom is made available not only to a daughter among the religious elite but also to one who is outcast and without a father. Each story contains poignant elements of characterization (more on this below). But the affective impact of their characterization is amplified by the intercalation of their shared vulnerability and the need for faith that courageously looks beyond the life-defying realities of the moment. Such plotting invites both sympathy from recipients and joy that a new future is made possible for these two women—and thus perhaps also for themselves—by God's reign in Jesus. Finally, the example of unbelief and collusion with Satan in the story of Ananias and Sapphira is disturbing on its own, but the passages preceding it enable Theophilus and others to recognize and feel more keenly how the actions of this couple constitute a tragic, perhaps even embarrassing, rejection of both the Spirit and the new community that reflects the ways of God's Kingdom.

WITHHOLDING RESOLUTION

Aristotle's description of a narrative as having a beginning, middle, and end has long been basic to the definition of plot offered by literary critics. Aristotle further defines the end as "that which does itself naturally follow from something else, either necessarily or in general, but there is nothing else after it."[4] In other words, narratives are expected to "go somewhere," to move toward a resolution, which in some clear manner follows from the beginning and middle of the plot. Most biblical narratives, both on a large and small scale, follow this teleological recipe for plotting. But on rare occasions the biblical authors deviate from it and leave us hanging, staring blankly at the final line of a story and asking, "Surely, there is more?"

One notable instance of withheld resolution receiving much attention in recent scholarship is the ending of Mark's Gospel (16:1–8). A common assertion since the critical study of Mark began has been that the original conclusion to the Gospel was lost when the end of its papyrus roll was torn. This view is still maintained by some, but many scholars now believe that the evangelist truly ended his Gospel with 16:8. Yet with 16:1–8 as the Gospel's final lines, the evangelist draws the plot to a close (or fails to) by reporting the women encountering the empty tomb, the angelic message announcing Jesus' resurrection, and the women's less than admirable response: "So they went out and fled from the tomb, for terror and amazement had seized them; and they said nothing to anyone, for they were afraid" (v. 8). Many conclude that this ending of Mark's narrative serves as an "invitation to finish the story" as recipients respond with surprise, dissatisfaction, and even dismay to its lack of resolution and the women's lack of faith.[5]

While individual pericopes in Luke-Acts may lack resolution (e.g., Luke 9:57–62 [do any of these "potential disciples" follow Jesus?]; 18:18–25 [what happens to the rich and sad ruler?]), one of the more notable instances of withholding resolution comes at the end of Luke's two-volume narrative. Most scholars believe that Acts was written long after Paul's death. So why did Luke choose to end his narrative short of that event? Why conclude with Paul sitting in Rome, awaiting his trial and possible condemnation, but also "welcom[ing] all who came to him" and "proclaiming the kingdom of God and teaching about the Lord Jesus Christ with all boldness and without hindrance" (Acts 28:31)? To me and many others it seems likely that Luke wished to emphasize

4. Aristotle, *Poetics* 5.1. This and the following references are from Aristotle, *Poetics*, trans. Malcolm Heath (New York: Penguin, 1996).

5. See Mary Ann Tolbert, *Sowing the Gospel: Mark's World in Literary-Historical Perspective* (Minneapolis: Fortress, 1989), 298–99. See also Cornelia Cross Crocker, "Emotions as Loopholes for Answerability in the Unfinalized Gospel according to Mark," *PRSt* 32 (2005): 281–94.

Paul as a paradigm of faithful witness, courageously proclaiming the gospel even in the face of a far-from-certain future, even surrounded by obvious manifestations of Roman power (see also Acts 20:17–35, esp. v. 24).[6] This is the dramatic image that Luke wanted reverberating in the minds and hearts of Theophilus and others as his kingdom story came to a close. They know what has happened to Paul; and the reality of Paul's martyrdom, along with Israel's ongoing resistance to the gospel, undoubtedly infuses this scene with a sense of sadness and tragedy. Yet it was more important for Luke to leave his recipients with this stirring image of Paul as the unrelenting champion of truth despite the trials that were sure to come (recall Acts 21:13). The Romans, as encouraged by some within Israel, may have killed this bold apostle, but they cannot kill the inspiration of his example, or silence the good news he proclaimed, or halt the advance of God's Kingdom, or dethrone the one—and the only one—who is to be hailed as Lord. Theophilus and others are called to continue this bold witness themselves, courageously sharing with all who may come to them the good news of which Kingdom and Lord they are to serve.

ASTONISHING INVERSION OF THE EXPECTED

Unexpected shifts and turns are common to narrative, but at times these shifts and turns are to such an extreme that they are designed to elicit astonishment and wonder in an audience. Aristotle referred to this narratological move as "reversal," involving "an astonishing inversion of the expected outcome of some action"[7] (I will borrow Aristotle's phrase "astonishing inversion of the expected" to refer to this technique and will continue to use "reversal" to refer to the inversion of culturally endorsed norms and worldviews). At times, the recipient has been prepared beforehand for such turns, and thus the focus is on the characters' astonishment, such as with Jesus' crucifixion ("We had hoped that he was the one to redeem Israel" [Luke 24:21]) and his resurrection ("The Lord has risen indeed!" [Luke 24:34]). At other times, Luke aims to lead recipients to astonishment over unexpected turns or twists in the plot. Such instances are not overly common, given the prominence of Luke's prophecy-fulfillment pattern throughout his account. Yet there are some.

One clear example occurs in Luke 1, when Zechariah fails to trust Gabriel's annunciation of John's birth despite praying for a child for years. Others include

6. So also French L. Arrington, *The Acts of the Apostles: Introduction, Translation, and Commentary* (Peabody, MA: Hendrickson, 1988), 273; Johnson, *Acts of the Apostles*, 476; Fitzmyer, *Acts of the Apostles*, 791; Wall, "Acts of the Apostles," 368; Witherington, *Acts of the Apostles*, 816.

7. See p. xxx of Malcolm Heath's introduction to his translation of the *Poetics*, cited above. See *Poetics* 6.3 for Aristotle's discussion on reversal.

the bold devotion of the "sinful woman" in Simon's house (Luke 7:36–50) and Mary abandoning Martha to assume the posture of a disciple (10:38–42). In Acts, Stephen's testimony before the Sanhedrin marks a stirring instance. At that incredible moment when Stephen is suddenly led by the Spirit to gaze into heaven, he beholds Jesus standing at the right hand of God and then announces his vision to all gathered! While similar to Jesus' own testimony before the Sanhedrin (Luke 22:69), Stephen's inspired outburst is startling and the first among several parallels to Jesus' crucifixion to follow (vv. 59–60). What recipients witness in Stephen is a powerfully passionate participation in the very same fate and faith as Jesus. The astonishing nature of Stephen's reenactment of Jesus' passion also includes a nostalgic dimension (see below) as it recalls the same poignant combination of faithful testimony and tragic rejection surrounding Jesus' trial and crucifixion.

Composing Conflict

Still another element related to plotting that serves an affective function in narrative is the composition of conflict. Conflict is, of course, a basic element in most narrative. Conflict between characters, competing cultures or world-views, or the forces of nature and human well-being form the core of most story lines coursing through our literature and all other forms of storytelling. By employing conflict and pairing it with characterization, authors create moments pregnant with tension and angst that lead recipients to invest themselves emotionally in the tale, respond in certain ways to its characters (positively or negatively), and align themselves with perspectives that are consistent with the views of characters who are portrayed as brave, noble, or just.

By reporting and staging conflict, authors of biblical narrative commonly accomplish at least two objectives. They are able to present conflict as something basic to the human experience, a manifestation of the depravity miring the human condition (e.g., Cain and Abel, David and Absalom). The portrayal of conflict in biblical narrative also draws attention to opposing commitments, with one party often representing perspectives consistent with the will of God, while others represent perspectives and actions at odds with God's intentions for humanity (e.g., Elijah vs. Jezebel and Ahab, Jeremiah vs. the false prophets, John vs. Herod, Jesus vs. the Pharisees, Paul vs. Roman elite).

Obviously, discord is no stranger to Luke-Acts. I will have more to say in chapter 10 about its function in Luke's narrative as we discuss the collision he composes between the hegemony of Rome, the faithlessness of many within Israel, and the emergence of God's Kingdom in Jesus and the ministry of the church. For now I will offer that Luke often employs conflict to contrast the ways of the Kingdom with the ways of this world and to compel a response from Theophilus and others. The conflict Luke portrays is so pervasive, raw, and at times tragic that it forces his recipients to decide with whom they are to side and for what they are to stand. For Luke, there is no middle ground.

Characterization

The casting of characters is among the most powerful rhetorical tools available to an author of narrative. While biblical narratives often (but not always) lack the level of characterization we commonly encounter in modern novels, biblical authors (like modern authors) play upon recipients' emotional connections or aversions to characters in order to draw them into their narratives. They also use these affective techniques to encourage recipients—subversively at times—to embrace their visions of the world.

INVITING SYMPATHY AND EMPATHY

Reader sympathy and empathy have been a topic of recent interest among psychologists and literary theorists addressing the impact of characterization on readers. Reader sympathy is typically defined as a reader's wishes for a character to achieve a beneficial state or to be delivered from some sort of threat or suffering. Reader empathy, in contrast, occurs when a reader becomes so engrossed with a character that the reader actually experiences the same emotions as the character, or at least similar ones, as those are either expressly stated or implied by the author or imagined by the reader.

To be sure, the extent to which readers sympathize or empathize with a character depends upon a whole host of factors relevant to the reader and beyond the control of the author (e.g., the reader's personality, reading skill, personal experience, gender, social location). But the likelihood that readers will sympathize or empathize with a character is greatly enhanced by the amount of attention and complexity given to a character by the author. In general, "round" (multidimensional) as opposed to "flat" (one-dimensional) characters are more likely to capture our interest. These are characters we encounter in a variety of situations. We see their struggles, strengths and weaknesses, triumphs and failures. We get a sense of what moves them, their hopes for themselves and others. In other words, we have the opportunity to "get to know them." Numerous biblical characters are sketched in such detail: several of the patriarchs and matriarchs, Moses, Joshua, Samson, Hannah, Samuel, Ruth, Naomi, Ahab, Jezebel, Elijah, Elisha, David, Solomon, Jeremiah, John the Baptist, Mary, John the apostle, Jesus, the Twelve, Nicodemus, Peter, Mary Magdalene, James, Stephen, Paul, and so on. At the same time, characters with only small parts in the biblical drama may also draw out our sympathy, especially if we encounter them in emotionally charged settings of injustice or vulnerability, such as Uriah or Naboth, Jephthah's daughter, Elizabeth and Zechariah, or those experiencing disease and illness, such as Jairus' daughter or the woman suffering from hemorrhaging.

INVITING READER IDENTITY

Reader identity has to do with the extent to which a reader considers himself or herself similar to a character in the narrative. By presenting a wide range of characters, authors of narrative provide readers with multiple opportunities to identify with at least some of those characters or some elements of their characterization. This feature of narrative draws readers more deeply into the story, as the reading of characters becomes a reading of one's self in relation to others and the world. Affectively, identification may lead readers to develop a sense of solidarity with characters, resulting in sympathy or even empathy, especially when these characters are at least in some ways admirable. On other occasions, however, authors may intentionally lead readers to identify with characters who are not portrayed in an admirable fashion. For example, in reading through Jesus' controversy dialogues with the Pharisees and scribes, recipients may come to the unpleasant realization that they are in some ways like Jesus' opponents, that they share some of their attitudes and values, and even engage in similar behaviors. But they can grudgingly make this connection without necessarily liking the Pharisees and the scribes or wishing them well in the pursuit of their goals. In short, when readers identify with characters that they don't admire, this creates cognitive and emotional dissonance and leads them to question the state of their own character.

Luke's characterization, I believe, reaches this level of sophistication. One example is found in the story of the sinful woman who crashes the dinner party of Simon the Pharisee (Luke 7:36–50). Consider Luke's description of the scene. His repeated mention of "Pharisees"/"Pharisee's house" in the opening verses (vv. 36–37) reinforces the atmosphere of high decorum and concerns for purity surrounding that space. Luke thus accentuates the scandalous nature of the uninvited guest's trespass, as "a woman in the city, who was a sinner," enters a domain forbidden to all like her (v. 37). The woman "comes into this scene like an alien, communicable disease."[8] Even more disturbing, this contagion of a person begins fawning over Jesus. Here the narrative slows as Luke encourages the recipient to attend to each of the woman's acts of humble yet indecorous devotion: standing behind Jesus at his feet and weeping, she continuously (note the imperfect tense in Greek) bathes his feet with her tears,

---

8. Green, *Gospel of Luke*, 307.

drying them with her hair, kissing his feet, and anointing them with costly perfume (vv. 37–38). Her actions could be viewed as a double offense: she is repeatedly touching and even depositing bodily fluids (tears) onto Jesus, thus rendering him unclean. Just as alarming, such intimate actions committed by a "sinful woman" (likely a prostitute or adulteress) could easily be taken in this cultural and social context as containing an erotic edge. No wonder Simon the Pharisee is beside himself and has reason to doubt Jesus' prophetic insight: "If this man were a prophet, he would have known who and what kind of woman this is who is touching him—that she is a sinner" (v. 39).

I think that the natural tendency of Theophilus and others of Luke's elite recipients would be to view the woman's entrance into this setting, along with her actions, as inappropriate, if not downright obscene. Luke presents to them a character who flagrantly transgresses social boundaries that they themselves are inclined to value and uphold. In doing so, Luke encourages them to identify—at least in part—with Simon, the disgruntled host offended by the woman's blatant indiscretion and understandably chagrined by Jesus' failure to reject the woman and her advances. Then, as the story unfolds, Luke (once again) leads his recipients to realize that Jesus sees things through a different set of eyes and finds so much joy in those whom others are inclined to disdain: "Do you see this woman? . . ." (vv. 44–47). In the immediately preceding verses, when accused of befriending sinners and tax collectors, Jesus said, "Wisdom is vindicated by all her children" (vv. 34–35). That statement continues to echo through this story, as Luke challenges Theophilus and others to consider what kind of wisdom they subscribe to. Are they those who, like Simon and his guests, cling to boundaries that divide and demean as measures of decency? Do they find little reason to respond to God and others with passionate gratitude and love? Or, like the indecent, sinful woman, will they recklessly toss all that is peripheral to the Kingdom aside, wantonly give themselves to Jesus and his ways above all else, and shamelessly embrace God's saving reign?

INVITING ADMIRATION OR DISDAIN

Still another common technique used to elicit an affective response to characters is to associate them with qualities or behaviors that invite either admiration or disdain. Justice, faithfulness, superior wisdom, power over threatening forces, compassion, courage—these and other attributes typically lead readers to admire the characters who possess them. Conversely, those displaying narcissistic self-interest, cruelty, ignorance, conceit, cowardice, or lack of mercy are typically disdained by readers. The rhetorical import of this technique is worth noting. Through such characterization an author may lead readers to admire certain characters and then use these characters to promote ideas the author wishes readers to adopt. Conversely, the author may associate characters whom readers likely disdain with a competing worldview he or she would have readers reject. Such techniques are apparent throughout Luke-Acts, as Luke presents a string of admirable characters who serve as spokespersons for the Kingdom, such as Gabriel, Elizabeth, Mary, Zechariah, the angelic host, Simeon, Anna, God, Jesus, the disciples (at least occasionally), Peter, Stephen, Philip, Paul, James, Barnabas, Priscilla, Aquila, and Apollos, amidst a host of unadmirable characters who in varying ways demonstrate allegiance to those dispositions and perspectives opposed to the arrival of God's salvation, such as Satan, the demonic, Pharisees, scribes, "civilized folk," chief priests, the Herodians, greedy merchants, stubborn Israelites, and most members of the ruling class. In doing so, Luke employs the rhetorical force of pathos and ethos in order to persuade recipients to entertain and even embrace the Kingdom story he sets before them.

At still other times, biblical writers may seek to elicit mixed feelings for certain characters, most often attributing negative actions or qualities to characters they otherwise find admirable. The resulting "affective dissonance" creates discomfort, may even be jarring, and focuses attention on the negative attributes or actions assigned to the characters. For example, the patriarchal-matriarchal narratives of Genesis contain numerous characters who display both remarkable trust in God and also moments of anxiety and doubt, dysfunctional conflict, and even sometimes deplorable treatment of others. David and Solomon would be two other notable examples among several in the Israelite scriptures. Within Luke-Acts, we could identify the mostly admirable but mixed portraits of Zechariah, the disciples, the early community (e.g., Acts 6:1–2; 11:1–4; 15:1–2), and even Paul and Barnabas (Acts 15:36–41). Not only do these moments of faithlessness and conflict add realism to Luke's account; they also help recipients to identify those dispositions and actions that could potentially circumvent one's embrace of and witness to the Kingdom. The affective dissonance accompanying such accounts makes them more memorable and rhetorically compelling.

Other Techniques Inviting an Affective Response

Besides those related to plotting and characterization, still other techniques inviting affective response are used by authors of biblical narrative.

Essential Relevance

This may be too obvious to merit mention, but well-composed narratives that revolve around matters essential to human well-being and fulfillment are more likely to gain the attention of their readers. The "stuff that really matters" throbs with pathos, calling readers to feel not only for the characters in the narrative but for themselves as well. Thus, as readers envision characters experiencing the deprivation or achievement of that which is central to blessing, they are likely moved not only for the sake of the characters in the story but also in response to the same realities that readers are invited to envision as possible for themselves.

From beginning to end, Luke claims that the "matters fulfilled among us" (Luke 1:1) are nothing less than the arrival of God's long-awaited Kingdom in the person and mission of Jesus. The astonishment, excitement, and jubilation of characters in the infancy narrative, in addition to their actual words, amplify the obvious and crucial significance of what is taking place in their midst. Jesus repeatedly hammers home the call to subordinate all claims and commitments to one's embrace of the Kingdom. Characters in Acts follow suit, combining the sublime jubilation and urgent call emerging from the Gospel to proclaim the dawn of a new age in venues as varied as houses, synagogues, riversides, prisons, town halls, and palaces.

Paradox

Paradox is the assigning of seemingly disparate attributes to a particular person or situation. Such mixing of incompatible categories creates cognitive dissonance in readers, leading them to question established ways of seeing the world and perhaps eventually to discover some truth about the ways of God. Yet when addressing matters deemed essential to human well-being and fulfillment, paradox is meant to encourage affective dissonance as well. The confounding of categories we use to order our view of reality is not only cognitively jarring but also emotionally stressing. Most of us zealously guard the security we enjoy when all is "in order" with our construal of the world and our perceived place in it. Consequently, we often respond to challenges to essential elements of our worldview with emotionally charged defenses. When the paradox is powerful or compelling enough to penetrate these defenses, the affective and cognitive "upset" we experience can lead us to recognize that something pivotal is at stake and can force us to seek resolution.

The biblical authors recognized that paradox compels these kinds of reactions. They often present characters emoting wonder, amazement, and disbelief in the face of what the characters perceive to be incompatible realities—for example, Peter's rebuke of Jesus after Jesus' first passion prediction (Mark 8:31–33); the wonder and joy of the disciples in Luke when they were finally able to grasp the paradoxical reality of Jesus' death and resurrection (Luke 24:52–53); the disbelief of Jesus' fellow Nazarenes that one from among them should be blessed with such authority, and then their anger when hearing that the Kingdom shall be welcomed among those they find unworthy (Luke 4:16–30); Mary's intense puzzlement at Gabriel's greeting and the news that she—an unwed peasant girl—would give birth to God's messiah, who is described as no mere mortal (Luke 1:26–38); and the Sanhedrin's befuddlement that "uneducated and ordinary men" would be able to heal in the name of Jesus—a crucified criminal of the state and convicted blasphemer—and then eloquently defend their actions (Acts 4:13–17).

Luke understood that the same paradoxical dimensions of the good news that challenged characters in his narrative would also challenge many of his audience. Indeed, Luke does not back down from presenting these seemingly incompatible realities to his recipients. By drawing such paradoxes sharply, and by presenting characters reacting to them with wonder or incredulity, Luke validates and even encourages this same kind of cognitive and emotional dissonance from Theophilus and others, in the hope that this upset will compel them to reconsider their assumptions about the world and make a choice for the Kingdom. At the same time, Luke provides his recipients with other affective and cognitive resources that encourage them to grasp or at least accept the paradoxical realties he relays. Back in chapter 4, I discussed how Luke invites recipients to identify with Mary's confusion regarding her son and to claim Mary as an ally, for these paradoxical notions about Jesus and his manner of conception really do strain notions of what many would conceive as possible. But then, when Mary hears what God has done for Elizabeth and hears the angel's profession about what is possible for God (Luke 1:36–37), Mary remarkably pulls out of her befuddlement and embraces Gabriel's words, or at least puts her faith in God despite her lingering uncertainty about the details concerning Jesus and his conception. In this Luke intends her to be an example for those who sympathize with her and perhaps even identify with her confusion. Gabriel's assurance—"For *nothing* will be impossible with God"—seems directed at doubting or confused recipients as much as it is at Mary. And the skeptical or confused recipient is invited to respond in a way that matches Mary's admirable trust and devotion: "Here am I, the servant of the Lord; let it be with me according to your word" (v. 38). Insofar as recipients relate to Mary via the sympathy or reader identity that Luke invites for her as one who is understandably unprepared for the wondrous, category-defying announcement she receives, and as they admire her for the courageous trust she nevertheless exhibits at the end, they are also prodded to join Mary in responding to these extraordinary claims with their own bold devotion. Likewise, Luke's extension of the threshold moment of Luke 24, as we saw above, invites his audience to participate in Jesus' frustration with his disciples. Moreover, it encourages recipients to set aside such doubt themselves and embrace the rather paradoxical and counterintuitive claim that God's messiah really did need to suffer the humiliation of the cross in order to fulfill the Scriptures and God's plan to save. The unceasing repetition of both of these claims throughout Acts by admirable characters further validates, and even to some extent normalizes, these paradoxical dimensions of the good news.

REVERSAL

Here I use "reversal" as we have employed it thus far to refer to the inversion of culturally endorsed norms and worldviews. Like paradox, reversal challenges readers to reassess their understanding of what truly matters, to see the world in a way that is consistent with the professions that Yahweh rules and Jesus is God's messiah, and to adopt values consistent with those professions. That biblical authors understood reversal as inviting emotional response is (as with paradox) indicated by the fact that they frequently portray or imply the affective reaction of characters (both positive and negative) to the announcement or occurrence of reversal within the narrative. In Luke-Acts, for instance, recall Jesus' embrace of marginal persons, or the ways in which Jesus recasts the law of Moses, or how the testimony of the early church and advance of the Kingdom upends established norms of honor and hierarchy, and how those opposing Jesus and his disciples respond.

As we have seen, Luke pulls no punches in his portrayal of the dramatic reversal inaugurated by the Kingdom's arrival. Along with Luke's use of conflict, such reversal sharply contrasts the ways of God with the ways of the world. This is meant to challenge Theophilus and others to understand that they cannot truly embrace the Kingdom while still participating in the norms and values of Rome. Such a challenge would most likely cause anxiety, fear, and perhaps even sadness (as it did for the rich ruler in Luke 18:18–25). But as with the more dramatic cases of paradox, Luke provides other resources that will hopefully lead Theophilus and others to overcome their fear and doubt. For Luke's persistent portrayal of reversal is accompanied by the equally persistent invitation to discover the blessing and joy of authentic community born of sacrifice, humility, equity, and compassion.

NOSTALGIA

The authors of biblical narrative are masters at weaving into their accounts allusions to other, most often past, biblical events and characters, and as we have seen in chapter 6, Luke is no exception. This recognition is, of course, basic to any serious engagement of biblical narrative. But scholars commonly overlook the fact that such allusion is often freighted with emotional appeal. Through these intertextual echoes, biblical authors sometimes transport some of the affective force of earlier stories (and what the stories have come to represent for their audience) into their own accounts in order to foster expectation, renew hope, color readers' perceptions of characters or events, and heighten readers' investment in what is taking place in the narrative. Biblical authors frequently present recitations of major events in Israel's history as eliciting some sort of emotion in the narrative's characters. It is thus likely that these biblical "summaries" (e.g., Josh. 24:1–15; Ezra 9:5–15; Neh. 9:6–37) were meant to prompt nostalgia in recipients, leading them to appreciate and commit themselves all the more to God's ways of blessing the characters in the story as well as themselves. Or in the case of Stephen in Acts 7, his review of Israel's history and the parallels Luke draws to Jesus' passion foreshadow the violent rejection Stephen will suffer at the hands of Israel and add to the painfully tragic nature of that event: the ignominious infidelity manifested all too often in Israel's distant and recent past continues still, even after the Kingdom has arrived.

On a more subtle but equally powerful level, the echoes to the story of Hannah and Elkanah (1 Sam. 1) in the naming of John (Luke 1:57–66) further accentuate the naming story's implication that in receiving a name outside his kin group, John—as was Samuel—is being set apart for service to the Lord, and from his own kin. This amplifies the element of sacrifice that also pervades this scene.[9] Like Hannah and Elkanah, Elizabeth and Zechariah accept God's will that their beloved son is called to a mission that will ultimately take him beyond their household and from them as parents. When Samuel was weaned, Hannah gathered up the child for whom she had desperately yearned and traveled back to Shiloh. "She left him there for the LORD" (1 Sam. 1:28). Here Zechariah and Elizabeth, in effect, do the same. Their naming of John was not a mindless recitation of Gabriel's command. The defiant tone of Elizabeth's "No" (v. 60) tells us that they realized well what was at stake. And yet recipients who have sympathized with Elizabeth and Zechariah and rejoiced in their blessing of a son are now led to recognize and participate in the sense of loss that also pervades this scene—to hear the sorrow mixed in with Elizabeth and Zechariah's righteous resolve. Luke reveals through this affectively laden moment that the restoration of Israel will be accompanied

9. For a more detailed discussion on Luke's use of pathos in this scene, see Karl Allen Kuhn, "Deaf or Defiant? The Literary, Cultural, and Affective-Rhetorical Keys to the Naming of John (Luke 1:57–80)," *CBQ* 75 (2013): 486–503.

by personal sacrifice. This is perhaps the first indication in Luke's narrative that God's Kingdom will come at a cost, not only for the proud and Israel's enemies, but for the faithful as well. Zechariah and Elizabeth prove up to the challenge, even if it means that they have to leave their beloved son, John, for the Lord. Theophilus is led to ask, "Would I do the same?"

CONTRASTING THE BEAUTIFUL AND THE UGLY, THE DESPERATE AND THE HOPEFUL

Still another technique employed by biblical writers to evoke an affective response from recipients is the juxtaposition within a scene of two sharply contrasting dispositions that represent the extremes of which humanity is capable. For example, the story of Solomon judging between the two women both claiming an infant as their son sets the sacrificial love of one woman against the callous, self-serving cruelty of the other (1 Kings 3:16–28). David's heart-wrenching angst over the death of his rebellious son Absalom movingly displays his paternal love for a troublesome child who sought David's own life, and yet also recalls David's own cruel sin against Uriah: "Now therefore the sword shall never depart from your own house" (2 Sam. 12:9–12). Jesus' cry on the cross, "Eloi, Eloi, lema sabachthani?" (Mark 15:34), captures both the desperation and the hope embodied in Psalm 22 as a whole.

Turning to Luke, we see the Gerasene demoniac's posture of discipleship and sincere resolve to follow Jesus after he has been healed standing in antithetical parallelism to the civilized city-folk's (and the demons'!) reaction to Jesus, wishing that he would leave them as soon as possible (Luke 8:26–39). As the Gospel unfolds and the conflict intensifies between Jesus and the elite, we see Jesus' courageous resolve to be faithful to God dramatically contrasted with the elite's desperate resolve to destroy him (22:39–53), embracing their "hour, and the power of darkness" (v. 53). Acts is filled with sharply opposing responses to the Kingdom's manifestation. Here, a few examples will suffice. At Pentecost, some onlookers perceived the Spirit's arrival, while "others sneered and said, 'They are filled with new wine'" (Acts 2:12–13). Stephen's heavenly vision and echo of Jesus' grace-filled words on the cross, "Father, forgive them; for they do not know what they are doing" (Luke 23:34), while he meets his own end dramatically contrast Stephen's confident hope in Jesus with the fearful, stiff-necked rejection of God's messiah and his followers by those who stone Stephen (Acts 7:54–60). The ministry of believers in Thessalonica leads "a great many of the devout Greeks and not a few of the leading women" to embrace Paul's testimony to the Kingdom (17:4), while jealous Israelites and "ruffians in the marketplaces" incite a violent mob that attacks Jason's home (17:5–7). Paul's ongoing, faith-filled witness to "all who came to him" (28:30) even while he awaited his trial and eventual death stands in sharp tension with the reality that others among God's people tragically continue to resist the arrival of God's new age. Joining with conflict and characterization, such dramatic contrast between the extremes of which humanity is capable heightens recipients' emotionally freighted sense of what is at stake in the choices they themselves make and calls them to consider to which lot they wish to belong.

An Additional Example

To illustrate further Luke's use of pathos to advance his rhetorical ends, I discuss below his portrayal of the Israelite elite in Acts 4:1–22.

In this stirring scene, Luke employs a number of the affective techniques we reviewed above to engage Theophilus, such as astonishing inversion of the expected, reversal, inviting admiration and disdain, portraying the best and worst of humanity, essential relevance, threshold moments, and nostalgia. As we saw in chapter 4, these verses are closely connected to the immediately preceding and following narrative and are also an integral part of a section spanning 3:1–4:31. This broader section begins with Peter and John going to the temple to pray, encountering and healing a lame man at the gate of the temple. Then in response to the amazement and pondering of the crowd, Peter offers a second speech explaining the source of his healing power (3:1–26).

Prior to Acts 4:1–22, Peter's speech in 3:12–26 rehearses the basic elements of the kerygma as formulated by Luke. Yet it also amplifies the tragic nature of Jesus' death at the hands of his own people. Peter employs pathos-laden language and a series of contrasting statements to underscore the astounding character and consequences of the people's response to Jesus. God has glorified his servant Jesus, whom they "handed over and rejected in the presence of Pilate" (3:13). Pilate found no reason to condemn Jesus, but they "rejected the Holy and Righteous One" (v. 14). More damning still, they asked for a murderer to be released to them, and in his place they killed "the Author of life" (v. 14).

God reverses the human no to Jesus, raising him from the dead. But through Peter we learn that Jesus' resurrection not only has the power to reverse the death of Jesus as the result of the people's wicked rejection; it also now affords the opportunity to reverse the character of the people's own hearts. Through Jesus, new life and salvation are made available to this formerly lame man and all who call upon Jesus for salvation, including those who were responsible for his death, *even* the elite (vv. 17–21). This astonishing offer of grace is accompanied by a stern warning. Citing from torah, Peter identifies Jesus as the awaited "prophet like Moses" (v. 22) and warns that from this point forward "everyone who does not listen to that prophet will be utterly rooted out of the people" (v. 23). Even so, the primary tone of this passage is that of mercy, offering forgiveness and the reclamation of the place that God's people are to have among all nations despite what they have done. Just before being interrupted by the temple elite, Peter cites the Abrahamic covenant (Gen. 12:1–3), announcing that God still intends to return blessing to all the nations of the earth through Israel and that it will all begin with God's people (vv. 24–26).

Therefore, leading up to 4:1–22, we encounter the joined emphases of Israel's wicked rejection of Jesus, leading nevertheless to this astonishing, new opportunity for grace, and God's undying commitment to bless God's people that they might fulfill their ancient calling to minister to the rest of humanity. With this dramatic narration, Luke guides Theophilus and others to an important threshold moment: How will the people and their leaders respond to these grace-filled words calling for repentance and reconciliation, despite all the wickedness they have committed?

Luke's recipients do not have to wait long to find out. Peter's gracious words are interrupted by an entourage of the Israelite elite, the guardians of the temple.[10] Beside themselves with "complete exasperation" (διαπονέομαι) because the apostles are proclaiming the resurrection of the dead in Jesus, they arrest Peter and John and put them in prison for the evening (4:2–3).[11] Luke's recipients are likely intended to discern two interconnected reasons for this reaction. Sadducees, as we know from Josephus and the Synoptics, including Luke (Luke 20:27; Acts 23:8), did not believe in the resurrection due to its perceived absence from their sacred traditions. Peter was proclaiming that such did indeed happen and was now made possible for others "in Jesus," a convicted blasphemer and enemy of the Roman state. Then, initiating an implied contrast that will only become sharper in the narrative to follow, Luke reports that from among the people, "many who heard the word believed." Their number was simply astounding, eclipsing by far the mass conversion at Pentecost: "about five thousand" (Acts 4:4).

The leaders, however, with their annoyance and seizure of Peter and John, have thus far shown no inclination to embrace Peter's claims regarding Jesus and his calls for repentance. Using the authority and power available to them,

10. Wall ("Acts of the Apostles," 83) points out that Acts includes several stories involving interrupted speeches or actions (2:37; 7:54; 8:39–40; 10:44; 17:32; 22:22; 26:24): "This literary device often introduces important elements into the story—a leading question, a principle player, a theological problem." One could add that it continues the challenge-riposte form so common in the Gospels to portray the opposition to Jesus and the Kingdom.

11. Witherington, *Acts of the Apostles*, 190.

they speedily silence Peter's testimony. One might hope that the morning light will inspire their clarity of mind and heart, as the Sanhedrin and other invested stakeholders among the elite now gather in full force to hold council: "The next day their rulers, elders, and scribes assembled in Jerusalem, with Annas the high priest, Caiaphas, John, and Alexander, and all who were of the high-priestly family" (Acts 4:5–6).[12] Instead, the dawn of day only illuminates the tragic, even maddening, impenetrability of their obduracy. Luke's shaping of the scene includes at least four features that cultivate an affective response from Theophilus.

A Dramatic Moment of Decision

As just mentioned above, Luke's plotting leads his recipients to a threshold moment, as they await the people's response to God's gracious offer of repentance and reconciliation. Despite the people's murder of God's Holy One, God will honor God's covenantal commitment and still desires to be reunited with them. Peter's grace-filled appeal and the essential relevance of this moment for the leaders of Israel charge this scene with a precipitously dramatic energy.

Tragic Obduracy in Contrast to Faithful Testimony

In the preceding narrative, Luke presents the healed man as a clear and apparent manifestation of God's power (Acts 3:12), and here he repeatedly juxtaposes that obvious "sign" with the elite's obstinate refusal to hear the word. Gathered the next day with Peter and John standing in their midst, the Sanhedrin themselves bring the sign into focus: "By what power or by what name did you do this?" they demand (4:5–7). Peter's defense likewise recalls the miracle he performed: "Rulers of the people and elders, if we are questioned today because of a good deed done to someone who was sick and are asked how this man has been healed . . ." (vv. 8–9). Peter then testifies to Jesus, offering a truncated version of the kerygma, proclaiming, "Let it be known to all of you, and to all the people of Israel, that this man is standing before you in good health by the name of Jesus Christ of Nazareth, whom you crucified, whom God raised from the

---

12. The precise membership of the Sanhedrin is debated by scholars and in reality may have been somewhat variable during this time (see *ABD* 5:975–80). Luke is apparently not interested in precision here, and he presents all the elite figures he mentions as "holding council" against Peter and John. Annas served as high priest from 6 to 15 CE, and his son-in-law, Caiaphas, from 18 to 36 CE. The use of the title "high priest" for Annas here by Luke may reflect a conventional way of referring to former holders of the office. "John" might be the "Jonathan" Josephus names as the son of Annas (*Ant.* 18.4.3 §95), who briefly served as high priest from 36 to 37 CE, but otherwise he and Alexander are unknown to us.

dead" (v. 10). Following Peter's defense, the elite "saw the man who had been cured standing beside them," and "they had nothing to say in opposition" (v. 14).

However, the elite's repeated examination and consideration of the sign, and their recognition of its reality and astounding character, are not enough to penetrate their disbelieving hearts. In so presenting the Israelite elite, Luke amplifies their stubborn and wicked obduracy. Their interrogation of the apostles brought to the fore the issues of power and authority: "By what power or by what name . . . ?" (v. 7). Luke crafts the passage to emphasize that it is the power and authority of the Spirit, Jesus, and God that are manifest in the ministry of Peter and John. "Then Peter, filled with the *Holy Spirit*, said to them . . . " (v. 8) prefaces Peter's testimony to "the *name of Jesus Christ* . . . whom *God* raised from the dead" (v. 10). Peter then grounds that reality in the testimony of Scripture, citing again from the stone-texts tradition of Psalm 118 (v. 11), before moving to the crescendo of his defense, proclaiming that "there is salvation in no one else, for there is no other name under heaven given among mortals by which we must be saved" (v. 12). All is now in place for the elite to cast aside their ignorance and see what is so plain before them. Peter and John speak with a boldness and eloquence that far transcend their background and stature; the man who has already been "saved" (σῴζω) by Jesus is standing right next to them; and the pattern of Jesus' ministry, rejection, and resurrection, along with the gift of the Holy Spirit among the people, was foretold by the Scriptures as a manifestation of God's plan to save Israel and "all the families of the earth" (Gen. 12:3). But the elite refuse Peter's cry to "let it be known" to them (v. 10). Rather than embrace and rejoice in God's offer of repentance and reconciliation, they dismiss Peter's testimony as a fraud and, in so doing, dismiss the manifestation of the authority and power of God among them. More wicked still, they try "to keep it from spreading further among the people" and order John and Peter "not to speak or teach at all in the name of Jesus" (vv. 17, 18). Thus, in rejecting this good news, they are not only rejecting the emergence of the Kingdom among them and the blessing that it offers them; they are obstructing the very purpose for which they were constituted as God's people in the days of Abram: to serve as a source of blessing for others. In sharp contrast, when Peter and John are informed of the Sanhedrin's verdict, they boldly counter by stating their unyielding commitment to the vocation demanded by the Kingdom's arrival: "Whether it is right in God's sight to listen to you rather than to God, you must judge; for we cannot keep from speaking about what we have seen and heard" (vv. 19–20; see also 5:29).[13] Luke draws the

---

13. Tannehill (*Narrative Unity*, 2:62) argues that Peter's shorter speeches here in 4:8–12 and 5:29–32 "are also important because they dramatically demonstrate *persistent* speaking in the

scene in compelling, black-and-white tones: the Sanhedrin's and the apostles' responses to the in-breaking of God's reign represent the extremes of which humanity is capable.

Nostalgic Intratextual Echoes

Finally, Luke imports into this account via parallelism the pathos of two earlier, affectively laden portions of the narrative. Commentators frequently note the similarities between this story and elements in Luke's passion narrative: the questioning of Jesus' authority by the chief priests, scribes, and elders in the temple ("Tell us, by what authority are you doing these things?" [Luke 20:1–2]); the parable of the wicked tenants to follow, which also applies the stone-texts tradition of Psalm 118 to the elite (20:9–19); Jesus' arrest (22:47–53) and trial before the Sanhedrin (22:66–71). Not noted by commentators but equally relevant, it seems to me, is Simeon's prophecy in Luke 2: "This child is destined for the falling and rising of many in Israel, and to be a sign that will be opposed so that the inner thoughts of many will be revealed" (2:34–35). As we mentioned in our discussion of that passage, the phrase "a sign [σημεῖον] that will be opposed" is taken by many to be an allusion to the very same stone-texts tradition cited here. Moreover, the centrality of the "sign" (σημεῖον; Acts 4:16, 22) embodied in the man who has been healed "in Jesus' name" provides another point of connection. Together, these allusions to earlier points of Luke's narrative lead Theophilus and others to perceive that the rejection of Jesus prophesied by Simeon and later enacted by Israel's elite is continuing in their ongoing resistance to the advent of God's Kingdom. The allusions also import into this scene the sense of tragedy introduced by Simeon's prophecy and manifested in the elite's collusion with the "power of darkness" (Luke 22:53).

These three affectively laden dimensions of the story conspire to provoke Theophilus and others to be filled with a sense of antipathy and loathing for the elite. I don't believe that it is an overstatement to say that Luke's characterization portrays the elite as ignorant, obstinate, self-important, and self-destructive. The repeated apposition of the irrefutable sign of the healed man with the elite's refusal to see and believe brings these elements of their character to the fore. At the same time, Luke is not interested in unveiling the astounding degree of the

---

face of opposition." Witherington (*Acts of the Apostles*, 197) suggests that the response of Peter and John to the council may echo Socrates' words when he was on trial before the Athenian judges and was ordered to desist from teaching: "I shall obey God rather than you, and while I have life and strength I shall never cease from the practice and teaching of philosophy" (Plato, *Apology* 29D).

elite's foolishness simply to invite disdain for those who reject the Kingdom's arrival. The gracious offer of God's forgiveness and the reminder of the vocation to which God's people have been called in the preceding narrative, along with the allusion to Simeon's prophecy in Luke 2, also invite Theophilus to taste (again) the bitter tragedy permeating this scene. Indeed, the falling and rising of many, opposition and rejection, these shall be markers of the Kingdom's arrival. Since Simeon's announcement, Theophilus and others have known this to be true. But that knowledge does not diminish, but rather enhances, the affective sting accompanying this latest, dramatic display of tragic resistance to God's reign. To be sure, there is great news relayed here as well: five thousand have been added to the number of the believers (Acts 4:4)! But there could be many more, if only the shepherds of God's people had not joined those conspiring "against the Lord and against his Messiah" (4:26).

Inviting Admiration

Finally, the courageous witness of Peter and John in the face of—and in contrast to—such obstinate opposition also invites Theophilus' admiration. These heralds of the Kingdom, here and repeatedly in the narrative to follow, boldly proclaim God's incredible overture of forgiveness, reconciliation, and blessing in the face of demonic opposition. Their witness is thus meant not only for the crowds but for Luke's patron as well. Which side, Theophilus, will you join?

Conclusion

Emotions play a crucial role in our reading of a narrative, in our engagement of its claims about the world, and in our willingness or not to recast our own storied worldviews in response to that encounter. *Affective appeal in varying forms is the means by which narratives compel us to enter their storied world and entertain the version of reality they present.* This is no less true for much of biblical narrative, and especially for Luke and Acts. By attending to the affective dimension of Luke's story, I believe that we can refine and sharpen our understanding of the narrative world—the kingdom story—into which Luke was inviting Theophilus and others.

Part 3

Luke's
Kingdom Story

I n chapter 2 I argued that Israelite and early Christian conceptions of God's
awaited Kingdom, for all their variety, are best viewed as narratives ani-
mating three essential claims. At their most basic level, these "kingdom
stories" proclaim the following:

1. Yahweh is King of Israel and Ruler of the universe.
2. The current order of creation and state of God's people are not in accord
   with God's will.
3. God will act to reorder creation into alignment with God's intentions.

These three basic features of Kingdom hope will guide us, as they did for our
brief review of Mark's narrative, in discerning and articulating the core con-
fessional commitments that energize Luke's own kingdom story. Moreover, by
paying close attention to how Luke distinctively shapes these elemental features
of his narrative, we will be in a good position to advance our understanding of
his primary rhetorical objectives. In pursuit of these two tasks, the chapters to

follow will engage each of these three fundamental, though richly elaborated, dimensions of Luke's witness.

Chapter 9 will review Luke's characterization of God and God's rule and its necessary corollary, Luke's characterization of Jesus and his sovereignty. Chapter 10 will first investigate the ills of this age that the evangelist unmasks, including the faithlessness of Israel, the degrading influence of the demonic, and the dehumanizing inequity spawned by Rome and the elite. It will then explore God's great counterstroke, which Luke claims has already begun to set the world to rights, leading those eager for a different kind of world and different Lord into a realm of extraordinary blessing. The concluding chapter will draw from the preceding discussion as I summarize my understanding of Luke's primary rhetorical objectives in conversation with the views of others.

9

Yahweh Is King and
Lord of All

Our exploration of Luke-Acts thus far has established that the confession of Yahweh, the God of Israel, as Creator and Sovereign of all that exists is a core feature of Luke's narrative. Even though this fundamental claim is more often implicit than directly stated, it is clearly embodied in Luke's and his characters' incessant insistence that the events to which they bear witness are initiated by God to fulfill God's promised deliverance of Israel and all humanity (recall, e.g., Luke 2:29–32; 24:47; Acts 17:30–31). However, when Paul speaks before the Areopagus, the pagan sophists of Athens who do not know the God of Israel, it becomes necessary for him to expressly articulate this core commitment:

> What therefore you worship as unknown, this I proclaim to you. The God who made the world and everything in it, he who is Lord of heaven and earth, does not live in shrines made by human hands, nor is he served by human hands, as though he needed anything, since he himself gives to all mortals life and breath and all things. From one ancestor he made all nations to inhabit the whole earth, and he allotted the times of their existence and the boundaries of the places where they would live. (Acts 17:23–26; see also Acts 7:48–50; 14:16–17)

Despite the emphasis placed on God's sovereign rule over creation in this passage and implied throughout the narrative, a dialectical tension characteristic

205

of most Israelite tradition is also amplified in Luke's narrative. Even though Yahweh is able to reverse the wrongs of humanity and the demonic, even though the rejection of Yahweh's own Son, Jesus, was a necessary part of the divine plan, even though God is now moving creation back into alignment with God's purposes, the accomplishment of God's saving purposes also hinges on humanity's trust and devotion. Both the Gospel and Acts make it abundantly clear that the Kingdom is to be an embodied reality: it is to be manifest in human communities of witness, service, and generosity (e.g., Luke 9:1–6, 10–17; 10:1–20; 19:1–10; Acts 2:43–47; 4:32–5:11). Consequently, as Luke emphasizes throughout his story, the advent of the Kingdom must be received and enacted by those who have prepared their hearts "for the way of the Lord." As the examples of many in Luke's story reveal, the unfolding of Yahweh's salvation in Jesus is not irresistible. The truthfulness of the faithful's testimony cannot be assailed (Luke 21:15), the Kingdom's manifestation is all but obvious (Acts 4:16), but it can be rejected through willful ignorance (recall the Israelite elite in Acts 3–4) or wickedness (recall Ananias and Sapphira in Acts 5). Luke's sense of both the essential and the problematic nature of human free will, and its consequences for not only Israel but all human history, is also implied in his account of the temptation story (Luke 4:1–13). As opposed to Adam, who failed to resist Satan's lure, Jesus is another "son of God" (3:38) who by his faithful resolve to fulfill God's will makes a new future for creation possible. His resolve is dramatically affirmed near the Gospel's close as he prays on the Mount of Olives, "Yet, not my will but yours be done" (22:41–42). Yahweh is indeed sovereign Creator, but the necessity of choice and trust as components of genuine relationship continues to complicate Yahweh's attempts to restore creation and its human creatures.

Other Key Dimensions of Yahweh's Character

In his portrayal of Yahweh as sovereign Lord, Luke emphasizes, along with his Israelite ancestors, several features of God's character.

God is intensely relational. Nearly every facet of Israelite sacred tradition characterizes Yahweh not only as transcendent Creator and Lord but also as one who is intensely relational and immanent. Similarly, Luke presents God as repeatedly engaging humanity through a variety of mediums: angelic appearances (e.g., Luke 1:5–20, 26–38; 2:8–15; Acts 10:1–8; 12:6–11), visions (e.g., Acts 7:55–56; 10:9–16), and direct speech (e.g., Luke 3:22; 9:35; Acts 9:3–6, 10–16). As we saw above, Luke also recalls numerous occurrences in which God guides and empowers characters through the Holy Spirit and enables them to grasp

God's intentions as revealed in the Scriptures. God is also revealed as deeply committed to the well-being of Israel and all humanity. One technique Luke employs to convey this concern is his repeated references to the Abrahamic covenant, which at the same time evokes God's covenantal commitment to Israel (e.g., Luke 1:55, 73; 3:8; 13:16; 16:23; 19:9; Acts 3:13; 7:2–8, 16–17, 32; 13:26) as well as God's intent that Israel become a source of blessing for all nations (see also Luke 2:29–32; Acts 3:24–25). Also typical of God in Israel's sacred tradition is Yahweh's intimate knowledge of and engagement in the lives of individuals. This is characteristic of Luke-Acts as well. Beyond his intimate relationship with Jesus, God hears Zechariah's and Elizabeth's prayers for a child (Luke 1:13); looks with favor on Mary (1:28–30, 46–50); reveals to the righteous Simeon and Anna the advent of God's awaited salvation; is aware of the extraordinary degradation of Ananias and Sapphira (Acts 5:1–11), Paul (9:1–9), and Herod (12:20–23); delivers first Peter (12:6–11) and then Paul and Silas (16:25–34) from prison; and instructs and guides Paul through the Spirit (16:10; 20:22–23; 21:11).

God is faithful to the covenant and promises made to Israel. Repeatedly in the preceding chapters, we have discussed God's faithfulness to the promises God has made as a key point of emphasis for Luke. It is one of the primary motifs implicitly or expressly stated in frequent citations and allusions to Israel's sacred traditions, and one of the standard elements of Luke's version of the kerygma. In addition to the references to the Abrahamic covenant noted above, Luke also frequently refers to Jesus' fulfillment of the promises to David (Luke 1:27, 32, 69; 2:4, 11; 18:38–39; 20:41–44; Acts 1:16; 2:25; 4:25; 13:22, 34–36) or to Israel's "ancestors" or "fathers" (Luke 1:55, 72; Acts 3:13, 25; 5:30; 7:32; 13:26, 32; 22:14; 24:14; 26:6).

God is a merciful and compassionate Savior. In chapter 6, while discussing Mary's and Zechariah's hymns, we paused to consider the characterization of God as a merciful and compassionate Savior, delivering the faithful from all that prevents their participation in God's blessing, including threat within and without. This is a fundamental dimension of God's character emphasized throughout Israel's scriptures, especially in the book of Exodus as God first delivers Israel from their enemies in Egypt and then from their own waywardness, manifested most dramatically in the golden calf affair (Exod. 32:1–34:28; see also Num. 14:18; Neh. 9:17, 31; Ps. 103:8). Throughout the remainder of Luke-Acts, God's mercy is apparent in the repeated announcement of forgiveness as integral to the arrival of the Kingdom (Luke 6:36; 18:13; 24:47; Acts 2:38–39; 3:17–20; 10:43). God's compassion is also evident in Jesus' and the disciples' ministries of healing that release humanity from its bondage to disease and the demonic—for example, in Luke 7:13: "When the Lord saw her, he had compassion for her and said to her, 'Do not weep'" (see also Luke 13:16; Acts 10:38).

God is a warrior and judge who overthrows oppressors, elite, and faithless. While discussing Mary's and Zechariah's hymns, we also noted that Yahweh's deliverance of the faithful will also entail the overthrow of the elite and powerful (Luke 1:51–53), the enemies of Israel (1:71, 73–74). This is still another feature of Yahweh unveiled in Israel's scriptures: God's identity as Savior is bound up with God's identity as divine Warrior (see Luke 1:49). Yet as Luke's narrative unfolds, we see that these early references to enemies, the proud, and the powerful who oppose God and the faithful of Israel are not simply ornamental carryovers from Israelite tradition. Rather, they enable us to recognize even at the narrative's beginning that the unfolding of God's deliverance for Israel and all humanity will be contested (recall also Simeon's pronouncement in 2:34–35).

God's response to such opposition is a combination of mercy and wrath. We will address Luke's portrayal of God's overthrow of evil in its various forms in chapter 10. For now, note that Luke, like much of Israelite apocalyptic tradition before him, including Mark and Paul, makes it clear that the consequences are dire for those of the demonic realm and among humanity who resist the manifestation of the Kingdom among them. As we have seen in the speeches of Acts, grace and forbearance persist in the wake of Israel's ignorant rejection of Jesus. But there is a limit to God's patience. As Peter and others announce, with the resurrection of Jesus and the advance of the Kingdom in their ministry, wicked faithlessness must end. For those who persist in such willful rejection of God, God's messiah, and his followers will be "utterly rooted out of the people" (Acts 3:23). Likewise, for gentiles, "while God has overlooked the times of human ignorance, now he commands all people everywhere to repent, because he has fixed a day on which he will have the world judged in righteousness by a man whom he has appointed" (Acts 17:30–31).

Already in Luke we have learned that evil days await those who have rejected the arrival of God's salvation. Recall Jesus' woes leveled at those towns refusing Jesus' disciples (Luke 10:13–16); his bitter denunciation of the Pharisees and lawyers (11:37–52); his warning about the necessity of repentance followed by the parable of the barren fig tree (13:1–9); his description of the cataclysms accompanying the arrival of the Son of Man at the end of times, including the separation of the righteous and wicked (17:22–37); his ominous prophecies about the fall of Jerusalem (19:41–44; 21:20–24) because it "did not recognize the time of [its] visitation" (19:44); and his equally ominous pronouncement that "everyone who falls on that stone will be broken to pieces; and it will crush anyone on whom it falls" (20:18).

These warnings and prophecies are neither pronouncements of unavoidable doom nor simply hyperbolic threats designed to scare Theophilus and others to true repentance. Instead, God's character as judge and the days of judgment that are due to arrive *underscore the inescapable reality of choosing either for or against the Kingdom, and the consequences that await each of those choices.* As Joel Green states regarding Luke 17:33 ("Those who try to make their life secure will lose it, but those who lose their life will keep it"): "At stake is the nature of one's disposition, one's commitments, one's attachments, one's ultimate loyalty."[1]

Yahweh Unveiled in Jesus

One simply cannot adequately assess Luke's characterization of God apart from an account of Luke's characterization of Jesus. Nearly all modern readers of Luke appreciate this on some level: because Jesus is sent by and acts on behalf of God, what Jesus says and does reflects God's will and thus also God's character. For instance, while I tried above to focus as much as possible on what Luke directly says about or attributes to God, at various points I also had to incorporate Jesus' teaching and actions into my analysis to offer a fuller picture of what Luke presumes and proclaims about Yahweh. As the mediator of God's will and the champion of God's Kingdom, Jesus represents the purpose and person of God. To put it in Jesus' words as recorded by Luke, "All things have been handed over to me by my Father; and no one knows who the Son is except the Father, or who the Father is except the Son and anyone to whom the Son chooses to reveal him" (Luke 10:22). Thus, to get a fuller picture of Luke's understanding of God, we also need to explore how his portrait of Jesus, including Jesus' teachings and actions, is meant to "reveal the Father." Here, however, we enter the contentious domain of Luke's Christology. Despite the widespread recognition among interpreters that Jesus' mission and person reflect God's character in Luke-Acts, there is significant disagreement among them on the specific contours of the evangelist's portrayal of Jesus.

The Debate about Luke's Christology

One fairly recent survey of scholarly perspectives on Luke's presentation of Jesus describes no less than eighteen different "controlling Christologies" that have been proposed for Luke-Acts, some of which have only one main

1. Green, *Gospel of Luke*, 635–36.

proponent.[2] Moreover, the views scholars espouse on key features of Luke's Christology are so variable that they defy easy classification into representative groupings. At the same time, many debates on Luke's Christology revolve around at least four major points.

1. Perhaps foremost among these areas of disagreement is the nature of the relationship between Jesus and God. While all recognize that Luke presents Jesus as an extraordinary individual called to play a pivotal role in the establishment of God's salvation, a number of scholars stress that Luke emphasizes Jesus' humanness and/or subordination to God.[3] Other scholars, in contrast, argue that Luke intends to present Jesus as divine and in many respects equal to God, while maintaining a distinction between the two.[4]

2. Closely related to the first is a disputed matter of emphasis: Does Luke set out to tell the story of Jesus the Savior, or does he intend to tell the story of God's salvation, in which Jesus serves as its primary mediator? In other words, is the focus of Luke-Acts on God's "salvation history" (as stressed by Hans Conzelmann and others) or on Jesus as the unique and exalted Savior who emerges as a central figure alongside God, not one peripheral to God?[5]

3. A third point of dispute addresses the timing of Jesus' exaltation as Messiah and Lord. Some argue, based on Peter's Pentecost sermon announcing, "God has made him both Lord and Messiah, this Jesus whom you crucified" (2:36), that Luke presents Jesus as first becoming Messiah and Lord after his resurrection and ascension. Consequently, Jesus' status as Messiah and Lord (whether divine or not) is bestowed upon him by God as a result, or at least

2. H. Douglas Buckwalter, *The Character and Purpose of Luke's Christology*, SNTSMS 89 (Cambridge: Cambridge University Press, 2005), 3–24. The overview I provide below is in many respects indebted to Buckwalter's survey.

3. See, e.g., Conzelmann, *Theology of St. Luke*, 178; Christopher Tuckett, *Christology and the New Testament: Jesus and His Earliest Followers* (Louisville: Westminster John Knox, 2001), 141; Eric Franklin, *Christ the Lord: A Study in the Purpose and Theology of Luke-Acts* (London: SPCK, 1975); Charles H. Talbert, "The Concept of Immortals in Mediterranean Antiquity," *JBL* (1975): 419–36.

4. See, e.g., Witherington, *Acts of the Apostles*, 147–53; Fitzmyer, *Acts of the Apostles*, 260; Buckwalter, *Luke's Christology*; Robert F. O'Toole, *Luke's Presentation of Jesus: A Christology*, SubBi 25 (Rome: Editrice Pontificio Istituto Biblico, 2004); C. Kavin Rowe, *Early Narrative Christology: The Lord in the Gospel of Luke* (Grand Rapids: Baker Academic, 2006); Richard Bauckham, *Jesus and the God of Israel: "God Crucified" and Other Studies on the New Testament's Christology of Divine Identity* (Grand Rapids: Eerdmans, 2008); Darrell L. Bock, *Proclamation from Prophecy and Pattern: Lucan Old Testament Christology*, JSNTSup 12 (Sheffield: JSOT Press, 1987), and more recently, *A Theology of Luke and Acts*, BTNT (Grand Rapids: Zondervan, 2012).

5. See, e.g., Buckwalter, *Luke's Christology*, 168–70; I. Howard Marshall, *Luke—Historian and Theologian*, 3rd ed. (Exeter: Paternoster, 1988), 19, 85–86, 116–17, 176–78; Ralph P. Martin, "Salvation and Discipleship in Luke's Gospel," *Int* 30 (1976): 367–72.

in the aftermath, of his sacrifice and exaltation. A term commonly used to identify this christological perspective is "adoptionist." It takes its name from the notion found in Israelite tradition that the Israelite king is "adopted" as God's son upon his enthronement and anointing (see Ps. 2:7).[6] Others argue that the exalted and divine identity of Jesus is already revealed in the infancy narrative, and that Acts "presents a messianic unveiling of what was announced of Jesus in Luke's Gospel right from the start."[7]

4. While nearly all readers of Luke-Acts recognize that the evangelist applies an array of images and titles to Jesus, scholars disagree on which of those images or titles should be regarded as primary for understanding Luke's presentation of Jesus' identity.

An Exploration of Luke's Christology

Offering an account of Luke's portrait of Jesus is kind of like trying to explain a richly textured, powerful, and compelling piece of artwork. The explanation is simply inadequate to the task and unavoidably reductionist. Nevertheless, the goals of this chapter require that we give it a go. As a means of ensuring that my attempt is relevant to the wider scholarly discussion, I am going to engage these four issues as I present my own understanding of Luke's characterization of Jesus. I will address the first three in the opening section on the person and work of Jesus in relation to the person and work of Yahweh, and the fourth in my discussion of Luke's portrayal of Jesus not only through the images and titles he employs but also through his depiction of Jesus' teachings, actions, and disposition.

The Person and Work of Jesus Is Interlaced with the Person and Work of Yahweh

In my analysis of several passages in the preceding chapters, I have claimed that Luke "blurs the lines of distinction" between Jesus and God or "converges" the missions and characters of Jesus and God. I noted several features of Luke's account as contributing to this convergence.

6. See John A. T. Robinson, "The Most Primitive Christology of All?," in *Twelve New Testament Studies* (London: SCM, 1962); Ferdinand Hahn, *The Titles of Jesus in Christology: Their History in Early Christianity* (London: Lutterworth, 1969), 107; Arie W. Zwiep, *Christ, the Spirit and the Community of God: Essays on the Acts of the Apostles*, WUNT 2.293 (Tübingen: Mohr Siebeck, 2010), 140–44.

7. Buckwalter, *Luke's Christology*, 189. So also Tannehill, *Narrative Unity*, 2:38–39; Rowe, *Narrative Christology*, 188–89; Witherington, *Acts of the Apostles*, 149; Bock, *Theology of Luke and Acts*, 182–84.

1. The point of the step-parallelism Luke employs in his infancy narrative is primarily christological: it invites recipients to discern that both God and Jesus are the "Lord" for whom John is preparing the way.

2. Gabriel's annunciation of Jesus' birth (1:32–35) describes Jesus in terms that just don't fit a mere mortal. He attributes to Jesus characteristics normally predicated of God in Israelite tradition: Jesus shall be "holy" and "great" without qualification. He defines Jesus' messiahship in terms of his identity as the divine Son, hailed by the titles "Son of the Most High" (v. 32) and "Son of God" (v. 35). Jesus' own rule (and not that of his lineage) will be eternal, and his very conception will be accomplished not by a normal union between a man and a woman but by the Holy Spirit. Israelite tradition, as we saw back in chapter 2, includes precedents for an agent of Yahweh imbued with divine-like characteristics and authority, and Luke may very well be drawing on one such tradition, 4Q246, in his composition of Gabriel's announcement. Considering all these features of the annunciation, the evangelist seems to present Jesus here as participating in his Father's divinity.

3. Luke employs several additional titles for Jesus suggesting that Jesus' identity transcends the human realm and is to be seen in direct connection to Yahweh. Most prominently, he uses "Lord" (κύριος) for both Jesus and God throughout Luke-Acts. Two factors indicate that Luke is using the title to interlace the characters of Jesus and God.[8] First, as I pointed out in chapter 2, the designation of Jesus as κύριος throughout the NT reflects the widespread confession among early believers that Jesus is divine and rules alongside Yahweh (cf. Phil. 2:5–11 and see esp. Acts 10:36).[9] Second, the use of the title for both Jesus and God, including frequent occasions when it is not clear to whom κύριος refers, suggests on some level the interchangeability of their identity and sovereignty.

We also saw that Luke similarly employs "Savior" (σωτήρ) for both God and Jesus. The title is used along with κύριος by Mary in Luke 1:46–47 in reference to Yahweh, calling to mind Yahweh's character as one who has both the will and power to save God's people. Then in 2:10–11 the two terms are, remarkably, both used of Jesus, appearing with "Christ" (Χριστός), as Luke forges the composite title "Messiah Lord" (Χριστὸς κύριος). In effect, Luke applies the ideas associated with Yahweh through the titles "Savior" and "Lord," which he has already awakened in Mary's Song, as a lens through which to view Jesus. Peter's use of "Savior" (σωτήρ) in Acts 5:31 suggests this exalted

8. For an illuminating account of Luke's portrayal of Jesus as κύριος and his characterization of Jesus as both distinct from and equal to God, see Rowe, *Narrative Christology*.

9. Hurtado, *One God, One Lord*, 108–9. So also Bauckham, *Jesus*, 129–30; Rowe, *Narrative Christology*, 41.

sense as well, as the title is combined with a description of Jesus exercising his sovereign rule alongside God: "God exalted him at his right hand [see also 2:33; 7:56] as Leader (ἀρχηγός) and Savior that he might give repentance to Israel and forgiveness of sins" (see also Acts 13:23). Also in Acts, Jesus is hailed as "Holy and Righteous One" (3:14)—another title normally reserved for Yahweh—and as "Author of life" (3:15), and he is described by Paul as the judge of creation (17:31).

4. As we saw in Zechariah's hymn (Luke 1:67–79), Luke utilizes parallelism to compose a convergence of mission and person between Jesus and God: the visitation of the Lord God (v. 68) is fulfilled by the visitation of the Messiah (vv. 78–79). Luke continues to remind recipients of this "dual visitation" in two passages to follow, Luke 7:16 and 19:44. Similarly, Luke alters Mark's conclusion to the story of the Gerasene demoniac to conflate the ministry and persons of Jesus and God: "'Return to your home, and declare how much *God* has done for you.' So he went away, proclaiming throughout the city how much *Jesus* had done for him" (8:39). A similar conflation between Jesus and God occurs in the account of Paul and Silas' divinely assisted escape from prison and their testimony to the jailer (Acts 16:25–34). After the jailer senses that the earthquake was a divine act, he beseeches Paul and Silas, "What must I do to be saved?" Paul replies, "Believe on the Lord Jesus, and you will be saved, you and your household" (vv. 30–31). Luke then tells us: "and he and his entire household rejoiced that he had become a believer in God" (v. 34).

5. In our discussion of Luke 24 and Peter's Pentecost sermon, we noted that Jesus' authority to bestow the Holy Spirit upon others is another manifestation of the convergence Luke composes between Jesus and God. The notion that Jesus would oversee the granting of the "power from on high" echoes John the Baptist's proclamation concerning Jesus' power in Luke 3:16 ("he will baptize you with the Holy Spirit"). It is similarly amplified as Peter proclaims, "Being therefore exalted at the right hand of God, and having received from the Father the promise of the Holy Spirit, he has poured out this that you both see and hear" (Acts 2:33). Just as noteworthy, Luke later refers to "the Spirit of Jesus" in apposition to "Holy Spirit" (16:6–7). As Buckwalter argues, Jesus' authority over the Spirit, as well as parallels between the work of Jesus and that of the Spirit, shows that "Luke perceives Jesus' relationship to the Spirit as fundamentally similar to Yahweh's relationship to his Spirit in the OT."[10]

6. We also considered in our examination of Luke 24 the statement that repentance and forgiveness of sins is to be proclaimed "in his name" (v. 47; see also 5:17–26; 7:36–50). As mentioned there, Larry Hurtado notes the

---

10. Buckwalter, *Luke's Christology*, 205.

traditional use of the expression "in his name" in the baptismal rites of the early church, and describes its function to identify Jesus as the exclusive agent of divine redemption.[11] Similarly, both in the Gospel and throughout Acts, the disciples heal and teach in Jesus' name (Luke 9:49; 10:17; Acts 3:6, 16; 4:10, 17; 5:28, 40).

Throughout this study and the preceding section, I have referred to Luke "blurring," "converging," and "interlacing" the work and person of Jesus and Yahweh. After summarizing here the evidence from Luke-Acts, it may now be appropriate to consider language suggested by others. Richard Bauckham, for instance, argues that Luke contributes to the NT's "assimilation of Jesus to God," "christological monotheism," and portrayal of "Jesus' participation in God's divine identity." His essential point is that Luke, along with other NT writers, bears witness to the early Christian commitment to "include Jesus in the unique divine identity as Jewish monotheism understood it."[12] C. Kavin Rowe similarly argues that Luke's use of κύριος and other features of Luke-Acts "narrate the relation between God and Jesus as one of inseparability, to the point that they are bound together in a shared identity as κύριος."[13] For Rowe, the shared identity Luke composes does not compromise the distinction between the two. The Lord God and the Lord Jesus are separate characters, but Jesus fully participates in the divine work, authority, and identity of Yahweh.[14] Buckwalter argues that Jesus "appears on equal footing with God by virtue of what he does and says in working alongside the Father in decreeing, preserving, and leading the church."[15] He is Yahweh's "co-equal" and "co-regent."[16]

If this understanding of Luke's portrayal of Jesus and God is correct, then it also addresses the second issue identified above: whether the focus of Luke's narrative is on the accomplishment of God's salvation, for which Jesus plays a central but supporting role as mediator, or on Jesus as the unique and exalted Savior. It addresses this issue by simply unveiling it for the false dichotomy that it is. The accomplishment of God's salvation, and Jesus' exalted character as Messiah, Savior, Son of God, and Lord whose person and work mirror that of God, are too integrally connected in Luke-Acts for us to discern any amplification of one over the other. Both are equally essential to Luke's kingdom story.

---

11. Hurtado, *One God, One Lord*, 108.

12. Bauckham, *Jesus*, 19.

13. Rowe, *Narrative Christology*, 27; Bauckham (*Jesus*, 55–56) argues that the revelation of God in Jesus reveals that divine identity can no longer be viewed by analogy as a single human subject, but must be regarded as an "intra-divine relationship."

14. See Rowe, *Narrative Christology*, 201.

15. Buckwalter, *Luke's Christology*, 192; so also O'Toole, *Luke's Presentation*, 223–24.

16. H. Douglas Buckwalter, "The Divine Saviour," in *Witness to the Gospel: The Theology of Acts*, ed. I. Howard Marshall and David Peterson (Grand Rapids: Eerdmans, 1998), 123.

We may also treat here the third issue identified above: At what point does Jesus' exaltation occur in Luke's narrative? As can be inferred from my preceding comments, I agree with those readers of Luke-Acts who argue that the evangelist presents Jesus as an exalted, divine personage from the time of his conception. Several features of the infancy narrative we have already addressed signal this. First is Gabriel's annunciation, which offers multiple indications of Jesus' divine character, including above all else his conception by the Holy Spirit: "We are not dealing with the adoption of a Davidid by coronation as God's son or representative; we are dealing with the begetting of God's Son through God's creative Spirit."[17] Other features of Luke's infancy narrative we have already addressed at length include Luke's use of "Lord" and "Savior" for both God and Jesus along with the step-parallelism he employs to signal the convergence of mission and person between them. In sum, the Israelite notion that the Davidic king was adopted by God as son upon his coronation simply does not sufficiently account for Luke's introduction of Jesus in his infancy narrative or for his portrayal of Jesus as Lord and divine Son in the narrative to follow.[18]

Indeed, it is possible that in Acts 2:33–36 Luke was drawing on the concept of adoption because it seemed to him that Peter would have found that a useful image to employ to explain Jesus' significance, character, and authority to his fellow Israelites.[19] As an analogy, note Paul's rather radical "tweaking" of the kerygma in his speech before the Areopagus in Acts 17. Moreover, Rowe argues (convincingly in my view) that Luke's use of the vocative form of κύριος by characters in reference to Jesus throughout his Gospel similarly functions on two levels. On the one hand, the vocative form in the mouths of characters could be seen simply as a form of polite address, as in "sir." This reflects Luke's penchant for historical verisimilitude and also his concern to

17. Brown, *Birth of the Messiah*, 312. Similarly, Strauss (*Davidic Messiah*, 93) concludes: "Luke seems to be consciously opposing the view that Jesus' sonship is merely 'functional'—a special relationship with God by virtue of his role as king. He is rather the Son of God from the point of conception, before he has taken on any functions of kingship."

18. For this reason, I also do not believe that Bock (*Theology of Luke and Acts*, 178–84)—while rejecting the notion that Luke promotes an adoptionist Christology—adequately accounts for the exalted portrait of Jesus already provided in the infancy narrative when he argues that the understanding of Jesus as divine and sovereign Lord becomes apparent for Luke's recipients only in Peter's Pentecost sermon.

19. On Luke's commitment to the Thucydidean principle of constructing speeches appropriate to the speaker and occasion as an explanation for variation in Luke's Christology, see Tuckett, *Christology and the New Testament*, 139–41. While I disagree with Tuckett's claim that Luke-Acts reflects a somewhat haphazard amalgam of christological imagery, I agree with his point that Luke's concern for historical verisimilitude may shape the christological statements he attributes to characters.

show that characters' understanding of Jesus as "Lord," along with other features of Jesus' mission and person, evolves throughout the narrative. On the other hand, Luke's recipients, by virtue of the nonvocative use of κύριος in the infancy narrative and throughout the Gospel (often occurring alongside its vocative forms), in addition to the other convergences of Jesus' and God's characters composed by Luke, would have been led to hear more in the use of κύριος than the characters themselves may intend.[20] Likewise—and returning now to Acts 2:33–36—for Luke's recipients who have the benefit of Luke's story leading up to the momentous day of Pentecost, Peter's words signal not the initial realization but the full manifestation of Jesus as Messiah and Lord—and Savior, Righteous One, Author of life, Son of God—in his resurrection and rule at the right hand of God.[21]

Luke's Portrait of Jesus: Guiding Principles

As noted above, the conclusions readers reach concerning the christological titles and images Luke applies to Jesus vary considerably. One reason for this is the tendency of scholars to emphasize the relevance of a select few titles and images Luke applies to Jesus while marginalizing others, along with widespread disagreement on which to privilege. To foster a more holistic approach, I suggest three interpretive guidelines for exploring Luke's attribution of images, titles, and actions to Jesus.

1. *Balancing Relevant Contexts.* The christological images and titles Luke attributes to Jesus need to be examined with an eye toward their Israelite and early Christian contexts. How those images and titles had been understood by those writing before Luke likely influenced how he used them. At the same time, those precedents also need to be balanced with how those images and titles are cast within the context of Luke's narrative and other features of his characterization of Jesus, such as Jesus' actions and teachings. For Luke is free to reshape, to some extent, the meaning of preexisting images and concepts in ways that conform to his own understanding of Jesus and the rhetorical objectives of his narrative.

2. *Avoiding the Redactional Fallacy.* For all its obvious benefits, redaction criticism has sometimes led scholars to the fallacious assumption that material that Luke takes over from Mark or Q is less significant, or even irrelevant,

20. See Rowe, *Narrative Christology*, 150–51, 202–5.
21. Tannehill (*Narrative Unity*, 2:39) points out that just as there are several stages in the life of monarchs in antiquity leading up to the assumption of their throne, so too in the life of Jesus according to Luke: "Although Jesus was called Lord and Savior previously, the full authority of these titles is granted only through death, resurrection, and exaltation."

for discerning Luke's intentions. Such an assumption overlooks the fact that the decision to *include* preexisting material is also a redactional one. This "redactional fallacy" has also led many scholars to downplay the significance of christological images and titles that appear in material that Luke borrows from an earlier source. This is not sound exegetical practice.

3. *Respecting the Diversity of Images Luke Employs.* Many scholars investigating Luke's portrait of Jesus seek to discern the one primary, controlling christological image Luke employs: Luke is understood to present Jesus as— above all else—Lord,[22] Son of God,[23] Servant,[24] Savior,[25] Prophet,[26] Messiah or King,[27] and so on. The other images Luke utilizes, if not simply dismissed, are then viewed as revolving around and supplementing this one essential feature of Jesus' identity and mission. I do not think this is a helpful approach. The widespread disagreement among scholars on the central element of Jesus' identity presented by Luke should suggest to us that Luke did not intend to present Jesus in such narrow terms. What we find instead is that Luke casts Jesus' character as a tapestry of multiple, interlaced images that complement and play off one another. One readily apparent manifestation of this mode of characterization is Luke's tendency to combine titles (e.g., "Messiah Lord," "Lord Jesus Christ") or to use them in very close proximity, sometimes even interchangeably. These images do not revolve around a single, controlling element as much as they mutually interpret one another and testify to the richly variegated, even paradoxical character that Luke understands Jesus to be.

Luke's Portrait of Jesus: Summary Statements

Guided by these principles, I offer now a series of summary statements, followed by a brief explanation for each, that seeks to integrate the various features of Jesus' identity and mission cast by Luke. The ordering I provide is not meant to indicate primacy or importance. Instead, I have tried to follow

22. Rowe, *Narrative Christology*, 197–218; Bock, *Theology of Luke and Acts*, 177–99.

23. Gerhard Voss, *Die Christologie der lukanischen Schriften in Grundzügen*, StudNeot 2 (Paris: Brouwer, 1965), 173–75; Malcolm Wren, "Sonship in Luke: The Advantage of a Literary Approach," *SJT* 37 (1984): 301–11.

24. E. Kränkl, *Jesus, der Knecht Gottes: Die heilsgeschichtliche Stellung Jesu in den Reden der Apostelgeschichte*, BU 8 (Regensburg: Pustet, 1972), 127, 210–11.

25. Marshall, *Luke—Historian and Theologian*, 19, 85–86, 116–17, 176–78; Martin, "Salvation and Discipleship," 367–72.

26. David Moessner, *Lord of the Banquet: The Literary and Theological Significance of the Lukan Travel Narrative* (Philadelphia: Fortress, 1989), 82; Johnson, *Gospel of Luke*, 18–21.

27. E. Earle Ellis, *The Gospel of Luke* (Eugene, OR: Wipf & Stock, 2003), 9–12, 31–36; A. R. C. Leaney, *The Gospel according to St. Luke*, 2nd ed., BNTC (London: Black, 1966), 34–37; Strauss, *Davidic Messiah*.

the order in which these notions first appear in Luke's narrative. Moreover, each of the statements below addresses an image, or persona, that Luke applies to Jesus, along with an element of Jesus' mission that Luke tends to associate with that image. I realize, however, that this may present things too neatly, for the activity that I assign to one image may also apply in varying degrees to others. I thus present these categories as useful *guides* to the primary contours to Luke's presentation of Jesus, while recognizing that these contours merge and meld as Luke's narrative portrait unfolds.

Jesus, the Messiah, fulfills God's long-standing promises to return a descendant of David to the throne and redeem God's people. Luke's presentation of Jesus as Messiah runs from the beginning (Luke 1:26–35) to the end (Acts 28:31) of his narrative. In much Israelite tradition leading up to the time of Jesus, the title "messiah" was employed to identify the one who would reclaim the throne of David and defeat God's enemies, thus ushering in the long-awaited era of God's rule over creation. The militaristic imagery that often characterized portraits of the Israelite messiah in preceding tradition is somewhat muted in Luke, though not completely (recall Mary's and especially Zechariah's hymns). Luke commonly employs the title and associated imagery (such as "horn of salvation" and "dawn from on high" in Luke 1:69, 78) in contexts that announce Jesus' role in inaugurating the awaited arrival of God's Kingdom and mediating God's salvation (e.g., Luke 2:11, 26; 3:15–17; 9:20; 22:29–30, 67; 23:35, 38–39; 24:26–27, 44–47; Acts 2:31–36; 3:19–26; 4:10–12; 10:34–43; 13:23–41; 17:1–3).

Jesus, the divine Son of God, conceived by the Spirit, is in intimate relationship with God and enacts his Father's will. We have already amply explored the programmatic text of Gabriel's annunciation (Luke 1:26–38). As we saw, Luke employs the annunciation along with the title "Son of God" to unveil Jesus' identity as the divine Son uniquely conceived by the Holy Spirit. Beyond the infancy narrative, Luke repeatedly reminds us of the centrality of Jesus' identity as the Divine Son, his intimate relationship with God, and his mission to enact his Father's will to save through the use of various forms of the title (e.g., Luke 3:22; 4:9, 41; 8:28; 10:21–22; 22:70; Acts 9:20) and through other statements referring to Jesus as the divine Son or to God as his "Father" (e.g., Luke 2:41–51; 20:13; 22:42; 23:34, 46; 24:49; Acts 1:4, 7; 2:33; 13:33).

Jesus, the Lord, is sovereign over creation and participates in the divine identity and mission of God. As discussed above, the title "Lord" occurs with extraordinary frequency throughout Luke-Acts. It serves a key role in Luke's repeated convergence of the characters of Jesus and God in terms of both their person and mission. Like other Christians before him, Luke adapts the Israelite convention of employing κύριος as a substitute for "Yahweh" to express his conviction that Jesus participates in the divine identity of God and is thus "Lord of all" (Acts 10:36). Although some instances of the term in Luke-Acts, especially those occurring in the vocative, may be intended by characters as a form of respectful address recognizing one of higher status, the exalted meaning Luke assigns to the title through his direct and ambiguous use of it in the infancy narrative, as well as his continued application of the title to Jesus in his third-person narration, recasts the meaning of even those mundane uses of the term for Jesus.[28] The unceasing cadence of characters and the narrator himself referring to Jesus as κύριος presents Jesus' divinity and sovereignty as key dimensions of his character.

Jesus is the Savior, whose mercy and power mirror the mercy and power of Yahweh to save Israel and all humanity. Though this title occurs less frequently than others, it appears in key contexts to associate Yahweh's character as merciful and powerful Savior with the person and mission of Jesus. As we noted in our discussion of the infancy narrative, not only does Luke present Jesus as the one who enacts the salvation of God the Savior (Luke 1:47) as the messianic "horn of salvation" (1:69: translated by the NRSV as "mighty savior"); he then goes on to apply the title "Savior" (σωτήρ) directly to Jesus in the proclamation of the heavenly host (2:11) as they announce the significance of Jesus for all humanity. This dimension of Jesus' identity is then amplified in Simeon's thanksgiving: in holding the infant Jesus, Simeon has now beheld God's "salvation [σωτηρία]," which God has "prepared in the presence of all peoples" (2:30–31). Beyond the infancy narrative, Jesus' identity as merciful and powerful Savior reverberates in Luke's description (citing from Isaiah and the Psalms) of John's role to prepare Israel for the coming day when "all flesh shall see the salvation of God" (3:6); it also echoes in Jesus' acts of healing and miraculous interventions on behalf of others and in all the various ways in which Jesus saves others—both Israelite and gentile—from their sin, the power of death, and the demonic (see esp. 7:11–17; 8:26–48; 9:37–43). In Acts, the title is twice used to indicate a primary feature of Jesus' person and mission: by Peter in reference to Jesus as one who "[gives] repentance to Israel and forgiveness of sins" (5:31), and again by Paul in 13:23 to summarize Jesus' significance. Moreover, Peter describes Jesus as one who performed all sorts of "deeds of power, wonders, and signs that God did through him" (2:22) and later proclaims that "there is salvation in no one else, for there is no other name under heaven given among mortals by which we must be saved" (4:12).

28. See, for example, Jesus' visit in the home of Martha and Mary (10:38–42), in which Martha's address of Jesus as κύριε (v. 40) is sandwiched between Luke's own references to Jesus as κύριος (vv. 39, 41). See also 12:41–42.

Accordingly, as we noted above, the disciples in Acts repeatedly announce forgiveness, baptize, and heal "in the name of Jesus."

Jesus is the Servant of Isaiah, whose humble suffering and vindication makes possible the servanthood and vindication of the faithful. A less prominent but still important dimension of Jesus' identity and mission presented by Luke is that of Servant, especially in relation to the Servant Songs of Isaiah.[29] The most obtrusive instances occur in Acts. Jesus is repeatedly hailed by Peter as "servant" (παῖς) in the opening chapters of Acts (3:13, 26; 4:27, 30). Luke also presents the Ethiopian eunuch puzzling over the meaning of Isaiah 53:7–8, which speaks of the Servant as "a sheep" who was "led to the slaughter" (Acts 8:32–33). Still, the humility, unjust condemnation, and vicarious suffering of the Servant conveyed in Isaiah 53 are also emphasized in Luke's passion narrative. In Luke 22:20, during the Last Supper, Jesus states that his life is given "for you" (ὑπὲρ ὑμῶν), a phrase that likely alludes to Isaiah 53:11–12.[30] Jesus also emphasizes to his disciples during the Last Supper—and in response to the disciples' argument over which of them is the greatest—that "I am among you as one who serves" (22:27). Shortly after this, when speaking about his imminent arrest and crucifixion, Jesus announces that "this scripture must be fulfilled in me, 'And he was counted among the lawless'" (22:37), citing Isaiah 53:12, which in typical Lukan fashion is then fulfilled in the following narrative as Jesus is hung between two criminals (23:32–33). Jesus' innocence is also amplified in Pilate's threefold assertion that he has found no guilt in Jesus (23:13–16, 20, 22), and above all in Luke's recasting of the centurion's confession, "Certainly this man was innocent" (23:47; cf. Mark 15:39). Moreover, near the start of his narrative, the evangelist alludes to the Servant Songs when revealing that Jesus has been called to bring light both to Israel and to the gentiles (Luke 2:29–32; cf. Isa. 42:6; 49:6, 9). Luke also includes the traditional designation of Jesus as the one "with whom I am well pleased" (3:22) and the "chosen one" (9:35), both commonly considered allusions to Isaiah 42:1.[31] Together, these references in the Gospel and Acts cast Jesus as the innocent and humble Suffering Servant, who in being raised by God paves the way for the faithful to denounce evil and take part in God's promised redemption: "When God raised up his servant, he sent him first to you, to bless you by turning each of you from your wicked ways" (Acts 3:26; see also 4:30). Yet

29. The Servant Songs, which celebrate the salvific ministry of a "servant" figure, include Isaiah 42:1–4; 49:1–6; 50:4–9; 52:13–53:12. For a helpful discussion of Luke's casting of Jesus as the Isaianic servant, see O'Toole, *Luke's Presentation*, 95–112.

30. Bock, *Theology of Luke and Acts*, 198.

31. Similarly, the leaders who mock Jesus also, and ironically, refer to Jesus as God's "chosen one" (Luke 23:35).

as the Servant, Jesus also calls upon his followers to embrace this ministry of service themselves, that they too may take up the Servant's call to be the light of salvation for all humanity:

> For so the Lord has commanded us, saying,
> "I have set you to be a light for the Gentiles,
> so that you may bring salvation to the ends of the earth."
> (Acts 13:47, citing Isa. 49:6; see also Luke 9:46–48; 22:26)

Jesus is the new Adam, faithful to God and calling forth a new kindred devoted to Jesus and one another. I stated above that the juxtaposition of Jesus' genealogy (tracing all the way back to "Adam, son of God") with the temptation story (showing Jesus, unlike Adam, faithfully resisting the wiles of Satan) suggests Luke's interest in presenting Jesus in the type of a "new Adam."[32] While Luke will not draw such a close association between Jesus and Adam in the remainder of his narrative, the importance of genealogies in establishing basic parameters of one's identity, along with the programmatic character of the temptation story showing the victory of Jesus, the "Son of God," over Satan, indicates that this dimension of Jesus' identity was significant to Luke.[33] It also seems likely to me that Luke's casting of Jesus as the new Adam, Son of God, is related to his portrayal of Jesus forming a new kindred devoted to God and one another. As we discussed above, several of Jesus' teachings emphasize that all commitments, including that of kinship, are to be subordinated to one's devotion to the Kingdom (e.g., 9:57–62; 11:27–28; 12:49–53; 14:25–27; 18:28–30). Among such statements, Luke 8:21 shows Jesus redefining kinship in relation to one's embrace of God's good news: "My mother and my brothers are those who hear the word of God and do it." Accordingly, the early community of believers in Acts functions as a fictive kinship group, of "one heart and soul," "devoted . . . to the apostles' teaching" (Acts 2:42), holding all things in common, gathering in homes, and sharing table with one another (2:41–47; 4:32–37).

Jesus is the Prophet who calls Israel back to faithfulness and suffers rejection. In chapter 5 we discussed the numerous parallels Luke composes between Jesus and leading prophetic characters of old, including Isaiah (Luke 4:16–21), Elijah (4:25–27; 7:11–17), and Moses (Acts 2:22–24; 7:37). Jesus' frequent prophetic testimony to events that are yet to come (as part of the prophecy-fulfillment pattern evident throughout Luke-Acts), along with accompanying

---

32. See also Ellis, *Gospel of Luke*, 11.
33. In his letters, Paul likewise applies an Adam typology to Jesus to amplify certain features of his person and significance (see Rom. 5; 1 Cor. 15).

calls for faithfulness and repentance, also contributes to Luke's presentation of Jesus as a prophetic figure. Likewise, Jesus' teaching ministry disclosing the true meaning of torah (e.g., Luke 6:17–49; 24:44–47) further underscores his prophetic role as one of calling Israel back into right relatedness with God. Moreover, just as God's own people have rejected the prophets that God has sent to teach and heal, so too will Jesus as prophet be rejected by his own people (e.g., Luke 2:34; 4:24–29; 13:31–34; Acts 7:51–53).

Jesus, the Son of Man, will suffer, die, be raised by God, and return. As in the other Synoptic Gospels, the title "Son of Man/Humanity" (ὁ υἱὸς τοῦ ἀνθρώπου) is the designation Jesus most commonly uses to refer to himself.[34] The title and the ideas associated with it convey the paradoxical nature of Jesus' mission and person. In several texts, the title is used in contexts that emphasize Jesus' exalted, even divine, character. Jesus as Son of Man possesses the authority to forgive sins (Luke 5:20–24) and to judge (9:26; 12:8, 40); is Lord of the Sabbath (6:5); shall come again to overthrow God's enemies and establish God's Kingdom (17:20–37); seeks and saves the lost (19:10); shall fulfill Daniel's prophecy of "one like a son of man" who arrives on the clouds and receives authority from the Ancient of Days to rule over creation at the end of the age (21:27; cf. Dan 7:13–14); and, now resurrected, stands at the right hand of God (Acts 7:56). By using the title, with its Danielic overtones, in contexts in which Jesus' authority is being intermingled with Yawheh's authority, Luke is inviting his recipients to associate Jesus with this larger-than-life, divine-like "son of man" foretold by Daniel, and perhaps also with the redeemer figures of other traditions, such as the Similitudes of 1 *Enoch* (*1 En.* 37–71), the *Aramaic Apocalypse* (4Q246), and 4 *Ezra*, which similarly cast Daniel's redeemer (see chap. 2).

However, Jesus also commonly uses the title to speak of his humiliation, suffering, death, and eventual exaltation: "The Son of Man must undergo great suffering, and be rejected by the elders, chief priests, and scribes, and be killed, and on the third day be raised" (Luke 9:22; see also 9:44, 58; 18:31–33; 22:22; 24:7). These uses amplify the literal meaning of the title "son of humanity" (i.e., human one) and invite comparison to Ezekiel's copious use of "son of man" (LXX: υἱὸς ἀνθρώπου; NRSV: "mortal") to emphasize the transient and inferior character of humanity relative to God. The title is thus a felicitous one for engaging the paradoxical nature of Jesus' identity and mission. The Son of Man, mighty and divine, is at the same time the humble human one, who will be rejected by God's own and face the humiliation and agony of a Roman cross.

---

34. Several of the many occurrences of the title are unique to Luke: Luke 6:22; 17:22; 18:8; 19:10; 21:36; 22:48; 24:7; Acts 7:56.

The Complexity of Luke's Portrait of Jesus and God

I trust that the preceding discussion has helped readers to appreciate the rich and variegated portrait of Jesus that Luke has composed. Not only do the various images of Jesus offer distinct resonances; they also overlap and interweave, creating a complex collage of identity and mission. At the same time, several of the resonances Luke sounds for Jesus are the same as those he sounds for God, to the extent that where the portrait of one ends and that of the other begins is not easy to discern. Consequently, as I argued at the start of this chapter, Luke's portrayal of Jesus reflects his understanding of God as Creator and Sovereign of the earth. Indeed, Luke leads his recipients to consider the surprising and paradoxical ways that the character of the one sovereign God—as faithful to the covenant, as intensely relational, and as the merciful and powerful Savior, Warrior, and Judge who overthrows all evil—is mirrored in the person and ministry of Jesus.

But, I wonder, what are we to make of those aspects of Jesus' character that don't seem to reflect divine identity, such as Jesus' clear and apparent humanity, humiliation, suffering, and death? It is one thing to present Jesus as possessing "God-like" qualities, but it is another to suggest that Jesus' experience as a human, limited by physical needs, growing up in Nazareth, and suffering a horrific execution at the hands of the Romans, also reflects divine identity. How far did Luke intend this shared identity to go? In my view, Luke does not provide us with enough material to render a confident verdict on the matter. While God's humiliation and suffering are amply displayed in Israel's sacred traditions (largely as a result of God's intensely relational character combined with Israel's stiff-necked rejection), the idea that God would somehow participate in human form and be subjected to death is not, and this would mark an extraordinary development in Israelite thought. So intentional is Luke in presenting Jesus as participating in divine identity that he may indeed suggest the logical corollary that humanity, humiliation, suffering, and death also become part of divine experience and identity in and through Jesus. But there are not, in my view, elements of Luke's narrative that clearly bring this notion to the fore, nor do we find precedents for this in Christian writings preceding Luke.

The Rhetorical Force of Luke's Christology: Jesus, Not Caesar, Is Savior, Lord, and King

What I think we can speak to with a little more confidence is how Luke's portrait of Jesus as one who participates in divine identity is connected to and facilitates his rhetorical objectives. As a means of exploring this, I suggest we stick our noses back into the text and examine the story of Jesus' birth in Luke 2. This pericope not only offers us another testimony to Jesus participating in God's mission and identity but also draws a poignant comparison between Jesus and Caesar, between Rome and the Kingdom of God, reinforcing one of the chief aims of Luke's narrative.

Throughout the preceding episodes of the infancy narrative, including Mary's hymn (1:46–56), we have seen that Luke employs reversal to help his recipients appreciate that the Kingdom inaugurated in the conceptions and births of John and Jesus is one that will turn the tables on the current world order. The climax in Luke's portrayal of this "upside-down" world in the infancy narrative takes place here in the story of Jesus' birth. With a concentration of dramatic artistry that is remarkable even for Luke, the evangelist invites Theophilus and others to discern, embrace, and praise the one who is truly Lord.

Yet as the passage opens, it is the one known as Lord throughout the Mediterranean region and beyond who speaks and moves "all the world" to action (2:1). Caesar Augustus, the Roman emperor and father of the empire, orders a census to be taken, and his underlings, such as Quirinius, governor of Syria, make it happen. Caesar wants to take stock of his subjects and possessions, the objects of his rule and sources of revenue. His word is spoken, and the world has no choice but to comply with this "penetrating symbol of Roman overlordship."[35] And so, "all went to their own towns to be registered" (v. 3). The father of Jesus is no exception: "Joseph also went from the town of Nazareth in Galilee to Judea, to the city of David called Bethlehem" (v. 4). Caesar's command rules the cosmos, or so it seems.

Scholars have long noted and debated a serious problem with Luke's chronology here. As many point out, reliable historical sources place the reign of Quirinius and the census undertaken while he was governor several years later in 6 CE.[36] We will not engage this debate except to note that scholars commonly view the census as a device to get Mary and Joseph to Bethlehem so that Jesus' birthplace fulfills Micah 5:2–4 (cf. Matt. 2:1–6). Luke's interest in Bethlehem for these reasons seems likely, but the census serves other interests as well. If Luke, along with Matthew, understands Jesus' birth in Bethlehem

---

35. Green, *Gospel of Luke*, 122. For a helpful discussion of how the census would be perceived by most Israelites as a particularly egregious instance of oppressive Roman hegemony, see Richard Horsley, *The Liberation of Christmas: The Infancy Narrative in Social Context* (New York: Crossroad, 1989), 33–38.

36. Helpful overviews of the debate can be found in Fitzmyer, *Luke I–IX*, 400–405; Nolland, *Luke 1:1–9:20*, 99–103; and Bock, *Luke 1:1–9:50*, 903–9.

as the divinely ordained fulfillment of Micah's prophecy, then notice how the mighty rule of Caesar is already being undercut in the opening verses of Luke's account. Ironically and unknowingly, Caesar Augustus, the world's venerated sovereign, puts into motion events that lead to the fulfillment of *God's* will for Israel and all the world.[37] Caesar may rule the cosmos, including Palestine, but Israel's messiah who will deliver Israel from its enemies is about to be born (cf. Luke 1:71, 74). And Caesar helps to bring it all to pass, unknowingly pushing the unborn Messiah to Bethlehem that he might be born just as God "spoke through the mouth of his holy prophets from of old" (1:70).

In her song of praise, Mary announced that the coming of her child would result in the bringing down of the powerful from their thrones and the lifting up of the lowly (Luke 1:52). But even this warning leaves the recipient unprepared for Luke's description of Jesus' birth and the humble state of his first resting place. In simple, unadorned prose, we are told that Jesus is born, wrapped in bands of cloth, and laid in a feedbox "because there was no place for them in the inn" (2:7). It can't get much lowlier than this. The inn (κατάλυμα), or hostel-like room adjoining a house, is full. None move aside so that the very pregnant and eventually laboring Mary can give birth in the security of even these very sparse quarters. So the young couple nestles in among the sheep, goats, and chickens, delivers their child, and employs a manger for a crib. Luke's recipients are confronted with an image of Israel's messiah that could not be more incongruous with the pomp and might of Emperor Augustus on his throne, commanding the world at will. The repeated references to the bands of cloth and manger and their function as the "sign" that identifies Jesus (2:7, 12, 16–17) keep these lowly elements in view even as Jesus is exalted by the heavenly host and found by the shepherds.

As the scene shifts from stable to darkened field, we once again encounter a setting far removed from Caesar's seat in Rome: shepherds tending their flocks by night. The lowliness of the shepherds and the locale of the angelic host's appearance to them continue the theme of reversal permeating the passage. Recall our discussion of Roman society and economy in chapter 1. Shepherds along with other agricultural workers were among the large peasant class whose economic servitude fueled the economy of empire and hegemony of Roman rule. Yet it is to such as these that the Kingdom is announced. The reversal inherent in the heavenly host's appearance targets the Israelite elite as well, for "God's glory, normally associated with the temple, is now manifest

---

37. As similarly noted by Brown, *Birth of the Messiah*, 415; Fitzmyer, *Luke I–IX*, 393; Green, *Gospel of Luke*, 121–22; Carroll, *Luke*, 66.

on a farm!"[38] While Jesus will engage both the Roman and Israelite elite on their own turf, the manifestation of God's reign will not be confined to their domain or controlled by their brokerage. Something radically new is taking place that defies elite control.

To be sure, the claim that the birth of this child of Israel, and his manifestation in this agrarian setting so far removed from the center of elite power, poses any sort of meaningful challenge to the elite's rule would—by nearly all sane accounts of the time—be simply laughable. But this is just the announcement that explodes from the heavenly messenger into the night. Luke crafts the angelic proclamation to once again amplify (in tandem with the preceding narrative) Jesus' divine identity as "Savior, Messiah Lord," while at the same time composing an implied, but quite apparent, repudiation of Caesar's reign. With a brazenness that goes beyond the subtlety of Paul's and Mark's challenges to Rome, Luke shapes the angel's testimony so that many of the things celebrated about Caesar and his birth by those allied with Rome are now attributed to this infant lying in a feedbox. In their decision to honor Augustus by beginning the new year on his birthday, the Roman provincial assembly announced the following:

> Whereas the providence which divinely ordered our lives created with zeal and munificence the most perfect good for our lives by producing Augustus . . . for the *benefaction of mankind*, sending us a *savior* who put an end to war . . . and whereas the *birthday* of the god marked *for the world* the beginning of *good tidings* through his coming . . .[39]

The parallels to the angel's announcement in 2:10–11 are apparent: "Do not be afraid; for see—I am bringing you *good news* of great joy for *all the people*: to you is *born this day* in the city of David a *Savior*, who is the Messiah Lord" (my translation). As Horsley comments, "any reader or hearer of this story in the Hellenistic-Roman world, particularly in Palestine, would have understood here a direct opposition between Caesar, the savior who had supposedly brought peace, and the child proclaimed as the savior, whose birth means peace."[40]

Beyond the Roman celebration of Augustus, there were other claims to Roman lordship that would have been scorched upon the hearts of those sympathetic to traditional Israelite hopes. In the aftermath of the Judean revolt,

---

38. Green, *Gospel of Luke*, 131.
39. Translation from S. R. F. Price, *Rituals and Power: The Roman Imperial Cult in Asia Minor* (Cambridge: Cambridge University Press, 1984), 54.
40. Horsley, *Liberation of Christmas*, 32–33.

Roman supporters added insult to tragedy by claiming that Vespasian, or his son, Titus—the Roman heroes in the defeat of Jerusalem who were later crowned emperors—were the ones who fulfilled the Israelite messianic prophecies of old! The Israelite general turned historian, Josephus, who entered into the service of Titus after the revolt, proclaimed:

> But what more than all else incited them [the Jews] to war was an ambiguous oracle, likewise found in their sacred scriptures, to the effect that at that time one from their own country would become ruler of the world. This they understood to mean someone from their own race, and many of their wise men went astray in their interpretation of it. The oracle, however, in reality signified the sovereignty of Vespasian, who was proclaimed Emperor on Jewish soil.[41]

In not-so-subtle contrast to the prevailing Roman propaganda of the day, Luke's challenge dramatically relayed is this: the Israelite infant lying in a feedbox among sheep, goats, cattle, and fowl undermines the significance of Caesar and Rome, because in his humility and lowliness this one named "Savior" and "Messiah Lord" manifests the identity and power of Yahweh. For this reason, his birthday, not Caesar's, is truly good news for all humankind. He, not Caesar, is Lord and Savior of the world. His reign, not Caesar's, will lead the heavens to erupt in praise of God and the celebration of enduring peace: "Glory to God in the highest heaven, and on earth peace among those whom he favors" (Luke 2:14). This, Luke shows, is how God's plan for the redemption of Israel, and even all humanity, unfolds. In this peasant infant, not Caesar or any other, divine identity and purpose come into the world and turn it upside down.

Thus, already near the start of his narrative, Luke puts Theophilus and the rest of his audience on notice that what God does in Jesus significantly undermines all other claims to mastery over humankind. In doing so, he also provides the *bidirectional*, comparative context for understanding the significance of the titles "Savior," "Christ," and "Lord" in the remainder of his narrative: as one who manifests the identity and mission of Yahweh, Jesus the lowly one, not Caesar, is Lord and Savior of all.

Another dramatic testimony to the sovereign rule of Yahweh in Jesus over against the elite of the Roman world occurs in Acts 4 as Luke concludes his account of Peter and John's arrest and release by the Israelite elite. Inspired by Psalm 2, the believers lift up a celebratory prayer proclaiming that all earthly

---

41. Josephus, *War* 6.312–13, cited in Winn, *Purpose of Mark's Gospel*, 161. The Roman historian Titus (*History* 5.13.1–2) claims that the prophecy is fulfilled by Vespasian and Titus.

dominion and power pales in comparison to that held by the "sovereign Lord" and "his Messiah":

> Sovereign Lord, who made the heaven and the earth, the sea, and everything in them, it is you who said by the Holy Spirit through our ancestor David, your servant:
>
>> "Why did the Gentiles rage,
>>   and the peoples imagine vain things?
>> The kings of the earth took their stand,
>>   and the rulers have gathered together
>>   against the Lord and against his Messiah."
>
> For in this city, in fact, both Herod and Pontius Pilate, with the Gentiles and the peoples of Israel, gathered together against your holy servant Jesus, whom you anointed, to do whatever your hand and your plan had predestined to take place. And now, Lord, look at their threats, and grant to your servants to speak your word with all boldness, while you stretch out your hand to heal, and signs and wonders are performed through the name of your holy servant Jesus. (4:24–30)

Luke may not be calling for open insurrection. But he is challenging his recipients' allegiances, urging them to forsake the life carved out for them by "the kings of the earth" and to "speak with all boldness" about life in a new Kingdom under a new King. The tide has turned, Luke announces. This new Kingdom is already beginning to overtake the old. And now that he has turned Theophilus' attention to Psalm 2, the implications ring clear: someday soon, God's messiah "shall break . . . with a rod of iron, and dash . . . in pieces like a potter's vessel" the foundations of Rome and all earthly claims to power (Ps. 2:8–9). Augustus, Titus, Vespasian, the Judean governors, and the Herods— their claims to sovereignty and beneficence are the source of divine derision and wrath (Ps. 2:4–5). God has set God's King on high (Ps. 2:6), and "there is salvation in no one else, for there is no other name under heaven given among mortals by which we must be saved" (Acts 4:12).

10

The Corruption
and Redemption
of Creation

A s a kingdom story, Luke-Acts devotes a good deal of attention to
the varied forms of corruption ailing God's creation and its human
creatures. For Luke, the world desperately needs deep and pervasive
transformation. But the good news announced in the testimony of numerous
characters is that God's long-awaited, promised deliverance has arrived and
continues to be manifest in the community and ministry of Jesus' followers
as they await his return to reclaim creation once and for all. This chapter will
explore how Luke shapes these two core dimensions of his kingdom story,
noting the features of creation's corruption and redemption that he amplifies
in his narrative.

The Corruption of Creation

Before engaging the evangelist's portrait of a world gone awry, it might be
helpful to review the ways this element is drawn in Israelite tradition preceding Luke-Acts. Doing so will aid our consideration of how Luke takes up and
recasts the visions of others before him.

Israelite Tradition

Our discussion in chapter 2 presented three common features of the degradation described in Israelite traditions leading up to and at the turn of the Common Era:

1. *Humanity's Ignorance and Wickedness.* On the whole, humanity fails to recognize Yahweh's sovereignty as Creator and Lord of all, and lives in ways that lead to cursing rather than blessing.

2. *Israel's Lack of Fidelity to Yahweh and Yahweh's Instruction.* Israel's traditions emphasize that many of God's own people participate in humanity's failure to honor Yahweh and Yahweh's instruction. Several Israelite traditions of the intertestamental era also pronounce that the temple cult and the temple itself have been perverted through the corruption and defilement of its leaders.

3. *The Destitution and Oppression of God's People.* The remnant of Israel continues to languish under foreign rule and socioeconomic victimization by both the Israelite elite and non-Israelite leaders. More apocalyptically minded texts often attribute this and other forms of oppression at least in part to the demonic. Satan and his minions actively seek to degrade the well-being of God's people and humanity in general, and they use human oppressors to accomplish these ends.

Mark's understanding of the present state of creation strikes similar chords. Mark shares with Israelite thought the basic conviction that the world in general, and humanity in particular, has gone incredibly awry. We identified four broad strokes to Mark's portrait of the corrupted creation.

1. *Cosmic Corruption.* As does apocalyptic thought, Mark holds that forces within and beyond the terrestrial realm are actively engaged in the degradation of God's creation.

2. *Life-Defying Insults of This Age.* The world has become a painfully inhospitable place: disease, maladies, evil spirits, hunger, and enmity plague humanity.

3. *Misaligned Values and Darkened Minds.* The life-defying forces degrading the world are in large measure the result of the misaligned values most have come to embrace. Darkness clouds the thoughts and hearts of humanity.

4. *Misaligned Rulers.* Greed and the fear of loss—loss of status, privilege, and even life—are reflected in the self-serving, oppressive actions and dispositions of the elite.

Luke's Portrait of a Misaligned Creation

The very same features that characterize Mark's account of a world gone awry are recapitulated in Luke-Acts. Accordingly, I will use these same four categories for organizing my discussion of this dimension of Luke's kingdom story. As I do so, however, I will note the emphases particular to Luke's kingdom story. While all four elements are central to Luke's portrait of a misaligned creation, Luke particularly emphasizes the role that darkened values, minds, and rulers have played in circumventing the blessing God intends for humanity.

Cosmic Corruption

Luke shares with Mark, Paul, and many other Christians and Israelites of his day the understanding that demonic entities significantly contribute to the corruption of humanity. A key text in this regard is the temptation story (Luke 4:1–13), which both Luke and Matthew expand significantly by relying on Q materials (cf. Mark 1:12–13; Matt. 4:1–11). Luke replaces Mark's terse account of Jesus' temptation in the wilderness with an extended challenge-riposte sequence in which Jesus faithfully deflects Satan's lures and remains true to his calling as the Son of God. Occurring at the forefront of Jesus' public ministry, and in conjunction with the narrative to follow, this scene also indicates the following about Luke's conception of the demonic:

1. The devil actively opposes the arrival of God's reign in Jesus, seeking to circumvent Jesus' ministry before it begins.
2. The devil attempts to mire Jesus and the rest of humanity in the lie of idolatry, claiming to be sovereign over creation and worthy of Jesus' and all of humanity's devotion (Luke 4:5–7); thus, we see Satan himself here claiming the authority that is reserved for Jesus.
3. The devil will continue to oppose Jesus and will make his next move at "an opportune time" (v. 13; see 22:3–6).

As the narrative progresses, another dimension of the demonic that emerges is the reality of demonic possession. We will say more about the degrading impact of demon possession in the next section. Here we must note that while the demons' recognition of Jesus' authority as "the Holy One of God" (4:34), "Son of God," and "Messiah" (4:41) ironically affirms Jesus' identity for recipients (as it does in Mark), it is not accompanied by their repentance or reverence (see also Acts 19:11–17). When confronted by Jesus, demons instead plead for their self-preservation and demand to be left alone (e.g., Luke 4:34; 8:26–33). The portrait that emerges of demonic entities, and one in concert with Israelite thought including Mark, is that they are agents unwilling to honor God's sovereignty and intentions for creation. Accordingly, the devil or Satan continues to be cast as one intractably opposed to God's will for human redemption and blessing. Fallen from heaven (Luke 10:18) and as Beelzebul, the ruler of demons, he marshals demonic forces against humanity (11:15–19; see also Acts 10:38).[1] He snatches "the word" from the hearts of those who hear it so that they "may not believe and be saved" (8:12). At the "opportune time" foreshadowed in the conclusion to the temptation account, he "entered into Judas called Iscariot" (22:3) and thus facilitated the machinations of the "chief priests, the officers of the temple police, and the elders" so that their "hour" enacted the "power of darkness" (22:52–53). Demonic resistance to the Kingdom continues in Acts: Satan inspires Ananias and Sapphira's lie against God (Acts 5:1–11), evil spirits resist the Kingdom and plague many (5:16; 8:7), and Paul describes his ministry as turning Israelites and gentiles alike "from darkness to light and from the power of Satan to God" (26:18).

Hard Living

The consequences of creation's corruption on the terrestrial sphere are widespread and debilitating. As with Mark, recipients of Luke's kingdom story are confronted with a world that mirrors the realities of life in the Roman Empire—a world where pain, suffering, and want were commonplace. Disease and ailments of various sorts, demon possession, enmity, social marginalization, poverty, and death litter the pages of Luke's narrative. Cursing, not blessing, pervades the fallen creation.

The evangelist seems particularly concerned to stress economic destitution and social marginalization as prominent features of a world gone awry. Early in the narrative, both are signaled in Mary's Song celebrating God's awaited reversal (Luke 1:52–53) and in John's instruction on what it means to live into the Kingdom (3:10–14). In the stories to follow, we are introduced to character after character on the edge—physically, socially, cultically, economically, and even ethnically (e.g., 4:25–27, 40; 5:27–6:11; 6:20–26; 7:11–16; 8:26–39). Jesus' own example of embracing the marginalized and calling others to do the same dominates his teaching and is a regular source of dispute between Jesus and the elite (more on this below). In Acts, social boundaries and economic disparity continue to cause conflict and depravation (e.g., Acts 3:1–3; 12:20–23). Even the believers initially struggle with the equitable distribution of resources among widows (6:1), the inclusion of gentiles (11:1–18), and the

---

1. Israelite tradition referred to leaders of the demonic forces opposed to God's will by several names, including "Beelzebul" (e.g., *T. Sol.* 3; 6). Jesus here equates Beelzebul with Satan.

observance of torah regulations among gentiles (15:1–21). Yet these growing pains are countered by the community's radical table sharing, economics of distribution according to need (2:41–47; 4:32–37; 6:1–6), and eventual recognition that gentiles are to be welcomed into the Kingdom (11:18; 15:22–29).

CORRUPTED HEARTS AND MINDS

Like Mark, Luke's narrative claims that the world needs a radical reorientation of values and perspectives. From the beginning to the end of Luke's account, the announcement of the coming Kingdom is resisted, and that resistance is met with the persistent call for characters to repent of their darkened hearts and minds and to open the way of the Lord in their midst.

The Failings of the Elite

On his way to Jerusalem, Jesus is journeying through the villages of Galilee teaching about the Kingdom. When a fellow Israelite asks him, "Lord, will only a few be saved?" (Luke 13:23), Jesus answers that on the day of judgment, many will be on the outside looking in, including many of his listeners (vv. 24–28)! "There will be weeping and gnashing of teeth when you see Abraham and Isaac and Jacob and all the prophets in the kingdom of God, and you yourselves thrown out" (v. 28). Even so, many shall also be welcomed in: "Then people will come from east and west, from north and south, and will eat in the kingdom of God. Indeed, some are last who will be first, and some are first who will be last" (vv. 29–30). Jesus' lament over Jerusalem to follow (vv. 33–35) provides a helpful context for discerning the intent of his warning to his fellow Israelites. Jesus, like many prophets before him, will be rejected by many of his own. Despite his efforts to gather the people of Jerusalem as a hen gathers her brood under her wings, despite his efforts to heal the hurts of Satan and lead his people back to God, they will take his life (vv. 32–33). One's entrance into the Kingdom will hinge on one's acceptance or rejection of Jesus and his teaching.

While those who oppose Jesus and the Kingdom include a wide-ranging group of folk, Luke particularly emphasizes the elite's lead role in resisting the Kingdom and embodying worldviews and values diametrically opposed to the ways of God. Even here in this same passage, Jesus is told by the Pharisees, "Get away from here, for Herod wants to kill you" (v. 31). In reply, Jesus refers to Herod as "that fox," adding another level of resonance to the "mother hen" imagery that Jesus will subsequently apply to himself. For now, Jesus will stay ahead of Herod and others seeking his life. But eventually, in the darkened confines of Jerusalem, the elite will catch up with Jesus and corner their prey.

Luke's portrayal of the corruption of the elite is painfully multifaceted. Here are some of the lowlights.

1. *Illegitimate and Ultimately Impotent Authority.* During the temptation account, Satan announces, "All this authority [of the kingdoms of the world] . . . has been given over to me, and I give it to anyone I please" (Luke 4:5–6). Such a claim, of course, runs counter to the fundamental Israelite conviction that Yahweh rules the world. I think that Luke's recipients, however, were meant to hear a hint of truth in Satan's audaciously false boast. Indeed, Caesar, for all practical purposes, does seem to rule the world (recall Luke 2). And in chapter 1 we learned that by the time Luke was writing his narrative, Romans had been worshiping this divinized Caesar and other emperors for over half a century. Here Luke seems to explain the source of Caesar's incredible power and perhaps even the source of the emperor cult itself: "All world rulers (chief among them the Roman Empire) govern at the behest of Satan and as an expression of idolatrous worship."[2] True to form and just like their demonic patron, these leaders also court divine favors and authority (4:7). Thus, Roman rule is not, as the Roman elite claim, the long-sought-after manifestation of divine will for the earth. Rather, the Roman Empire manifests the depraved reality that many have turned aside from the basic human calling: "Worship the Lord your God, and serve only him" (4:8).

Accordingly, throughout Luke-Acts the Israelite and gentile elite frequently claim authority without acknowledging Yahweh's sovereignty or Jesus' lordship, and their authority is therefore unmasked as illegitimate, impotent, and ultimately transient. One such dramatic display of the elite's illegitimate use of authority is their arrest and trial of Jesus and their manipulation of Pilate. As we noted above, the elite's plotting and use of power manifests the "power of darkness" (22:53), the "opportune time" when Satan seeks Jesus' destruction through them. Their actions follow on the heels of Jesus' parable of the wicked tenants (20:9–19). Aimed at the scribes and chief priests, the parable presents them as seeking to usurp God's anointed and to take over the Kingdom for themselves (v. 14). Here too the stone-texts tradition is used to provide a scriptural precedent for their rebellion against God, and Jesus then adds these ominous words warning them of their peril and the inefficacy of their attempts to resist the advance of the Kingdom: "Everyone who falls on that stone will be broken to pieces; and it will crush anyone on whom it falls" (v. 18). Jesus also knows that the desperate, ultimately vain, and tragic attempts of the elite to oppose the Kingdom will not cease with his death and resurrection. While the elite plot his destruction, Jesus instructs his followers to expect similar treatment in the days to come (21:7–36), for they too will be arrested, persecuted, and accused "before kings and governors" because of Jesus' "name" (v. 12). But

2. Carroll, *Luke*, 401.

rather than responding to such occasions with fear, even though their lives may be at stake, believers are to regard the occasions as an "opportunity to testify" (v. 13). Nor are believers to worry about what they will say in defense, for "I will give you words and a wisdom that none of your opponents will be able to withstand or contradict" (vv. 14–15). The elite might be able to put some of the faithful to death, but Jesus assures them, "Not a hair of your head will perish. By your endurance you will gain your souls" (vv. 18–19; see also 12:11–12).

As we saw in previous chapters, Jesus' prediction of elite resistance met by faithful testimony is dramatically depicted in Acts 4. Peter and John announce that the unbelieving Israelite and gentile elite have killed Jesus, God's anointed, just as in the past they have killed the prophets God has sent. In response to the Israelite elite's continuing attempt to circumvent the spread of the word, the apostles hail Jesus as the cornerstone of God's Kingdom and proclaim that "there is no other name under heaven given among mortals by which we must be saved" (4:12). When the Sanhedrin forbids them to speak any further about Jesus, Peter and John bring the issue of authority to the fore: "Whether it is right in God's sight to listen to you rather than to God, you must judge; for we cannot keep from speaking about what we have heard" (vv. 18–20). Later, when the elite again threaten the apostles because of their ongoing witness to Jesus, Peter and the others answer, "We must obey God rather than any human authority" (5:29). What becomes clear is that the elite are powerless to control the advance of God's reign. For all their pomp and self-importance, for all their ability to reject, imprison, and even kill those sent by God, they cannot keep Peter, John, or anyone else from speaking to what they have seen and heard. Fittingly, as the gathered believers give thanks to God for the apostles' bold testimony and consider the threats of the elite, they celebrate the unassailable authority of their sovereign Lord and Messiah over all those—Israelite and gentile elite alike—who in vain try to oppose God (4:24–26).

With even greater poignancy, the murder of Stephen strikes a very similar chord. As the Israelite elite stone him to death in order to silence his testimony to Jesus and maintain their self-affirming worldviews, Stephen proclaims his vision of Jesus sitting at the right hand of God (Acts 7:55). With dramatic irony, the elite are doing everything they can to silence "the word," but even when they kill in order to stop this testimony to Jesus, the message only spreads faster and farther, and their resistance only serves to confirm the truth they so zealously resist. For the death of Stephen and the severe persecution it inspires result in the scattering of the disciples "throughout the countryside of Judea and Samaria" (8:1), and these scattered ones "went from place to place, proclaiming the word" (v. 4). The elite-sanctioned program of persecution, much like Caesar's census in Luke 2, serves the unfolding of the divine will:

Jesus had told the disciples that they were to be his witnesses "in Jerusalem, in all Judea and Samaria, and to the ends of the earth" (Acts 1:8). Now, the elite's attempt to eradicate this witness fosters its fulfillment.

Another stirring example of the elite's vain attempt to thwart the Kingdom's advance and to claim authority that is not their own occurs in Acts 12 with Herod Agrippa I, grandson of Herod the Great. Herod seizes James, the brother of John, and has him killed. When he sees that this act pleases some of the Israelite elite, he has Peter arrested and plans to bring him to trial. Peter's angel-assisted escape from prison foils Herod's plan, and in his anger Herod has the guards put to death (12:1–19). Then Herod receives a desperate delegation from the people of Tyre and Sidon who have come to sue for reconciliation with Herod lest he cut off their allotment of food. Luke makes note of Agrippa donning his "royal robes" (12:21) as he prepares to hear his subjects' pleas. Josephus tells us that the robes were made entirely of silver, causing them to radiate and shimmer with the reflective glory of the sun (*Ant.* 19.343–44).[3] Accordingly, as Herod offers his address, he gladly receives the petitioners' ostentatious accolades, "The voice of a god, and not of a mortal!" (v. 22). The evangelist clearly casts Herod in these scenes as one "playing God," dealing out both death and life and desiring the people's homage in return. The true Lord's response is swift: "And immediately, because he had not given the glory to God, an angel of the Lord struck him down, and he was eaten by worms and died" (v. 23).

One more example will suffice. As we noted above, the temple system was—ideally—meant to function as an institutionalized embodiment of Yahweh's presence and mercy. However, Luke joins with a number of his apocalyptic contemporaries in viewing those who administered the cult as bereft of true piety. As John Elliott summarizes,

> The temple, once a holy house of prayer, had become a "den of thieves" (Luke 19:46). The guardians of the temple law, purity, and power had become preoccupied with status and class determination (Luke 11:43, 52; 15:2; 16:5; 18:11). They imposed heavy burdens (Luke 11:46), ignored the needy (Luke 10:29–37), neglected justice and the love of God (Luke 11:42), were full of extortion and wickedness (Luke 11:39), and devoured widows' houses (Luke 20:7).[4]

By virtue of its endorsement of values that are intensely opposed to the will and ways of God, the temple establishment can no longer claim legitimate

---

3. I owe this reference to Spencer, *Journeying through Acts*, 139.
4. John H. Elliott, "Temple versus Household in Luke-Acts: A Contrast in Social Institutions," in *The Social World of Luke-Acts: Models for Interpretation*, ed. Jerome H. Neyrey (Peabody, MA: Hendrickson, 1991), 236.

authority over the affairs of God's people or the ministrations of sacred worship. In fact, Elliott adds, "Precisely because it had failed in the *redistribution* not only of material resources but also justice, mercy and peace, the entire system and its chief symbol, the temple, was destined by God for destruction (Luke 11:34–35; 19:41–44; 21:5–6, 20–24)."[5]

2. *Greed: For Wealth and Honor.* Another common characteristic of the elite in Luke-Acts is their self-serving pursuit of "riches and the pleasures of life" (Luke 8:14). As is often noted by modern readers of Luke-Acts, the evangelist carries over a number of passages from Mark or Q and adds or redacts several others to emphasize the problematic pursuit of honor and excessive wealth in a society of great need.[6] As we have noted repeatedly, Mary's canticle signals near the narrative's beginning that God's new age will not abide elite hegemony over power, status, and possession (1:51–53). Moreover, numerous elements of Luke's account stress that relief for the poor and marginalized is a central feature of the Kingdom's arrival. John the Baptist commands all his followers to share with those in need, and calls those who serve as retainers to abandon the socioeconomic strategies and dispositions of their elite masters (3:10–14). Luke alone records Jesus citing the Isaian oracles announcing the deliverance of the poor, the release of captives and the oppressed, and the year of jubilee (which includes release from debt and the return of ancestral lands seized by the elite) as a summation of his ministry (4:16–22). Later, the ministry of the disciples in Acts is similarly depicted as bringing hope, comfort, and healing to the poor and diseased, echoing Jesus' own ministry to the marginalized in the Gospel (Acts 3:1–10; 5:12–16; 8:4–8; 9:36–42; 14:8–17; 19:12). Luke's version of the Beatitudes is accompanied by a set of corresponding woes that together offer a striking manifestation of the radical reversal Mary first announced (Luke 6:20–26; see also 14:7–14). As the sermon continues, Jesus also instructs his followers to leave behind the patronage system and to give without calculation (6:27–36), thereby becoming "children of the Most High; for he is kind to the ungrateful and the wicked" (v. 35).

As the Gospel unfolds, Luke continues to portray Jesus taking direct aim at the elite's preoccupation with honor and wealth. Jesus' woes against the Pharisees and scribes name their concern with outward appearance as opposed to inward piety (11:39–41) and their love for seats of honor and admiration

5. Ibid.

6. For three helpful discussions of Luke's criticism of wealth and the wealthy, see Walter E. Pilgrim, *Good News to the Poor: Wealth and Poverty in Luke-Acts* (Minneapolis: Augsburg, 1978), 87–146; Richard Cassidy, *Jesus, Politics, and Society: A Study of Luke's Gospel* (Maryknoll, NY: Orbis, 1978), 20–62; Luise Schottroff and Wolfgang Stegemann, *Jesus and the Hope of the Poor*, trans. Matthew J. O'Connell (Maryknoll, NY: Orbis, 1986), 67–120.

(v. 43) as among their warped features. Particularly instructive is Luke's version of Jesus' exhortation leading up to and including the banquet parable in Luke 14 (cf. Matt. 22:1–13). The evangelist sets the scene in a completely different context than it appears in Matthew and shapes its content to address the damning implications of elite interests. The setting is the house of a "leader of the Pharisees" to which Jesus has been invited on the Sabbath. While by conventional standards such an invitation should signal the Pharisees' honor and respect for Jesus, Luke makes their ulterior motives clear, as an attentive recipient would suspect: "they were watching him closely" (14:1). If it is controversy they want, Jesus does not disappoint. Immediately, Jesus heals a man with dropsy and challenges their prioritization of outward piety over truly righteous work on the Sabbath (vv. 2–6). Then, noticing how the guests clamor over the seats of honor, Jesus turns the tables on their contrived sense of worth: "For all who exalt themselves will be humbled, and those who humble themselves will be exalted" (v. 11). Jesus then addresses the one who had invited him. By holding such a banquet, the leader could expect to be praised by his guests for his generosity and to receive similar invitations from them in the future. Yet Jesus explains that such calculated reciprocity is not true generosity, nor the kind of hospitality worthy of the Kingdom. Instead of inviting members of his social class that can offer returns on his benefaction, the host should invite "the poor, the crippled, the lame, and the blind" (v. 13). One who does this will truly be blessed and will receive the proper reward from God's benefaction at the resurrection of the righteous (v. 14).

In response to Jesus' instruction, one of the dinner guests exclaims, "Blessed is anyone who will eat bread in the kingdom of God!" (v. 15). It is unclear whether the guest's statement is meant as an affirmation of Jesus' teaching or a challenge. The controversy-imbued setting of the passage, however, as well as the ubiquity of challenge-riposte sequences in Greco-Roman culture,[7] suggests an antagonistic response on the part of the guest. If a challenge, perhaps its emphasis is on the notion that *anyone* who eats in God's Kingdom is to be blessed, not just those who act in accordance with Jesus' instruction—to paraphrase: "We Pharisees, as righteous guardians of the sacred and social order, will be eating there as well, Rabbi!" But the banquet parable to follow goes on to identify the characteristic pursuits of the elite as distracting them from the invitation to eat bread in the Kingdom: land acquisition (v. 18), equipment needed to farm a large estate (five yoke of oxen: v. 19), preoccupation with family status and obligations (v. 20). Others will be invited to fill the spots of the guests who have spurned the master's offer to dine, and the house will be filled, for the

---

7. Recall our discussion of the "challenge and response" exchange in chap. 1.

master will persist until no room is left at his table (v. 21–23). Yet the cost of the original invitees' preoccupation with possession and patronage is severe: "For I tell you, none of those who were invited will taste my dinner" (v. 24).

Later, upon hearing Jesus' parable of the unconventional manager (unique to Luke; 16:1–13), the Pharisees, "who were lovers of money" (v. 14), ridiculed him. Jesus' response is a damning summary of their character and interests: "You are those who justify yourselves in the sight of others; but God knows your hearts; for what is prized by human beings is an abomination in the sight of God" (unique to Luke; 16:15–16; see also 18:11). Jesus then follows up with the parable of Lazarus and the rich man, also unique to Luke. Through this chilling example story, Jesus condemns the elite for luxuriating in their wealth while others starve at their gates, and warns of their damnation should they fail to repent and embrace what Moses and the prophets make clear to them (16:19–31). Later in the Gospel, Jesus will castigate the scribes' pursuit of honor and wealth in equally scathing tones:

> In the hearing of all the people he said to the disciples, "Beware of the scribes, who like to walk around in long robes, and love to be greeted with respect in the marketplaces, and to have the best seats in the synagogues and places of honor at banquets. They devour widows' houses and for the sake of appearance say long prayers. They will receive the greater condemnation." (20:45–47)

The evangelist also shares with Theophilus the Markan story of the wealthy ruler (18:18–25). While faithful to torah, the ruler still lacked one thing: setting aside his wealth to follow Jesus. He was greatly saddened by Jesus' call, "for he was very rich." Although, somewhat characteristically, Luke does not tell us what the rich ruler ultimately decides (see also 9:57–62), the moment becomes an occasion for Jesus to make an astounding and, for some, heartbreaking claim about the corruption spawned by the pursuit and possession of wealth: "How hard it is for those who have wealth to enter the kingdom of God! Indeed, it is easier for a camel to go through the eye of a needle than for someone who is rich to enter the kingdom of God" (18:24–25).

In Acts, Luke continues to provide examples of the elite's misguided quest for wealth and honor. Simon the magician, dubbed by the least to the greatest as "the power of God that is called Great," offers the apostles money for the power to confer the Holy Spirit on others (8:9–24). Peter rebukes him, crying, "May your silver perish with you, because you thought you could obtain God's gift with money! You have no part or share in this, for your heart is not right before God" (vv. 20–21). Paul and his associates are assailed by the owners of a highly lucrative, fortune-telling slave girl after Paul casts out her spirit of divination

(16:16–24). Luke presents Governor Felix as fearful, immoral, and money hungry, as he hoped to secure a bribe for Paul's release (24:24–27). When King Agrippa II and his wife, Bernice, arrive to hear Paul's case at the invitation of Governor Felix, Luke tells us that they "came with great pomp, and they entered the audience hall with the military tribunes and the prominent men of the city" (25:23).

In marked contrast to the priorities of the elite, Jesus' teachings on discipleship call followers to sacrifice themselves and forsake the ways of the world (Luke 9:23–27, 57–58; 10:7; 11:43), to put service to the Kingdom above family honor and loyalty (9:59–62; 12:49–53). Jesus also calls his disciples to take stock of what their commitment to him and the Kingdom will entail, using the parables of one who builds a tower and a king who goes out to war to illustrate the importance of counting the cost (14:25–32). But then Jesus describes that cost in very personal, economic terms: "So therefore, none of you can become my disciple if you do not give up all your possessions" (14:33). Consistent with the radical reversal characterizing the Kingdom, Jesus also calls his disciples to adopt an understanding of greatness that no longer blindly follows the misaligned prejudices of the elite:

> A dispute also arose among them as to which one of them was to be regarded as the greatest. But he said to them, "The kings of the Gentiles lord it over them; and those in authority over them are called benefactors. But not so with you; rather the greatest among you must become like the youngest, and the leader like one who serves. For who is greater, the one who is at the table or the one who serves? Is it not the one at the table? But I am among you as one who serves." (Luke 22:24–27; see also 9:46–48)

3. *Disregard for and Abuse of Others.* Luke frequently connects the elite's pursuit of wealth and honor and their abhorrent treatment of others. The citation from Elliott above captures well Luke's portrayal of the abusive practices of the Israelite elite serving as guardians of torah piety and the temple (Luke 10:29–37; 11:39, 42, 46; 20:7). Other examples include their misreading of torah, which puts misplaced piety above the needs of those who are suffering (6:6–11; 10:25–37; 13:10–17), their ostracizing of those they regard as sinful and unclean (7:36–50; 18:9–14), their neglect of the hungry (16:19–31), and their anemic generosity (21:1–3). Of course, both the Israelite and Roman elite also commit tremendous acts of oppression when they perceive that their worldviews or privileged stations are being challenged, having Jesus and his followers arrested, imprisoned, and killed.

4. *Inability to See the Kingdom among Them.* With few exceptions, the elite in Luke-Acts fail to recognize the arrival of God's Kingdom in Jesus and the

ministry of the early church. This failure is especially pronounced among the leadership of Israel. Recall that throughout the Gospel, Jesus' understanding of torah and his authority are challenged at nearly every turn by representatives from the Pharisees, scribes, lawyers, and Herod (see chap. 6). Recall also our discussion of the elite's response to the apostles' preaching in Acts 3–4 (chap. 8). These chapters of Acts poignantly capture the obduracy of the Israelite elite: despite the amazing reality that God's grace continues to be offered to the leaders of Israel after their rejection and murder of God's messiah and divine Son, they still refuse to acknowledge the presence of God's redeeming power made manifest in their midst through his name. While Gamaliel's wise counsel in Acts 5 shows a member of the elite as having the capacity to at least reserve judgment on the apostles, lest the leaders be "found fighting against God" (5:39), this turns out to be only a brief reprieve in their persecution of the Way. The apostles are still flogged and again told not to speak in the name of Jesus (5:40). Luke then transitions into the story of Stephen. Stephen's murder and the subsequent persecution of believers by authorities demonstrate the elite's unrelenting ignorance and ruthless resolve to obstruct the testimony to the Kingdom.

Other elite respond similarly. While Pilate recognizes Jesus' innocence and sues for clemency, he chooses to "save himself" by acquiescing to the demands of the Israelite elite and the crowds they have stirred, and he hands Jesus over to be crucified (Luke 23:13–25). As noted above, Herod Agrippa I has James, the brother of John, killed and seeks to do the same to Peter. Most of the elite of Athens, embodied in the Areopagus, scoff at Paul's witness to the resurrection of Jesus (Acts 17:32). Mired in a pagan worldview, they struggle to make sense of Paul's strange babbling (17:18–20), and most are unwilling to radically retool their sense of reality (17:32–33). In response to Paul's testimony to Jesus, Festus exclaims, "You are out of your mind, Paul! Too much learning is driving you insane!" (26:24).

Resistance to the Kingdom by Others

While Luke presents the elite as the primary opposition to the arrival of the Kingdom in Jesus, he also reveals others resisting the values and mission of Jesus and his followers. When Jesus challenges his fellow Nazarenes' sense of entitlement based on ethnic prejudice or pedigree, they are so enraged that they attempt to cast him off a precipice (Luke 4:23–30). As just mentioned, "the people" join with their leaders in calling for Jesus' condemnation (Luke 23:13, 18): the "power of darkness" compromises the sensibilities of elite and peasant alike. Along with the scribes and elders, Israelites from the Synagogue of the Freedmen stir up the people against Stephen and bring him before the

Sanhedrin (Acts 6:8–15). Nameless "Jews" resist the newly converted Saul's preaching and eventually plot to have him killed (Acts 9:22–25), initiating a pattern of resistance that Paul will face throughout his ministry. While many Israelites respond positively to Paul's message, others vehemently resist it (e.g., Acts 13:45–51; 14:2, 19–20; 17:5–9; 18:6; 19:9), including at the very end of Acts as Paul preaches to Israelites who visit him in prison (28:24–28).

Paul also meets resistance from gentiles. In Lystra, Paul heals a man lame from birth, and he and Barnabas barely succeed in preventing the amazed crowds from worshiping them as manifestations of Zeus and Hermes (14:8–18). Then, inflamed by Israelites from Antioch and Iconium, a largely gentile mob stones Paul and leaves him for dead (vv. 19–20). We noted above the angry response from the owners of a slave girl from whom Paul cast out a spirit of divination (16:16–40). Moreover, a riot in Ephesus is started by silversmiths who rightly perceive that Paul's teaching against idolatry would be bad for business (19:23–41). Just as a misaligned embrace of their own tradition leads Israelites to resist the Kingdom's arrival, so too does the misaligned view of the world endemic to paganism prevent many gentiles from perceiving the truth that Paul and other believers proclaim about this pivotal moment in human history.[8]

Some resistance to Jesus comes from his own followers. Luke includes several stories from Mark revealing the hardheadedness of the disciples (e.g., Luke 8:22–25 [Mark 4:35–41]; 9:46–48 [Mark 9:33–37]; 22:24–27 [Mark 10:41–45]). To these he adds the stories of James and John asking Jesus whether they should call down fire from heaven to consume a Samaritan village (9:51–55); the hesitancy of three marginal followers (9:57–62); Jesus' rebuke of Martha (10:38–42); and the disciples' need for repeated instruction from Jesus after his resurrection (Luke 24). As we just discussed, slowness to implement Kingdom values in full measure also occurs among believers in Acts, as revealed in the story of Ananias and Sapphira (5:1–11); the need for the community to regulate closely the daily distribution of food (6:1–6); the initial resistance to welcoming gentile believers into the fold (11:1–18); the dispute over the gentiles' responsibility to torah (15:1–21); and the disagreement between Paul and Barnabas, which is so sharp that they decide to separate (15:36–41). However, there is an important difference between most of these incidents of resistance and that displayed by the enemies of the Kingdom: having been corrected by Jesus or the testimony of the Spirit, these moments of resistance morph into moments of transformation for those involved. They become examples of divine grace, embodied in rebuke and forgiveness, received with repentance.

8. On the importance of recognizing the pagan setting for Acts, see C. Kavin Rowe, *World Upside Down: Reading Acts in the Graeco-Roman Age* (Oxford: Oxford University Press, 2009), esp. 17–51.

Returning the World to Blessing

Indeed, there is much that ails God's cosmos and the sentient creatures who inhabit it. Yet, above all else, Luke's narrative is about God's good news! Luke joins with his fellow believers in proclaiming that God's age-long intention to reclaim his recalcitrant creation is now unfolding in the ministry of Jesus and his followers.

Readers of Luke-Acts typically note Luke's concern to present the arrival of the Kingdom against the backdrop of God's relationship with Israel, and with a view to what God will yet accomplish as history courses toward its culmination. In other words, the evangelist narrates the origination of God's plan to redeem creation in the promises made to God's people to rescue them from the world's (and their own) corruption, that plan's emergence and advance in the ministry of Jesus and that of his followers, and its final consummation when Jesus returns. Because of Luke-Acts' emphasis on the unfolding of God's will in and through human history, the work is often characterized as offering a "salvation history." Moreover, like Mark and the other Gospels, Luke stresses the present and future dimensions of God's saving reign: the Kingdom has arrived and is present in the witness and actions of Jesus and his followers, but its full manifestation and victory over evil are yet to be achieved. Luke understands that in Jesus' day and in the days thereafter, humankind lives in a liminal age, experiencing the very real ministrations and premonitions of life in the Kingdom while also suffering the ongoing reality of life in a degraded, misaligned world. Scholars commonly call this view of God's salvation an "inaugurated eschatology": inaugurated in Jesus and experienced in the present, God's Kingdom and all its blessings are yet to arrive in fullness.

Although Luke's interest in providing a "salvation history" that stresses the past, present, and future dimensions of God's Kingdom is widely recognized, scholars debate the precise contours of the chronological scheme underlying Luke's narrative. As we saw above, Hans Conzelmann argues that the evangelist shapes his account according to a tripartite periodization of history, dividing the time from creation to the end of the world into three epochs: the time of Israel, the time of Jesus' earthly ministry, and the time of the church.[9] While Conzelmann's proposal has influenced generations of scholars—who have embraced, rejected, and modified it—and many find Luke's narrative presuming a periodization of some sort, many agree that Conzelmann's divisions are far too rigid: they neglect to account for Luke's much more fluid understanding

9. Conzelmann, *Theology of St. Luke*, 16.

of the "stages" in which God's Kingdom unfolds and for Luke's emphasis on the continuity between those stages.

In my view, two features of Luke's account present a conceptual challenge for comprehending the chronological character of Luke's salvation history. On the one hand, Luke presents a developmental understanding of the Kingdom in successive "movements": God's redemption is preconceived in the heart of a Savior God and foretold by the prophets, arrives in Jesus' ministry, advances in Jesus' death and resurrection, which inaugurate the Spirit-empowered ministry of his followers, and will reach its consummation when Jesus returns. On the other hand, Luke emphasizes the interconnection between these movements by patterning them in similar ways. In chapter 5 we examined Luke's penchant for patterns and his use of intertextual parallelism on both a small and large scale to emphasize the continuity between Israel's past and the unfolding of God's salvation in the "matters fulfilled among us." As we saw, some of the broader Israelite themes that Luke emphasizes in his account of the Kingdom's arrival in Jesus include the following:

1. God's character as Savior who rescues and acts mercifully toward Israel
2. God's promises to restore Israel to blessing and God's calls for Israel's return to righteousness through the prophets
3. The mixed response of faithfulness on the part of some and violent rejection on the part of many
4. God's merciful resolve to honor God's commitment to Israel and the world, despite the faithlessness of many

The intertextual connections that Luke makes to these motifs enable him to amplify what he sees as characteristic patterns in God's dealings with Israel, as well as Israel's response to God, while he presents the unfolding of God's salvation in the events he records. Luke is thus able to emphasize both that crucial developments in God's salvation have occurred, are taking place, and will yet arrive, *and* that these developments reenact much of what has been going on throughout Israel's age-long relationship with Yahweh.

In addition to these intertextual parallels, we also saw that Luke composes and amplifies intratextual parallels between Jesus and his followers: Jesus' Spirit-empowered ministry of teaching, healing, and confronting evil and suffering is taken up in the Spirit-empowered ministry of his disciples, as his journey becomes their journey. These parallels reveal that Jesus and his followers, through their Spirit-directed ministries, are together implementing one and the same Kingdom. Similarly, Luke *interlaces* the major movements of salvation history by intercalating elements of later developments into earlier ones: the specific contours of Jesus' birth, ministry, suffering, death, resurrection, and sending out of the Spirit are anticipated in the testimony of Israel's prophets; the disciples' journey of witness begins with Jesus during his earthly ministry; and the blessings of the future Kingdom are already being experienced in the present. Building on this discussion, it seems to me that Luke's unfolding of salvation history could be profitably diagrammed something like this:

God's Initiative	Human Response
PAST	
Pivotal Events: God's past acts of delivering and instructing Israel	
God repeatedly saves Israel; through the prophets, God calls them to righteousness and promises to deliver them from their waywardness and the evils of this age.	faithfulness and hope vs. wicked ignorance and violent rejection
Pivotal Events: the birth, ministry, and resurrection of Jesus	
The Kingdom arrives in Jesus and is powerfully manifested in the Spirit-empowered ministry of the Lord and Savior: calling all people to return to righteousness, delivering them from the ills of this evil age, and suffering for his bold witness to the Kingdom. The Kingdom advances in Jesus' resurrection from the dead, leading to . . .	faithfulness and hope vs. wicked ignorance and violent rejection
PRESENT	
Pivotal Events: the bestowal of the Spirit and the bold witness of the faithful	
. . . the Spirit-empowered ministry of his followers: calling all people to return to righteousness, delivering them from the ills of this evil age, and suffering for their bold witness to the Kingdom.	faithfulness and hope vs. wicked ignorance and violent rejection
FUTURE	
Pivotal Events: the return of Jesus and deliverance of the faithful	
God's resolve to save Israel and all humanity will be fulfilled and God's Kingdom fully enacted as Jesus returns to gather the faithful and defeat evil once and for all.	faithful hope leading to vindication vs. wicked rejection leading to condemnation

This table's account of Luke's historical vision divides human history into broad temporal periods of past, present, and future to convey Luke's sense of the advancement of God's plan of salvation. Yet it does not attempt to periodize history into distinct epochs or stages. Rather, it reflects Luke's more dynamic portrait of God's Kingdom pulsing forward and manifesting more fully within the pivotal events achieved in Jesus, the divine Son, the Spirit, and his followers. Second, as noted above, the history Luke tells unfolds according to characteristic patterns involving God, Jesus, and the varied response to God's sovereign will by God's people. In this regard, Luke's historical vision has a cyclical quality to it, not in the sense of a closed circle but more like a repeating cadence spiraling toward climactic resolution. As John Nolland states, "Luke knows nothing of sharply delineated periods in salvation-history; for Luke the same story keeps repeating, but in different keys and with a definite sense of escalation towards a climax represented by the parousia."[10]

Another feature of Luke's account also needs to be addressed, and one that is very similar to the intercalation I just described. As critical as all the pivotal events are to the unfolding of God's Kingdom, especially the resurrection, I think Luke takes pains to stress that many of the blessings of the Kingdom's arrival in Jesus are made manifest—if not in degree, then at least in kind—from the moment of Jesus' conception. There is clearly advancement and escalation in the manifestation of the Kingdom beyond this point (such as in the resolution of the disciples' misunderstanding and their transformation into witnesses, and the bestowal of the Spirit at Pentecost), but with Jesus' conception it is possible for the faithful to enter into the Kingdom's current and in a substantial (even if penultimate) sense participate in God's saving reign. This is why Elizabeth, Mary, and Zechariah can celebrate the arrival of God's salvation and their experience of it even before the births of John and Jesus; why the angelic host, the shepherds, Simeon, and Anna do the same upon beholding the infant Messiah; and why these characters can bear Spirit-empowered witness to the Kingdom. This is why John can proclaim a baptism of repentance for the forgiveness of sins, "the word" can be preached, and the life-altering blessings of the Kingdom's power—including forgiveness, healing, exorcism, defeat of death (widow's son, Jairus' daughter), bold witness, and "salvation" (recall Zacchaeus)—can be received by characters before Jesus' death and resurrection. This is why Jesus can tell the robber hanging next to him, "Truly I tell you, today you will be with me in Paradise" (Luke 23:43), though it occurs long before the parousia. The blessed markers of the Kingdom's arrival—though hinging on God's radical intervention in history through Jesus' birth, ministry, suffering, death, resurrection, ongoing reign, and return—are made real and available from the *very* beginning of Jesus' advent.

10. John Nolland, "Salvation History and Eschatology," in *Witness to the Gospel: The Theology of Acts*, ed. I. Howard Marshall and David Peterson (Grand Rapids: Eerdmans, 1998), 70.

Cadences of the Kingdom

We will now review the blessings made possible by the Kingdom's advance in Jesus that are celebrated by Luke. As Luke's portrayal of the world's corruption took up many of the same motifs stressed by Mark and other Israelite precedents, so is this the case with Luke's portrayal of God's salvation. Luke, however, emphasizes the following features of God's reign: the exaltation of the lowly, the rescue and instruction of the faithful, the bold witness of believers and resistance to the world zealously guarded by Rome, and the Kingdom blessings of forgiveness, healing, deliverance from evil, and eternal life.

Welcoming and Exalting the Meek and Marginalized

Already at the start of his narrative, Luke stresses the exaltation of the meek and marginalized as an essential consequence of the Kingdom's arrival. Mary, a peasant girl, is hailed in terms calling to mind Israel's heroes of old. She is then told by Gabriel that she will bear Yahweh's awaited Messiah, and her song celebrating Jesus' conception announces world-upending reversal. After Mary bears her son, the first to hear the good news of Jesus' birth—from an angelic host of heaven—are not Israel's elite but lowly shepherds tending their flocks in the hills. We have seen that such reversal is also one of the primary features of Jesus' ministry. In sharp contrast to the callous and neglectful tendencies of the elite, Jesus and his followers minister to the lowly and elite alike with the blessings of the Kingdom, offering healing, sustenance, and hope. Jesus rejects the elite's formulations of Israelite tradition that have used torah to keep many on the margins and to create an avenue for bolstering the elite's own honor. While Luke appears to find some of the markers of Israelite piety important, such as a less rigorous version of the dietary codes, these function for him as a way to maintain the community's sense of unity and continuity with its Israelite heritage (e.g., Acts 15:1–35) rather than as a mechanism for shame and exclusion.

Just as important, Jesus calls the marginalized to join in his ministry, entering into fellowship with him and others longing for the Kingdom's arrival. Sinners, tax collectors, and other displaced persons seem to compose the lion's share of Jesus' wider retinue. Women are also recognized as disciples, traveling with Jesus and the twelve. Some of them with means support Jesus' ministry, and some from among their number are the first to hear and announce the good news of Jesus' resurrection.[11] The eclectic character of Jesus' followers

---

11. As Richard Cassidy (*Jesus, Politics, and Society*, 37) helpfully summarizes, "Luke's description indicates that Jesus had adopted a pattern of behavior that implicitly opened the way

continues in Acts, even as more people of means are added to their number. Gentile believers are welcomed into the fold, despite the challenges this creates for some. As already discussed, unlike his fellow elite, Luke also makes it clear that the authority to proclaim the mysteries of God resides not in a select few but in an ever-expanding group of ministers. While the ministry of the twelve receives focused attention in the Gospel and early in Acts, the pattern presented in both volumes is that testimony to the Kingdom is to be taken up by many others as well (as is foreshadowed by the outpouring of the Spirit at Pentecost in accord with Joel 2). As we saw earlier in this chapter, the authority claimed by the elite is revealed as illegitimate and impotent in comparison to the bold, Spirit-empowered testimony of these persons who have truly received heaven's mandate to disclose and mediate divine truth and blessing.

Jesus' Rescue of the Faithful and Instruction of Followers

Both Mary's and Zechariah's songs speak of God's victory over those who oppose the faithful. Simeon announces that Jesus' ministry will cause some to fall and others to rise as Jesus unveils the intentions of human hearts. And one of the major themes of Luke's narrative is the resistance and violent rejection that Jesus Messiah and his followers will suffer, primarily at the hands of both the Israelite and gentile elite, but also by Jesus' hometown folk, other Israelites and gentiles, and above all, Satan. In the midst of this violent resistance and rejection, God's deliverance and purposes prevail. Jesus emerges from his time of temptation victorious and proceeds to bind "the strong man" in his acts of healing, casting out demons "by the finger of God" (Luke 11:20), and teaching about the Kingdom. The disciples in both the Gospel and Acts share in this power and ministry. Though the elite may prevail for a day, and even put Jesus, the Son of God, Author of life, and Suffering Servant, to death along with some of his followers, their oppression of the righteous only leads to greater acts of deliverance and further advances the purpose and plan of God. Jesus is raised from the dead! As resurrected Lord and Savior, he oversees and empowers the further unfolding of God's reign as his followers take up his ministry of healing and witness despite the resistance and even natural trials they face (e.g., Acts 27:31; 27:43–28:6). Similarly, the elite's martyrdom of Jesus' followers in Acts in order to halt the Way only leads to the good

---

to a new personal identity and social standing for women." While women in Luke's narrative still function within a largely patriarchal context, their role and importance in Jesus' ministry and that of the early church transcends—even transgresses—the norms of the first-century Mediterranean world. The extent to which the early church would later follow through with (or circumvent) this new identity and social standing for women is, of course, another matter!

news advancing to the rest of Judea, Samaria, and beyond. The "hour of darkness," though persistent and pervasive and manifested in varying forms, is no match for the light that brings salvation "to the ends of the earth" (Acts 13:47) and turns humanity from "the power of Satan to God" (26:18). For the ultimate outcome of those who entrust themselves to Jesus and the Kingdom is not in doubt. Jesus, the glorious Son of Man, will return, all evil shall be vanquished, and the faithful will share in the eternal banquet of God's realm (see Luke 6:20–26; 14:15–24; 17:27–30; 18:28–30; 21:25–28; Acts 1:11; 3:12–19; 13:46).

As we have seen, Luke also emphasizes Jesus countering elite values and wickedness through his teaching and example. Very likely, this is to ensure that Theophilus and others do not themselves get caught up in the corrupting quest for wealth, honor, and power. Instead, Luke calls them to orient their lives according to the values of the Kingdom, embracing humility, compassionate service, bold witness, and sacrifice as they follow Jesus to Jerusalem and beyond. And so this becomes another means by which evil is to be overcome and the faithful rescued.[12] As part of the instruction the evangelist relays, he makes it clear that Jesus advocated reliance on God's intervention to establish the Kingdom of God and demanded nonviolent resistance to Rome of his followers. Jesus repeatedly rebuked his disciples when they suggested violence as a response to the persecution they faced (e.g., Luke 9:51–55; 22:38), even when his life was at stake (22:49–51). Note also that in Luke, Jesus' instruction on "turning the other cheek," among others, applies specifically to how believers are to respond to their enemies. These instructions follow immediately on the heels of Jesus' announcement concerning the stark, eschatological reversal that will accompany the dawning of the Kingdom in a contrasting series of beatitudes and woes (6:20–26).

> Then he looked up at his disciples and said:
> "Blessed are you who are poor,
> for yours is the kingdom of God.
> "Blessed are you who are hungry now,
> for you will be filled.
> "Blessed are you who weep now,
> for you will laugh.
> "Blessed are you when people hate you, and when they exclude you,
> revile you, and defame you on account of the Son of Man. Rejoice

---

12. In the lament psalms, it is common for the psalmist to call for God's deliverance from oppressors, as well as for the wisdom and fortitude needed to avoid the sins of those very same wicked ones (see, e.g., Ps. 25).

> in that day and leap for joy, for surely your reward is great in heaven;
> for that is what their ancestors did to the prophets.
> "But woe to you who are rich,
>   for you have received your consolation.
> "Woe to you who are full now,
>   for you will be hungry.
> "Woe to you who are laughing now,
>   for you will mourn and weep.
> "Woe to you when all speak well of you, for that is what their ancestors
> did to the false prophets."

These blessings and woes are a powerful testimony to the drastic reversal that shall accompany the dawning of God's new age. Indeed, the enemies to whom Jesus refers in these and related instructions are the elite who oppress and persecute the faithful. God will bring about their defeat and humiliation. But in the meantime, followers must resist them not only with bold witness but also with outlandish love and goodness, even if such as these threaten them with persecution and death: "But I say to you that listen, Love your enemies, do good to those who hate you, bless those who curse you, pray for those who abuse you. If anyone strikes you on the cheek, offer the other also; and from anyone who takes away your coat do not withhold even your shirt" (6:27–29).

Spirit-Empowered Community of Prayer, Provision, Bold Witness, and Sacrifice

We have repeatedly noted that Jesus' followers in the Gospels and especially the early believers in Acts display communal life marked by earnest and joyful prayer, devotion to the apostles' teaching, bold witness, and social relations characterized by intimacy and inclusivity. Moreover, "resources were not directed under compulsion to a distant center and redistributed according to the interests of those in power, but were shared directly according to availability and need (Luke 6:30–36; 11:5–13; 12:33; 15:3–32; 18:22; 19:1–10; Acts 2:44–47; 4:32–37; 6:1–6)."[13] We also emphasized in chapter 4 that all these features of community life are underscored by Luke as being empowered by the Spirit and essential to believers' participation in the life of the Kingdom. Still another is sacrifice. Implied already in the controversy surrounding John's naming, and reinforced in Simeon's ominous words to Mary, the coming of the Kingdom

---

13. Elliott, "Temple versus Household," 236. See also Halvor Moxnes, "Patron-Client Relations and the New Community in Luke-Acts," in *The Social World of Luke-Acts: Models for Interpretation*, ed. Jerome H. Neyrey (Peabody, MA: Hendrickson, 1991), 266.

will come with a cost not only for God's enemies but also for the faithful. Jesus, the Servant, serves as the paradigm for this call to forsake all for the Kingdom, including the renunciation of wealth and the marginalization of all other commitments, even one's own life. Such is part of the bold vocation of embracing the Kingdom in a world gone terribly awry—it is not simply an unfortunate reality to be endured. For this reason, after being imprisoned and flogged, the apostles "rejoiced because they were considered worthy to suffer dishonor for the sake of the name" (Acts 5:41). Similarly, the risen Lord Jesus tells Ananias concerning Paul, "I myself will show him how much he must suffer for the sake of my name" (9:16), and Paul later speaks to the Ephesian elders of the trials the Spirit shall call him to endure, saying, "But I do not count my life of any value to myself, if only I may finish my course and the ministry that I received from the Lord Jesus, to testify to the good news of God's grace" (20:23–24). Faithful resistance to the world's varied forms of corruption is going to result in vicious reprisal. Jesus lived and prepared his disciples for this reality, and in Acts they encounter it. Such will not cease until the Son of Man returns (see Luke 21:12–18).

Forgiveness, Healing, Deliverance from Evil, and Eternal Life

As noted repeatedly in the preceding pages, Luke emphasizes God's forgiveness as an essential feature of God's saving reign. John announced a baptism of repentance and forgiveness, and Jesus freely pronounced release from sins for those who entrusted themselves to his care. Even to those who killed the Author of life or his followers, forgiveness and "times of refreshing . . . from the presence of the Lord" are offered (Luke 23:34; Acts 3:20; 7:60). Through faith in Jesus, forgiveness is conferred apart from temple and cult. As Peter announces to Cornelius, "All the prophets testify about him that everyone who believes in him receives forgiveness of sins through his name" (Acts 10:43). Scholars have long debated Luke's understanding of Jesus' death. Many, however, conclude that the evangelist presents Jesus' death as an act of atonement while not emphasizing its atoning significance.[14] At the Last Supper, Jesus says, "This is my body, which is given for you," and, "This cup that is poured out for you is the new covenant in my blood" (Luke 22:19–20). There are resonances of the Passover meal in this language, and so Jesus' role as the "prophet like Moses" inaugurating a new exodus may be intended here. Yet the atoning

---

14. See I. Howard Marshall, "The Place of Acts 20.28 in Luke's Theology of the Cross," in *Reading Acts Today: Festschrift for Loveday Alexander*, ed. Steve Walton et al., LNTS 427 (London: T&T Clark, 2011), 154–70.

character of Jesus' death is also implied. Likewise, in Acts 20:28 Paul speaks of God constituting the church "with the blood of his own son." Even so, it is above all else Jesus' resurrection that makes possible and empowers the proclamation of God's mercy to the ends of the earth.

"Salvation" for Luke, however, includes a broader array of benefits than just forgiveness, even if these might be experienced only in part before the arrival of God's reign in fullness: "Jesus offers *aphesis* (Luke 4:18–19), a 're-lease' variously conceived and enacted."[15] Healing from disease, release from demonic spirits, deliverance from oppression, return of dignity, restoration to one's community, abundant provision, and the eventual defeat of death itself—basically all that is wrong with this world and all that circumvents the blessing God intends for it shall be overcome. Luke, like the other evangelists, provides little detail on the state of God's future realm for the faithful. Yet his portrayal of the blessings that God's reign confers through Jesus and the com-munity of believers in the present reveals signs of the "Paradise" that awaits all eager for Jesus to come into his Kingdom (Luke 23:42–43).

Summary

The ills of this age that Luke amplifies are countered by the vision of salva-tion he proclaims. Luke shares the apocalyptic view that the entire cosmos is embroiled in conflict, as demonic powers seek to undermine God's designs for creation and work their wiles through corrupted humans. But Luke announces that the world enacted by those powers shall not stand and is already being fatally undermined by the Kingdom's arrival. Not unlike what we see with the covenanters of Qumran, who believed that their oppressed and beleaguered community embodied the true, spiritual temple of God, Luke maintains that the privilege and ideological commitments of the elite are being countered by the community of the Kingdom emerging into the Roman world. Those whom the elite have oppressed are filled with God's presence, blessing, and power. Their resources are not zealously horded and enjoyed by a few but are distributed according to need and lent without the expectation of reciprocity. The good news and ways of relating that offer salvation to humankind are being announced and lived out by apostles who are "unlearned men" (Acts 4:13), and they are being given voice by an ever-expanding group of witnesses from across the social spectrum. Theirs is a community dismissive of the agonistic quest for honor and the system of patronage that merely perpetuates the status

15. Carroll, *Luke*, 10.

quo. Instead, its members redefine their understanding of greatness as service, humility, and sacrifice. In short, the world misshaped by Satan and the elite is to be undone by the advent of the Kingdom in Jesus and its advance in the mission of the early church.

Yet Luke's depiction of the community established by Jesus' followers lacks the exclusivity characterizing the eschatological visions of Qumran and other Israelites. Not only are the poor, lowly, and marginalized welcomed into the community participating in God's new age, but so are the "sinful" and even gentiles. Also unlike the Essenes of Qumran and others who lamented the present state of the temple, Luke (as with Mark) does not envision the restoration of the current temple or the creation of a new one. Instead, the sanctifying work of God's Spirit can be fully embodied in the community of believers who live out and call others to embrace the ways of the Lord's new realm.

Accordingly, the reality-upending work that Jesus inaugurates not only targets those entities unremittingly resistant to the Kingdom's arrival but also transforms those with hearts open to receiving the word he and his followers proclaim. For centuries, the prophets had announced that the dawn of God's new age would be marked by a return to righteousness by at least a remnant of Israel. For some of these later prophetic and apocalyptic sages, God's Spirit would come upon the faithful with a breadth and intensity never before experienced to inspire their devotion to God's instruction and embolden their embrace of the Kingdom. Jesus' teaching, ongoing ministry as resurrected Lord, and sending out of the Spirit upon believers enable Jesus' fearful, ignorant, and small-minded disciples, along with a zealous persecutor of the Way and countless others, to morph into bold and eloquent champions of God's mercy and deliverance. Their endurance in the face of evil enables them not only to "gain their souls" (Luke 21:19) but also to share this good news of salvation to the ends of creation, fulfilling Israel's ancient calling, which God first announced to Abram, saying, "And in your descendants all the families of the earth shall be blessed " (Acts 3:25).

Conclusion

Discerning Luke's Purpose

If the preceding section offers an adequate assessment of what Luke found wrong with the world and how God was setting it to rights through the ministry of Jesus and his followers, what might it tell us about Luke's reasons for scribing his two-volume work? What, in other words, was the "truth" that Luke was especially concerned for Theophilus to discern regarding the instruction he had already received? Since the introduction of this work, I have maintained that one of Luke's chief objectives was to call Theophilus and other members of the elite to abandon their privileged stations and their allegiance to Rome and to embrace the Kingdom of God and Jesus as Lord. It is now time to test that thesis by reviewing what we have discovered in the preceding chapters and engaging in conversation with other interpreters. I will also discuss here a second objective Luke sought to address.

In what follows, I first catalogue various proposals scholars have offered concerning Luke's primary interests. In doing so, I have tried to provide a representative overview of the more commonly held assessments of Luke's purpose, but readers should be aware that the diversity of such proposals transcends those covered here.[1] I then present a more detailed review of various perspectives on Luke's regard for Roman rule and authority, since this matter is central to the understanding of Luke-Acts I present in this study. Finally, summarizing ma-

---

1. The number of objectives scholars have found Luke pursuing are truly legion. For a more detailed review of many of these proposals and a few others, see Mark Allen Powell, *What Are They Saying about Luke?* (New York: Paulist Press, 1989), 42–59, and *What Are They Saying about Acts?* (New York: Paulist Press, 1991), 38–79. In composing this catalogue of views, I have been greatly assisted by Powell's discussions.

255

terial we have already engaged, I present my case, in conversation with these other viewpoints, for the two aims I believe dominate Luke's narrative rhetoric.

Some Proposals on Luke's Purpose

Hans Conzelmann believed that Luke's primary concern was to address believers' perceived delay in Jesus' return and to instruct the church on how to live in the current age.[2] In sharp contrast, A. J. Mattill argues that Luke's Jesus fervently instructs his disciples to proclaim the nearness of the Kingdom and to ready themselves for Jesus' return because the evangelist thinks the parousia is imminent.[3] Charles Talbert proposes that Luke wrote to combat an early form of gnosticism in the church that promoted a docetic view of Christ.[4] In response, Luke emphasizes the existence of Christ in human form, the corporeal reality of both his crucifixion and resurrection, and the apostles as the legitimate witnesses to Jesus and authoritative interpreters of Scripture. Schuyler Brown argues that Luke focuses on the persecution experienced by Christians.[5] Luke responds by affirming the reliability of the church's witness and depicting the church as faithfully steadfast in resisting Satan's onslaught. While sharing the view that one of Luke's primary aims is to encourage believers in the face of tribulation and suffering, David Tiede finds that Luke directs his audience to the Israelite scriptures to explain the reality of persecution, and especially the humiliation and suffering resulting from the fall of Jerusalem.[6] Just as did Israel in the past, so too are God's people now experiencing a divinely ordained pattern of prophecy-rejection-punishment-vindication. And just as the prophets and Jesus (as the Suffering Servant) share in the punishment that God levels on Israel, so too are Jewish Christians now sharing in the suffering of all Jews as a result of Jerusalem's rejection of Jesus. Thus, while Brown understands that Luke's main goal is to exhort believers to remain steadfastly committed to the ministry of the church despite its persecution, Tiede finds that Luke also wants to explain why believers are experiencing persecution, while encouraging them to await the vindication that is to surely come.

2. Conzelmann, *Theology of St. Luke.*
3. A. J. Mattill, *Luke and the Last Things: A Perspective for the Understanding of Lukan Thought* (Dillsboro: Western North Carolina Press, 1979).
4. Charles H. Talbert, *Jesus and the Gnostics: An Examination of the Lucan Purpose* (Nashville: Abingdon, 1966).
5. Schuyler Brown, *Apostasy and Perseverance in the Theology of Luke,* AnBib 36 (Rome: Pontifical Biblical Institute, 1969).
6. David L. Tiede, *Prophecy and History in Luke-Acts* (Philadelphia: Fortress, 1980).

A number of scholars have argued that one of Luke's primary concerns is to account for, as Luke Timothy Johnson puts it, "the very existence of a messianic sect in the Gentile world."[7] Robert Maddox, for example, proposes that Luke's primarily gentile community was facing an identity crisis. Jewish detractors were challenging the legitimacy of gentiles' belief in Jesus as Messiah in light of the fact that so few Jews shared it.[8] In response, the evangelist shapes his narrative to show the continuity between Christianity and Israelite tradition, while at the same time emphasizing that Israel has consistently rejected God's plan for God's people and the rest of humanity. By now rejecting Jesus and the early Christian witnesses, Jews have once again turned away from God's attempt to redeem them, and they are now experiencing God's judgment for their continued faithlessness. In the meantime, God's salvation has been embraced by the gentile Christians.[9] Taking Luke's apparently negative view of Judaism several steps further, Jack T. Sanders claims that Luke's narrative is anti-Semitic. Sanders finds that Luke's invective against Judaism targets the tradition in general and not simply members of the religious elite.[10] Luke even shows antipathy for Jewish Christians who, like those in Acts 15:5, insist that gentile believers must be circumcised and follow the laws of Moses. Accordingly, one of Luke's main concerns is to defend his community from these Christian "Judaizers" who threaten the integrity of the Christian faith. Jacob Jervell, however, challenges the claim that Luke presents such a negative view of the Jewish response to the gospel and Jews in general.[11] He points out that Luke presents the early community as composed mostly of Jews and that Luke repeatedly shows Jews becoming members of the Way. It is from this Jewish-Christian community—representing the faithful remnant of Israel—that the mission to the gentiles emerges, and the resounding success of that mission affirms that those Jews are now fulfilling their promised role as stewards of God's salvation for all humanity.

Still others have argued that Luke's narrative emphasizes the need for his Christian community to show compassion to the marginalized and oppressed as part of a radical call for social reversal.[12] For example, Luise Schottroff and Wolfgang Stegemann claim that the evangelist writes for Christians across the

7. Johnson, *Gospel of Luke*, 10. So also Carroll, *Luke*, 12.

8. Robert Maddox, *The Purpose of Luke-Acts*, SNTW (Edinburgh: T&T Clark, 1985).

9. Stephen G. Wilson (*The Gentiles and the Gentile Mission in Luke-Acts*, SNTSMS 23 [Cambridge: Cambridge University Press, 2005]) offers a similar assessment of Luke's main concerns while focusing less on Jewish rejection and more on the gentile mission and acceptance of the gospel as a primary thrust of Luke's narrative. See also Johnson, *Gospel of Luke*, 10.

10. Jack T. Sanders, *The Jews in Luke-Acts* (Philadelphia: Fortress, 1987).

11. Jacob Jervell, *Luke and the People of God* (Minneapolis: Fortress, 1972).

12. See John R. Donahue, "Two Decades of Research on the Rich and Poor in Luke-Acts," in *Justice and the Holy: Essays in Honor of Walter Harrelson*, ed. Douglas A. Knight and Peter J.

social spectrum but is particularly concerned to call the rich and respectable to an awareness of how the gospel contravenes the pursuit of wealth and status common to the elite. Rather than the "evangelist to the poor," Luke "is an exceptionally keen critic of the rich and wants their conversion, which is possible only by way of radical renunciation (renunciation of half of their possessions) and unpleasant specific actions (risky loans, cancellation of debts, gifts)."[13] Similarly, Walter E. Pilgrim finds that while the basic message of Jesus' ministry in Luke's Gospel centers on the theme of good news to the poor, Jesus' "extensive discussion of wealth and poverty is addressed primarily to the rich."[14] Possessions, Jesus teaches, pose a "radical danger to Christian discipleship," and Luke formulates the Jesus traditions at his disposal (such as the Lukan woes and parables) to question "whether or not wealth and discipleship have anything in common."[15] Through his depiction of Jesus' teaching and the early community in Acts, Luke asks all Christians, and especially the wealthy, to freely give of and, if necessary, even abandon their possessions for the sake of the needy within and beyond their communities of faith. In sum, "the challenge of the Jerusalem church is that of a new kind of community, where there is neither rich nor poor, where economic needs are met by practical and costly action."[16]

Luke's Understanding of Jesus and the Kingdom in Relation to Rome

One issue complicating attempts to discern Luke's purpose is the extent to which the evangelist advocates accommodation or resistance to Roman rule. Across the landscape of studies engaging this matter, scholars have collectively composed (as might be guessed!) a wide spectrum of views. We will begin by returning to a scholar whose work has influenced and served as a point of departure for much scholarly conversation on Luke's objectives in relation to Rome.

Hans Conzelmann proposed that Luke had three crucial aims. First, as noted above, he argues that the chief issue Luke confronted was the delay in Jesus' return to consummate the Kingdom: "Luke is confronted by the situation in which the Church finds herself by the delay of the Parousia and her existence

---

Paris (Atlanta: Scholars Press, 1989), 129–44, for a helpful survey of works (prior to 1989) and key interpretive issues related to Luke's casting of the rich and poor.

13. Schottroff and Stegemann, *Jesus and the Hope of the Poor*, 117. Originally published as *Jesus von Nazareth—Hoffnung der Armen* (Stuttgart: Verlag W. Kohlhammer, 1978).

14. Walter E. Pilgrim, *Good News to the Poor: Wealth and Poverty in Luke-Acts* (Minneapolis: Augsburg, 1981), 163.

15. Ibid., 164.

16. Ibid., 165–66. See also David Peter Seccombe, *Possessions and the Poor in Luke-Acts*, SNTSU (Linz: A. Fuchs, 1983).

in secular history, and he tries to come to terms with the situation by his account of historical events."[17] As we saw in the previous chapter, Conzelmann thus argues that Luke provides a reshaping of "salvation history" into three distinct epochs: the period of Israel, the period of Christ, and the period of the church.[18] In so periodizing God's redemptive plan, Luke establishes a rationale for the parousia's delay: salvation history was indeed unfolding as God had intended, and in the present period believers are required to remain steadfast and patient, relying on the Spirit to empower their ministry of witness, which now extends to all peoples of the world.[19]

Conzelmann argues that a second, related objective thus follows: as those who are required to persevere and minister within the present period, the church must find a way of living in harmony with Roman order. Accordingly, we must understand that the claims of lordship and kingship that Luke makes of Jesus function on a religious, not political, level. For instance, Luke shapes Jesus' messianic identity in key texts such as Jesus' announcement in Nazareth (Luke 4) and his triumphal entry (Luke 19) in a "nonpolitical" sense.[20] Moreover, just as Luke shows that Jesus was not in conflict with the existing political order but proclaimed devotion to an apolitical, religious realm, so too must believers recognize the legitimacy of Roman rule, at least in the current era of history. Thus, when dealing with the empire, Christians "should render to Caesar what is Caesar's, and to God what is God's."[21] Similarly, Conzelmann concludes that "Luke emphasizes that to confess oneself to be a Christian implies no crime against Roman law."[22] In his commentary on Acts, he adds that Luke provides a "demonstration that Christian preaching does not impinge upon the power of empire."[23]

This second objective is closely related to a third. Conzelmann also assumes that Luke intended his work to be engaged by at least some Roman officials, and therefore Luke shapes his account not only to instruct the church but also to pursue an apologetic aim: "Whereas in the original eschatological perspective it was felt that the State had to be withstood, now the attempt is made to enter into conversation with it, in order to achieve a permanent settlement."[24] While Conzelmann does not elaborate on this third objective in detail, he nevertheless argues (building on the work of earlier scholars, such as Loisy,

---

17. Conzelmann, *Theology of St. Luke*, 14.
18. Ibid., 16.
19. Ibid., 135–36.
20. Ibid., 139.
21. Ibid., 148 (quoting Mark 12:17//Matt. 22:21//Luke 20:25). See also pp. 139–40, 188–89.
22. Ibid., 139–40.
23. Conzelmann, *Acts of the Apostles*, xlvii.
24. Conzelmann, *Theology of St. Luke*, 138.

Goguel, Dibelius, and Cadbury) that Luke "sets out to show that Christianity is the most authentic form of Judaism, and that by virtue of this it has a right to enjoy from the Roman authorities the same tolerance as does Judaism."[25]

Paul Walaskay has advocated Conzelmann's second objective, arguing that Acts calls Christians to seek peaceable relations with Rome. He claims that Luke has "a high regard for the imperial government and those who administer it."[26] According to Luke, "the state is ordained by God to use its power for the benefit of all by obtaining peace and maintaining harmony among the diverse nations of the world."[27] Others have embraced Conzelmann's third objective and made it central to their understanding of Luke's rhetoric. For example, B. S. Easton and Ernst Haenchen have similarly argued that Luke intended to present Christianity as politically benign in order to convince the Roman authorities that the tradition should be granted status as a legitimate religion alongside Judaism.[28] While later writers have recognized that there is scant evidence that Rome classified religions as legal or illegal in the first century, many agree with Conzelmann and others that Luke cast Christianity as a movement that could exist peaceably within the Roman Empire.[29]

Several scholars have roundly rejected the notion that Luke intended to promote the early church as a politically benign entity posing no challenge to Roman rule. Richard Cassidy stresses that the words and actions Luke ascribes to Jesus in his narrative are so revolutionary that no first-century recipient would view

25. Ibid., 137.

26. Paul Walaskay, "And So We Came to Rome": The Political Perspective of St. Luke, SNTSMS 49 (Cambridge: Cambridge University Press, 1983), 25.

27. Ibid., 66. These quotations from Walaskay were culled from Powell, What Are They Saying about Acts?, 73.

28. B. S. Easton, "The Purpose of Acts," in Early Christianity: The Purpose of Acts and Other Papers, ed. C. F. Grant (Greenwich, CT: Seabury Press, 1954), 31–118; Ernst Haenchen, The Acts of the Apostles: A Commentary, 14th ed. (Philadelphia: Westminster, 1971).

29. See, e.g., Alan Richardson, The Political Christ (Philadelphia: Westminster, 1973); Charles Homer Giblin, The Destruction of Jerusalem according to Luke's Gospel: A Historical-Typological Moral (Rome: Biblical Institute, 1985); Philip Esler, Community and Gospel in Luke-Acts: The Social and Political Motivations of Lucan Theology, SNTSMS 57 (Cambridge: Cambridge University Press, 1987); Johnson, Gospel of Luke, 9; Gregory E. Sterling, Historiography and Self-Definition: Josephos, Luke-Acts, and Apologetic Historiography, NovTSup 64 (Leiden: Brill, 1992); Brigitte Kahl, "Acts of the Apostles: Pro(to)-Imperial Script and Hidden Transcript," in In the Shadow of Empire: Reclaiming the Bible as a History of Faithful Resistance, ed. Richard A. Horsley (Louisville: Westminster John Knox, 2008), 137–56; Dean Pinter, "The Gospel of Luke and the Roman Empire," in Jesus Is Lord, Caesar Is Not: Evaluating Empire in New Testament Studies, ed. Scot McKnight and Joseph B. Modica (Downers Grove, IL: IVP Academic, 2013), 101–15; Keener, Acts, 1:441–58. J. C. O'Neil (The Theology of Acts in Its Historical Setting [London: SPCK, 1961]), followed by F. F. Bruce (The Book of Acts, rev. ed., NICNT [Grand Rapids: Eerdmans, 1988]), argues that Luke's attempt to show Christianity's compatibility with Roman rule is more than simply apologetic. It is also part of Luke's strategy to convert pagans to the faith.

Jesus or his followers as harmless to Roman order.[30] First, Cassidy points out that Luke presents Jesus as incredibly disruptive of existing social patterns. This disruption is manifested in Jesus' concern for the poor, the sick, women, and other marginalized persons and in his teachings honoring their dignity and welcoming them into the Kingdom. Luke also presents Jesus as calling for radical modifications in how wealth was viewed and used, castigating those who hoarded surplus possessions and refused to aid those in need. Furthermore, Jesus rejected the use of violence to maintain the social order and criticized the gentile kings for their practice of dominating their subjects. In stark contrast, Jesus insisted that "social relationships be governed by the themes of service and humility."[31]

Second, Cassidy argues that Luke casts Jesus as a serious threat to the Roman Empire because he refused to cooperate with the various political officials who were responsible for maintaining the social pattern he rejected. Whether it be Herod, Pilate, or the various representatives of the Israelite elite, Jesus does not defer to or even recognize their authority, and he outspokenly criticizes them. Cassidy concludes:

> Was Jesus dangerous to the Roman empire? The two factors that we have just elaborated make it clear that he was, at least potentially, a serious threat to the continuance of Roman rule in Palestine and to the empire itself. If large numbers of people ever came to support the new social patterns that Luke portrays Jesus advocating, and if large numbers came to adopt his stance toward the ruling political authorities, the Roman empire (or indeed, any other similarly-based social order) could not have continued.[32]

For this reason, Cassidy argues, both Herod and Pilate were ironically *incorrect* when they pronounced Jesus innocent of any threat against Roman rule. The point of Luke's narrative, in fact, is to call believers to follow Jesus' lead in resisting the Roman elite insofar as they try to prevent believers from proclaiming and living out the radical form of community that Jesus enacted. In doing so, believers follow Jesus in inaugurating God's Kingdom, a "new social order in which neither the Romans nor any other oppressing group would be able to hold sway."[33]

Following Cassidy's work, several scholars have similarly emphasized the ways in which Luke's narrative undermines the Roman social order, though in varying degrees. In several of his writings, Richard A. Horsley stresses that the Gospels, including Luke, portray Jesus' radical, though nonviolent, resistance

30. Cassidy, *Jesus, Politics, and Society*.
31. Ibid., 78.
32. Ibid., 79.
33. Ibid.

to Roman rule and Jesus' proclamation that God would soon restore the world to the kind of community proclaimed by Israel's prophets.[34] As noted above, Schottroff and Stegemann find Luke's interest in establishing a "concrete social utopia" reflected in his narrative.[35] This community was to be separate from the rest of Roman society and deeply countercultural, focused on material and social equality and responsive to the needs of the poor. But at the same time, Luke "is far from offering a political program for a comprehensive redistribution of property throughout society."[36] Moreover, Luke calls members of his community "to abandon any illegal behavior."[37]

More recently, C. Kavin Rowe has argued that, on the one hand, Luke does not present the Christian mission as a "counter state" seeking to replace Rome. While the followers of Jesus are accused in Acts of plotting sedition (see especially the speech by Tertullus, the lawyer for the Israelite high priest and elders seeking Paul's death in 24:1–9), Luke has the opponents of the Way raise this charge "precisely so that such an understanding of the Christian mission can be narrated out of the realm of interpretive possibility. To follow Luke's narrative is to read Christianity not as a call for insurrection but as a testimony to the reality of the resurrection."[38] At the same time, the early Christian proclamation of Jesus as Messiah and the embodiment of his reign in the countercultural practices of the church's mission—made possible by the resurrection—also reveal Luke's understanding that the Kingdom's arrival in Jesus is ultimately incompatible with the lordship of Caesar and the manner of his rule. What we thus encounter as the chief objective of Luke's narrative, according to Rowe, is neither accommodation with nor stringent resistance against Rome, but the unveiling of God's new realm that simply transcends the Roman world.

> Because he knows that Jesus is the κύριος πάντων, Luke proclaims him, in contrast to the emperor, as "another King," as one whose salvific claim upon his subjects results in a new, worldwide, and publically identifiable form of communal life. And because of the peacemaking character of Jesus' Lordship, Luke also proclaims—via the mouths of his Roman officials—that Christians are innocent of the charges of sedition and treason. The universal Lordship of God in Jesus leads to neither an *apologia* to (or for) Rome nor to an anti-Rome polemic. It is simply, but really, a different way (Acts 18:25, 26; cf. 9:2; 19:9, 23;

---

34. See, e.g., Horsley, *Liberation of Christmas*; *Jesus and the Powers: Conflict, Covenant, and the Hope of the Poor* (Minneapolis: Fortress, 2011); *Jesus and the Politics of Roman Palestine* (Columbia: University of South Carolina Press, 2013). See also Moxnes, "Patron-Client Relations."
35. Schottroff and Stegemann, *Jesus and the Hope of the Poor*, 67–120.
36. Ibid., 117.
37. Ibid., 116.
38. Rowe, *World Upside Down*, 87–88.

24:22). Reading Acts as a document that explicates "the Way of the Lord" (Acts 18:25) thus allows us to see that Luke's redescription of cultural dissolution as the gracious act of God in bringing the pagan world out of darkness—his insistence that Christianity is not a governmental takeover but an alternative and salvific way of life—is a reading of the world in deeply and ultimately Christian terms.[39]

In a detailed study of Luke's passion narrative, Yong-Sung Ahn somewhat similarly concludes that Luke presents Jesus "in between anti- and pro-Roman stances." For him, "the Lukan Jesus is not in accord with the religious/political system of the Empire but envisions an alternative system, the Reign of God (22:24–30)."[40] In the end-time discourse (21:5–36), Jesus foresees and announces the end of the empire through the fall of Jerusalem, the stronghold of the imperial system set against him in the narrative (22:28–30).[41] Yet Jesus "does not explicitly resist Empire," and Luke is concerned to demonstrate that Jesus, while resistant to Rome, is not an insurrectionist and is innocent of the charges leveled against him by his fellow Israelites.[42]

Finally, Amanda C. Miller approvingly cites Rowe's study, similarly arguing that Luke had a complex and multifaceted relationship with Rome. It was neither entirely resistant nor entirely complicit and conciliatory, but rather accepting (for now) of imperial dominance while also determined to proclaim and enact the radically different values and practices of God's reign in the midst of the opposing Roman status quo.[43] Miller also claims, particularly in reference to the scene in the Nazareth synagogue (4:16–30), that while "the Lukan Jesus critiqued the imperial status quo and its unjust domination of non-elites," Jesus also "sought to disrupt social divisions and prejudices among the subordinate groups themselves."[44]

The Primary Purposes of Luke-Acts

As with most writers of narratives as rich and complex as Luke-Acts, the evangelist likely composed his two volumes with several objectives in mind. Among them, it seems to me that two were paramount and received the focus of Luke's rhetorical energy.

39. Ibid., 136.
40. Yong-Sung Ahn, *The Reign of God and Rome in Luke's Passion Narrative: An East Asian Global Perspective* (Leiden: Brill, 2006), 192.
41. Ibid., 194.
42. Ibid., 192. So also Carroll, *Luke*, 398–404.
43. Miller, *Rumors of Resistance*, 255.
44. Ibid., 254.

Calling Theophilus to Embrace a Different Lord and a Different Realm

One of Luke's primary aims was to challenge Theophilus and others to leave behind their lives and stations as elites, to acknowledge Jesus, not Caesar, as Lord of all, and to embrace the reality and values of the Kingdom of God, rather than the ways of Rome, by entering into community with other believers. Here I will overview features of Luke's context and narrative that together manifest this critical objective, gathering up several of my observations in the preceding chapter on the evangelist's understanding of what was wrong with the current world order, along with other observations I presented in earlier chapters. I will also engage the views we have just considered.

APPRECIATING LUKE'S HISTORICAL AND SOCIAL CONTEXTS

One of the limitations I find in studies arguing that Luke stressed the compatibility between the church's mission and Roman rule is that they fail to engage adequately, or at all, the agonistic and oppressive character of the Roman world as well as the tensions that likely existed between Rome and messianic movements in the aftermath of the Israelite revolt. As we discussed in chapter 1, Rome depended on an elite-controlled economy fueled by aggressive taxation and slavery, characterized by a gross disparity of resources, and resulting in widespread poverty for the vast majority of the population. Moreover, undergirded by unmatched military might, Rome and its client kings were quick to respond to any challenge to their rule through violent reprisal, and they had done that to Jesus of Nazareth, many of his followers, and others who cited their own kingdom stories as a basis for revolt against Rome. In light of this social and historical setting, I find it highly unlikely that Luke's two volumes were meant to assure Christians that Rome was their friend as they proclaimed Jesus as Messiah, Savior, and Lord of all *and* proclaimed his call for a way of life radically out of rhythm with the pulse of the empire. I find it equally unlikely that Luke-Acts was a narrative designed to convince elite persons used to squashing resistance to their rule that the Christian movement was compatible with Rome's maintenance of elite wealth, status, and control.

Furthermore, views stressing the compatibility between Luke's vision of the Kingdom and Roman rule assume an anachronistic dichotomy between religion and politics in the ancient world. They assume that Luke's recipients and the Roman elite would have recognized that the "religious" devotion to Jesus and the Kingdom that Luke championed somehow belonged to a separate realm of human activity with no implications for the "secular" world ordered by Rome and those who ruled it, as if these domains of human thought and experience were distinct. But as we also saw in chapter 1, such a dichotomy was most unlikely in the ancient world: the claims of lordship and legitimation, and the social structures deriving from those claims, were inescapably and inextricably political and religious at the same time. In order to be convincing, let alone intelligible, Israelites and Christians seeking to promote amicable relations with Rome during this period would have had to create formulations of their faith that overtly incorporated Roman rule into God's plan for God's people and the rest of humanity. We clearly see this with Josephus, who went so far as to speak of Vespasian as fulfilling Israelite messianic prophecy! There are also precedents for such advocacy of foreign rulers in Israelite tradition, such as with Cyrus in 3 Isaiah; Persian lords in Ezra, Nehemiah, and Esther; and, in a more limited sense, the Romans in 1 Maccabees 8. But Luke fails to provide such an apology. To the contrary, he stresses how severely *incongruous* the visions of reality promoted by Rome and early Christian testimony really are.

In sum, a historically tenable backdrop for engaging Luke's rhetorical interests must include as its primary features the following: (1) Rome's zealously cultivated and guarded economic circulatory system ensuring abundant wealth for an elite few and a life-sustaining wage for their retainers while resulting in widespread poverty for the masses; (2) client kings and governors wary of any threats to their social and economic control; (3) the elite's readiness to use violence to repress those threats, perhaps exacerbated by the tension-filled years following the Israelite revolt; (4) the inherently religious dimensions of elite attempts to legitimize their social, political, and economic mastery over others; and (5) the ample prophetic and apocalyptic precedents within Israelite religious traditions challenging elite injustice, socioeconomic oppression, and their illegitimate authority. Against this backdrop, the following features of Luke's narrative together suggest that Luke is calling Theophilus to recognize the incompatibility between the ways of Rome and the ways of the Kingdom, and to urge him to embrace the latter.

THE COUNTER-ROMAN DIMENSIONS OF THE KINGDOM

1. With a few exceptions (which I address below), Luke provides a largely uncomplimentary portrait of both the Israelite and Roman elite. As we saw in preceding chapters, the elite are mired in worldviews that prevent them from recognizing the true identity of Jesus and the reality of the Kingdom's advent, even when it is plainly manifested before them. Beyond their ignorance, the elite mirror Satan by exerting illegitimate and abusive authority over others in order to serve their own ends rather than God's will for creation. They are portrayed by Luke as greedy, self-serving, honor-seeking, idolatrous, violent, and murderous, yet ultimately impotent. It is difficult to imagine how such a

portrait of the elite would encourage Christians to consider Roman rulers as their allies or encourage the Roman elite to think kindly of Christians.

2. Luke repeatedly depicts Jesus and his followers suffering persecution at the hands of the Israelite and Roman elite. According to the evangelist, such resistance to the Kingdom is consistent with how the elite have responded to the righteous in the past, and it will persist until the Son of Man returns. This feature of the narrative not only characterizes the elite unfavorably; it also shows Luke's community why such persecution is taking place (as recognized by Tiede) and encourages them to persevere in response (as recognized by Brown). This feature of the narrative makes sense only if Luke expected such elite antagonism and persecution to continue.

3. As we discussed in chapter 8, Luke uses characterization as a key rhetorical technique to engage his recipients' emotions and to guide their response to his kingdom story. The two features of his narrative that I just discussed make it clear that Luke employs such characterization not to call Theophilus to an admirable view of the elite, or to a recognition of the compatibility between the ways of the Kingdom and the ways of Rome, but to convince Theophilus of the exact opposite. Rather, the ones whom Luke lures Theophilus to admire and emulate are unlearned peasants, the persecuted, the recklessly generous, and others who unashamedly contravene the social order by embracing the reality and values of the Kingdom. While a few elite characters also invite reader admiration, they do so by eschewing the normal order of things and recognizing the presence of God's rule in the ministry of Jesus or his followers (more on this below).

4. Luke also regards the hoarding of resources by the elite as central to the perversion of the current world order. Jesus problematizes wealth in a society where many struggle to survive. He also emphasizes the transitory character of wealth and the shallowness of luxurious living, and repeatedly calls upon current and potential followers to cast off the allure of possessions and embrace the Kingdom as the true source of blessing. The new world the Kingdom is calling into being—already manifest in the lives of believers—is one in which resources shall be distributed according to need, not social location. In no uncertain terms, Luke demonstrates that equitable access to God's provision is an essential dimension of life in God's new age, and one that is to be embraced by the faithful in the present. Those who cannot abide this new economy will be "brought down . . . from their thrones" and "sent . . . away empty" (Luke 1:52–53). They will find that the places at the Great Banquet prepared for them have been filled by others (14:23–24). They will be separated from God's realm by a chasm that cannot be crossed (16:26).

5. Repeatedly, Jesus and his followers make it clear that one's choice for or against the Kingdom and Jesus is a matter of life and death (recall Ananias and

Sapphira!). They also make it clear that one's devotion to the Kingdom and Jesus must transcend any other marker of identity or commitment. Any allegiance to wealth, kin, honor, or ruler that compromises one's devotion to Jesus, the Kingdom, and the marginalized must be cast aside. Such behavior would be seen by most in the Roman world, and especially the elite, as moronic, shameful, and even treasonous. But such devotion is to characterize those of the Way.

6. Luke exalts Jesus as Son of God, Lord, Savior, and Son of Man and with other lofty titles. He also presents him as a faithful prophet and servant of Yahweh who at the same time possesses divine power and authority and is the one (and the only one) through whom salvation comes to humanity. Not only do these characterizations resonate powerfully (even if paradoxically) within an Israelite context; they also carry the clear implication for members of the Roman world that if Jesus is the divine Lord and Savior, then Caesar is not. As we have seen, Luke carefully constructs pivotal scenes (such as Jesus' annunciation and birth in Luke 1–2 and the conflict of Acts 4) and shapes many others to converge the characters of Jesus and Yahweh while also contrasting Jesus with the rulers of this world. This bidirectional, comparative characterization of Jesus—stressing the alignment between Jesus and Yahweh *and* the misalignment between Jesus and the Roman/Israelite elite—is basic to Luke's Christology and a central thread in his narrative rhetoric. Along with the other features of Luke's narrative I just discussed, this characterization also proves untenable the claim that Luke is calling for one's religious devotion to Jesus while promoting one's political devotion to Caesar. On the contrary, *any* others who claim mastery over humankind, Luke reveals, are demonic pretenders. The one Lord and Savior of all—of heaven *and* earth—is the Messiah, the King of Israel, whose mission and person are intricately interwoven with the mission and person of Yahweh.

The Function of the "Good" Elite in Luke's Rhetoric

Against the backdrop of the first-century Roman world, these features of Luke's narrative indicate that the evangelist is advocating not that Theophilus embrace Rome as friend and protector but that he come to see it as an embodiment of allegiances and patterns of behavior that oppose God's purposes for creation and lead to destruction. Still, we must also account for the elements of Luke's narrative that appear to cast members of the elite in a somewhat, if not wholly, positive light. The centurion whose servant Jesus heals built a synagogue for local Israelites and exhibits a faith found not even in Israel (Luke 7:1–10). Zacchaeus, a chief tax collector, spurns his wealth and receives God's salvation (19:1–10). Another centurion recognizes Jesus' innocence as Jesus breathes his last (23:46–47). In Acts, an Ethiopian official receives the good news (Acts 8:26–40), and the centurion Cornelius and his household are described by Luke as devout gentiles, worshipers of Yahweh, who are led by Peter to faith in Jesus (10:1–48). Sergius Paulus, a proconsul, is led by Paul and Barnabas to resist the wayward teachings of the magician, Elymas, and to believe in "the teaching of the Lord" (13:4–12). Other gentiles of means join the community, including Lydia and her household (16:14–15), a jailer (16:25–34), other leading women (17:4), and "men of high standing" (17:12); and Apollos, described as "an eloquent man, well versed in the scriptures" (18:24), may also have been a member of the elite. On several occasions in Acts, Christians are delivered by Roman rulers from the hands of their enemies (18:12–17; 19:35–41; 23:6–35). Both Jesus and Paul are declared innocent by rulers judging their cases (Luke 23:13–16; Acts 26:30–32). Paul also appeals to Caesar with the expectation that justice will be done (Acts 25:11–12).

In light of Luke's typically negative portrait of the elite, the positive reception of the gospel by some is certainly notable. However, the accounts of elite persons exhibiting faith in Jesus and joining the Christian community are perfectly consistent with Luke's rhetorical objectives as I have described them. If Luke is seeking to encourage Theophilus to commit himself to the Way, the examples of other elite who have recognized Jesus' identity as Lord (Luke 7:6–9), devoted their households to the faith (Acts 10:44–48; 16:14–15, 33), and offered Paul and others hospitality (16:15, 34, 40) could only further enhance Luke's effort.

The declarations of Jesus' and Paul's innocence by some elite are notable as well. The centurion at the foot of the cross seems to function as another elite character who at least begins to recognize something essential of Jesus' identity. However, the Roman rulers who find that neither Jesus' nor Paul's case constitutes a capital offense certainly do not emerge from Luke's account as admirable defenders of the faith or even adequate defenders of justice. Herod the Great has Jesus "treated with contempt and mocked" and jokingly clothed with an elegant robe before returning him to Pilate. Presumably, Herod's treatment of Jesus and his deferral to Pilate's judgment served as the bonds of newly awakened friendship between the two rulers (Luke 23:12). Despite his and Herod's recognition of Jesus' innocence, Pilate still allows Jesus to be crucified! Gallio simply dismisses the case against Paul, (incorrectly) sensing that it pertains only to Israelite customs, but then stands idly by as the Jews retaliate by beating Sosthenes, the official of the synagogue, perhaps because he, like Crispus, has become a follower of the Way (Acts 18:17, 18).[45] Felix, as noted above,

---

45. As Tannehill (*Narrative Unity*, 2:229) observes, "Paul is released by Gallio, and this is the result of the Lord's promised protection. Nevertheless, the human instrument of this protection is no model of just and enlightened policy."

lacks self-control and panders for a bribe. Festus and Herod Agrippa II (son of Herod Agrippa I, who put James to death [Acts 12:1–5]) might seem to be cast a little less negatively since they consider Paul innocent of the charges leveled against him and admit to themselves that he could have been released had he not appealed to Caesar (26:32). Yet Festus leaves Paul in prison in order to "grant the Jews a favor" and later declares Paul insane, while Agrippa dismisses Paul's attempts to make him a Christian (vv. 26–29). Keep this in mind as well: Theophilus knows what the ultimate outcome of Paul's journey to Rome and appearance before Caesar will be. In the end, Caesar disregards Paul's testimony to the Kingdom and continues the barbarism of Roman injustice.

In light of the myriad ways that Luke's narrative challenges the ethos of Roman society and the legitimacy of elite claims to mastery and also presents Roman rulers as despicable characters, these few instances in which the elite's handling of conflict or deliberation on charges benefits Paul (or at least delays his condemnation) hardly establish the Roman elite as trustworthy advocates of justice or the Christian movement as socially benign. Rather, having been primed by the preceding narrative, recipients are far more likely to perceive these acts of "justice" as additional incidents when the elite unwittingly promote the purpose and plan of God. Just as Caesar's overtly hegemonic act of the census led the unborn Messiah to Bethlehem as foretold by the prophets, just as Pilate's fear-driven impotence led to Jesus' crucifixion as was foretold by Jesus and the Scriptures, just as the Israelite elite's attempts to exterminate the Way in Jerusalem led to its spread throughout Judea and Samaria (see Acts 1:8), so too does Festus and Agrippa's decision to defer Paul's case to Caesar fulfill Paul's resolve (19:21) and God's call for him "to bear witness in Rome" (23:11; see also 20:22–24).

At the same time, the irony inherent in these verdicts, as I think Cassidy rightly discerns, is richer than simply these elites' unwitting advancement of God's plan. These Roman elite do not yet recognize the Christian community as seditious because they do not yet know enough to realize the full implications of what members of the Way practice and proclaim.[46] Others, however, are a bit more astute and thus more hostile. The Israelite elite accuse Jesus of "perverting our nation, forbidding us to pay taxes to the emperor, and saying that he himself is the Messiah, a king" (Luke 23:2), charges that parallel those leveled against Paul by Tertullus, who calls Paul a "pestilent fellow, an agitator among all the Jews throughout the world, and a ringleader of the sect of

---

46. Even though Luke tells us that Felix is rather well informed about the Way (Acts 24:22), he also lets us know that Felix was unprepared for the implications its teachings posed for him as a member of the elite: when Paul later speaks to Felix about "justice, self-control, and the coming judgment," Felix becomes frightened and sends Paul away (24:25).

the Nazarenes" (Acts 24:5). Earlier, Paul and his associates are maligned for "advocating customs that are not lawful for us as Romans to adopt or observe" (16:21). We recall that in Thessalonica, Jason and other believers are seized by a mob and accused of "turning the world upside down," for they are "acting contrary to the decrees of the emperor, saying that there is another king, Jesus" (17:6–7). Similarly, the silversmiths in Ephesus discern that if the Way makes any significant inroads into their city, more will be led astray by Paul's teaching that "gods made with hands are not gods," and as a result the "the temple of the great goddess Artemis will be scorned" (19:25–27).

In sum, Luke takes great pains to show Theophilus throughout the Gospel and Acts that the advent of the Kingdom in Jesus and the ministry of his followers is deeply disruptive not only of the elite-controlled forms of Israelite tradition (e.g., Luke 19:45–48; Acts 18:12–13; 21:27–28; 24:4–7) but also of Mediterranean society, the Roman social order, and eventually Roman rule itself when Jesus returns. Some of the Roman elite during the time of Paul's ministry were ignorant of this reality. Following Paul's execution in Rome and the Israelite revolt, that may no longer be the case. Perhaps it is for this reason that Luke redacts Jesus' warning about trials to come so as to include the specific agents of oppression Jesus' disciples will face: "When they bring you before the synagogues, the rulers, and the authorities . . ." (Luke 12:11; cf. Mark 13:11; Matt. 10:19). In response, members of the Way are to remain steadfast in their devotion to Jesus and the glorious Kingdom he has inaugurated among them, no matter the cost.

Addressing the Tragedy of Israel's Faithlessness

The second major issue Luke sought to address as he composed Luke-Acts was the reality that many among Israel refused to embrace Jesus as God's messianic Savior, divine Son, and Lord and recognize the arrival of the Kingdom in his and the church's ministry. As we noted above, a number of scholars identify this as one of Luke's primary concerns, and we may also suppose that it was a concern for Theophilus and others for whom Luke wrote. It seems to me that as Luke engages the reality that many in Israel have refused to embrace Jesus and the church's testimony to the Kingdom, he emphasizes five dimensions: (1) the origins of these developments in the promises of God as announced through the prophets; (2) the emergence of these events among the people and institutions of Israel; (3) the stiff-necked culpability of those Israelites who rejected Jesus and continue to reject the Way; (4) the tragic nature of their refusal to believe; and (5) the advancement of the Kingdom among both Israelites and gentiles despite this tragic resistance. Since we have addressed most of these elements on one or more occasions in the preceding chapters, I will be able to treat this objective in a rather economical fashion.

1. *Origins of God's Saving Acts.* We noted in the introduction that from the prologue of the Gospel onward, Luke-Acts tells us a story of "the matters fulfilled among us" (Luke 1:1–4). Whether it be through his use of Septuagintal style in the infancy narrative mimicking the cadence and character of Israel's scriptures; his widespread use of scriptural citation and allusion; the subtle to obvious parallels between characters in his narrative and those of Israel's sacred history; or Jesus' and later his followers' repeated assertions that all these events took place in fulfillment of the testimony of Israel's prophets and sacred traditions, Luke incessantly insists that the matters he records originate in the will of Yahweh to redeem Israel and all humanity.

2. *Emergence of the Kingdom in Jerusalem and Judea.* When "the chief priests, the officers of the temple police, . . . the elders," and their strongmen come to arrest Jesus, he says to them, "Have you come out with swords and clubs as if I were a bandit? When I was with you day after day in the temple, you did not lay hands on me. But this is your hour, and the power of darkness!" (Luke 22:52–53). This passage, of course, illuminates the cowardly and despicable character of the elite's actions, but along with still other passages it amplifies another very important dimension of the Kingdom's emergence for Luke. The advent of the Kingdom did not occur in a vacuum, nor was it confined to the obscure villages of Galilee. Luke's telling of the gospel story privileges Jerusalem and its environs as the epicenter of the Kingdom's arrival and of key moments in Jesus' and the early church's ministry.

We discussed above this essential element of Luke's plotting. The evangelist's narrative begins in Jerusalem—in the temple, no less—among the most faithful of Israel, and the holy city and Judea are the setting for nearly all the events relayed in the infancy narrative. While Luke follows Mark's lead in setting many of the events of Jesus' ministry in Galilee, from 9:51 onward he uses the journey motif to highlight Jesus' movement toward Jerusalem, and then again uses the motif to highlight the movement of witnesses away from Jerusalem in Acts. This movement to and from Jerusalem underscores the centrality of Jerusalem in God's plan of salvation. Jerusalem is to be the place of Jesus' suffering, rejection, death (Luke 9:22, 44), and resurrection (9:22, 31). Afterward, it is in that sacred city that the arrival of the Holy Spirit testified by the prophets occurs, leading thousands of Israelites to believe (Acts 2:1–36), and from there that the message of God's salvation spills out to the rest of the world (Acts 1:8). This feature of Luke's plotting not only underscores the rootedness of God's deliverance of humankind in God's relationship with Israel; it also makes clear that God's revelation of Jesus and the Kingdom took place in the geographical and spiritual heart of Israel, a point that Peter and others repeatedly make in their testimony to fellow Israelites (e.g., Acts 2:22–24; 3:11–16; 5:29–32).

3. *Stiff-Neckedness of the Faithless*. The rootedness of the Kingdom's arrival in Israel's relationship with Yahweh and its manifestation within the epicenter of Israelite faith together underscore the culpability of those Israelites who reject and crucify Jesus, and even more so those who refuse to see the emergence of God's reign in the life and testimony of the early believers (recall our earlier discussions of Acts 4). The attention Luke gives to these features of his narrative is what rightly leads many recipients to perceive that the evangelist is explaining the failure of so many of God's own people to join the Way.[47] For in conjunction with these elements, Luke repeatedly characterizes the people's faithless resistance to Jesus and the Kingdom as a continuation of their ancestors' stubborn, ignorant, and even violent rejection of God's prophets. These faithless of Israel are doing what the faithless of Israel have always done, and the price for their disobedience and betrayal is not only the destruction of Jerusalem but—should they persist in it—their eternal separation from the realm of God (see Acts 3:23).

4. *Tragedy*. As helpfully noted by Robert Tannehill, there is a note of tragedy pulsing throughout Luke's account.[48] While Luke provides Theophilus and others with the resources they need to make sense of the rejection of God and the Kingdom by many of Israel—explaining it as a continuation of the very same faithlessness Israel has displayed in the past—a sense of tragic loss also often pervades these scenes of rejection and judgment. Simeon's prophecy connects the falling, rising, and judgment of many in Israel with the excruciating pain that Mary herself will experience (Luke 2:34–35). Moreover, Jesus' ongoing resolve to engage the Pharisees and others despite their resistance, rudeness, and mounting agitation parallels Yahweh's own resolve to maintain relational bonds with Israel and to continue instructing them despite their persistent stiff-necked disposition and wayward behavior (Acts 7:51–53). Luke tends not to identify Jesus' states of emotion, but pronounced pathos washes through Jesus' lament over Jerusalem's inability to recognize "the things that make for peace" and its impending destruction (Luke 19:41–44). As we have seen, Peter's rebuke of the Israelite elite in Acts 3–4 includes a tragic dimension: even though they have murdered the Author of life, God is willing to regard it as an act born of ignorance. Incredibly, repentance, forgiveness, even "times

47. As Luke Timothy Johnson (*Gospel of Luke*, 10) helpfully puts it, Luke is providing a theodicy, a defense of the word and work of God in history, that accounts for the acceptance of the gospel by many more gentiles than Israelites.
48. Tannehill, *Narrative Unity*, 2:344–57.

of refreshing from the presence of the Lord" (Acts 3:20) and their participation in God's universal salvation are all still available to them (4:17–21). Yet despite this generous overture of grace and an opportunity for yet another new beginning, the elite of Israel refuse it. Later, while Paul is preaching in Antioch, he urges his fellow Israelites and "brothers" (13:26) not to be those whom Habakkuk said would refuse to believe in God's deliverance (13:40–41; cf. Hab. 1:5). Then, at the end of the narrative, Paul once again turns to the prophets, not only to warn his fellow Israelites but also to help them see that the same sort of seemingly impenetrable resistance to Yahweh that has characterized Israel's past continues still—and all the more tragically so now, so close to the end of the age when God intends for them to understand and be healed (28:26–27; cf. Isa. 6:9–10).

5. *Nevertheless, the Joyous Advancement of the Kingdom.* Even though Luke wants Theophilus and others to appreciate the tragedy of Jesus' rejection and passion, Jerusalem's ruin, and the persistent refusal of many in Israel to believe, Luke also wants them to know—through Israel's history (see also Luke 21:22), Simeon's prophecy, and Jesus' predictions—that this tragedy is *expected* as part of the collision between the reign of God and the desperate ways of this world. Just as important, Luke emphasizes that the tragedy of Jesus' rejection by many within Israel does not ultimately undermine or overcome the joyful proclamation of the salvation God will accomplish in Jesus: both "a light for revelation to the Gentiles, and for glory to your people Israel" (2:32). This tragic element is added to Simeon's hymn as a painful countermelody—a piercing reminder of Jerusalem's destruction and the suffering and faithlessness of many; but in the end this countermelody cannot keep up with the dominant currents of the song. And so, Simeon's proclamation and the good news shared by many others to follow stand as testimony that tragedy and sadness are part of the story of God's salvation, but not more so than that salvation's triumph over evil and its joyous welcome of both Jews and gentiles into the realm of God's rule and blessing.

Conclusion

Indeed, tragedy is not the end of the story Luke tells. Many have rejected God's messiah, the temple is now gone, many have been killed or exiled, and Jerusalem lies in ruin. But the gospel has been embraced by *many* from Israel (e.g., Luke 10:21–24; Acts 2:41; 4:4; 6:7; 13:43; 14:1; 16:11–15; 17:4; 18:20; 28:24) while also being proclaimed to the gentiles, many of whom also see it for the good news it truly is. Even though Paul repeatedly threatens unbelieving

Israelites that he will now turn to the gentiles, who will surely believe (e.g., Acts 13:46–47; 18:6–7), this doesn't prevent Paul from returning to the synagogue to preach to his fellow Israelites in the next village or city he encounters (e.g., 14:1; 19:8) *and* continuing to win converts among Israel up to the very end of his ministry (28:24). And so, while the words of Isaiah near the close of Luke's narrative might seem to give tragic judgment the final stroke in Luke's regard for the unfaithful of Israel, the pattern that has been exhibited in the ministries of Jesus, Peter, Stephen ("Lord, do not hold this sin against them" [Acts 7:60]), and Paul indicates otherwise. For even after Paul issues this final threat to his fellow Israelites (28:28), we are then immediately told that this indefatigable witness "welcomed *all* who came to him, proclaiming the kingdom of God and teaching about the Lord Jesus Christ with all boldness and without hindrance" (vv. 30–31). Luke reveals to Theophilus that where the slimmest possibility of repentance and redemption exists, Jesus' followers are compelled to witness to the arrival of God's reign in the Lord Messiah, the crucified and resurrected Son of God. As is most often the case in Israelite tradition, so too for Luke—grace and hope, not judgment, have the final word.

Bibliography

Achtemeier, Paul J., Joel B. Green, and Marianne Meye Thompson. *Introducing the New Testament: Its Literature and Theology*. Grand Rapids: Eerdmans, 2001.

Ahn, Yong-Sung. *The Reign of God and Rome in Luke's Passion Narrative: An East Asian Global Perspective*. Leiden: Brill, 2006.

Alexander, Loveday. "Luke's Preface in the Context of Greek Preface-Writing." *NovT* 28 (1986): 48–74.

Argyle, A. W. "The Greek of Luke and Acts." *NTS* 20 (1973–74): 441–45.

Aristotle. *Poetics*. Translated by Malcolm Heath. New York: Penguin, 1996.

Arrington, French L. *The Acts of the Apostles: Introduction, Translation, and Commentary*. Peabody, MA: Hendrickson, 1988.

Attridge, Harold W. "Josephus and His Works." In *Jewish Writings of the Second Temple Period*, edited by Michael E. Stone, 185–232. Philadelphia: Fortress, 1984.

———. *The Interpretation of Biblical History in the "Antiquitates Judaicae" of Flavius Josephus*. HDR 7. Missoula, MT: Scholars Press, 1976.

Aune, David E. *The New Testament in Its Literary Environment*. LEC. Philadelphia: Westminster, 1987.

Balch, David L. "Acts as Hellenistic Historiography." In *Society of Biblical Literature Seminar Papers* 24, edited by Kent H. Richards, 429–32. Atlanta: Scholars Press, 1985.

Barbour, Robin, ed. *The Kingdom of God and Human Society: Essays by Members of the Scripture, Theology and Society Group*. Edinburgh: T&T Clark, 1993.

Barrett, Charles K. "Paul Shipwrecked." In *Scripture, Meaning and Method*, edited by B. P. Thompson, 51–63. Hull, England: Hull University Press, 1987.

Bauckham, Richard. *Jesus and the God of Israel: God Crucified and Other Studies on the New Testament's Christology of Divine Identity*. Grand Rapids: Eerdmans, 2008.

Beard, Mary. "Writing and Religion: Ancient Literacy and the Function of the Written Word in Roman Religion." In *Literacy in the Roman World*, edited by Mary Beard, Alan K. Bowman, and Mireille Corbier, 35–60. Journal of Roman Archaeology Supplementary Series 3. Ann Arbor, MI: Journal of Roman Archaeology, 1991.

Beard, Mary, Alan K. Bowman, and Mireille Corbier, eds. *Literacy in the Roman World*. Journal of Roman Archaeology Supplementary Series 3. Ann Arbor, MI: Journal of Roman Archaeology, 1991.

Beavis, Mary Ann. *Jesus and Utopia: Looking for the Kingdom of God in the Roman World*. Minneapolis: Fortress, 2006.

Ben-David, A. *Talmudische Ökonomie: Die Wirtschaft des jüdischen Palästina zur Zeit der Mishna und des Talmud*. Hildesheim: Olms, 1974.

Blomberg, Craig L. *Interpreting the Parables*. 2nd ed. Downers Grove, IL: IVP Academic, 2012.

Bock, Darrell L. *Jesus according to the Scriptures: Restoring the Portrait from the Gospels*. Grand Rapids: Baker Academic, 2002.

———. *Luke 1:1–9:50*. BECNT 3a. Grand Rapids: Baker, 1994.

———. *Luke 9:51–24:53*. BECNT 3b. Grand Rapids: Baker, 1996.

———. *Proclamation from Prophecy and Pattern: Lucan Old Testament Christology*. JSNTSup 12. Sheffield: JSOT Press, 1987.

———. *A Theology of Luke and Acts*. BTNT. Grand Rapids: Zondervan, 2012.

Bovon, François. *A Commentary on the Gospel of Luke 1:1–9:50*. Translated by Christine M. Thomas. Hermeneia. Minneapolis: Fortress, 2002.

———. *Luke the Theologian: Thirty-Three Years of Research (1950–1983)*. Allison Park, PA: Pickwick Press, 1987.

Brawley, Robert. *Luke-Acts and Jews: Conflict, Apology, and Conciliation*. Atlanta: Scholars Press, 1987.

Brooke, George. "Luke-Acts and the Qumran Scrolls: The Case of the MMT." In *Luke's Literary Achievement*, edited by C. M. Tuckett, 72–90. JSNTSup 116. Sheffield: Sheffield Academic Press, 1995.

Brown, Raymond. *The Birth of the Messiah: A Commentary on the Infancy Narratives in the Gospels of Matthew and Luke*. Rev. ed. New York: Doubleday, 1993.

Brown, Schuyler. *Apostasy and Perseverance in the Theology of Luke*. AnBib 36. Rome: Pontifical Biblical Institute, 1969.

———. "'The Secret of the Kingdom of God' (Mark 4:11)." *JBL* 92 (1973): 60–74.

Bruce, F. F. *The Book of Acts*. Rev. ed. NICNT. Grand Rapids: Eerdmans, 1988.

———. "The Significance of the Speeches for Interpreting Acts." *SwJT* 33 (1990): 20–28.

Buckwalter, H. Douglas. *The Character and Purpose of Luke's Christology*. SNTSMS 89. Cambridge: Cambridge University Press, 2005.

———. "The Divine Saviour." In *Witness to the Gospel: The Theology of Acts*, edited by I. Howard Marshall and David Peterson, 107–23. Grand Rapids: Eerdmans, 1998.

Burridge, Richard A. *What Are the Gospels? A Comparison with Graeco-Roman Biography*. SNTSMS 70. Cambridge: Cambridge University Press, 1992.

Cadbury, H. J. *The Making of Luke-Acts*. London: SPCK, 1961.

———. "The Speeches in Acts." In *The Beginnings of Christianity: Part 1, The Acts of the Apostles*, edited by F. J. Foakes Jackson and Kirsopp Lake, 402–27. Grand Rapids: Baker, 1966.

Carroll, John T. *Luke: A Commentary*. NTL. Louisville: Westminster John Knox, 2012.

Carter, T. L. "The Irony of Romans 13." *NovT* 46 (2004): 209–28.

Carter, Warren. *The Roman Empire and the New Testament: An Essential Guide*. Nashville: Abingdon, 2006.

Cassidy, Richard. *Jesus, Politics, and Society: A Study of Luke's Gospel*. Maryknoll, NY: Orbis, 1978.

Charlesworth, James H., ed. *The Old Testament Pseudepigrapha*. 2 vols. New York: Doubleday, 1983–85.

Clark, Andrew C. *The Acts of the Apostles*. Oxford: Clarendon, 1993.

———. "The Role of the Apostles." In *Witness to the Gospel: The Theology of Acts*, edited by I. Howard Marshall and David Peterson, 169–90. Grand Rapids: Eerdmans, 1998.

Clements, Ronald. "Poverty and the Kingdom of God—An Old Testament View." In *The Kingdom of God and Human Society: Essays by Members of the Scripture, Theology and Society Group*, edited by Robin Barbour, 13–27. Edinburgh: T&T Clark, 1993.

Coleridge, Mark. *The Birth of the Lukan Narrative: Narrative and Christology in Luke 1–2*. JSNTSup 88. Sheffield: JSOT Press, 1993.

Collins, Adela Yarbro. *Mark*. Hermeneia. Minneapolis: Fortress, 2007.

Collins, John J. *The Apocalyptic Imagination: An Introduction to Jewish Apocalyptic Literature*. 2nd ed. Grand Rapids: Eerdmans, 1998.

————. *Jerusalem and the Temple in Jewish Apocalyptic Literature of the Second Temple Period*. Lecture presented at the International Rennert Guest Lecture Series, Bar-Ilan University, 1998.

————. "Models of Utopia in the Biblical Tradition." In *A Wise and Discerning Mind: Essays in Honor of Burke O. Long*, edited by Saul M. Olyan and Robert Culley. Brown Judaic Studies 325, 51–67. Atlanta: Scholars Press, 2000.

————. *The Scepter and the Star: Messianism in the Light of the Dead Sea Scrolls*. 2nd ed. Grand Rapids: Eerdmans, 2010.

Conzelmann, Hans. *Acts of the Apostles*. Translated by James Limburg et al. Hermeneia. Philadelphia: Fortress, 1987.

————. *The Theology of St. Luke*. Translated by Geoffrey Buswell. New York: Harper & Row, 1961.

Cosgrove, Charles H. "The Divine ΔEI in Luke-Acts: Investigations into the Lukan Understanding of God's Providence." *NovT* 26 (1984): 168–90.

Crenshaw, James L. *Education in Ancient Israel: Across the Deadening Silence*. New York: Doubleday, 1998.

Crocker, Cornelia Cross. "Emotions as Loopholes for Answerability in the Unfinalized Gospel according to Mark." *PRSt* 32 (2005): 281–94.

Croix, G. E. M. de Ste. *The Class Struggle in the Ancient Greek World: From the Archaic Age to the Arab Conquests*. Ithaca, NY: Cornell University Press, 1980.

Darr, John A. *On Character Building: The Reader and the Rhetoric of Characterization in Luke-Acts*. Louisville: Westminster John Knox, 1992.

de Boer, M. C. "Paul and Apocalyptic Eschatology." In *The Continuum History of Apocalypticism*, edited by Bernard McGinn et al., 166–94. New York: Continuum, 2003.

Dillon, Richard J. *From Eye-Witnesses to Minsters of the Word: Tradition and Composition in Luke 24*. AnBib 82. Rome: Biblical Institute Press, 1978.

————. "Previewing Luke's Project from His Prologue (Luke 1:1–4)." *CBQ* 43 (1981): 205–27.

Doble, Peter. *The Paradox of Salvation: Luke's Theology of the Cross*. Cambridge: Cambridge University Press, 1996.

Donahue, John R. "Two Decades of Research on the Rich and Poor in Luke-Acts." In *Justice and the Holy: Essays in Honor of Walter Harrelson*, edited by Douglas A. Knight and Peter J. Paris, 129–44. Atlanta: Scholars Press, 1989.

Donahue, John R., and Daniel J. Harrington. *The Gospel of Mark*. Sacra Pagina. Collegeville, MN: Liturgical Press, 2002.

Drury, John. *Tradition and Design in Luke's Gospel: A Study in Early Christian Historiography*. Atlanta: John Knox, 1976.

Dupont, Jacques. "La portée christologique de l'évangélisation des nations d'après Luc 24,47." In *Neues Testament und Kirche*, edited by J. Gnilka, 125–43. Freiburg: Herder, 1974.

————. "The Meal at Emmaus." In *The Eucharist in the New Testament: A Symposium*, edited by J. Delorme, 104–24. Baltimore: Helicon Press, 1964.

Easton, B. S. "The Purpose of Acts." In *Early Christianity: The Purpose of Acts and Other Papers*, edited by C. F. Grant, 31–118. Greenwich, CT: Seabury Press, 1954.

Elliott, John H. "Jesus the Israelite Was Neither a 'Jew' nor a 'Christian': On Correcting Misleading Nomenclature." *JSHJ* 5 (2007): 119–54.

————. "Temple versus Household in Luke-Acts: A Contrast in Social Institutions." In *The Social World of Luke-Acts*, edited by Jerome H. Neyrey, 211–40. Peabody, MA: Hendrickson, 1991.

Elliott, Neil. *The Arrogance of the Nations: Reading Romans in the Shadow of Empire.* Paul in Critical Contexts. Minneapolis: Fortress, 2008.

Ellis, E. Earle. *The Gospel of Luke.* Eugene, OR: Wipf & Stock, 2003.

Esler, Philip. *Community and Gospel in Luke-Acts: The Social and Political Motivations of Lucan Theology.* SNTSMS 57. Cambridge: Cambridge University Press, 1987.

Evans, C. F. *Saint Luke.* London: SCM, 1990.

Farris, Stephan. *The Hymns of Luke's Infancy Narrative: Their Origin, Meaning, and Significance.* JSNTSup 9. Sheffield: JSOT Press, 1985.

Ferguson, Everett. *Backgrounds of Early Christianity.* 2nd ed. Grand Rapids: Eerdmans, 1993.

Fiensy, David A. *The Social History of Palestine in the Herodian Period: The Land Is Mine.* Studies in the Bible and Early Christianity 20. Lewiston, NY: Edwin Mellen, 1991.

Fitzmyer, Joseph A. *The Acts of the Apostles.* AB 31. New York: Doubleday, 1997.

———. "4Q246: The 'Son of God' Document from Qumran." *Bib* 74 (1993): 153–74.

———. *The Gospel according to Luke I–IX.* AB 28. New York: Doubleday, 1981.

———. *The Gospel according to Luke X–XXIV.* AB 28a. New York: Doubleday, 1985.

———. *Luke the Theologian: Aspects of His Teaching.* Mahwah, NJ: Paulist Press, 1989.

Franklin, Eric. *Christ the Lord: A Study in the Purpose and Theology of Luke-Acts.* London: SPCK, 1975.

Friesen, Steven J. "Poverty in Pauline Studies: Beyond the So-Called New Consensus." *JSNT* 26 (2004): 323–61.

Fuller, Reginald H. *The Formation of the Resurrection Narratives.* New York: Macmillan, 1971.

Gärtner, B. *The Areopagus Speech and Natural Revelation.* ASNU 21. Lund: C. W. K. Gleerup, 1955.

Gasque, W. Ward. *A History of the Interpretation of the Acts of the Apostles.* 2nd ed. Peabody, MA: Hendrickson, 1989.

———. "The Speeches of Acts: Dibelius Reconsidered." In *New Dimensions in New Testament Study,* edited by Richard Longenecker, 232–50. Grand Rapids: Zondervan, 1974.

George, Augustin. *Études sur l'oeuvre de Luc.* Paris: Gabalda, 1978.

Giblin, Charles Homer. *The Destruction of Jerusalem according to Luke's Gospel: A Historical-Typological Moral.* Rome: Biblical Institute, 1985.

Gill, David H. "Observations on the Lukan Travel Narrative and Some Related Passages." *HTR* 63 (1970): 199–221.

Gordon, Richard. "From Republic to Principate: Priesthood, Religion and Ideology." In *Pagan Priests: Religion and Power in the Ancient World,* edited by M. Beard and J. North, 179–98. Ithaca, NY: Cornell University Press, 1990.

Gottschall, Jonathan. *The Storytelling Animal: How Stories Make Us Human.* New York: Mariner Books, 2013.

Goulder, Michael D. "The Chiastic Structure of the Lucan Journey." In *Studia Evangelica,* 2 vols., edited by F. L. Cross, 2:195–202. Berlin: Akademie Verlag, 1964.

Grant, Michael. *The Ancient Historians.* New York: Scribners, 1970.

Green, Joel B. *The Gospel of Luke.* NICNT. Grand Rapids: Eerdmans, 1997.

———. "The Social Status of Mary in Luke 1,5–2,52: A Plea for Methodological Integration." *Bib* 73 (1992): 457–71.

———. *The Theology of the Gospel of Luke.* Cambridge: Cambridge University Press, 1995.

Green, Joel B., and Michael C. McKeever. *Luke-Acts and New Testament Historiography.* Grand Rapids: Baker, 1994.

Hadas-Lebel, Mireille. *Jerusalem against Rome.* Translated by Robyn Fréchet. Interdisciplinary Studies in Ancient Culture and Religion 7. Leuven; Dudley, MA: Peeters, 2006.

Haenchen, Ernst. *The Acts of the Apostles: A Commentary*. Translated by Bernard Noble and Gerald Shinn. Philadelphia: Westminster, 1971.

———. "'We' in Acts and the Itinerary." In *The Bultmann School of Biblical Interpretation: New Directions?*, edited by James M. Robinson et al., 590–68. Journal for Theology and the Church 1. Tübingen: Mohr; New York: Harper, 1965.

Hahn, Ferdinand. *The Titles of Jesus in Christology: Their History in Early Christianity*. London: Lutterworth, 1969.

Hamel, Edouard. "Le Magnificat et le Renversement des Situations." *Greg* 60 (1975): 55–77.

Hamel, Gildas. "Poverty and Charity." In *The Oxford Handbook of Jewish Daily Life in Roman Palestine*, edited by Catherine Hezser, 308–26. Oxford: Oxford University Press, 2010.

Hamerton-Kelly, R. G. "The Temple and the Origins of Jewish Apocalyptic." *VT* 20 (1970): 1–15.

Hanson, K. C., and Douglas E. Oakman. *Palestine in the Time of Jesus: Social Structures and Social Conflicts*. 2nd ed. Minneapolis: Fortress, 2008.

Harland, Phillip A. "The Economy of First-Century Palestine: State of the Scholarly Discussion." In *Handbook of Early Christianity: Social Science Approaches*, edited by Anthony J. Blasi et al., 511–27. Walnut Creek, CA: Alta Mira Press, 2002.

Harris, William V. *Ancient Literacy*. Cambridge, MA: Harvard University Press, 1989.

Hezser, Catherine. *Jewish Literacy in Roman Palestine*. Texts and Studies in Ancient Palestine 81. Tübingen: Mohr Siebeck, 2001.

Hilgert, Earle. "Speeches in Acts, and Historical Canons of Historiography and Rhetoric." In *Good News in History: Essays in Honor of Bo Reicke*, edited by L. Miller, 83–110. Atlanta: Scholars Press, 1993.

Hock, Ronald F., and Edward N. O'Neil. *The Chreia in Ancient Rhetoric: Volume 1: The* Progymnasmata. Atlanta: Scholars Press, 1986.

Hopkins, Keith. *Conquerors and Slaves*. Sociological Studies in Roman History. Cambridge: Cambridge University Press, 1978.

———. "Conquest by Book." In *Literacy in the Roman World*, edited by Mary Beard, Alan K. Bowman, and Mireille Corbier, 33–158. Journal of Roman Archaeology Supplementary Series 3. Ann Arbor, MI: Journal of Roman Archaeology, 1991.

Horsley, Richard. *Hearing the Whole Story: The Politics of Plot in Mark's Gospel*. Louisville: Westminster John Knox, 2001.

———. "High Priests and the Politics of Roman Palestine: A Contextual Analysis of Evidence in Josephus." *JSJ* 17 (1986): 435–63.

———, ed. *In the Shadow of Empire: Reclaiming the Bible as a History of Faithful Resistance*. Louisville: Westminster John Knox, 2008.

———. *Jesus and the Powers: Conflict, Covenant, and the Hope of the Poor*. Minneapolis: Fortress, 2011.

———. *The Liberation of Christmas: The Infancy Narrative in Social Context*. New York: Crossroad, 1989.

———. "The Slave Systems of Classical Antiquity and Their Reluctant Recognition by Modern Scholars." *Semeia* 83/84 (1998): 19–66.

Hur, Ju. *A Dynamic Reading of the Holy Spirit in Luke-Acts*. London: T&T Clark, 2004.

Hurtado, Larry W. *Lord Jesus Christ: Devotion to Jesus in Earliest Christianity*. Grand Rapids: Eerdmans, 2003.

———. *One God, One Lord: Early Christian Devotion and Ancient Jewish Monotheism*. Philadelphia: Fortress, 1988.

Jaffee, Martin. *Torah in the Mouth: Writing and Oral Tradition in Palestinian Judaism, 200 BCE–400 CE*. New York: Oxford University Press, 2001.

Jervell, Jacob. *Luke and the People of God*. Minneapolis: Fortress, 1972.

Jewett, Robert. *Romans: A Commentary*. Hermeneia. Minneapolis: Fortress, 2007.

Johnson, Luke Timothy. *The Acts of the Apostles*. Sacra Pagina 5. Collegeville, MN: Liturgical Press, 1992.

———. *The Gospel of Luke*. Sacra Pagina 3. Collegeville, MN: Liturgical Press, 1991.

Just, Arthur A. *The Ongoing Feast: Table Fellowship and Eschatology at Emmaus*. Collegeville, MN: Liturgical Press, 1993.

Kahl, Brigitte. "Acts of the Apostles: Pro(to)-Imperial Script and Hidden Transcript." In *In the Shadow of Empire: Reclaiming the Bible as a History of Faithful Resistance*, edited by Richard Horsley, 137–56. Louisville: Westminster John Knox, 2008.

Keener, Craig S. *Acts: An Exegetical Commentary*. Vol. 1, *Introduction and 1:1–2:47*. Grand Rapids: Baker Academic, 2012.

Kränkl, E. *Jesus, der Knecht Gottes: Die heilsgeschichtliche Stellung Jesu in den Reden der Apostelgeschichte*. BU 8. Regensburg: Pustet, 1972.

Kuhn, Karl A. "Beginning the Witness: The αὐτόπται καὶ ὑπηρέται of Luke's Infancy Narrative." *NTS* 49 (2003): 237–55.

———. "Deaf or Defiant? The Literary, Cultural, and Affective-Rhetorical Keys to the Naming of John (Luke 1:57–80)." *CBQ* 75 (2013): 486–503.

———. *Having Words with God: The Bible as Conversation*. Minneapolis: Fortress, 2008.

———. *The Heart of Biblical Narrative: Rediscovering Biblical Appeal to the Emotions*. Minneapolis: Fortress, 2009.

———. *Luke: The Elite Evangelist*. Collegeville, MN: Liturgical Press, 2010.

———. "The 'One Like a Son of Man' Becomes the 'Son of God.'" *CBQ* 69 (2007): 22–42.

———. "The Point of the Step-Parallelism in Luke 1–2." *NTS* 47 (2001): 38–49.

Kurz, William S. *The Acts of the Apostles*. Collegeville Bible Commentary 5. Collegeville, MN: Liturgical Press, 1983.

———. "Narrative Models for Imitation in Luke-Acts." In *Greeks, Romans and Christians: Essays in Honor of Abraham J. Malherbe*, edited by Wayne A. Meeks et al., 171–89. Minneapolis: Fortress, 1990.

———. *Reading Luke-Acts: Dynamics of Biblical Narrative*. Louisville: Westminster John Knox, 1993.

Landry, David T. "Narrative Logic in the Annunciation to Mary." *JBL* 114 (1995): 65–79.

Laurentin, René. *Structure et Théologie de Luc I–II*. Paris: Gabalda, 1957.

Leaney, A. R. C. *The Gospel according to St. Luke*. 2nd ed. BNTC. London: Black, 1966.

Lee, Doohee. *Luke-Acts and "Tragic History."* WUNT 346. Tübingen: Mohr Siebeck, 2013.

Lenski, Gerhard E. *Power and Privilege: A Theory of Social Stratification*. 2nd ed. Chapel Hill: University of North Carolina Press, 1984.

Levison, John R. *The Spirit in First Century Judaism*. New York: Brill, 1997.

Longenecker, Bruce W. "Exposing the Economic Middle: A Revised Economy Scale for the Study of Early Urban Christianity." *JSNT* 31 (2009): 243–78.

Maddox, Robert. *The Purpose of Luke-Acts*. SNTW. Edinburgh: T&T Clark, 1985.

Malbon, Elizabeth Struthers. *Mark's Jesus: Characterization as Narrative Christology*. Waco: Baylor University Press, 2009.

Malina, Bruce J. *The New Testament World: Insights from Cultural Anthropology*. Rev. ed. Louisville: Westminster John Knox, 2001.

Marcus, Joel. *The Way of the Lord: Christological Exegesis of the Old Testament in the Gospel of Mark*. Louisville: Westminster John Knox, 1992.

Marshall, I. Howard. *The Gospel of Luke: A Commentary on the Greek Text*. NIGTC 3. Grand Rapids: Eerdmans, 1978.

———. *Luke—Historian and Theologian*. 3rd ed. Exeter: Paternoster, 1988.

———. "The Place of Acts 20.28 in Luke's Theology of the Cross." In *Reading Acts Today: Festschrift for Loveday Alexander*, edited by Steve Walton et al., 154–70. LNTS 427. London: T&T Clark, 2011.

Marshall, I. Howard, and David Peterson, eds. *Witness to the Gospel: The Theology of Acts*. Grand Rapids: Eerdmans, 1998.

Martin, Ralph P. "Salvation and Discipleship in Luke's Gospel." *Int* 30 (1976): 366–80.

Mather, P. Boyd. "Paul in Acts as 'Servant' and 'Witness.'" *Journal of the Chicago Society of Biblical Research* 30 (1985): 23–44.

Mattill, A. J., Jr. "The Jesus-Paul Parallels and the Purpose of Luke-Acts: H. H. Evans Reconsidered." *NovT* 27 (1975): 15–46.

———. *Luke and the Last Things: A Perspective for the Understanding of Lukan Thought*. Dillsboro: Western North Carolina Press, 1979.

Mays, James Luther. "The Language of the Kingdom of God." *Int* 47 (1993): 174–76.

McCann, J. Clinton. *A Theological Introduction to the Book of Psalms: The Psalms as Torah*. Nashville: Abingdon, 1993.

McKnight, Scot, and Joseph B. Modica, eds. *Jesus Is Lord, Caesar Is Not: Evaluating Empire in New Testament Studies*. Downers Grove, IL: IVP Academic, 2013.

Meier, John Paul. *A Marginal Jew: Rethinking the Historical Jesus*. Vol. 2, *Mentor, Message, and Miracles*. New York: Doubleday, 1994.

Menzies, Robert P. *Empowered for Witness: The Spirit in Luke-Acts*. Journal of Pentecostal Theology Supplement Series 6. Sheffield: Sheffield Academic Press, 1994.

Metts, H. Leroy. "The Kingdom of God: Background and Development of a Complex Discourse Concept." *CTR* 2 (2004): 51–82.

Miller, Amanda C. *Rumors of Resistance: Status Reversal and Hidden Transcripts in the Gospel of Luke*. Emerging Scholars. Minneapolis: Fortress, 2014.

Miller, Norma P. "Dramatic Speech in the Roman Historians." *Greece & Rome* 22 (1975): 45–56.

Moessner, David P., ed. *Jesus and the Heritage of Israel: Luke's Narrative Claim upon Israel's Legacy*. Harrisburg, PA: Trinity Press International, 1999.

———. *Lord of the Banquet: The Literary and Theological Significance of the Lukan Travel Narrative*. Philadelphia: Fortress, 1989.

Moore, Ann. *Moving beyond Symbol and Myth: Understanding the Kingship of God of the Hebrew Bible through Metaphor*. Studies in Biblical Literature 99. New York: Peter Lang, 2009.

Morgan, Teresa. *Literate Education in the Hellenistic and Roman Worlds*. Cambridge Classical Studies. Cambridge: Cambridge University Press, 1998.

Morgenthaler, R. *Die lukanische Geschichtsschreibung als Zeugnis*. 2 vols. ATANT. Zurich: Zwingli, 1948.

Moxnes, Halvor. "Patron-Client Relations and the New Community in Luke-Acts." In *The Social World of Luke-Acts: Models for Interpretation*, edited by Jerome H. Neyrey, 241–70. Peabody, MA: Hendrickson, 1991.

Mussies, Gerard. "Variation in the Book of Acts." *Filologia Neotestamentaria* 4 (1991): 165–82.

Myers, Ched. *Binding the Strong Man: A Political Reading of Mark's Story of Jesus*. Maryknoll, NY: Orbis, 1988.

Newsom, Carol A. *Songs of the Sabbath Sacrifice*. Atlanta: Scholars Press, 1985.

Neyrey, Jerome H. *The Passion according to Luke: A Redaction Study of Luke's Soteriology*. New York: Paulist Press, 1985.

————, ed. *The Social World of Luke-Acts: Models for Interpretation*. Peabody, MA: Hendrickson, 1991.

Nolland, John. *Luke 1:1–9:20*. WBC 35a. Dallas: Word, 1989.

————. *Luke 9:21–18:34*. WBC 35b. Dallas: Word, 1989.

————. *Luke 18:35–24:53*. WBC 35c. Dallas: Word, 1989.

————. "Salvation History and Eschatology." In *Witness to the Gospel: The Theology of Acts*, edited by I. Howard Marshall and David Peterson, 63–81. Grand Rapids: Eerdmans, 1998.

Oakman, Dennis E. "Cursing Fig Trees and Robbers' Dens: Pronouncement Stories within Social-Systemic Perspective; Mark 11:12–15 and Parallels." *Semeia* 64 (1993): 253–72.

————. *Jesus and the Peasants*. Matrix: The Bible in Mediterranean Context. Eugene, OR: Cascade, 2008.

Olbricht, Thomas H. "*Pathos* as Proof in Greco-Roman Rhetoric." In *Paul and Pathos*, edited by Thomas H. Olbricht and Jerry L. Sumney, 8–22. SBL Symposium Series 16. Atlanta: Society of Biblical Literature, 2001.

Oliver, H. H. "The Lucan Birth Stories and the Purpose of Luke-Acts." *NTS* 10 (1963–64): 202–26.

O'Neil, J. C. *The Theology of Acts in Its Historical Setting*. London: SPCK, 1961.

O'Toole, Robert F. "Activity of the Risen Jesus in Luke-Acts." *Bib* 63 (1981): 471–98.

————. *Luke's Presentation of Jesus: A Christology*. SubBi 25. Rome: Editrice Pontificio Istituto Biblico, 2004.

————. *The Unity of Luke's Theology*. GNS 9. Wilmington, DE: Glazier, 1984.

Parsons, Mikeal. *The Departure of Jesus in Luke-Acts: The Ascension Narratives in Context*. JSNTSup 21. Sheffield: JSOT Press, 1987.

————. "Narrative Closure and Openness in the Plot of the Third Gospel: The Sense of an Ending in Luke 24:50–53." In *Society of Biblical Literature Seminar Papers* 26, edited by Kent H. Richards, 201–23. Atlanta: Scholars Press, 1986.

Parsons, Mikeal C., and Richard I. Pervo. *Rethinking the Unity of Luke and Acts*. Minneapolis: Fortress, 1990.

Patrick, Dale. "The Kingdom of God in the Old Testament." In *The Kingdom of God in 20th-Century Interpretation*, edited by Wendell Willis, 67–79. Peabody, MA: Hendrickson, 1987.

Perrin, Nicholas. *Jesus the Temple*. Grand Rapids: Baker Academic, 2010.

Perrin, Norman. *Jesus and the Language of the Kingdom: Symbol and Metaphor in New Testament Interpretation*. Philadelphia: Fortress, 1980.

Pervo, Richard I. *Profit with Delight: The Literary Genre of the Acts of the Apostles*. Philadelphia: Fortress, 1987.

Philip, Finny. *The Origins of Pauline Pneumatology*. WUNT 94. Tübingen: Mohr Siebeck, 2005.

Pilgrim, Walter E. *Good News to the Poor: Wealth and Poverty in Luke-Acts*. Minneapolis: Augsburg, 1981.

Pinter, Dean. "The Gospel of Luke and the Roman Empire." In *Jesus Is Lord, Caesar Is Not: Evaluating Empire in New Testament Studies*, edited by Scot McKnight and Joseph B. Modica, 101–15. Downers Grove, IL: IVP Academic, 2013.

Porter, Stanley. "Thucydides 1.22.1 and Speeches in Acts: Is There a Thucydidean View?" *NovT* 32 (1990): 121–42.

Portier-Young, Anathea. *Apocalypse against Empire: Theologies of Resistance in Early Judaism*. Grand Rapids: Eerdmans, 2011.

Powell, Mark Alan. *What Are They Saying about Acts?* New York: Paulist Press, 1991.

————. *What Are They Saying about Luke?* New York: Paulist Press, 1989.

————. *What Is Narrative Criticism?* Edited by Dan O. Via. Minneapolis: Fortress, 1990.

Price, S. R. F. *Rituals and Power: The Roman Imperial Cult in Asia Minor*. Cambridge: Cambridge University Press, 1984.

Ravens, David. *Luke and the Restoration of Israel*. JSNTSup 119. Sheffield: Sheffield Academic Press, 1995.

Rhoads, David. "Losing Life for Others in the Face of Death: Mark's Standards of Judgment." In *Gospel Interpretation: Narrative-Critical and Social-Scientific Approaches*, edited by Jack Dean Kingsbury, 83–94. Harrisburg, PA: Trinity Press, 1997.

———. "Mission in the Gospel of Mark." *CurTM* 22 (1995): 340–55.

Rhoads, David, Joanna Dewey, and Donald Michie. *Mark as Story: An Introduction to the Narrative of a Gospel*. 2nd ed. Minneapolis: Fortress, 1999.

Richardson, Alan. *The Political Christ*. Philadelphia: Westminster, 1973.

Rives, James B. *Religion in the Roman Empire*. Malden, MA: Blackwell, 2007.

Robbins, Vernon K. "By Land and by Sea: The We Passages and Ancient Sea Voyages." In *Perspectives in Luke-Acts*, edited by C. H. Talbert, 215–42. Edinburgh: T&T Clark, 1978.

Robinson, B. P. "The Place of the Emmaus Story in Luke-Acts." *NTS* 30 (1984): 481–87.

Robinson, John A. T. "The Most Primitive Christology of All?" In *Twelve New Testament Studies*, 139–53. London: SCM, 1962.

Rohrbaugh, Richard. "The Social Location of the Markan Audience." In *The Social World of the New Testament: Insights and Models*, edited by Jerome H. Neyrey and Eric C. Stewart, 141–62. Peabody, MA: Hendrickson, 2008.

Rowe, C. Kavin. *Early Narrative Christology: The Lord in the Gospel of Luke*. Grand Rapids: Baker Academic, 2006.

———. *World Upside Down: Reading Acts in the Graeco-Roman Age*. Oxford: Oxford University Press, 2009.

Sanders, Jack T. *The Jews in Luke-Acts*. Philadelphia: Fortress, 1987.

Satterthwaite, P. E. "Acts against the Background of Classical Rhetoric." In *The Book of Acts in Its First Century Setting*, edited by Bruce Winter and Andrew D. Clarke. Vol. 1, *Ancient Literary Setting*, 337–80. Grand Rapids: Eerdmans, 1993.

Scheid, John. *An Introduction to Roman Religion*. Translated by Janet Lloyd. Bloomington: Indiana University Press, 2003.

Schmidt, Daryl. "The Historiography of Acts: Deuteronomistic or Hellenistic?" In *Society of Biblical Literature Seminar Papers* 24, edited by Kent H. Richards, 417–27. Atlanta: Scholars Press, 1985.

Schottroff, Luise, and Wolfgang Stegemann. *Jesus and the Hope of the Poor*. Translated by Matthew J. O'Connell. Maryknoll, NY: Orbis, 1986.

Schürmann, H. *Das Lukasevangelium I. Kommentatar zur Kap 1,1–9,50*. HTKNT 3. Freiburg: Herder, 1969.

Scott, James C. *Domination and the Arts of Resistance: Hidden Transcripts*. New Haven: Yale University Press, 1992.

Seccombe, David Peter. *Possessions and the Poor in Luke-Acts*. SNTSU. Linz: A. Fuchs, 1983.

Shepherd, W. H., Jr. *The Narrative Function of the Holy Spirit as a Character in Luke-Acts*. SBLDS 147. Atlanta: Scholars Press, 1994.

Siverstev, Alexei. "The Household Economy." In *The Oxford Handbook of Jewish Daily Life in Roman Palestine*, edited by Catherine Hezser, 229–45. Oxford: Oxford University Press, 2010.

Snyder, H. Gregory. *Teachers and Texts in the Ancient World: Philosophers, Israelites and Christians*. Religion in the First Christian Centuries. New York: Routledge, 2000.

Soards, Marion. *The Speeches in Acts: Their Content, Context, and Concerns*. Louisville: Westminster John Knox, 1994.

Spencer, F. Scott. *Journeying through Acts: A Literary-Cultural Reading.* Peabody, MA: Hendrickson, 2004.

Sterling, Gregory E. *Historiography and Self-Definition: Josephos, Luke-Acts, and Apologetic Historiography.* NovTSup 64. Leiden: Brill, 1992.

Storkey, Alan. *Jesus and Politics: Confronting the Powers.* Grand Rapids: Baker Academic, 2006.

Strauss, Mark L. *The Davidic Messiah in Luke-Acts: The Promise and Its Fulfillment in Lukan Christology.* JSNTSup 110. Sheffield: Sheffield Academic Press, 1995.

Strelan, Rick. *Luke the Priest: The Authority of the Author of the Third Gospel.* Burlington, VT: Ashgate, 2008.

Talbert, Charles H. "The Concept of Immortals in Mediterranean Antiquity." *JBL* (1975): 419–36.

———. *Jesus and the Gnostics: An Examination of the Lucan Purpose.* Nashville: Abingdon, 1966.

———. *Literary Patterns, Theological Themes and the Genre of Luke-Acts.* Atlanta: Scholars Press, 1974.

———, ed. *Luke-Acts: New Perspectives from the Society of Biblical Literature.* New York: Crossroad, 1984.

———, ed. *Perspectives on Luke-Acts.* Perspectives in Religious Studies: Special Studies Series 5. Edinburgh: T&T Clark, 1978.

———. "The Place of the Resurrection in the Theology of Luke." *Int* 46 (1992): 19–30.

———. "Promise and Fulfillment in Lucan Theology." In *Luke-Acts: New Perspectives from the Society of Biblical Literature*, 91–103. New York: Crossroad, 1984.

———. "Prophecies of Future Greatness: The Contribution of Greco-Roman Biographies to an Understanding of Luke 1:5–4:15." In *The Divine Helmsman: Studies on God's Control of Human Events, Presented to Lou H. Siberman*, edited by James L. Crenshaw and Samuel Sandmel, 129–41. New York: Ktav, 1980.

———. *Reading Luke: A Literary and Theological Commentary on the Third Gospel.* New York: Crossroad, 1982.

———. *What Is a Gospel? The Genre of the Canonical Gospels.* Philadelphia: Fortress, 1977.

Tannehill, Robert C. *Luke.* Abingdon New Testament Commentaries. Nashville: Abingdon, 1996.

———. "The Magnificat as Poem." *JBL* 93 (1974): 263–75.

———. *The Narrative Unity of Luke-Acts: A Literary Interpretation.* 2 vols. Minneapolis: Fortress, 1986, 1990.

Tiede, David L. *Prophecy and History in Luke-Acts.* Philadelphia: Fortress, 1980.

Tolbert, Mary Ann. *Sowing the Gospel: Mark's World in Literary-Historical Perspective.* Minneapolis: Fortress, 1989.

Tuckett, Christopher. *Christology and the New Testament: Jesus and His Earliest Followers.* Louisville: Westminster John Knox, 2001.

Tyson, Joseph B. "The Birth Narratives and the Beginning of Luke's Gospel." *Semeia* 52 (1990): 103–20.

van Unnik, W. C. "Luke's Second Book and the Rules of Hellenistic Historiography." In *Les Actes des Apôtres: Tradition, Rédaction, Théologie*, edited by J. Kremer, 37–60. BETL 48. Leuven: Leuven University Press, 1979.

Varneda, Pere. *The Historical Method of Flavius Josephus.* Leiden: Brill, 1986.

Vermes, Geza. *The Complete Dead Sea Scrolls in English.* London: Penguin, 2004.

Viviano, B. T. "The Kingdom of God in the Qumran Literature." In *The Kingdom of God in 20th-Century Interpretation*, edited by Wendell Willis, 96–107. Peabody, MA: Hendrickson, 1987.

Voss, Gerhard. *Die Christologie der lukanischen Schriften in Grundzügen.* StudNeot 2. Paris: Brouwer, 1965.

Walaskay, Paul W. *"And So We Came to Rome": The Political Perspective of St. Luke*. SNTSMS 49. Cambridge: Cambridge University Press, 1983.

Wall, Robert W. "The Acts of the Apostles." In vol. 10 of *The New Interpreter's Bible*, edited by Leander E. Keck, 1–368. Nashville: Abingdon, 2002.

Wehnert, Jürgen. "The Claims of the Prologues and Greco-Roman Rhetoric: The Prefaces to Luke and Acts in Light of Greco-Roman Rhetorical Strategies." In *Jesus and the Heritage of Israel: Luke's Narrative Claim upon Israel's Legacy*, edited by David P. Moessner, 63–83. Harrisburg, PA: Trinity Press International, 1999.

———. *Die Wir-Passagen der Apostelgeschichte: Ein lukanisches Stilmittel aus jüdischer Tradition*. Göttingen: Vandenhoeck & Ruprecht, 1989.

Wenell, Karen J. "Contested Temple Space and Visionary Kingdom Space in Mark 11–12." *BibInt* 15 (2007): 323–37.

Wenham, J. "The Identification of Luke." *EvQ* 63 (1991): 3–44.

Wheelwright, Philip. *Metaphor and Reality*. Bloomington: Indiana University Press, 1962.

Willis, Wendell, ed. *The Kingdom of God in 20th-Century Interpretation*. Peabody, MA: Hendrickson, 1987.

Wilson, Stephen G. *The Gentiles and the Gentile Mission in Luke-Acts*. SNTSMS 23. Cambridge: Cambridge University Press, 2005.

Winn, Adam. *The Purpose of Mark's Gospel: An Early Christian Response to Roman Imperial Propaganda*. WUNT 245. Tübingen: Mohr Siebeck, 2008.

Wiseman, T. P. *Clio's Cosmetics: Three Studies in Greco-Roman Literature*. Totowa, NJ: Rowman & Littlefield, 1979.

Witherall, Carol S., Hoan Tan Tran, and John Othus. "Narrative Landscapes and the Moral Imagination: Taking the Story to Heart." In *Literacy, Society and Schooling: A Reader*, edited by Suzanne De Castell, Allan Luke, and Kieran Egan, 39–49. New York: Cambridge University Press, 1995.

Witherington, Ben, III. *The Acts of the Apostles: A Social-Rhetorical Commentary*. Grand Rapids: Eerdmans, 1998.

———. *History, Literature and Society in the Book of Acts*. Cambridge: Cambridge University Press, 1996.

———. *New Testament History: A Narrative Account*. Grand Rapids: Baker Academic, 2001.

Wren, Malcolm. "Sonship in Luke: The Advantage of a Literary Approach." *SJT* 37 (1984): 301–11.

Wright, N. T. *The New Testament and the People of God*. Minneapolis: Fortress, 1992.

———. "Putting Paul Together Again: Toward a Synthesis of Paul's Theology." In *Pauline Theology*. Vol. 1, *Thessalonians, Philippians, Galatians, Philemon*, edited by Jouette Bassler, 183–211. Minneapolis: Fortress, 1991.

———. *The Resurrection of the Son of God*. Minneapolis: Fortress, 2003.

Zias, Joseph. "Death and Disease in Ancient Israel." *BA* 54 (1991): 146–59.

Zwiep, Arie W. *Christ, the Spirit and the Community of God: Essays on the Acts of the Apostles*. WUNT 2.293. Tübingen: Mohr Siebeck, 2010.

Index of Subjects

Abraham, 122, 132–33
  God's covenant with, 28, 92, 117, 172, 197, 207
Adam, Jesus as, 221
admiration, narrative and, 189–90, 201
Aeschylus, 103
affect, narrative and, xvi–xvii, 179–96
affective dissonance, 190
affirmations, general, 118
agents, divine, 35–39
Alexander Jannaeus, 5
Alexander the Great, 4, 79n9
allusions, intertextual, 117. *See also* parallelism
analogy, parables and, 85–87
Ananias and Sapphira, 101–2, 183, 206–7, 232, 242, 266–67
angels
  Gabriel, 37, 125, 190
    and annunciation of Jesus' birth, 91–97, 106–7, 119–20, 122, 124, 131–33, 144, 192, 212, 215, 218, 247
    and annunciation of John's birth, 91, 106, 121, 137, 185, 194
  Michael, 30, 37
  Raphael, 37
  Sariel, 37
Anna, 107, 190, 207, 246
Annas (high priest), 198, 198n12
annunciation form, 79–80, 91–97
Antiochus IV, 4–5, 32
apocalyptic literature, 34–35, 52–53, 120–21
Apollonius of Tyana, 79n9

Areopagus, 205, 215, 241
Aristobulus II, 5
Aristotle, 180, 184, 185
Augustus, Caesar, 6, 8, 19, 50, 64, 68, 102, 117, 224–28, 234–35, 259, 262, 264, 267. *See also* emperors, Roman: Octavian
authority, worldly, 234–37
authorship, Lukan, xviii–xix, xx–xxi, 55–64

baptism, 167, 213–14
Barnabas, 100–101, 108, 124, 174, 190, 242, 268
beginning-middle-end trajectory, 74–75
Benedictus, 129, 137. *See also* Zechariah's Canticle
biography, ancient, xxi–xxii
birth announcements, 79–80, 91–97
bracketing, narrative, 182
branch, messianic, 136

Caiaphas, 198, 198n12
challenge-response, 21–22, 83
characterization
  of the elite, 266
  of Jesus, 209–22
  narrative and, xxi–xxii, 76–77
  parallelism and, 119, 124–25
  pathos and, 187–90
  speech and, 127–39
  of Yahweh, 206–9
chreia form, 82–83
Christology
  adoptionist, 210–11, 215–16

287

Index of Authors

293

Index of Scripture
and Other Ancient Sources

Printed and bound by CPI Group (UK) Ltd, Croydon, CR0 4YY

13/04/2025

14656461-0002